Read *to* Achieve

Read *to* Achieve
GATEWAY TO ACADEMIC READING

David Rothman
Queensborough Community College

Jilani Warsi
Queensborough Community College

Boston   Columbus   Indianapolis   New York   San Francisco   Upper Saddle River
Amsterdam   Cape Town   Dubai   London   Madrid   Milan   Munich   Paris   Montreal   Toronto
Delhi   Mexico City   São Paulo   Sydney   Hong Kong   Seoul   Singapore   Taipei   Tokyo

Senior Sponsoring Editor: Nancy Blaine
Assistant Editor: Amanda Dykstra
Editorial Assistant: Jamie Fortner
Senior Development Editor: Gillian Cook
Executive Marketing Manager: Thomas DeMarco
Senior Supplements Editor: Donna Campion
Executive Digital Producer: Stefanie Snajder

Digital Project Manager: Janell Lantana
Production Manager: S.S. Kulig
Project Coordination, Text Design, and Electronic Page Makeup: PreMediaGlobal
Cover Designer/Manager: John Callahan
Cover Art: Ifong/Shutterstock
Senior Manufacturing Buyer: Roy Pickering
Printer/Binder: Courier Corporation
Cover Printer: Lehigh-Phoenix Color

This title is restricted to sales and distribution in North America only.

Credits and acknowledgments borrowed from other sources and reproduced, with permission, in this textbook appear on the appropriate page within text or on pages 475–479.

Lexile® is a trademark of MetaMetrics, Inc., and is registered in the United States and abroad. The trademarks and names of other companies and products mentioned herein are the property of their respective owners. Copyright © 2012 MetaMetrics, Inc. All rights reserved.

Library of Congress Control Number: 2012955142

10 9 8 7 6 5 4 3 2 1—CRK—16 15 14 13

Student ISBN 10: 0-205-57806-3
Student ISBN 13: 978-0-205-57806-1
A la Carte ISBN 10: 0-321-87184-7
A la Carte ISBN 13: 978-0-321-87184-8

www.pearsonhighered.com

Brief Contents

Contents

Chapter 3   Personal Finance   83

Chapter 4   Economics   127

Chapter 5 Literature   173

Chapter 6 Mathematics   227

Chapter 9 U.S. History 375

Preface

Read to Achieve was inspired by the philosophy that four critical goals for a reading textbook series (*Read to Succeed* is the upper-level book in the series) could be met with a thematic, content-based approach. We realize that it is imperative that developmental readers be fully engaged in content as they acquire the college reading skills that are pivotal to their academic success. This multifaceted approach enables students to become active readers, develop academic vocabulary, increase their reading comprehension, and to prepare for readings across the disciplines. What follows is a brief description of these four critical goals of RTA:

- **Encouraging active reading.** First and foremost, *Read to Achieve* aims to spur developmental readers to become active readers by fostering intellectual inquiry through an exploration of contemporary themes related to academic disciplines. All too often college students are uninspired as they read textbooks that focus on isolated skills and are thus unmotivated to invest their time and effort in reading them. *Read to Achieve* takes the approach that there is no substitute for high-interest, cohesive content that engages students and taps into their natural curiosity. After all, reading should be a pleasant experience!

- **Building vocabulary.** Secondly, *Read to Achieve* offers a strong focus on building vocabulary development skills. Research shows that reading students have mature thoughts and ideas, but that they lack sufficient vocabulary to express them. One of the strongest features of *Read to Achieve* is its emphasis on vocabulary development. This heavy emphasis on vocabulary building should eliminate the need to adopt an additional vocabulary text.

- **Increasing comprehension skills.** Thirdly, *Read to Achieve* helps students develop their reading comprehension skills in preparation for standardized reading tests. Unlike most reading textbooks, *Read to Achieve* offers in-depth reading skills foci integrated into each chapter's thematic content focus. In this way, students are motivated to work with these critical reading skills, as it is the improvement of these skills that will help them gain a deeper understanding of the chapter's content-based readings.

- **Preparing students for reading across disciplines.** Finally, *Read to Achieve* helps prepare students for the challenges of the 100-level survey courses that lie just beyond their developmental coursework. By focusing chapters across a wide array of academic disciplines (sociology, biology, economics, literature, mathematics, occupational therapy, and so on) and having students work with authentic textbook excerpts, they are exposed to the college-level material they will be working with in their credit courses. This gives *Read to Achieve* readers a valuable edge in their academic preparation. Moreover, many students in the developmental stage of their college careers are undecided about their majors, and reading across the curriculum introduces them to the most popular academic disciplines and helps them explore potential areas of academic interest.

Content Overview

Read to Achieve is organized into ten chapters, each focusing on a different academic discipline. A critical reading skill focus is integrated into each thematic unit:

Chapter	Academic Discipline	Reading Skill in Focus
Chapter 1	SOCIOLOGY	VOCABULARY IN CONTEXT
Chapter 2	BIOLOGY	TOPIC AND MAIN IDEA
Chapter 3	PERSONAL FINANCE	SUPPORTING DETAILS
Chapter 4	ECONOMICS	INFERENCE
Chapter 5	LITERATURE	AUTHOR'S TONE AND PURPOSE
Chapter 6	MATHEMATICS	LOGICAL RELATIONSHIPS
Chapter 7	ARCHITECTURE	FACTS AND OPINIONS
Chapter 8	OCCUPATIONAL THERAPY	PATTERNS OF ORGANIZATION
Chapter 9	U.S. HISTORY	AUTHOR'S BIAS
Chapter 10	TRAVEL AND TOURISM	COMBINED SKILLS

Beyond the many activities offered within the chapters, there are endless opportunities for instructors to go deeper into a given academic discipline of high interest to students. Faculty guest speakers can give overviews of their respective academic areas, and students can do further online research on an academic major of interest.

Special Features of *Read to Achieve*

Each chapter in *Read to Achieve* contains a variety of elements designed to engage students and support the principle features: themes relevant to academic disciplines, a variety of genres, extensive vocabulary support, as well as overall reading improvement.

How *Read to Achieve* Introduces Students to a Variety of Academic Disciplines

Each chapter in *Read to Achieve* focuses on an academic discipline such as sociology, finance, or occupational therapy. All of the reading selections in the chapter relate to the various aspects of the academic discipline as do the following features:

- **Introduction to the Discipline of (Discipline):** Each chapter begins with a brief passage to introduce students to a particular academic area. The passage gives a historical overview of the academic discipline, offers controversial topics related to the discipline, and explains the subtopics students will read in the chapter.

- **Reading into a Photo:** In this section, students are asked to examine a photo that relates to the academic area they are learning about. Students are asked to answer two open-ended questions about the photo either in pairs or in small groups.

- **Key Terms in the Field of (Discipline):** *Read to Achieve* introduces students to some key terms that are germane to a particular field. In other words, they learn typical words from an academic area that are used by experts, professors, and university students.

- **Landmark in the Field of (Discipline):** A significant landmark in each of the academic fields is profiled. In the sociology chapter, students learn about the evolution of chat rooms; in the biology chapter, they read about the development of organ transplants; and in the personal finance chapter, online banking is profiled. After each of the landmark readings, students are asked to research another important landmark in the academic field. Students are thus exposed to the connections between an academic discipline and its "real world" applications.

- **An Interview with a Student in the Field of (Discipline):** Students have the opportunity to read interviews with successful individuals who are majoring in the academic discipline that is the focus of the chapter. The interviewees discuss what inspired them to major in their field and how they overcame obstacles in their academic journey. The students also discuss their career plans for after graduation from college and alternative career options for which their degree prepares students. These personal accounts of academic success help students visualize their own future in college and beyond.

- **Textbook Application:** Each chapter contains a textbook reading from an introductory text in the discipline. Students have the opportunity to listen to the text read in lecture style (via an audio file or instructor reading aloud) as a preview before interacting with the written text. Research has shown that this listening skill component is critical in developing intermediate-level readers' reading proficiency. Students thus learn how to navigate textbook reading and are given ample practice to check their comprehension with multiple-choice questions after each textbook selection.

- **Panel Discussion:** Several chapters provide students with an opportunity to participate in a panel discussion and articulate their thoughts on a controversial topic in the discipline. Unlike a debate in which two teams argue for and against a controversial topic, a panel discussion is a forum whereby the panelists express their points of view without being subjected to the expectations of winning or losing an argument. For example, in Chapter 1, Sociology, the discussion focuses on whether playing violent video games can cause imitative behavior among children and teenagers. This activity gives students practice making a presentation and raising and responding to questions.

How *Read to Achieve* Develops Students' Vocabulary

Research on vocabulary acquisition shows that developmental readers have mature thoughts and ideas, but that they do not have a strong vocabulary to articulate them. It is clear that vocabulary development is crucial to academic success, and *Read to Achieve* provides students with many opportunities to improve their vocabulary.

- **Word Form and Context Clues:** Chapter 1 introduces students to morphological forms such as prefixes, roots, and suffixes and context clues. Students do vocabulary exercises and learn how to determine meaning from context.

- **Key Terms in the Field:** Each respective academic discipline has a set of high-frequency key terms used in the field. *Read to Achieve* includes a discipline-specific vocabulary list and vocabulary-building activities for each academic area covered. By the end of the course, students have been introduced to a wide range of academic terms.

- **Pre- and Post-Reading Vocabulary Exercises:** Each reading selection is preceded by a vocabulary exercise whereby students practice guessing meaning from context and a post-reading vocabulary exercise that gives students the opportunity to solidify their newly acquired vocabulary.

How *Read to Achieve* Engages Students' Interest with a Variety of Genres

Read to Achieve offers students a variety of reading genres such as Web articles, blog posts, magazine articles, news articles, poems, and textbooks, as well as a scene from a play, the first chapter of a novel, and an interview. In addition to the longer reading selections, the text has numerous discipline-specific short paragraphs and passages throughout every chapter. All longer selections include the Flesch-Kincaid grade level and a Lexile measure in the *Annotated Instructor's Edition.*

- **Immersion in Reading:** With up to six reading selections per chapter, *Read to Achieve* provides students with ample opportunity to develop key reading skills and be exposed to different genres.

- **Internet Fact Search:** Students develop their online Web research skills by seeking out statistical information and fast facts related to each academic discipline. This online exercise gives them a chance to obtain information from a wide range of genres.

- **Reading Levels in Annotated Instructor's Edition** A Lexile® measure—the most widely used reading metric in U.S. schools—provides valuable information about a student's reading ability and the complexity of text. It helps match students with reading resources and activities that are targeted to their ability level. Lexile measures indicate the reading levels of content in MyReadingLab and the longer selections in the Annotated Instructor's Editions of all Pearson's reading books. See the Annotated Instructor's Edition of *Read to Achieve* and the *Instructor's Manual* for more details.

How *Read to Achieve* Helps Students Achieve Overall Academic Improvement

Read to Achieve helps students improve their academic preparedness by giving them opportunities to learn college reading skills, brainstorm open-ended discipline-specific questions, and explore their thoughts in writing in response to the many reading selections as follows:

- **Skill Focus:** Every chapter provides in-depth instruction for a key reading skill. Students interact with exercises and examples to develop these critical skills, and then work to apply them in the context of authentic reading passages within each discipline focus.

- **Follow Your Interests:** This feature gives students the opportunity to review some of the questions experts in a specific field such as sociology or biology may explore. Students choose three or four questions that pique their interest and discuss them with their peers in small groups.

- **College Study Skills:** This feature guides students toward better college preparedness. College Study Skills focuses on critical applications such as "how to highlight a text" or "how to build your vocabulary using index cards," and so on.

- **Readiness for College Success:** Readiness for College Success offers students helpful hints on how to be successful in college with advice on "how to communicate with your professor" or "how to build a weekly study plan."

- **Writing Connections:** Most chapters include this feature, which helps students make a conscious link between reading and writing and explore their thoughts in writing. The writing assignment changes from chapter to chapter, introducing students to specific types of writing. For example, students practice freewriting in a reflective journal in Chapter 2, and they learn to build a financial plan in Chapter 3. The rationale behind this feature is that reading and writing are integrated skills, and that reading students need to practice writing in response to the various selections they read and analyze.

The features and activities described above form the core part of *Read to Achieve*, an academically oriented and content-based textbook designed to mirror a college-level mainstream course. We believe that *Read to Achieve* will not only improve students' reading proficiency, but it also will increase their familiarity with the North American higher education system and prepare them to succeed in college.

Book-Specific Ancillary Materials

- **Annotated Instructor's Edition for *Read to Achieve*:** (ISBN 0-321-87224-X/ 978-0-321-87224-1) Identical to the student text, but with answers printed directly on the page where questions and exercises appear and marginal ELL notes that provide tips for teaching the content to second language learners.

- **Instructor's Manual and Test Bank for *Read to Achieve*:** (ISBN 0-205-58533-7 / 978-0-205-58533-5) The Instructor's Manual/Testbank includes comprehensive post-reading discussion questions as well as writing, research and classroom activities to accompany each chapter and is available both in print and for download on the Instructor Resource Center. The Test bank includes multiple choice tests based on the skill focus of each chapter. Test questions are focused on reading passages from each chapter. Instructor's Manual and Test Bank written by Julie Shuchman.

- **MyTest Bank for *Read to Achieve*:** (ISBN 0-321-87203-7 / 978-0-321-87203-6) Pearson MyTest is a powerful assessment generation program that helps instructors easily create and print quizzes, study guides, and exams. Questions designed to accompany *Read to Achieve* or from other writing test banks are included. You can also create and add your own questions. Save the finished test as a Word document or PDF or export it to WebCT, Blackboard, or other CMS systems. Available at www.pearsonmytest.com.

- **PowerPoint Presentation for *Read to Achieve*:** (ISBN 0-321-87227-4 / 978-0-321-87227-2) This PowerPoint presentation set consists of chapter-by-chapter classroom-ready lecture outline slides, lecture tips and classroom activities, and review questions. It is available for download from the Instructor Resource Center.

- **Answer Key for *Read to Achieve*:** (ISBN 0-321-87226-6 / 978-0-321-87226-5) The Answer Key contains the solutions to the exercises in the student edition of the text. Available for download from the Instructor Resource Center.

MyReadingLab™ Where better practice makes better readers!

www.myreadinglab.com

MyReadingLab, a complete online learning program, provides additional resources and better practice exercises for developing readers.

What makes the practice in MyReadingLab better?

- **Diagnostic Testing.** MyReadingLab's diagnostic Path Builder test comprehensively assesses students' reading skills. Students are provided an individualized learning path based on the diagnostic's results, identifying the areas where they most need help.

- **Progressive Learning.** The heart of MyReadingLab is the progressive learning that takes place as students complete the Overview, Animations, Recall, Apply, and Write exercises along with the Posttest within each topic. Students move from preparation (Overview, Animation) to literal comprehension (Recall) to critical understanding (Apply) to the ability to demonstrate a skill in their own writing (Write) to total mastery (Posttest). This progression of critical thinking, not available in any other online resource, enables students to truly master the skills and concepts they need to become successful writers.

- **Online Gradebook.** All student work in MyReadingLab is captured in the Online Gradebook. Instructors can see what and how many topics their students have mastered. They can also view students' individual scores on all assignments throughout MyReadingLab, as well as overviews of student and class performance by module. Students can monitor their progress in new Completed Work pages, which show them their totals, scores, time on task, and the date and time of their work by module. They can also open and review any of their assignments directly from these pages.

- **Where Print and Media Connect.** Students can also complete all the pre- and post-reading exercises and activities related to the longer reading selections in each chapter of the printed text within the *Read to Achieve* book-specific module in MyReadingLab. These unique activities are clearly identified in the print text by the MyWritingLab logo and the exercise icon shown in the margin.

MyReadingLab™

Complete this **Exercise** at **myreadinglab.com**

- **eText.** The *Read to Achieve* eText is accessed through MyReadingLab. Students can highlight important material in the eText, tab pages and areas of importance, and add notes to any section for reflection and/or further study.

From the Authors

Many dedicated individuals have contributed to *Read to Achieve*, and it would have been impossible for us to complete the book without their guidance and much-needed support. First and foremost, we wish to thank our reviewers, who offered their valuable suggestions for improvement during the course of writing our book:

Valerie Bolaris
Evergreen Valley College

Napoleon Brooks
Union County College

Kathy Daily
Tulsa Community College

Georgia Gaspar
Rio Hondo College

Dr. Judy Leavell
St. Edward's University

Inna Newbury
El Camino College

Mary Nielsen
Dalton State

Debbie Spradlin
Tyler Junior College

Marguerite Stark
Monterey Peninsula College
Connie Tucker, Citrus College

Brian White
Texas Southern University

We are also grateful to the meticulous students who contributed their personal stories to the "Interview with a Student" feature:

Jaymee Castillo
UCLA – Biology

Jamie Chow
Cornell – Architecture

Jeanelle Hope
California State University Long Beach
—History

Dominic Jaramillo
Cal Poly Pomona—Hospitality
Management

Kim Jones
University of Southern California—
Occupational Therapy

Katrina Lin
Baruch College (CUNY)—Personal
Finance

Rebecca Martin
Michigan State University—Math

Paul Saltz
Columbus State
Community College—Sociology

Nidhi Shah
University of Maryland Baltimore
County—Economics

Rean Valere
Queens College—Literature

We owe special thanks to Nancy Blaine, our acquisitions editor, for her expert advice, support, and encouragement. We are also thankful to Gill Cook, our development editor, for coming to our rescue at the eleventh hour. We express our gratitude to Jamie Fortner for fulfilling our numerous requests on short notice. We also would like to thank our Pearson and PreMediaGlobal production team, particularly Marie Desrosiers, project manager; Jorgensen Fernandez, image researcher; and Jen Roach, permissions project manager. We are also grateful to Melissa Sacco for her timely intervention and expert advice. Last but not least, Jilani Warsi would like to thank Shabana, his life partner, for her patience, understanding, and constant support throughout the writing of this book. David Rothman would like to thank Zlati, his wife, for her unwavering support of the often-tedious project. We are greatly indebted to all of these individuals who made *Read to Achieve* a reality.

Sincerely,
Jilani Warsi & David Rothman

A Guide to Genre

Read to Achieve offers students a wide range of text genres, and the genre of each reading is indicated in the text. It is critically important that students are aware of both the source and genre of the selection they are about to peruse. Reading a given text without knowing its genre is akin to turning the ignition of a vehicle with little or no knowledge of whether one is driving a plane, a boat, or a truck. The genre of a text offers a clear context for the reader, often determines the author's purpose for writing, and keys the reader into such elements as the author's tone and bias and, perhaps more fundamentally, the kind of vocabulary that one could expect within a given genre.

For example, if you are reading an *editorial* about the situation in the Middle East, you can predict that the author's goal is to persuade the reader to share his or her opinion. Thus, the author of an editorial will use persuasive language to convince the reader. However, if you are reading a newspaper article on the situation in the Middle East, the author's purpose will be to provide information objectively and to expose the reader to a number of different perspectives on the issue. That is not to say that newspaper articles are neutral and show no bias. This is clearly not the case. What is true is that editorials, by definition, are written with the primary purpose of expressing a viewpoint. This distinction between one genre (editorial) and another (newspaper article) is critical, and fluent readers fully understand this. Notice that the topic may be the same, but it is ultimately the author's intended goal and text genre that can change the overall effect on the reader.

A list of all of the genres offered in *Read to Achieve* follows, with a brief description of each genre type and some strategies on how best to approach them as a reader.

Genres in *Read to Achieve* Reading Selections

Internet blog—an Internet chat forum designed and moderated by an individual who may not be an expert in the topic area. A fluent reader using critical thinking skills can easily distinguish between an incoherent piece of writing (often with basic grammar and spelling errors) and a well-written piece. Keep in mind that you should not have to accept the blogger's opinion just because it appears on the Internet. By the same token, it does not mean that you should take amateur writing lightly. Come to think of it, the beauty of most blogs is that they offer readers the opportunity to share perspectives with others in an informal forum.

Interview—a question-and-answer session. Often famous people or experts in a particular field are interviewed in magazines and newspapers. In *Read to Achieve*, there are interviews with students who are pursuing academic disciplines covered in this text. As in reading a memoir, the key is to understand the interviewed student's perspective and some of the points he or she is trying to make. If you have some background information on the specific discipline, it will make it much easier to follow what the student has to say.

Memoir—autobiographical writing. It is crucially important for readers to understand the general context of a memoir. Is this a famous person who you would like to learn more about, or is it someone whose life experience you would like to know more about? Pay close attention to the memoirist's life perspectives and to key turning points in his or her life experience and the precious life lessons that can be learned from them.

Newspaper/magazine/online article—reports on a current topic or event, usually in an objective manner. Readers must understand the general theme, context, and topic area of news articles before trying to make sense of the supporting details. As you read a newspaper article, consider how the subtopics and specific examples provided key you into the author's bias.

Novel—a work of fiction. It is usually extensive in length. In first entering a novel, consider the setting (time and location), theme(s), characterization, plot, and the voice of the narrator. Robert Scholes's words about reading novels are instructive in this regard:

> In considering the voices within this text, students will be encouraged to ask who speaks it, where they come from, and what values that they share are embodied in their speech … [W]ho is speaking to us? What kind of voice is that? Does it present itself as reliable, trustworthy? How does it establish its authority? How does that voice compare to the voices of characters as they are represented? Is the narrator a character? Is the narrator the author? Do characters speak always in one voice, or in more than one? How do different characters speak to one another? The length of a novel requires prolonged engagement. One needs time to read it, time to discuss it, time to write responses to it, but one set in a time and place that is accessible by means of other texts … The point is not to find the answers to fictional questions in the author's life or in the history of a time and place, but to use such information to ask more interesting questions about that novel.

Online advice column—experts in certain fields such as psychology or finance offer their advice in response to Internet readers' questions. The advice columnist's language is usually comforting and reassuring as it is the goal of advice columnists to guide readers through difficult situations. As you read an advice column, focus mostly on the main points of advice offered.

Poetry—literary work often in metrical form. The key to reading and understanding poetry is to pay close attention to symbolic meaning and to the author's word choice. Remember that different readers can understand the same poem differently as a poem is a matter of subjective interpretation.

Scene from a play—excerpt from a theater script. Keep in mind that you are reading direct speech in this genre. Pay attention to conversational style, as it often keys readers into the characters' emotional state and how they interact with other characters in the play. You will notice deviations from standard language (regional dialects, slang, or idiomatic expressions).

Textbook reading—discipline-specific academic content. Textbook chapters are usually assigned for mainstream college courses. The content of a text chapter often reinforces material discussed in class, so the more active of a learner you are during your course lectures, the easier it will be to work with the textbook readings. Good highlighting and annotation skills are essential in focusing on key terms and concepts.

SOCIOLOGY

1

Learning Objectives

IN THIS CHAPTER, YOU WILL LEARN TO . . .

1. Describe the discipline of sociology
2. Define key terms in the field of sociology
3. Use index cards to build your vocabulary
4. Describe what makes a successful college student
5. Analyze roots, prefixes, and suffixes to understand the meaning of words
6. Find the meaning of words from their contexts

INTRODUCTION TO THE DISCIPLINE OF SOCIOLOGY

① LEARNING OBJECTIVE
Describe the discipline
of sociology

Sociology is the study of human behavior in society, including the study of the organization, institutions, and development of human society. As you can tell, human behavior is quite complex, so sociologists study various aspects of it such as race and ethnicity, gender and age, families, education and religion, and environment and urbanization. In this chapter, you will read several reading selections dealing with a wide range of topics such as gender differences in communication, social networking and teenagers, choosing a life partner, successful parenting, and parenting teenagers. We hope that after completing the chapter, you will arrive at a basic understanding of how different social factors determine and influence human behavior.

Reading into a Photo

Working in a small group, examine the following photograph and answer the questions that follow.

1. In your opinion, what do these people seem to be watching?
2. What message does this image convey to you?

Collaboration

Follow Your Interests

Review the set of questions below that sociologists might explore. Check off the three to four questions that are most interesting to you.

1. How have cell phones and texting changed the way people communicate?
2. How are men and women different? How have gender roles in society changed in the last 50 years?

3. What are the secrets of happiness and success?

4. In what ways do wealthy people behave differently than poorer people?

5. What factors make more people move to big cities?

6. Why do teenagers often have trouble relating to their parents?

7. How do people choose their life mate?

8. Why is the divorce rate so high in the United States? What makes a good marriage?

9. What causes racism?

10. What factors lead young people into a life of crime?

11. Why are so many people changing their religions in the United States?

12. How do people act differently when they are in a large group compared to how they behave when they are alone?

13. What are some reasons why people immigrate to another country?

14. What is culture shock, and how can immigrants best assimilate into a new culture?

Now, share your choices with a small group of classmates and explain why these particular questions are most interesting to you. You may wish to discuss these questions with them and ask which questions they found interesting.

Key Terms in the Field of Sociology

LEARNING OBJECTIVE
Define key terms in the field of sociology

The following key terms are frequently used in the discipline of sociology. If you take a college-level course in sociology, it will be important for you to remember these words and to use them in your speech and writing. Review the words below and answer the multiple-choice questions that follow.

acculturation	deviance	social class
assimilation	mores	social justice
competition	peer group	social networking
conflict	polygamy	status
cultural relativism	prejudice	survey

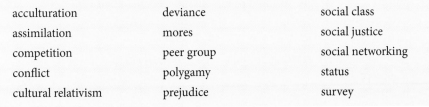

EXERCISE 1   Inferring Meaning from Context

Read each sentence below and try to derive the meaning of the italicized key terms from the context. Circle the correct definition of each italicized term.

1. The *conflict* between Israelis and Palestinians has been going on for many years.
   a. friendship
   b. prolonged struggle
   c. argument
   d. indifference

2. The servant and the master are members of different *social classes*.
   - a. geographic units
   - b. teams
   - c. economic groupings
   - d. educational units

3. In many cultures a person's *status* in society is considered more important than their salary.
   - a. furnishing
   - b. independence
   - c. position
   - d. defense

4. Many people believe that *competition* pushes people to perform at a higher level.
   - a. inflation
   - b. enhancement
   - c. division
   - d. rivalry

5. The man was *prejudiced* against his new Latino neighbors and wanted them to move out.
   - a. angry
   - b. held unfavorable opinions
   - c. judgemental
   - d. ready to take legal action

6. For some, like Martin Luther King, *social justice* is the goal of all protest movements.
   - a. criminal release
   - b. legal network
   - c. fair treatment by society
   - d. revolutionary

7. An immigrant family in America celebrating Thanksgiving is an example of *acculturation*.
   - a. acceptance of a new culture
   - b. rejection of a new culture
   - c. abandoning your culture completely
   - d. expanding

8. To be accepted in a new society, one has to understand the *mores* of the culture. For example, in India public kissing is considered rude.
   - a. superstitious beliefs
   - b. accepted behaviors
   - c. disagreements
   - d. liberalism

9. In most societies, stealing is considered a *deviant* act.
   - a. acceptable
   - b. stringent
   - c. abnormal
   - d. loose

10. Communicating with friends and family on Facebook is a form of *social networking*.
    - a. behavioral norms
    - b. gossiping
    - c. searching for a job
    - d. connecting socially within a defined group

11. A recent *survey* showed that many Americans watch more than four hours of television every day.
    - a. formal questionnaire
    - b. status citation
    - c. governance
    - d. view

12. An American living in China is practicing *cultural relativism* if he doesn't judge Chinese people for eating dogs or for being very strict with their children.
    a. arguing to support one's cultural norms
    b. accepting cultural standards outside a familiar norm
    c. discriminating against foreigners
    d. eating healthily

13. At all stages of life, from childhood to their senior years, people tend to feel most comfortable among their own *peer group*.
    a. family members
    b. mentors you respect
    c. people of similar age
    d. disabled veterans

14. The immigrant *assimilated* into American culture by learning English well, playing baseball every weekend, and working in an office with mostly American peers.
    a. culturally integrated
    b. disqualified himself
    c. successfully applied
    d. became an American

15. A man in California was arrested for practicing *polygamy*.
    a. being married to one spouse
    b. speaking many languages
    c. having multiple wives
    d. fraud

EXERCISE 2 **Writing Meaningful Sentences with the Key Terms**

Working with a partner, choose five of the key terms in sociology and write an original sentence about each one.

Collaboration

1. Word = _____

   _____

   _____

2. Word = _____

   _____

   _____

3. Word = _____

   _____

   _____

4. Word = _____

   _____

   _____

5. Word = _____

   _____

   _____

3 LEARNING OBJECTIVE
Use index cards to build
your vocabulary

COLLEGE STUDY SKILLS
Building Vocabulary with Index Cards

Introducing the Skill

One of the keys to improving reading comprehension is to work on building a richer vocabulary. An excellent technique for reviewing unfamiliar words is to keep an organized set of index cards to study from. To work effectively with this strategy, you will need index cards that are blank on one side and lined on the other.

You will learn many new words as you read your way through *Read to Achieve*. Of course, it is improbable that you can learn each and every unfamiliar word you come across. However, if you set a goal of learning **25 new words** in each chapter using the index card technique, then by the time you finish the ten text chapters you will have learned **250 words**! This is a respectable goal.

Putting the Skill into Action

Examine the index card below.

Annoyed

1. **Source:** <u>You Just Don't Understand: Women and Men in Conversation</u>, p. 12, para. 1

2. **Pronunciation:** /əˈnɔɪd/

3. **Meaning:** be bothered or disturbed

4. **Part of speech:** adjective

5. **Example:** He is **annoyed** with his professor, because he got a low grade.

This card shows how we would like you to organize your vocabulary index cards. You will need a good dictionary in order to do this activity. For each word, fill in the card with the following information:

1. **Source:** What is the name of the reading selection where this vocabulary term appeared? Exactly where in the reading did you locate it?

2. **Pronunciation:** Most dictionaries phonetically transcribe words. Some on-line dictionaries pronounce words for you.

3. **Meaning:** Words often have several meanings. Write the definition that is closest to the meaning of how the word is used in the sentence in which you found it.

4. **Part of Speech:** Is the word a noun, a verb, an adjective, or an adverb?

5. **Example:** Use the word in an original sentence.

The Last Word

Buy a set of loose index cards. Try to choose words that seem interesting to you. Select vocabulary terms from various readings throughout the chapter. Review your collection of new words periodically and follow the guidelines laid out by your instructor in terms of vocabulary reviews and quizzes. Enjoy the process and in the end, if you follow through, you should have an index card set of up to 250 words!

READINESS FOR COLLEGE SUCCESS
The Successful College Student

4 LEARNING OBJECTIVE
Describe what makes a successful college student

Each chapter of the text will offer you an interactive opportunity to explore the critical topic of "college readiness" and will give you a chance to consider what it takes to make it in college.

Working with a partner, consider the characteristics of successful college students and fill in the list below. An example is given to lead you on your way.

Collaboration

Six Characteristics of Successful College Students

Characteristic	Explanation
1. *Successful college students attend every class.*	*These students are present in every class, both mentally and physically.*
2.	
3.	
4.	
5.	
6.	

After you and your partner have completed the list, compare your choices with another pair of classmates before sharing your ideas with your instructor and the entire class.

VOCABULARY BUILDING
Prefixes, Suffixes, and Roots

5 LEARNING OBJECTIVE
Analyze roots, prefixes, and suffixes to understand the meaning of words

You may have noticed that words are of differing lengths. The reason for this is that words are made up of parts, namely prefixes, suffixes, and roots. **Roots** carry the primary meaning, **prefixes** come before roots and alter their meaning, and **suffixes** come after roots and change the tense or part of speech of words.

Consider the following example:

Word: insatiable		
Prefix	*Root*	*Suffix*
in-	sate	-able
"not"	"satisfy"	"can be"
Meaning: "cannot be satisfied"		

In the word *insatiable*, the root is *sate*, which means "to satisfy." In addition, the suffix *-able* means "can be done" or in this case "can be satisfied." Finally, the prefix *in-* is attached before *satiable*, giving it a different meaning, "cannot be satisfied." As you can see, knowing how words are formed can help you determine meaning easily. Let's first look at prefixes. Then we will consider suffixes and roots.

Prefixes

The following prefixes all have something in common. They all mean "not," negating the meaning of the words they are attached to. These prefixes are *il-*, *im -*, *ir-*, *un-*, *in-*, *dis-*, *mis-*, and *non-*. For example, if we attach the prefix *il-* to the word *legal*, we get *illegal*, meaning "not legal."

EXERCISE 3   **Using Prefixes**

Now use each of the prefixes below to make up at least three words that have a negative meaning. The first one has been completed as an example.

Prefix	Example 1	Example 2	Example 3
il-	illicit	illegal	illogical
im-			
ir-			
un-			
in-			
dis-			
mis-			
non-			

Suffixes

Unlike prefixes, which always come before the root, suffixes are attached after the root. However, just like prefixes, suffixes also change the meaning of the words they are attached to. Let's see how this works.

Word: unfriendly		
Prefix	*Root*	*Suffix*
un-	friend	-ly
"not"	"friend"	"in a way that is"
Meaning: "not friendly"		

The word *unfriendly* consists of the root *friend*, the suffix *-ly*, and the prefix *un-*. The adverbial suffix *-ly* means "in a way that is," so *friendly* means "in a way that is like a friend." It should be noted, though, that there is a precise order in which words are formed. For example, we cannot use the prefix *un-* before attaching the suffix *-ly* to *friend*. Doing so would give us a non-word, *unfriend*. Remember that the prefix can only be attached to *friendly*. You learned previously that the prefix *un-* means "not." Can you guess what the word *unfriendly* means? You guessed it right. It means "not a friendly person."

Another important point to remember is that there are different types of suffixes. Some are noun suffixes, others are verb suffixes, and yet others are adjective suffixes. Let's look at each of them:

- **Noun suffix.** When *-ian* is attached to the word *magic*, it gives the extended noun *magician*, which means "someone who does magic."
- **Verb suffix.** When *-ize* is added to the word *final* it gives the verb *finalize*.
- **Adjectival suffix.** Some suffixes form adjectives when attached to nouns. The adjectival suffix *-y* when attached to a noun such as *rain* produces the adjective *rainy*.

EXERCISE 4   Using Suffixes

Working with a classmate, write at least three words using each of the noun suffixes below.

Collaboration

Noun suffix	Example 1	Example 2	Example 3
-ian	technician		
-ary			
-tion			
-ness			
-ment			
-ence			
-ist			

Now try making up words using these verb suffixes. After you finish, compare your examples with those of your classmates.

Verb Suffix	Example 1	Example 2	Example 3
-ify	satisfy		
-ize			
-ate			
-en			

Finally, practice forming adjectives by using the suffixes below. Be sure to make at least three words using the same adjectival suffix.

Adjectival Suffix	Example 1	Example 2	Example 3
-y	dreamy		
-ish			
-ous			
-ful			
-less			
-ent			
-al			
-ic			

After doing the above exercises, you should have gained a fair understanding of how words are formed using different prefixes and suffixes. Now let's take a look at the roots.

Roots

Most roots in English are derived from Latin and Greek, and a basic knowledge of their meanings will help you figure out unfamiliar words. As mentioned previously, roots carry the primary meaning, and prefixes and suffixes are attached to them to change meaning. For example, the root *mort* means "death." However, we can use different suffixes to give rise to different forms. Notice that the words *mortal*, *mortuary*, *mortician*, *mortally*, and *immortal* are all extended forms of the root *mort*.

EXERCISE 5   Using Roots

Using your knowledge of roots, create at least three words using each of the following roots. If you do not know some of these roots, try to recall some words you know that contain these roots. If need be, work with a dictionary.

Root	Example 1	Example 2	Example 3
ped	biped		
sol			
mar			
sate			
vis			
soc			
agri			

EXERCISE 6   Identifying Prefixes, Suffixes, and Roots

This final exercise gives you an opportunity to break down words into prefixes, roots, and suffixes. The first example is done for you. Where there is no prefix, simply put an X in the Prefix column.

Word	Prefix(es)	Root	Suffix(es)
hospitalization	X	hospital	-ize, -ation
invisibly			
reinforcement			
dysfunctional			
inconsiderate			
postcolonial			
asymmetrical			
hypersensitivity			
interdependence			

WEB CONNECTION

If you want to study prefixes, roots, and suffixes further, the following Web pages can be useful resources. Use a search engine like Google or Yahoo to locate them.

- Wikipedia has an entry on Greek and Latin roots in English.
- English Language Roots Reference provides a chart of roots, prefixes, and suffixes, their meanings, and examples.

READING

Reading Selection **1**

Book Excerpt

You Just Don't Understand: Women and Men in Conversation

Preview Questions

1. In what ways do men and women communicate differently? How can some of these differences cause conflicts between the sexes?

2. Some people believe that as we move deeper into the twenty-first century the roles of men and women in American society have become nearly identical. What is your opinion about the male and female roles in modern society?

3. How best can men learn how to understand women, and vice versa? Offer some advice.

MyReadingLab™
Complete this Exercise
at **myreadinglab.com**

Collaboration

Pre-Reading Vocabulary:
Focus on Some Key Terms

Working with a partner, try to guess the meaning of these words from the context. Then look up the words in a dictionary.

Word	Your Definition	Dictionary Definition
take place		
preference		
obvious		
genuine		
confront		

Adapted from *You Just Don't Understand: Women and Men in Conversation*

By Deborah Tannen (2004)

Deborah Tannen is a world-famous linguist who has studied the differences in male and female conversational styles. The following is adapted from her best-selling book on this subject.

1   In an article I wrote for the *Washington Post,* I presented a conversation that had taken place between a couple in their car. The woman had asked, "would you like to stop for a drink?" Her husband had answered truthfully, "No," and they hadn't stopped. He was later frustrated to learn that his wife was annoyed because she had wanted to stop for a drink. He wondered, "Why didn't she just say what she wanted? Why did she play games with me?" From his point of view, he had not made a demand; he had simply answered her question literally. The wife, I explained, was annoyed not because she had not gotten her way, but because her preference had not been considered. From her point of view, she had shown concern for her husband's wishes, but he had shown no concern for hers.

2   A woman I'll call Diana often begins statements with "Let's." She might say, "Let's go out for brunch today," or "Let's clean up now, before we start lunch." This makes Nathan angry. He feels she is ordering

him around, telling him what to do. Diana can't understand why he takes it that way. It is obvious to her that she is making suggestions, not demands. If he doesn't feel like doing what she proposes, all he has to do is say so.

3   Conversational style differences do not explain all the problems that arise in relationships between men and women. Relationships are sometimes threatened by psychological problems, true failures of love and caring, genuine selfishness and real effects of political and economic inequity. But there are also innumerable situations in which groundless allegations of these failings are made, simply because partners are expressing their thoughts and feelings, and their assumptions about how to communicate, in different ways. If we can sort out differences based on conversational style, we will be in a better position to confront real conflicts of interest and to find a shared language in which to negotiate them.

Adaptation of text from pages 15, 18, 151 from *You Just Don't Understand* by Deborah Tannen, reprinted by permission of HarperCollins Publishers and ICM

Reading Comprehension Check

MyReadingLab™
Complete this **Exercise**
at **myreadinglab.com**

1. What caused the fight between the husband and wife in the first example?
   a. He was tired and frustrated.
   b. The couple misunderstood each other.
   c. The husband wanted to stop for a coffee.
   d. The wife wanted an instant decision.

2. In the sentence, "Conversational style differences do not explain all the problems that **arise** in relationships between men and women," *arise* means _____.
   a. give up   c. come up
   b. gain something   d. take into consideration

3. In the sentence starting "But there are also **innumerable** situations …" (para. 3) the term *innumerable* could be replaced with _____.
   a. some   c. no
   b. numbers of   d. many

4. Tannen writes, "If we can *sort out* differences based on conversational style …" (para. 3) In this context, the expression *sort out* means _____.
   a. figure out
   b. organize
   c. manage
   d. win an argument

5. In the example given in the second paragraph, why is Nathan upset?
   a. He wants to give all the orders for the couple.
   b. Men don't like female proposals.
   c. He feels he is being told what to do.
   d. He doesn't want to do any cleaning.

Collaboration

Exploring the Topic

Discuss the following questions to review the content of the book excerpt you have just read.

1. In your understanding, if a friend says, "Let's park over there," would you consider this an order or a proposal? Explain.

2. Deborah Tannen believes that the best way for males and females to reduce conflict between them is to better understand how the opposite sex communicates. Do you think this type of understanding can solve relationship problems? Explain.

Post-Reading Vocabulary

Without using a dictionary, determine the meaning of the bolded words from the context.

1. "He was later **frustrated** to learn that his wife was annoyed because she had wanted to stop for a drink." (para. 1)

   Frustrated means _____

2. "From her **point of view,** she had shown concern for her husband's wishes ..." (para. 1)

   Point of view means _____

3. "It is obvious to her that she is making **suggestions,** not demands." (para. 2)

   Suggestions means _____

READING

Reading Selection **2**

Blog

MyReadingLab™
Complete this **Exercise**
at **myreadinglab.com**

To Teens, Tweens and the People Who Love Them: It's Time to Get "Social Smarts"

Preview Questions

1. How important are social network Web sites like MySpace and Facebook in your life? Explain.

2. Do you think parents have the right to investigate their teenage children's Web activity? Why or why not?

Pre-Reading Vocabulary: Focus on Some Key Terms

Collaboration

Working with a partner, try to guess the meaning of these words. Then look up the words in a dictionary.

Word	Your Definition	Dictionary Definition
compelled		
intercepted		
creepy		
to bail out		
damage		

To Teens, Tweens, and the People Who Love Them: It's Time to Get "Social Smarts"

By Joellyn Sargent

I normally blog on business issues, but something happened at my house yesterday that compelled me to write this post. Please share it with the people in your life who use social media. Everyone needs some social smarts.

Dear Friend,

1.   We haven't met yet IRL *(in real life)*, but I've seen you online and … we need to talk.

2.   You are growing up in a world where privacy is an old-fashioned concept. Almost everything you do is recorded, watched or monitored somehow.

3.   We have cameras on our computers and cell phones, in stores, parks and on the highway. We check in on Facebook and Foursquare and whatever other check-in app you choose. Your phone goes everywhere you go, and the GPS on your phone *always* knows where you are.

4.   Invasion of privacy used to mean my brother read my diary or the teacher intercepted a note about a cute guy and read it in front of the class. Times sure have changed.

5.   Maybe you've been on social media since before you were born. *(Did your mom or dad post those ultrasound pics on Face-book or MySpace or Flikr? I thought so.)* Your whole life is there.

6.   Yes, this is your world. It seems nor-mal, I'm sure, because you've never known anything else. Maybe that's why you don't think twice before posting that crazy video on You Tube, or using those words *(yes, the*

dirty ones that make your mother blush) on Twitter, and "OMG, did she really say that to him on Facebook?"

7   You're in a relationship with social media and "It's Complicated."

8   Most of your parents don't get it. *(Sorry parents, it's true.)*

9   Well, let me tell you the hard truth that you don't like to think about:

People are watching.

10   That creepy guy at the mall?

11   *Yep, he's online and he can read your Twitter stream.*

12   That jerk you wish you never met?

13   *He can Google you and get your life story in a flash.*

14   Yes, Google indexes your Facebook feeds and your tweets and lots of other things you forget about 5 minutes after you post them.

The Internet never forgets.

15   I heard on the news that the FCC (*people who set the rules for the Internet*) have decided it's OK for people to do social media background checks.

16   That means that 10 or 15 years from now when you apply for that really cool job that you've been dreaming about since your were, oh, *the age you are right now,* the people thinking about hiring you can pull up all those old message you forgot about and WOW … won't they be surprised?

17   Is that what you want for your future you?

What about right now?

18   Would you stand up in front of a million people today and do that sexy dance or act like an idiot or talk about how you drank too much when you weren't old enough to drink at all? Really? 1,000,000 people? What about 1,000 people? Or even 15 people? Probably not.

19   Well, tweet about it and you have the power to reach a lot more than 1 million people. PEOPLE. YOU. DON'T. KNOW.

20   Just because you don't see them doesn't mean they aren't out there. <u>They are</u>. Ask former Rep. Weiner. Or Gilbert Gottfried. Lots of people saw their messages, and look where it got them.

It's not a secret.

21   Maybe your mom and dad don't know you are on Twitter. You went behind their back and created that account, so no one will ever know except the 1579 friends you've collected on Facebook (including the ones you've never met).

22   How many of those people are who they say they are? You can be anyone you want to be online, right? Do you really know your *"friends"*?

My point is that you need to be CAREFUL online.

23   I'm not that old, but the world sure has changed since I was a kid. People used to talk about being "street smart," which meant that you knew a thing or two about life and weren't likely to be taken advantage of or do something that could get you in trouble—and I mean real trouble, not just the kind where you get grounded for a week or have your phone taken away.

24   The new "street smart" is "social smarts." There's <u>way</u> more trouble online, just waiting for you if you're careless. And you might not see it coming.

I'm not trying to scare you, but wake up.

25   Protect your privacy online. Be careful what you post. Think twice.

26   *Would you want your grandma to see that?* Then it probably shouldn't be online.

27   It's really hard to undo social media mistakes. Mom and Dad can't bail you out. You can't buy your way back from a bad reputation. Poor judgement will follow you, because the Internet never forgets and yes, people *are* watching.

28   Don't get me wrong. I'm a big fan of social media. It's a great tool for sharing, communicating and staying in touch. But any tool, when it's misused, can create a lot of damage.

29   Don't let that happen to you.

30   Have fun, but be careful out there. Please.

Reading Comprehension Check

1. What is writer's view about privacy in modern times?
   a. it has increased
   b. it depends on the person
   c. it no longer exists
   d. it has changed all adults

2. The writer mentions 'that creepy guy at the mall' to make the point that
   a. he is not computer savvy.
   b. he may be online and reading your Twitter posts.
   c. his Twitter account may have expired.
   d. privacy involves security.

3. Why does the author ask the question, "Would you stand up in front of a million people today and do that sexy dance or act like an idiot or talk about how you drank too much when you weren't old enough to drink at all?" (para. 18)
   a. to make the point that you should only act silly in private
   b. to explain the concept of luck
   c. to show the beneficial power of social media in finding a job
   d. to make the point that what is appropriate in private may not be appropriate in public.

4. What advice does the writer offer?
   a. Friend your family members on Facebook.
   b. Protect your privacy by being more careful online.
   c. Always be open and completely honest online.
   d. Spend more money on social media.

5. The writer says she is a big fan of social media because
   a. you can show the world everything about yourself.
   b. you can share and stay in touch with evil strangers.
   c. it is a money-saving tool.
   d. it's a great tool for sharing, communicating, and staying in touch.

Exploring the Topic

Collaboration

Discuss the following questions to review the content of the blog entries you have just read.

1. The writer offers several arguments for why you need to be more careful online. Which of her points do you most agree with? Which do you disagree with? Explain.

2. In your opinion, how have social networking Web sites, such as Facebook, changed the way we communicate and meet new people?

Post-Reading Vocabulary Exercise

Without using a dictionary, determine the meaning of the bolded words from the context.

1. "… not just the kind where you get **grounded** for a week or have your phone taken away." (para. 23)

   Grounded means _____

2. "There's way more trouble online, just waiting for you if you're **careless**." (para. 24)

   Careless means _____

3. "You can't buy your way back from a bad **reputation**." (para. 27)

   Reputation means _____

Paul Saltz   An Interview with a Student in the Field of Sociology

Columbus State Community College

1. How did you find your path to majoring in sociology?

I have a passion for social justice, beginning with my grandfather's commitment to community service. I want to study social problems in order to create solutions.

2. What was the biggest obstacle you faced in your study of sociology?

Time management. Many sociology texts are very word heavy with very lengthy chapters, sometimes taking an hour or more to read them.

3. What area(s) of sociology in particular do you find most interesting?

I love examining social problems. I also find law and other social constructs very fascinating.

4. What specific skills are required of students who study sociology?

A student needs to keep an open mind, recognizing their preconceived ideas as was taught to them via socialization. They also need to be mindful of other cultures and social constructs.

5. Other than teaching sociology, what other career avenues are available for sociology majors?

While I personally want to teach higher education, I know that sociology majors also tend to work for non-profit and government organizations.

READING

Reading Selection **3**

Web Article

MyReadingLab™
Complete this **Exercise**
at **myreadinglab.com**

Is This the One? Choosing the Right Mate

Preview Questions

1. In the past, family members played an instrumental role in helping one choose a spouse. Discuss how this social practice has changed over time. In other words, what has brought about the change in how we choose a mate?

2. If you were to look for the five most important qualities in a life partner, what would they be? Discuss why these qualities would be important for you.

3. Do you think that men and women have different requirements when they choose their life partners? If so, what factors cause these differences in their respective agendas? Give specific reasons for your answer.

Pre-Reading Vocabulary: Focus on Some Key Terms

As you have done before, try to guess the meaning of these words below with a classmate. Then consult a dictionary to determine how accurate you were.

Collaboration

Word	*Your Definition*	*Dictionary Definition*
soulmate		
mission		
consulting		
potential		
intriguing		

Is This the One? Choosing the Right Mate

By Janice Allen

6:36 P.M. EDT, October 28, 2011
GRAND RAPIDS, Mich.—

1   Mr. Right. A Soulmate. 'The One'.

2   No matter what you call it, chances are you or someone you know is on a mission to find the right mate.

3   According to the U.S. Census Bureau, there are more than 99 million unmarried Americans. That's 44 percent of the adult population.

4   The quest to find love is big business on dating websites and the subject of songs, movies, and hit reality TV shows.

5   Is there a formula to follow when it comes to finding and picking your perfect partner? FOX 17 took that question to longtime matchmaker Kim Kanoza. Kanoza has been in the business of matching singles for over 20 years and currently serves as the executive director of Matchmaker Michigan.

6   "There is a lid to go with every pot, I solely believe it," said Kanoza. "I've believed it as long as I've been doing this job."

7   Kanoza spends her time consulting with people looking for love. She matches them up with other singles based on what qualities and values they're looking for. With hundreds of success stories under her belt, she has some advice on what to look for in a lifelong partner.

8   "We all kind of grew up around Cinderella. We read the fairy tales about Prince Charming, our knight in shining armor, well that's not really how it ends," Kanoza told FOX 17. "There's not always gonna be the 6'4" guy that comes along, the tall dark guy that sweeps you off your feet."

9   "When it comes to finding a futuristic mate, you have to have some kind of ideal guy or girl that you're looking for," said Kanoza. She added that means taking into account more than the superficial traits you desire in a potential mate.

10   "The reality of it is, what's going to make you happy? A lifelong partner, someone monogamous, somebody stable in their environment financially?" explained Kanoza. She advises listing out personality traits and other items that may be deal breakers (i.e. different religion, morals, family values)

11   You know the saying opposites attract? Kanoza says there's truth to that. "To a degree, I think opposites can attract because it's intriguing to us. We can be kind of curious … they're different than me, let me kind of pursue that, see where it goes."

12   "The chemistry doesn't come on the first date always," said Kanoza. "It may not come on the second date, nor sometimes the third or the fourth."

13   The number one thing Kanoza says to evaluate before choosing a mate is *yourself*. She says, "You first of all have to like yourself and feel good about who you are individually. You have to be comfortable in your environment."

14   Kanoza finally advises singles who are seeking love to keep looking and keep the faith.

15   "There are great [people] out there. They're out there just like you … They're doing the same thing, just like you," said Kanoza.

16   With some patience, it could lead to something priceless.

17   Kanoza says "Once you're in love and you have your best friend, and you know you're gonna wake up to them for the rest of your life, and they are the one … it's a life changing experience."

Fox 17 News, October 28, 2011. Reprinted by permission.

Reading Comprehension Check

1. FOX 17 asked Kim Kanoza if there was a formula to finding and picking one's perfect partner because
   a. she is a FOX 17 employee.
   b. Kanoza saves marriages from falling apart.
   c. she has been a successful matchmaker for 20 years.
   d. she has been married to the same person for 20 years.

2. In the sentence, "With hundreds of success stories **under her belt**, she has some advice on what to look for in a lifelong partner," (para. 6) the expression *under her belt* means

a. she wears hundreds of belts.

b. she wears a tight leather belt.

c. she has a big heart.

d. she has lots of experience.

3. "The chemistry doesn't come on the first date always," said Kanoza. "It may not come on the second date, nor sometimes the third or the fourth." In this sentence, the word *chemistry* means

a. the science dealing with the composition of matter.

b. the positive interaction of one personality with another.

c. the lack of connection between two people.

d. the chemical properties of two people.

4. "We can be kind of curious … they're different than me, let me kind of **pursue** that, see where it goes." (para.11) The word *pursue* in this context means

a. chase.   c. seek or attain.

b. ignore.   d. think about.

5. "The **chemistry** doesn't come on the first date always," said Kanoza. "It may not come on the second date, nor sometimes the third or the fourth." In this context, the word *chemistry* means

a. a chemistry professor on the fourth date.

b. a major crisis between the first date and the second.

c. an argument between two single Americans.

d. the interaction of one personality with one another.

Exploring the Topic

Collaboration

Discuss the following questions to check your comprehension of the article you have just read.

1. When people ask Kanoza for advice on how to choose a mate, why does she ask them to be realistic about what they are looking for in a potential partner?

2. Why does Kanoza advise her clients to have some kind of ideal guy or girl in mind that they are looking for?

3. In addition to the advice offered by Kanoza, what advice would you give to someone who was looking for a mate? Be specific.

Post-Reading Vocabulary

Without using a dictionary, determine the meaning of the bolded words from the context.

1. "A lifelong partner, someone **monogamous**, somebody stable in their environment financially?" (para. 10)

Monogamous means _____

2. "She added that means taking into account more than the superficial **traits** you desire in a potential mate." (para. 9)

   Traits means _____

3. "The number one thing Kanoza says to **evaluate** before choosing a mate is yourself." (para. 13)

   Evaluate means _____

SKILL FOCUS
Vocabulary in Action

6 LEARNING OBJECTIVE
Find the meaning of words
from their contexts

As you read college textbooks, you are likely to come across many unfamiliar words. Come to think of it, your academic success will depend, to a large extent, on your strong vocabulary. Keep in mind that each discipline has its own unique vocabulary, and sociology is no exception. It will be important for you to be able to recognize discipline-specific vocabulary. You will most probably be required to use some, if not all, of these new words in the academic papers you write and the formal presentations you give.

When faced with a new word, there are various ways to determine its meaning. Often you will not have the access or the time to look up the word in a dictionary, in which case you will need to depend on the context to guess its meaning. Let's go over two strategies to figure out the meaning of new words.

Strategy 1: Using Context Clues

When you come across an unfamiliar word, pay attention to the context in which the word appears. The context can be just a sentence or an entire paragraph containing the unfamiliar word. Consider the words appearing before and after the word you do not know. More often than not, it is the context that will enable you to unlock the meaning of the new word.

Let's look at an example of how this is done.

> Most of these values, such as success, hard work, and efficiency, are clearly related to one another, showing cultural **integration**, the joining of various values into a coherent whole.
>
> from Alex Thio, *Sociology: A Brief Introduction*, 7e, p. 47

Let's suppose that you do not know the meaning of **integration**. By closely looking at the context, which in this case is the whole sentence, we can readily see the clues such as "success, hard work, and efficiency … clearly related to one another … joining of various values … a coherent whole." We can then make a correct conclusion that the word **integration** means bringing together various things to make up a whole.

Strategy 2: Using Your Knowledge of Prefixes, Suffixes, and Roots

Earlier in this chapter, you learned about how words are formed by combining prefixes, suffixes, and roots. Your knowledge of these word parts will come in handy when you encounter an unfamiliar word. For example, if you recognize a verb suffix in an unfamiliar word, then you will at least know that it is an action. Similarly, if you see that there is a noun suffix in a new word, you can conclude that it is most likely a thing, a place, a phenomenon, so on and so forth. Finally, if the unfamiliar word contains an adjectival suffix, you can safely conclude that the word provides additional information about a noun.

Consider the following example to understand this strategy further.

> In the past 25 years, the typical adult's leisure time has shrunk to less hours a week and the work week has swelled to more hours, largely a result of the greater demands of employers and the rise of **addictive** consumerism.
>
> from Alex Thio, *Sociology: A Brief Introduction*, 7e, p. 47

Notice the *-ive* suffix in the bolded word. It indicates that the word is an adjective. Recall other adjectives with the same suffix such as *relative, active, passive,* and *massive*. As you know, adjectives provide additional information about the nouns they modify. In the above context, it is a type of consumerism that is **addictive**. If you know anything about an addiction such as drug use or smoking, you can perhaps draw a conclusion that **addictive** most probably means a desire that is difficult to control. In this context, it is consumerism—the act of buying products and services—that is difficult to control.

EXERCISE 7   Finding Meaning from Context in Sentences

Collaboration

Now it is time for you to practice determining meaning from context at the sentence level. You will have a chance to look at larger contexts, but let's focus on a single sentence containing a new word. With a classmate, read the following sentences carefully and figure out the meaning of the bolded word by using the two strategies you have learned so far.

1. Culture is a design for living or, more precisely, a complex whole consisting of objects, values, and other characteristics that people **acquire** as members of a society.

   from Alex Thio, *Sociology: A Brief Introduction*, 7e, p. 43

   Acquire means _____

2. The **tangible** objects make up the material culture, which includes every conceivable kind of physical object produced by humans, from spears and plows to cooking pots and compact discs.

   from Alex Thio, *Sociology: A Brief Introduction*, 7e, p. 43

   Tangible means _____

3. The high standards of living in modern societies may be **attributed** to their advanced knowledge and sophisticated technology.

from Alex Thio, *Sociology: A Brief Introduction*, 7e, p. 43

Attributed means _____

4. These shared ideas are usually the basis of a society's **norms,** social rules that specify how people should behave.

from Alex Thio, *Sociology: A Brief Introduction*, 7e, p. 43

Norms means _____

5. If we believe in the value our society places on freedom of religion, we are likely to follow the norm against religious **intolerance**.

from Alex Thio, *Sociology: A Brief Introduction*, 7e, p. 45

Intolerance means _____

Collaboration

EXERCISE 8   Finding Meaning from Context in Paragraphs

You have practiced guessing meaning from context at the sentence level. Now try doing the same at the paragraph level. In the paragraphs below, certain words are highlighted. Working in small groups, read the paragraphs carefully and pay attention to the context to figure out the meaning of the highlighted words.

1. As children grow older, they become **increasingly** involved with their **peer** group, a group whose members are about the same age and have similar interests. As a socializing **agent**, the peer group differs from both the family and the school. Whereas parents and teachers have more power than children and students, the peer group is made up of equals.

from Alex Thio, *Sociology: A Brief Introduction*, 7e, p. 79

Increasingly means _____
Peer means _____
Agent means _____

2. At home, children are treated as **unique** special persons. At school, they are treated more **impersonally**, the same as all their schoolmates. One of their first tasks at school is to learn to fit in by **getting along** with others. In fact, the school often provides children with their first training in how to behave in secondary groups.

from Alex Thio, *Sociology: A Brief Introduction*, 7e, p. 79

Unique means _____
Impersonally means _____
Getting along means _____

3. Are children like **clay**, waiting to be shaped in one way or another? The roles of nature (**heredity** or what we inherit) and nurture (environment or what we learn) in making us what we are have long been argued. To the seventeenth-century philosopher John Locke, the mind of a child was a tabula rasa (blank slate). People became what they were taught to be. By the second half of the nineteenth century, however, a quite different view was popular. Instead of looking to **nurture**—what people are taught—to explain human behavior, many social scientists looked to nature—what people **inherit**. The pendulum of opinion has swung back and forth ever since.

from Alex Thio, Sociology: A Brief Introduction, 7e, p. 62

Clay means _____

Heredity means _____

Nurture means _____

Inherit means _____

4.   When Americans talk, they tend to express directly what is on their minds. People in many other cultures are more likely to speak indirectly. In China, if you visit an **acquaintance** on a hot day and feel thirsty, you would not ask your host point-blank, "May I have a glass of water?" Instead, you would **convey** the same request by saying "Isn't it hot today?" In Japan, if at the end of a lengthy business meeting you ask, "Do you then agree to do business with us?" the Japanese will always say "yes" even if they mean "no." They are **reluctant** to say "no" directly in order to save others' face and spare them **embarrassment**. Used to directness in speech, many Americans cannot understand how "yes" can possibly mean "no." But the Japanese can say "yes" in a certain way to mean "yes" and then say "yes" in another way to mean "no."

from Alex Thio, Sociology: A Brief Introduction, 7e, p. 95

Acquaintance means _____

Convey means _____

Reluctant means _____

Embarrassment means _____

5.   In India, which has the largest number of cattle in the world, there are many poor and starving people, yet the slaughter of cows is **forbidden**. Moreover, their 180 million cows are treated as **divine**. They are given right of way in the street. They are even affectionately retired to "old-age homes" when they begin to become **infirm**. Why doesn't India feed its starving human population by killing these animals for food? The popular explanation is simply that the Hindus consider their cows **sacred**. But why?

The reason suggested by the functionalist perspective is that the sacred cows serve several important, practical functions. First, they produce oxen which Indian farmers desperately need to plow their fields and pull their carts. Second, when the cows die naturally, their beef is eaten by the poor lower castes and their **hides** are used by non-Hindu Indians to maintain one of the world's largest leather industries. Third, the cows produce an enormous amount of **manure**, which is used as fertilizer and cooking fuel. Fourth, the cows are tireless **scavengers**, eating garbage, stubble, and grass between railroad tracks, in ditches, and on roadsides. Thus, it costs nothing to raise the cows, and they provide many things of value. India's **peasant** economy depends heavily on the cows. If the Indians ate their cows, many more people would starve to death. In short, by enabling the cows to do all those things, the Hindu belief in their sacredness ultimately serves the function of saving the lives of people, thereby helping to ensure social order and stability in India.

from Alex Thio, Sociology: A Brief Introduction, 7e, p. 54

Forbidden means _____

Divine means _____

Infirm means _____

Sacred means _____

Hides means _____

Manure means _____

Scavengers means _____

Peasant means _____

As you work through this chapter, you will have many opportunities to practice and strengthen this very important reading skill. You will notice that as you build your vocabulary, your reading comprehension will also improve. Keep practicing determining meaning from context throughout the rest of the chapter.

LANDMARK IN THE FIELD OF SOCIOLOGY

Chat Rooms

Not many years ago, before text messaging and online chatting, if someone wanted to communicate with another person in writing they had to write a letter and mail or fax it. Thus, if the letter was mailed, there would be a significant gap in time from the composition of the message to its reception. This was particularly true if the receiver was in another part of the world. The ability to communicate via e-mail and chat sessions fundamentally changed written communication.

Online chat is a form of communication in which people send text messages to other people in the same chat room in real time. Some chat rooms now offer both text and voice simultaneously, as well as live video capability.

The first online chat rooms were created by an English college student named Roy Trubshaw in 1978. Trubshaw's program allowed others to play a fantasy game called Multi-User Dungeon (MUD) from their home computers. MUD spread from Trubshaw's network of friends. It inspired others to create their own versions. By the mid-1990s, there were hundreds of MUDs on the Internet covering all kinds of shared interests.

In 1991, a team of computer engineers began work on an Internet programming language. This eventually became what is known today as Java. Java chat was distinct in that it allowed people to participate in chat rooms from their Internet browser. Java technology advanced over the years. By 2003 its usage reached over 500 million computers. Java chat now has many uses, from recreational and personal chatting to customer service chat rooms.

Instant messaging, such as Yahoo! Messenger, soon developed, and private chat room users could invite others into their chat sessions. More recently, voice chat combined with video conferencing has allowed users to both see and hear one another during chat sessions.

Chat rooms have changed our perceptions of what it means to communicate with someone both in written and in spoken form. They have blurred the distinction between telephone-like conversation and written messages. People can send and receive written responses as fast as they can type them or text them through cell phones. Chat rooms are in many ways the updated telephone of the twenty-first century. They connect us instantly to those in our own social networks and to strangers with shared interests.

Considering the Topic

Collaboration

Answer the following questions with a partner.

1. In what ways have chat rooms changed the way people communicate?

_____

_____

2. Do you think this is a positive or negative change? Explain.

_____

_____

3. Can you imagine another technological development that will further change the way we communicate and interact? Explain.

_____

_____

Internet Connection

Research another landmark in the field of sociology, and fill out the section below.

Internet dating	school busing
the birth control pill	the National Origins Act
the Green Movement	African American English

Landmark: _____

Question	Answer
When did this landmark become a reality?	
Who was involved in developing this landmark?	
What made this landmark special?	
How did this landmark change the way people interact?	

Reminder: Are you on your way to learning at least 25 unfamiliar words for this chapter?

READING

Reading Selection **4**

Web Article

MyReadingLab™
Complete this **Exercise**
at **myreadinglab.com**

Ten Keys to Successful Parenting

Preview Questions

1. Do you believe that successful parenting can produce caring and responsible members of society? Why or why not? Give specific reasons for your answer.

2. Some people believe that human behavior is mostly influenced by environmental factors such as good parenting, quality education, etc. Others think that much of human behavior is genetically determined, and that the environment plays little or no role in influencing it. What is your position on this issue?

3. Does parenting come naturally to most people, or do you think people should be required to take courses in parenting before they become parents? In other words, should the government require expecting parents to attend parenting workshops? Why or why not?

Collaboration

Pre-Reading Vocabulary: Focus on Some Key Terms

As you have done before, try to guess the meaning of these words below with a classmate. Then consult a dictionary to determine how accurate you were.

Word	Your Definition	Dictionary Definition
self-esteem		
hassle		
consequences		
pleas		
pouting		

Ten Keys to Successful Parenting

By Kathryn Kvols

1   It is important that we discipline in a way that teaches responsibility by motivating our children internally, to build their self-esteem and make them feel loved. If our children are disciplined in this respect, they will not have a need to turn to gangs, drugs, or sex to feel powerful or belong.

2   The following ten keys will help parents use methods that have been proven to provide children with a sense of well-being and security.

3   **1. Use Genuine Encounter Moments (GEMS)**

Your child's self-esteem is greatly influenced by the quality of time you spend with him—not the amount of time that you spend. With our busy lives, we are often thinking about the next thing that we have to do, instead of putting 100% focused attention on what our child is saying to us. We often pretend to listen or ignore our child's attempts to communicate with us. If we don't give our child GEMS throughout the day, he will often start to misbehave. Negative attention in a child's mind is better than being ignored.

It is also important to recognize that feelings are neither right nor wrong. They just are. So when your child says to you, "Mommy, you never spend time with me" (even though you just played with her) she is expressing what she feels. It is best at these times just to validate her feelings by saying, "Yeah, I bet it does feel like a long time since we spent time together."

4   **2. Use Action, Not Words**

Statistics say that we give our children over 2000 compliance requests a day! No wonder our children become "parent deaf"! Instead of nagging or yelling, ask yourself, "What action could I take?" For example, if you have nagged your child about unrolling his socks when he takes them off, then only wash socks that are unrolled. Action speaks louder than words.

5   **3. Give Children Appropriate Ways to Feel Powerful**

If you don't, they will find inappropriate ways to feel their power. Ways to help them feel powerful and valuable are to ask their advice, give them choices, let them help you balance your checkbook, cook all or part of a meal, or help you shop. A two-year-old can wash plastic dishes, wash vegetables, or put silverware away. Often we do the job for them because we can do it with less hassle, but the result is they feel unimportant.

6   **4. Use Natural Consequences**

Ask yourself what would happen if I didn't interfere in this situation? If we interfere when we don't need to, we rob children of the chance to learn from the consequences of their actions. By allowing consequences to do the talking, we avoid disturbing our relationships by nagging or reminding too much. For example, if your child forgets her lunch, you don't bring it to her. Allow her to find a solution and learn the importance of remembering.

7   **5. Use Logical Consequences**

Often the consequences are too far in the future to practically use a natural consequence. When that is the case, logical consequences are effective. A consequence for the child must be logically related to the behavior in order for it to work. For example, if your child forgets to return his video and you ground him for a week, that punishment will only create resentment within your child. However, if you return the video for him and either deduct the amount from his allowance or allow him to work off the money owed, then your child can see the logic to your discipline.

8   **6. Withdraw from Conflict**

If your child is testing you through a temper tantrum, or being angry or speaking disrespectfully to you, it is best if you leave the room or tell the child you will be in the next room if he wants to "Try again." Do not leave in anger or defeat.

9   **7. Separate the Deed from the Doer**

Never tell a child that he is bad. That tears at his self-esteem. Help your child recognize that it isn't that you don't like him, but it is his behavior that you are unwilling to tolerate. In order for a child to have healthy self-esteem, he must know that he is loved unconditionally no matter what he does. Do not motivate your child by withdrawing your love from him. When in doubt, ask yourself, did my discipline build my child's self-esteem?

10   **8. Be Kind and Firm at the Same Time**

Suppose you have told your five-year-old child that if she isn't dressed by the time the timer goes off, you will pick her up and take her to the car. She has been told she can get dressed either in the car or at school. Make sure that you are loving when you pick her up, yet firm by picking her up as soon as the timer goes off without any more nagging. If in doubt, ask yourself, did I motivate through love or fear?

11   **9. Parent with the End in Mind**

Most of us parent with the mindset to get the situation under control as soon as possible. We are looking for the expedient solution. This often results in children who feel overpowered. But if we parent in a way that keeps in mind how we want our child to be as an adult, we will be more thoughtful in the way we parent. For example, if we spank our child, he will learn to use acts of aggression to get what he wants when he grows up.

12   **10. Be Consistent, Follow Through**

If you have made an agreement that your child cannot buy candy when she gets to the store, do not give in to her pleas, tears, demands or pouting. Your child will learn to respect you more if you mean what you say.

from www.incaf.com.

MyReadingLab™
Complete this **Exercise**
at **myreadinglab.com**

Reading Comprehension Check

1. The author suggests that parents should
   a. spank their children to teach discipline.
   b. help their children build self-confidence through love and respect.
   c. make children understand that there will be dire consequences for their misbehavior.
   d. punish children severely whenever they make a mistake.

2. "Your child's self-esteem is greatly **influenced** by the quality of time you spend with him—not the amount of time that you spend." The meaning of *influenced* in this context is
   a. disturbed.   c. affected.
   b. interfered.   d. decimated.

3. In the sentence, "If we **interfere** when we don't need to, we rob children of the chance to learn from the consequences of their actions," the word *interfere* means

 a. support. c. resolve.

 b. encourage. d. intrude.

4. "For example, if your child forgets to return his video and you **ground** him for a week, that punishment will only create resentment within your child." In this sentence, the word *ground* means

 a. surface. c. reward.

 b. floor. d. punish.

5. "Most of us parent with the mindset to get the situation under control as soon as possible. We are looking for the expedient solution. This often results in children who feel **overpowered**." In this passage, the word *overpowered* means

 a. strengthened. c. energized.

 b. helpless. d. powerful.

Exploring the Topic

Collaboration

Working in a small group, discuss the following questions. Write brief answers to the questions and be prepared to share them with your classmates.

1. According to the author, why is it crucially important that parents teach their children discipline with love and respect? What are the consequences of not doing so?

2. The article suggests that it is the quality of time, not the quantity of time, spent with children that helps them build their self-esteem. Do you agree with this view? Give specific reasons for your answer.

3. Contrary to an old expression, "spare the rod, spoil the child," the author warns us of the consequences of punishing children. Do you believe that punishing a child can cause negative feelings in her or him? Why or why not?

Post-Reading Vocabulary

Without using a dictionary, determine the meaning of the bolded words from the context.

1. "We often **pretend** to listen or ignore our child's attempts to communicate with us." (para. 3)

 Pretend means _____

2. "For example, if your child forgets to return his video and you ground him for a week, that punishment will only create **resentment** within your child." (para. 7)

 Resentment means _____

3. "For example, if we spank our child, he will learn to use acts of **aggression** to get what he wants when he grows up." (para. 11)

Aggression means _____

Reading Selection **5**

Advice Column

Trouble with Raising Teenage Son

Preview Questions

MyReadingLab™
Complete this **Exercise**
at **myreadinglab.com**

1. What kinds of trouble do some teenage boys get into? How should a parent deal with a teenage boy in crisis?

2. Are parents generally stricter with their boys or with their girls? Explain.

3. In the following reading, a concerned parent writes an advice columnist for ideas on how best to deal with her son? Do you believe that advice columnists play an important role in society? Explain. If you felt that you needed help in dealing with a situation, would you share your concerns with an advice columnist? Why or why not?

Collaboration

Pre-Reading Vocabulary: Focus on Some Key Terms

As you have done before, try to guess the meaning of the words below with a classmate. Then consult a dictionary to determine how accurate you were.

Word	Your Definition	Dictionary Definition
endure		
craving		
warden		
modifications		
exasperation		

Trouble with Raising Teenage Son

Ethnically Speaking *by* **Larry Meeks**

1   Dear Larry: I am African-American and a single mother with three children, ages 15, 10 and 8. All of them are boys. I am having a lot of problems with them, especially the eldest.

2   He argues with me about almost everything. He thinks he is the man/boss of the house. He wants to do things his way. The biggest thing we have disagreements about is his failure to follow my instructions regarding the time he must be home and in the house.

3   The home is becoming an unhappy place. It is getting to the point that I hate to go home because I do not want to get into an argument.

4   My other sons are starting to act out because of the fighting and hollering that is happening. I do not know how to handle the situation.

5   I would like to give my son to his father, but I have no idea where he is. Also, his father never wanted to have anything to do with his son. The father of the other two children is not helpful. He does not want to get involved and probably would be happy to get rid of his stepchild.

6   We have had counseling, but it has not worked.

7   I would appreciate any information or advice. I am desperate.

— Tired Mom

8   Dear Tired Mom: Don't give up. You are experiencing the same thing millions of other mothers have had to endure. Your son is growing into an adult, and he is craving his freedom. He sees you as more of a warden than a mother. You are the one who always tells him "no" and what he should be doing. You are the one who is stopping him from doing what he wants to do.

9   The best possible advice is for you to follow the advice of a qualified counselor who has the opportunity to speak to both of you.

10   The counselor can give advice, see how things are progressing and make modifications as the situation develops.

11   Other than that, all I can do is tell you how I handled a similar situation with my son.

12   I knew from my own experience growing up that freedom is what teens crave the most. Parents don't give their children freedom because they are fearful their children will make the wrong decisions and get in trouble.

13   There is always a push-pull between parents and children. It gets worse as the children get older. There is constant bickering until the parents finally, in exasperation, let go and grudgingly back away.

14   I decided with my son to let him have freedom when he finished high school. I chose that time because that was when he would go away to college, where kids typically have total freedom from their parents.

15   I decided to give my son a four-year freedom, or emancipation, plan. We started when he was in ninth grade. In ninth grade, he could decide where he wanted to go from after school until 6 p.m. The only stipulation was he had to tell me where he was going and why he was going there. The other part of the plan was that his decisions had to be free of any problems or trouble.

16   He knew that if there were no problems, his freedom time would be extended. If he had made wrong decisions, his freedom time would have been shortened.

17   I am happy to report that I never had to subtract time from my son's freedom time. When he finished high school and went away to college, freedom from parents was nothing new.

18   My method allowed him to have freedom with me there for counseling, support and advice. It takes a great amount of faith to let go of a child, and there is a lot of trepidation. I wish you the best. Write me and let me know what you decide.

Reading Comprehension Check

1. Which of her sons is giving the mother the hardest time?
    a. she only has one child
    b. her oldest son
    c. her youngest son
    d. each is challenging her equally

2. Why doesn't the mother get the children's father involved?
    a. She doesn't want to bother him.
    b. He is already very involved.
    c. She cannot find him.
    d. She would rather deal with this situation on her own.

3. What does the advice columnist mean when he writes, "There is always a push-pull between parents and children"? (para. 13)
    a. Parents should discipline their children more.
    b. Children should never push their parents.
    c. Children control the home situation.
    d. There is often a power struggle going on.

4. Why did the advice columnist give his son four years of freedom?
    a. because his son demanded it
    b. He couldn't control him anymore.
    c. to trick him into a new form of control
    d. to teach his son self-discipline

5. Why does the advice columnist share his own parenting story?
    a. He likes to talk only about himself.
    b. so that the single mother may learn something from his experience
    c. to make the point that she should be tougher with her son
    d. to disempower her

Collaboration

Exploring the Topic

Working in a small group, discuss the following questions. Write brief answers to the questions and be prepared to share them with your classmates.

1. In your own words, what exactly is the problem the single-mother is having with her eldest son?

2. The single mother makes it clear that the child's father is not around to offer any support during her parenting crisis. Why, in your view, do many fathers run away from their parenting responsibilities?

3. The advice columnist seems to believe that sometimes it is best to give a teenager a greater sense of freedom. Do you share his view? Why or why not?

Post-Reading Vocabulary

Collaboration

Working with a partner, determine the meaning of the bolded words from the context.

1. "There is constant **bickering**." (para. 13)

    Bickering means _____

2. "… until the parents finally, in exasperation, let go and **grudgingly** back away." (para. 13)

    Grudgingly means _____

3. "It takes a great amount of faith to let go of a child, and there is a lot of **trepidation**." (para. 18)

    Trepidation means _____

Panel Discussion on the Role of Video Games and Violent Behavior

Many parents and social activists are deeply concerned that violent video games can cause imitative behavior in teenagers. Participate in a panel discussion and discuss if there is a correlation between violent video games and crimes committed by teenagers. You can create a profile for yourself and play a specific role as you express your view on the controversial topic. What follows are some possible profiles for the panelists. Feel free to brainstorm other profiles with your instructor and peers.

1. a single mother
2. a teenage delinquent
3. a police chief
4. a high school teacher
5. the CEO of a company that produces violent video games
6. a priest
7. a doctor
8. a single father
9. a victim of a violent crime
10. the owner of a store that sells video games

As you participate in the panel discussion, try to address the following questions. You can formulate your own questions as well and ask other panelists to respond to them.

1. Who makes the decision(s) to produce and market violent video games?
2. How and why are these decisions made?
3. Who stands to gain from these decisions?
4. What can be done to protect our young children from violent video games?

Your instructor will give you specific guidelines on how to participate in a panel discussion. Read the guidelines carefully and come fully prepared to participate in the panel actively.

TEXTBOOK APPLICATION   **Sociology in the United States**

In this section of each chapter, you will practice reading excerpts from college textbooks. The purpose of this exercise is to get you acquainted with the type of reading you will be required to do in college. First, listen to the lecture and take notes. You can listen to the lecture by scanning the QR code on the next page with your smart phone. Your professor may also read the selections or play the audio file in class. Make sure that you write down the important points of the lecture.

Collaboration

Group Discussion

Working in small groups of three to four students, answer the following questions. Your instructor may ask you to share your answers with your classmates. As you refer to your notes, it is best to write brief answers to each of the questions below using your own words. After the discussion, you will have an opportunity to share your findings with your peers.

1. At the beginning of the twentieth century, how did American sociologists deal with social problems differently than their European counterparts?
2. What was the name of the center that Jane Addams opened in Chicago?
3. Why was Addams awarded the Nobel Peace Prize in 1931? Name at least two government programs that Jane Addams helped establish.
4. Why did W. E. B. DuBois move to Ghana in 1961?
5. Do you agree with the view that sociology must remain a basic science only, an idea that gained currency in the early twentieth century? Please give specific reasons for your answers.
6. What factors brought about a change in the perception of sociology in the 1960s?
7. Why has sociology been divided into numerous specialties in the twenty-first century?

Now that you have discussed the highlights of the lecture with your class-mates, read the following selection and answer the multiple-choice questions that follow.

Sociology in the United States

1   By the turn of the twentieth century, sociology had made its way from Europe to the United States. Like their European predecessors, the first U.S. sociologists tried to understand and solve the problems of their time, such as crime and delinquency, broken homes, poor neighborhoods, and racial problems. But they dealt with social problems differently. The Europeans were more interested in developing large-scale social theories. So they examined the fundamental issues of social order and social change, trying to discover the causes of social problems as a whole. In contrast, the U.S. sociologists were more pragmatic. They were more inclined to focus on specific problems, such as prostitution, street gangs, or racial discrimination in employment, and to treat each problem separately (Ross, 1991).

 Scan this code using your smart phone to listen to an audio version of this reading

2   A good example was Jane Addams (1860–1935), one of the founders of U.S. sociology and social work. In Chicago, she set up and directed a center for social reform and research, which she named Hull House. Most of the social activists working at Hull House were women. Their goal was to solve social problems using sound sociological theory and research. In their projects, Addams and her colleagues would first identify a certain problem, gather data documenting the nature of the problem, and then formulate a social-action policy based on the data. Their final step was to organize citizens and lobby political and community leaders to eliminate or alleviate the problem. They dealt with a wide array of social ills, including poverty, worker exploitation, child labor, and juvenile delinquency. Addams was thus able to play a significant role in establishing many government programs—most notably, Social Security, the Children's Bureau, and workers' compensation—and various government regulations affecting health and safety standards. For all these contributions, Addams was awarded the Nobel Peace Prize in 1931 (Ross, 1991; Deegan, 1988).

3   Another sociologist with the same dedication to improving society was W. E. B. DuBois (1868–1963), an African American. He graduated from Fisk University in Tennessee and became the first African American to receive a doctorate of sociology. He soon began a highly productive academic career that included, among many other things, founding two scholarly journals and writing numerous books and articles. He focused his research and writing on the racial problems in the United States. At the same time, however, he worked hard to apply his enormous knowledge to improving society. He founded the Niagara Movement, an organization of African American intellectuals fighting for racial equality. He also helped create the National Association for the Advancement of Colored People (NAACP) and edited its influential magazine, *Crisis*. Later, he became a revolutionary Marxist, advocating the use of force to achieve racial equality. Finally, seeing little improvement in race relations, he moved in 1961 to the African nation of Ghana, where he died two years later.

4   For about 40 years after 1900, most U.S. sociologists, such as Addams and DuBois, concentrated on studying and solving social problems. However, the prosperity that followed World War II masked many social problems, causing the reformist fervor to begin to cool. Some sociologists turned their attention to general theories of society. The idea grew that sociology should be a *basic science*, seeking knowledge only, not an *applied science*, which puts knowledge to use. Moreover,

many people believed that sociology must be objective and free of values. This left no room for a commitment to reform society according to certain values. From about 1945 to 1965, sociology was dominated by the attempt to develop scientific methods that could be applied to the study of societies and social behavior. During these two decades, sociologists developed increasingly sophisticated research techniques.

5   In the 1960s, however, the ideal of objective, value-free knowledge came under fire in just about all fields, including sociology. Renewed awareness of poverty and years of social unrest—marked by race riots, student revolts, and controversy about the Vietnam War—put pressure on sociologists to attack society's ills once again. Meanwhile, attitudes toward the major theoretical perspectives in sociology were also shifting. The conflict perspective, which emphasizes social conflict as a constant fact of social life, was becoming popular at the expense of the functionalist perspective, which stresses the persistence of social order.

6   American sociology has thus developed into a diverse discipline. Today, it is both a basic and an applied science, and sociologists use both objective and subjective methods. The soaring number of sociologists—from only about 3,000 in the 1960s to over 20,000 today—has further splintered sociology into numerous specialties, such as mathematical sociology, organizational research, and race and ethnic relations. Each of these specialties has been differentiated into many subspecialties. The specialty of race relations, for example, has broken down into studies of African Americans, Hispanics, Asians, and other specific minorities in the United States. Underlying the diversity of those studies are certain theoretical perspectives that sociologists employ to study and understand social behavior.

from Alex Thio, *Sociology: A Brief Introduction*, 7e, pp. 9–10

MyReadingLab™
Complete this **Exercise**
at **myreadinglab.com**

Reading Comprehension Check

1. In the sentence, "Like their European predecessors, the first U.S. sociologists tried to understand and solve the problems of their time, such as crime and **delinquency**, broken homes, poor neighborhoods, and racial problems," (para. 1) the word *delinquency* means
   a. obeying the law.   c. breaking the law.
   b. trusting the law.   d. paying a debt.

2. "So they examined the fundamental issues of social order and social change, trying to discover the causes of social problems as a whole. In contrast, the U.S. sociologists were more **pragmatic**." (para. 1) In this passage, the word *pragmatic* means
   a. inconsistent.   c. disinterested.
   b. inexperienced.   d. practical.

3. In the introductory paragraph, we read, "They were more **inclined t**o focus on specific problems, such as prostitution, street gangs, or racial discrimination in employment, and to treat each problem separately." In this context, the word *inclined* means
   a. uninterested.
   b. disposed.
   c. having no preference.
   d. unlikely.

4. In the sentence, "Their final step was to organize citizens and **lobby** political and community leaders to eliminate or alleviate the problem," (para. 2) the word *lobby* means
   a. influence.
   b. discourage.
   c. instigate.
   d. block.

5. "At the same time, however, he worked hard to apply his **enormous** knowledge to improving society." (para. 3) In this sentence, the word *enormous* is opposite in meaning to
   a. vast.
   b. little.
   c. gigantic.
   d. massive.

6. In the sentence, "For about 40 years after 1900, most U.S. sociologists, such as Addams and DuBois, **concentrated** on studying and solving social problems," (para. 4) the meaning of the word *concentrated* is
   a. ignored.
   b. avoided.
   c. focused.
   d. diverged.

7. "However, the prosperity that followed World War II masked many social problems, causing the reformist **fervor** to begin to cool." (para. 4) In this sentence, a synonym for the word *fervor* is
   a. powerful emotion.
   b. weak emotion.
   c. unconcerned emotion.
   d. negative emotion.

8. In the sentence, "Renewed awareness of poverty and years of social **unrest**—marked by race riots, student revolts, and controversy about the Vietnam War—put pressure on sociologists to attack society's ills once again," (para. 5) the word *unrest* means
   a. calm condition.
   b. easy condition.
   c. peaceful condition.
   d. troubled condition.

9. "The conflict perspective, which emphasizes social conflict as a constant fact of social life, was becoming popular at the expense of the functionalist perspective, which stresses the **persistence** of social order." (para. 5) In this sentence, the word *persistence* means
   a. termination of a condition.
   b. disruption of a condition.
   c. continuance of an effect.
   d. discontinuance of an effect.

10. In the concluding paragraph, we read, "The soaring number of sociologists—from only about 3,000 in the 1960s to over 20,000 today—has further **splintered** sociology into numerous specialties, such as mathematical sociology, organizational research, and race and ethnic relations." In this context, the word *splintered* means
    a. joined.
    b. conjoined.
    c. conflated.
    d. divided.

INTERNET FACT SEARCH

Sociology

The Internet can be a powerful and effective research tool once you have learned how to successfully limit your information searches and have learned how to interpret the results of your search with a critical lens.

Two Quick Tips

1. **Be Specific in Your Search Headings**

   If you wanted to find out how many Chinese Americans are living in California, what would you type in the search box of the search engine you were working with? Write a good search heading for finding this information on the line below:

   _____

   If you typed in as your search, "Chinese Americans in California," you might get an article about famous Chinese Americans in California or a source about the history of Chinese Americans in California. What you probably wouldn't find with this search is the number of Chinese Americans living in California.

   If you used the search heading, "population of Chinese Americans," you would probably get data about the number of Chinese Americans in the entire United States.

   Be specific and accurate. The search heading that would most likely lead you to the information you are looking for would be: Population of Chinese Americans in California.

2. **Interpret Search Results with a Critical Lens**

   The World Wide Web is a big world indeed, filled with Web sites with varying degrees of legitimacy and professionalism. When sifting through the information contained in your list of "search results," always consider the quality of your sources. Try to establish the identity of each of the Web sites you are working with. Are you examining the Web site of a well-known news source such as the *New York Times*, *USA Today*, or CNN, or perhaps an official U.S. government data resource? Or is the Web site you are working with the personal Web site of an angry guy named Jim? These distinctions are critical in your ability to locate accurate, verifiable information. You may want to check the data you receive from one Web source against the data offered by a second legitimate Web source.

Instructions: First try to use logic and background knowledge in guessing the correct answers to the following data questions. Then, go online and search for the relevant data. Be sure to write the Web source below your research finding.

1. What is the divorce rate in the United States?

   a. 10%   c. 50%
   b. 25%   d. 75%

   Your guess: _____   Research finding: _____

   Websource: _____

2. How many people are incarcerated in American prisons?
   a. 1,000,000+   c. 100,000
   b. 500,000   d. 25,000

   Your guess: _____   Research finding: _____

   Websource: _____

3. What is the largest minority group in the United States?
   a. African Americans   c. Hispanics
   b. Native Americans   d. None of the above

   Your guess: _____   Research finding: _____

   Websource: _____

4. Which country has the highest percentage of women in Congress or Parliament positions?
   a. The United States   c. Sweden
   b. Japan   d. France

   Your guess: _____   Research finding: _____

   Websource: _____

5. What is the average age of marriage for females in Kebbi State, Nigeria?
   a. 11   c. 21
   b. 18   d. 25

   Your guess: _____   Research finding: _____

   Websource: _____

FORMAL PRESENTATION PROJECTS

You will be given the opportunity to present on a topic of your interest pertinent to one of the text's chapter disciplines. Topics could relate to one of the questions you checked off in the "Follow Your Interests" section at the beginning of the chapter. Your instructor may ask you to browse through the chapters to guide you toward a given discipline focus.

MyReadingLab™   For more help with **Building Vocabulary**, go to your learning path in **MyReadingLab.com**.

2

BIOLOGY

Learning Objectives

IN THIS CHAPTER, YOU WILL LEARN TO . . .

1. Describe the discipline of biology
2. Define key terms in the field of biology
3. Highlight text effectively
4. Use college advising services
5. Recognize the topic and stated main idea of a text
6. Use a reflection journal

INTRODUCTION TO THE DISCIPLINE OF BIOLOGY

Biology is the study of life and of all living organisms, including their function, growth, origin, evolution, and distribution. Biologists study human biology as well as carbohydrates, lipids, proteins, structure and function of cells, ecosystems, evolution, and the origin of life. In this chapter, the reading selections address several topics such as cloning, weight loss, genetically modified foods, reversing the process of aging, and organ donation. After reading the selections in this chapter, you will have a deeper appreciation of the variety of life, the role of science in society, and how human activities affect the lives of all living organisms.

1 LEARNING OBJECTIVE
Describe the discipline of biology

Reading into a Photo

Working in a small group, examine the following photograph and answer the questions that follow.

1. What significance does this photo have for biology? In other words, which aspect of biology is addressed in this image?
2. In your opinion, what is the underlying message of this photo?

Collaboration

Follow Your Interests

Review the set of questions below that biologists might explore. Check off the three or four questions that are most interesting to you.

1. How do germs spread?
2. Is human cloning scientifically possible?
3. Would you be willing to donate your vital organs after death? Why do you think an individual might object to having an organ donated?
4. Is liposuction—a surgery performed to remove body fat—a realistic way to lose that belly? Can you think of healthier ways to reduce fat?
5. How do performance enhancement drugs improve sports performance?
6. Will cancer continue to be the #2 cause of death in America, or will doctors find a cure for most cancers?
7. Is DNA reliable evidence for criminal prosecution? Why or why not?
8. With the advancements in science and technology, some experts believe that it is possible to live over one hundred years. How do you think science can reverse the aging process?
9. Many experts in the field of human genetics believe that in the future scientists will be able to predict an individual's eventual cause of death. What methods do you think scientists will use to accomplish this task?
10. With the growing global food crisis, do you believe that genetically modified food is the answer? If not, what other effective ways can be adopted to feed the hungry?
11. How can medical authorities most fairly decide who qualifies to receive donated organs?
12. MP3 players, smart phones and other portable electronic devices are wildly popular among young people. There is some evidence that these technologies can harm one's hearing. What can be done to prevent a generation of hearing-impaired youth?

Now, share your choices with a small group of classmates and discuss why these particular questions are most interesting to you. You may wish to discuss these questions with them and ask which questions they found interesting.

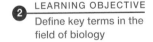

LEARNING OBJECTIVE
Define key terms in the field of biology

Key Terms in the Field of Biology

The following key terms are frequently used in the discipline of biology. Be sure to familiarize yourself with these words and practice using them often. Review the words below and answer the multiple-choice questions that follow.

anemia	cloning	molecule
antioxidants	genetics	neurons
arteries	hormones	organisms
cancerous	immune	plasma
cardiac	leukemia	transplant

EXERCISE 1   Inferring Meaning from Context

Read each sentence below and try to derive the meaning of each of the italicized key terms from the context. Circle the correct definition of each italicized term.

1. Biologists study living *organisms*.
   a. dead tissues
   b. lung cancer
   c. heart disease
   d. forms of life

2. Scientists interested in human *cloning* want to make multiple copies of an individual.
   a. producing exact replicas
   b. dividing up a cell
   c. damaging tissues
   d. cell structure

3. The main function of *arteries* is to transport blood away from the heart.
   a. red blood cells
   b. white blood cells
   c. blood vessels
   d. small tissues

4. Water is the most essential *molecule* to life since it accounts for 60% of body weight.
   a. body temperature
   b. small particle
   c. living organism
   d. hydrogen

5. A person with *cardiac* disease may need to see a heart specialist.
   a. relating to the heart
   b. relating to the kidneys
   c. relating to the lungs
   d. relating to the liver

6. Our *immune* system protects us from disease or infection.
   a. defense
   b. urinary
   c. respiration
   d. circulation

7. Some scientists believe that much of human behavior is influenced by *genetics*.
   a. inherited traits
   b. biology
   c. blue jeans
   d. blood cells

8. Blood *plasma* mainly consists of water, gases, and nutrients.
   a. antibodies
   b. the solid part of blood
   c. the liquid part of blood
   d. white blood cells

9. *Neurons* are cells of the nervous system that are specialized for communication.
   a. nervous cells
   b. brain cells
   c. dysfunctional cells
   d. impulse-conducting cells

10. Peter's liver is not functioning, so he desperately needs an organ *transplant*.
    a. to remove from one person and destroy
    b. to transfer from one person to another
    c. to move a family from one place to another
    d. to leave an organ in a person's body

11. Gregory's uncle is suffering from *anemia*, and the number of his red blood cells is decreasing.
    a. a reduction in red blood cells
    b. an increase in red blood cells
    c. a rapid growth of red blood cells
    d. a rapid growth of white blood cells

12. *Hormones* are chemical messenger molecules that are produced by the endocrine system to carry out specific functions in the human body.
    a. products of dead cells
    b. products of living cells
    c. solid particles in blood
    d. liquids in the bloodstream

13. Some experts claim that vitamins, minerals, and certain food extracts contain *antioxidants*, which reduce the risk of illnesses such as heart disease and cancer.
    a. substances that fight disease
    b. inorganic substances that cause disease
    c. organic substances that cause disease
    d. substances that do not help fight disease

14. Diego's doctor has suggested chemotherapy because he has *leukemia* and his body has stopped manufacturing red and white blood cells.
    a. a system manufacturing white blood cells
    b. a system manufacturing red blood cells
    c. a condition improving blood-forming organs
    d. a disease affecting blood-forming bone marrow

15. Medical experts believe that cells that become *cancerous* lose control of their functions and structures.
    a. properly functioning
    b. lacking cancer cells
    c. relating to a growth or tumor
    d. well-developed structures

Collaboration

EXERCISE **2**   Writing Meaningful Sentences with the Key Terms

Working with a partner, choose five of the key terms in biology and write an original sentence about each one.

1. Word = _____

_____

_____

2. Word = _____

_____

_____

3. Word = _____

_____

_____

4. Word = _____

_____

_____

5. Word = _____

_____

_____

COLLEGE STUDY SKILLS
Highlighting Key Terms and Concepts in a Text

3 LEARNING OBJECTIVE
Highlight text effectively

Active reading is one of the secrets of success in developing better reading comprehension skills and connecting with the challenging academic reading you will do in college. Active readers do not sit silently flipping through the pages of their assigned readings (this is an easy way to find yourself taking a nap). No, they interact with the text they are focusing on in a number of productive ways. **Active readers** connect with academic text through such methods as outlining, annotation, and highlighting. In this chapter, we will examine the critical skill of highlighting key terms and concepts and in subsequent chapters focus on outlining and annotating relevant text.

Introducing the Skill

Most likely in high school you marked class readings with a brightly colored highlighter. Many students get confused when using a highlighter about which sections of a text they should highlight and which they should not. Some students end up highlighting large sections of text. Later on when they want to review a chapter for an exam, they realize that their highlighting work hasn't simplified the process of understanding the material at all.

Effective highlighting should guide you toward the key terms and concepts that will help you grasp the material you are studying. Highlighting, when carefully done, will

- aid your comprehension as you actively read and choose which terms and concepts are most important to remember, *and*
- save you time during your review session as you will have a visual code of which sections of the text are important to review.

Imagine you are reading a five-page section of your introduction to biology textbook. You have a bright green highlighter in hand and you are ready to begin. What should you consider highlighting?

- Highlight vocabulary that relates to key ideas and concepts.
- Highlight main ideas, not small details or examples.
- Highlight important phrases or sentences that you feel will help you to understand the reading.

Practice: Guided by the above tips, read the paragraph below and work with a highlighter. It is recommended that you first read through the passage and then go back and highlight what is important to remember and review.

> Mitochondria are the organelles responsible for providing most of this usable energy; they are often called the cells' "power plants." Not surprisingly, their number within different cells varies widely according to the energy requirements of the cells. A cell with a high rate of energy consumption, such as a muscle cell, may contain over 1,000 mitochondria.
>
> from Michael D. Johnson, *Human Biology*, 6e, p. 63

Collaboration

Now, compare what sections of the text you chose to highlight with a friend, and discuss your choices. Remember, when discussing highlighting preferences, there is no exact right answer. Needless to say, there are wise choices however. Please examine the highlighted text below.

Mitochondria are the organelles responsible for providing most of this usable energy; they are often called the cells' "power plants." Not surprisingly, their number within different cells varies widely according to the energy requirements of the cells. A cell with a high rate of energy consumption, such as a muscle cell, may contain over 1,000 mitochondria.	*Clear definition and function of important term, "mitochondria"* *"Power plant" describes the role of mitochondria* *Example gives a sense of number of mitochondria in a cell*

Putting the Skill into Action

It is up to you to develop a consistent system of highlighting that works for you. You may decide to highlight the main points of a passage in one color and the key terms you want to remember in another. The best way to find out if highlighting works for you as an information organizing system is to get your highlighter(s) out and practice!

Let's read a section of the article found on page 53, "What's the Best Way to Lose Belly Fat?" Work with a highlighter to locate key terms and concepts in the passage.

> The idea is to exercise vigorously in sprints and then rest. Get your heart rate up then wait for it to come back down. To burn off belly fat exercise for about 30 seconds then rest for around 3 minutes; then repeat. Since everyone is different, interval and recovery times can vary, so listen to your body and adapt your training according to your own fitness level.

> Any type of exercise, including cycling, skiing exercise (jumping back and forth), jumping rope, push-ups, jumping up and down, sprinting, or pushing a wall can help get rid of belly fat, which is the most dangerous type of fat even for people whose weight is normal.
>
> If you've been sedentary, Berg warns you should not engage in high intensity interval training, nor should you exercise vigorously if you're tired.
>
> For people who aren't physically fit, Berg advises starting with a simple walking program to gradually increase your exercise tolerance. Speak with your doctor first if you have any health conditions or haven't been exercising.

Once you have finished this highlighting exercise, explain your choices in the table below.

Words or Phrases Highlighted	Reason for Highlighting

The Last Word

Highlighting is a way to break a text down into easier-to-follow points. Highlighting keeps you physically active as you read and helps focus your attention on the material at hand. As with any other study tool, the more you practice highlighting, the more confident and effective you will be in the execution of this activity. Together with text annotation and article outlining, highlighting will push you to be a more active and engaged reader.

READINESS FOR COLLEGE SUCCESS
Meeting with an Advisor

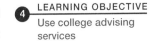

LEARNING OBJECTIVE
Use college advising services

When they begin college, most students do not have a clear sense as to what major they want to pursue. Some of them end up taking courses that do not apply toward their diploma or degree. Often when students think they are about to graduate, they are informed they still need to take more courses in order to obtain their intended degree. As a result, students are frustrated and lose the motivation to continue their education.

To avoid this rather unfortunate situation, most colleges in the United States have an Office of Advisement where experienced advisors guide incoming students step by step. They tell these students exactly which courses are required for a specific degree and help them register for the courses so that students can graduate in a timely fashion. These advisors usually prefer to meet with students at the beginning and end of a semester. They keep track of students' academic progress and make sure that they manage their time effectively and graduate as planned.

As you can see, it is imperative that you make an appointment with a seasoned advisor to understand what the college requires of you in order to graduate. Before you embark on your intellectual journey, make sure that you call the Office of Advisement and set up an appointment with an advisor to receive guidance. You are better off making the appointment as early as possible. You will realize that you are more sure of yourself after receiving advisement, and that you are taking courses that apply toward your degree.

Working with a classmate, brainstorm some of the most important questions you would like to ask your advisor, and fill in the table below. The first example is done for you.

Collaboration

Some Questions to Ask an Advisor

1. *What courses do I need to take for a Liberal Arts degree?*
2.
3.
4.
5.
6.
7.

After you formulate questions with your classmate, share them with the instructor and the entire class.

READING

Reading Selection **1**

Poem

MyReadingLab™
Complete this **Exercise**
at **myreadinglab.com**

An Ode to Dolly Re: Global Warming

Preview Questions

1. Do you believe scientists will ever have the ability to perfectly clone a human being? Explain.

2. In your opinion, are there risks involved in the effort to clone humans? Explain.

3. Can you think of any advantages or disadvantages of having a perfect copy of you (a clone) walking around?

Pre-Reading Vocabulary:
Focus on Some Key Terms

Collaboration

As you have done before, try to guess the meaning of the words below with a classmate. Then consult a dictionary to determine how accurate you were.

Word	*Your Definition*	*Dictionary Definition*
ode		
sacrilegious		
wondrous		
accomplish		
matters		

An Ode to Dolly Re: Global Warming

By Valerie Coskrey

December 31, 2008

(A science poem about the first cloned mammal, Dolly the sheep clone, and the nature of the culture wars between religion and science.)

1   Dolly had a little lamb.
     It came the natural way.
     Now everything that Mary's can
     A clone can do today.

2   "To clone," you say, "is playing God.
     'Tis sacrilegious. Nay.
     We'll lose our Faith, you know we will,
     If we use tech that way."

3   But "He helps him who helps himself"
Encourages men to plan
The use of nature in wondrous ways
To accomplish all we can.

4   What matters most in this age
Of stress from hotter days,
Is saving genes that work for us
No matter what the ways.

By Valerie Coskrey © 2006 . Reprinted by permission of the author.

Reading Comprehension Check

1. "We'll lose our **Faith**, you know we will." The word *faith* could be replaced by
   _____.
   a. not living   c. belief
   b. skepticism   d. neutrality

2. According to the poem, what "encourages men to plan"?
   a. their sense of fear
   b. The idea that cloning will lead to their destruction.
   c. The idea that they should help themselves and not rely on faith
   d. cloning sheep

3. Which idea is NOT mentioned in the poem?
   a. losing faith   c. using technology
   b. accomplishing all we can   d. GM crops

4. What does the line, "What matters most in this age of stress from hotter days" refer to?
   a. cloning animals
   b. global warming
   c. encouraging future generations
   d. making money

5. What is the message of this poem?
   a. Scientists could produce hundreds and hundreds of clones.
   b. Global warming is causing cloning.
   c. We must save our genes at all costs.
   d. Clones offer society many benefits.

Collaboration

Exploring the Topic

Discuss the following questions to check your comprehension of the poem you have just read.

1. Do you think a poem or a story can sometimes be a more effective way to explore a topic than a news article? Consider this question in relation to the poem you just read on cloning.

2. This is a poem about science that focuses on visions of what the future will look like. Share some ideas about how life will be different a hundred or two hundred years from now.

3. Read the poem for a second time. Which line of the poem do you think is most interesting? Explain why.

What's the Best Way to Lose Belly Fat?

Preview Questions

1. There are many people who have tried and tried again to lose belly fat, but can't seem to do so. What are the secrets of losing belly fat and keeping it off?

2. When you are choosing what to eat, do you consider the calorie count of food items? Explain.

3. Some people believe that genetics and lifestyle play an equal role in determining one's body size. In your opinion, is body size more a question of nature or of nurture? Explain your position clearly.

MyReadingLab™
Complete this **Exercise**
at **myreadinglab.com**

Pre-Reading Vocabulary: Focus on Some Key Terms

As you have done before, try to guess the meaning of these words below with a classmate. Then consult a dictionary to determine how accurate you were.

Collaboration

Word	Your Definition	Dictionary Definition
nutrition		
intense		
hormone		
vigorously		
adapt		

What's the Best Way to Lose Belly Fat?

By Kathleen Blanchard RN on September 4, 2012—9:24 AM

1   If you're looking for the best way to lose belly fat and not just weight, Dr. Eric Berg has some advice. Berg, who is chiropractor specializing in weight loss and nutrition says you can burn the most belly fat with intense interval training. The good news is you can start out slowly if you're deconditioned and there are a variety of ways to train for a slimmer waistline.

2   Berg, who is also an active member of the Endocrinology Society and on the advisory panel for the Health Science Institute, explains interval training burns belly fat because it increases levels of growth hormone by 450%.

3   The idea is to exercise vigorously in sprints and then rest. Get your heart rate up then wait for it to come back down. To burn off belly fat exercise for about 30 seconds then rest for around 3 minutes; then repeat. Since everyone is different, interval and recovery times can vary, so listen to your body and adapt your training according to your own fitness level.

4   Any type of exercise, including cycling, skiing exercise (jumping back and forth), jumping rope, push-ups, jumping up and down, sprinting or pushing a wall can help get rid of belly fat, which is the most dangerous type of fat even for people whose weight is normal.

5   If you've been sedentary, Berg warns you should not engage in high intensity interval training, nor should you exercise vigorously if you're tired.

6   For people who aren't physically fit, Berg advises starting with a simple walking program to gradually increase your exercise tolerance. Speak with your doctor first if you have any health conditions or haven't been exercising.

7   Berg seems to especially like hopping exercises that engage the whole body. The idea is to use large muscle groups to stimulate growth hormone and burn fat in the abdomen. Hopping engages the large muscles in the legs and is aerobic. It's important to start out small. Berg says you can start by using your stairs at home or just a small platform.

8   Interval training is anti-aging because it releases hormones that help cells in the body rejuvenate. Dr. Berg says it's the best way to burn belly fat. Human growth hormone (HGH) is released in response to exercise. Growth hormone has many roles in the body including muscle building, collagen turnover and overall increased fat metabolism.

EmaxHealth.com

Reading Comprehension Check

1. What is the topic of the reading?
   a. losing weight
   b. losing belly fat
   c. burning calories
   d. Overweight people need to do at least one hour of physical exercise per day.

2. What is the main idea of the reading passage?
   a. It is recommended that most people do at least one hour of physical exercise per week.
   b. Most people try to lose weight but can't seem to do it.
   c. Interval training is most effective in burning belly fat.
   d. Intensive interval training is not recommended for thin people.

3. In the sentence, "For people who aren't physically fit, Berg advises starting with a simple walking program to gradually increase your exercise **tolerance,**" (para. 6) the word *tolerance* could be replaced by
   a. inability to endure something.
   b. capacity to endure something.
   c. frequency of physical exercise.
   d. tendency to avoid something.

4. In the sentence, "Berg seems to especially like **hopping** exercises that engage the whole body," (para. 7) the word *hopping* means
   a. jumping so both feet are up in the air.
   b. rolling over on the floor.
   c. lying down quietly.
   d. jumping or making a short leap.

5. According to the article, growth hormones have many roles in the body EXCEPT
   a. muscle building.
   b. collagen turnover.
   c. intensive interval training.
   d. increased fat metabolism.

Exploring the Topic

Collaboration

Discuss the following questions to check your comprehension of the article you have just read.

1. The writer states, "If you're looking for the best way to lose belly fat and not just weight, Dr. Eric Berg has some advice." Discuss how it is possible to lose weight but not belly fat and why it is so hard to lose belly fat. Be specific.

2. According to Berg, we "can burn the most belly fat with intense interval training." Do you think this is reasonable advice? What are some examples of 'intense interval training'?

3. The article states, "If you've been sedentary, Berg warns you should not engage in high intensity interval training, nor should you exercise vigorously if you're tired." Why does he warn against "high intensity interval training"? Give specific reasons for your answer.

Post-Reading Vocabulary

Without using a dictionary, determine the meaning of the bolded words from the context.

1. "Any type of exercise, including cycling, skiing exercise (jumping back and forth), jumping rope, push-up, jumping up and down, sprinting, or pushing a wall can help **get rid of** belly fat that is the most dangerous type of fat even for people whose weight is normal." (para. 4)

   The expression *get rid of* means _____

2. "If you've been **sedentary**, Berg warns you should not engage in high intensity interval training, nor should you exercise vigorously if you're tired." (para. 5)

   Sedentary means _____

3. "The idea is to use large muscle groups to **stimulate** growth hormones and burn fat in the abdomen." (para. 7)

   Stimulate means _____

Jaymee Castillo   An Interview with a Student in the Field of Biology

UCLA

1. How did you find your path to majoring in biology?

I came into UCLA as a Neuroscience major, and when I realized that the course load was too much, and that I may not be able to graduate in time with that major, my Life Science professor suggested switching to biology. I always knew I was interested in general biology, and realized that it may be the more suitable path for me.

2. What was the biggest obstacle you faced in your study of biology?

Finding the right classes that interested me was the hardest part.

At UCLA, the biology major falls under the Ecology and Evolutionary Biology Department, so the classes offered a range from plant physiology to animal behavior.

3. What area(s) of biology in particular do you find most interesting?

I actually find the conservation biology portion of my major most interesting, especially since it is very relevant to my generation currently. It's amazing analyzing the relationship between humankind and the natural world, and how the Earth has evolved throughout the millennia.

4. What specific skills are required of students who study biology?

As a biology major, I learn about a vast number of topics dealing with general biology. It's essential to not only know about the details of plant, animal, and human biology (as well as basic chemistry and physics fundamentals), but to look at the bigger picture and how they are all related and interact.

5. Other than teaching biology, what other career avenues are available for biology majors?

Biology majors are open to a great number of career avenues, including becoming medical doctors, dentists, nurses, researchers, lawyers, and more.

SKILL FOCUS
Recognizing Topic and Stated Main Idea

⑤ LEARNING OBJECTIVE
Recognize the topic and stated main idea of a text

Understanding the Concept of Topic

Examine the paragraph below:

> We all know that smoking is bad for your health. Cigarette smoke contains a whole host of known or suspected **carcinogens**. Numerous scientific studies have shown convincingly that smoking is the single leading cause of lung cancer in the world. Hardly anyone would dispute these facts today.

> from Michael D. Johnson, *Human Biology*, 6e, p. 236

As a reader trying to get a handle on an unfamiliar reading passage, what is the first thing you should try to make sense of? If you answered "the topic," you are absolutely correct!

What exactly does the term *topic* mean? With a partner, try to think of a few synonyms for the word *topic* and write them below.

Topic = _____

If as a reader you cannot recognize the topic of a reading passage, it makes it that much more difficult to enter a text and comprehend the text's finer details. It also makes the reading much less interesting if you don't have a general sense of what the piece is about. So, for example, if the topic of a passage you are reading is *illnesses suffered by professional football players* and you cannot recognize the subject matter, how can you possibly be expected to connect with the material and comprehend the article? The answer is, you can't! Therefore, recognizing the topic of a passage should be your first order of business.

Examine the paragraph at the beginning of this section (p. 56) again. What, in your opinion, is the topic, or subject, of the passage? Another way to think about the concept of "topic" is to consider how you would respond if a classmate asked you, "What is the paragraph about?"

Well, you could say the topic is "smoking," but this might be too general. The paragraph is not about "the act of smoking" or "the benefits of smoking" or, for that matter, "the different kinds of products you can smoke." The topic is a little more specific and has to do with "smoking and health."

EXERCISE 3   Developing Topics

Collaboration

To get a better sense of how we label different topics, work with a partner to fill in the following chart.

What are some topics typically discussed among friends in high school?	*What are some topics typically discussed among friends who are senior citizens?*

EXERCISE 4   Identifying Topics

Read the following passages and try to determine the topic of each reading.

1.   A rapid loss of 30% or more of blood volume strains the body's ability to maintain blood pressure and oxygenate tissues. When this happens, survival may depend on receiving blood from others. About 15 million units of blood are given every year. Almost 5 million people receive donated blood. Most people

who donate blood get nothing more (and nothing less) than the satisfaction of knowing they have helped someone in need.

from Michael D. Johnson, *Human Biology*, 5e, p. 396

The topic of the passage is _____

2.   Do you enjoy taking your music with you? Join the club; portable music players like the Discman, and MP3 players, such as the iPod, are more popular than ever. Apple has sold more than 150 million iPods. However, some music fans have sued the company, claiming that the iPod's design endangers listeners' hearing by exposing them to loud noise levels.

from Michael D. Johnson, *Human Biology*, 5e, p. 293

The topic of the passage is _____

3.   Today expectant parents may be able to discover the gender of a fetus as early as five weeks. They may even be able to select gender (and several other genetic traits) ahead of time. If you were going to have a child, would you want to know whether it's a boy or girl ahead of time?

from Michael D. Johnson, *Human Biology*, 5e, p. 396

The topic of the passage is _____

4.   Who owns your genetic data—you? Your physician? The company that performed the test? The insurance company that paid for it? Consider your existing medical records, which are widely available. They are available to your insurance company, all doctors you have consulted and all hospitals you have ever used, including clinical and clerical personnel. Should your genetic data become part of this data?

from Michael D. Johnson, *Human Biology*, 5e, p. 459

The topic of the passage is _____

5.   And yet, people do recover from cancer. There are known risk factors for most types of cancer and things we can do to reduce our risk. There are treatments for many cancers, some of which work rather well. The death rate from some cancers is even declining as we learn more about the disease.

from Michael D. Johnson, *Human Biology*, 5e, p. 423

The topic of the passage is _____

Recognizing an Author's Stated Main Idea

When a friend who didn't come to school yesterday asks you, "What was the main point of the history lecture?" or another friend calls you and asks you to tell her or him what happened in the episode of their favorite TV drama last night (and they only have time to listen to a one-sentence explanation!), what they are expecting you to tell them is the main idea of the lecture and of the TV show. They may not have time for the details, but they do want to get a sense of the key message. Perhaps the main idea, or main point, of the history lecture was that "many countries in Africa achieved independence in the 1960s." The main idea of the TV episode may have been that "Debbie no longer loves Bobbie."

It is important to keep in mind, when listening to a lecture or reading a text, that the main idea may be directly stated, indirectly stated, or implied, by the speaker or author. In this text, we will focus our attention on recognizing an author's stated main idea.

Examine the paragraph below:

> It's a good idea to combine any athletic activity with stretching exercises. Gentle stretching before exercise increases your heart rate gradually. This pumps additional blood to your muscles and prepares you for more strenuous exertion. This lowers your risks of sprains and pulled muscles. After exercising, let your heart rate and breathing return gradually to normal as you walk slowly and do more stretching. Regular stretching improves joint mobility and range of motion.
>
> from Michael D. Johnson, *Human Biology*, 5e, p. 133

How can you most easily determine the stated main idea of the above paragraph? Ask yourself:

- Which sentence contains an idea that the rest of the paragraph supports with details?
- Which sentence is general enough to be a main point, and not simply an example or detail?
- Which sentence acts as the focus of the entire paragraph?

These questions should guide you to the logical conclusion that the first sentence in the paragraph, *"It's a good idea to combine any athletic activity with stretching exercises,"* is the main idea.

EXERCISE 5   Identifying the Stated Main Idea

Read the following paragraphs and try to locate the sentence that contains the main idea of the passage. Remember, the main idea can be found in the beginning, middle, or at the end of a given passage.

1.   [1]Mothers with newborns have to make the decision whether to breast-feed their baby or to feed their child with formula milk. [2]One advantage of breast-feeding is that breast milk contains colostrums, which are rich in antibodies and protect the child as their immune system develops. [3]Breast-feeding has also been shown to increase the baby's intelligence quotient (IQ) by about seven points, on average. [4]Finally, breast-fed babies suffer fewer allergies. [5]Clearly, there are many benefits of newborn babies being breast-fed.

   The stated main idea is found in sentence _____

2.   [1]Will a healthy lifestyle that includes exercise and a proper diet slow the aging process? [2]The answer is far from certain. [3]However, regular exercise and healthy nutrition can certainly help us age better. [4]Exercise and a healthy diet improve cardiovascular and skeletomuscular fitness and reduce your risk of major killers such as cancer and other diseases. [5]A healthy lifestyle also improves

your quality of life. [6]It provides you with a heightened sense of well-being and increased energy and vigor.

adapted from Michael D. Johnson, Human Biology, 5e, p. 502

The stated main idea is found in sentence _____

3.   [1]Lyme disease is an infectious disease caused by a bacterium inside of certain ticks (e.g., deer ticks). [2]It can be spread to humans by the bite of an infected tick. [3]There are several common symptoms of Lyme disease. [4]Victims might develop a skin rash, which appears from three days to several weeks after the bite. [5]Later they may have a fever and suffer joint and muscle pain. [6]If left undetected for a longer period of time, Lyme disease can cause arthritis and affect the victim's central nervous system.

The stated main idea is found in sentence _____

4.   [1]Genetic testing can promote healthy childbirth. [2]Couples can be tested to determine whether they are carriers of recessive disorders. [3]This can help them to make an informed decision about whether to have a child. [4]Prenatal genetic testing can also examine the cells of the fetus to screen for about 40 genetic defects.

adapted from Michael D. Johnson, Human Biology, 5e, p. 458

The stated main idea is found in sentence _____

5.   [1]Deficiencies of one or more nutrients can produce specific effects. [2]For example, years of vitamin A deficiency lead to eye damage and night blindness. [3]In children undernutrition stunts growth and increases chances of infection. [4]Severe undernutrition, or starvation, is still the leading cause of malnutrition around the world. [5]Nearly 20 million people die every year of starvation, or related disease. [6]Most of them are children.

adapted from Michael D. Johnson, Human Biology, 5e, p. 344

The stated main idea is found in sentence _____

EXERCISE 6   Distinguishing between Topic and Main Idea

As you read the following paragraphs, first consider the topic, and then try to determine the stated main idea of the text. Remember that the topic is more general than the main idea and, unlike the main idea, can be described in just a few words. The first example is done for you.

1.   Bio-fuels are produced directly from living organisms or from their metabolic by-products. They must contain greater than 80% of renewable materials to be considered bio-fuels. They can be in the form of solids, liquids or gases. It may seem that the use of renewable materials for fuel is advantageous. However, there are pros and cons to be considered for each application.

adapted from Michael D. Johnson, Human Biology, 5e, p. 553

Topic	*Main Idea*

2.   An important property of water is that it can absorb and hold a large amount
of heat energy with only a modest increase in temperature. In fact it absorbs heat
better than most other liquids. Water thus may prevent large increases in body
temperature when excess heat is produced. Water also holds heat well when
there is a danger of too much heat loss. An example of this would be when you
go outside wearing shorts on a cool day. The ability of water to absorb and hold
heat helps prevent rapid changes in body temperature when changes occur in
metabolism or in the environment.

adapted from Michael D. Johnson, *Human Biology*, 5e, p. 30

Topic	Main Idea

3.   All cells in a multicellular organism have a specialized function that benefits
the organism in some way. However, specialization is not enough. The specialized
functions must be organized and integrated if they are to be useful. As an example,
the activity of a single cell in your heart is insignificant because the cell is so small.
The beating of your heart requires that hundreds of thousands of cells be arranged
end to end. In this way, their functions are coordinated to produce a single heartbeat.

from Michael D. Johnson, *Human Biology*, 5e, p. 79

Topic	Main Idea

4.   The human body is capable of a great variety of physical activities. With training some individuals can run a mile in less than four minutes, or lift more than
their own weight. Sensitive motor skills allow us to thread a needle, turn our head
to focus on a single star, and throw a baseball into the strike zone. Considered
individually, any one of these activities may not seem amazing. However, for
a single structure (the human body) to be capable of all of them is remarkable
indeed.

adapted from Michael D. Johnson, *Human Biology*, 5e, p. 101

Topic	Main Idea

5.   Fifty years ago, an aspiring athlete needed only a set of weights, a place to
train and a lot of determination and hard work. Not today. In an era where winning brings big endorsement contracts, sports have gone high tech. Downhill
ski racers and speed skaters are studied in wind tunnels. Digital video cameras,
remote sensors and computer programs analyze athletes' motion patterns for

speed, power and direction. Researchers in genetics, bio-chemistry and exercise training are unlocking the secrets of athletic success on a cellular level. They are applying what they learn to young athletes in training.

adapted from Michael D. Johnson, *Human Biology*, 5e, p. 132

Topic	*Main Idea*

LANDMARK IN THE FIELD OF BIOLOGY

Organ Transplant

In the nineteenth century, if a person's organs, such as the heart, liver, kidneys, or lungs, failed to function, there was not much doctors could do to save his or her life. The patient was usually given medicine to treat the ailing organ, but had no choice but to await a slow and painful death. Family members prayed for recovery, but there was no way around it. Death was coming.

The beginning of the twentieth century brought about a revolution in the field of medical science. Eduard Konrad Zirm, an Austrian, performed the first successful cornea transplant on December 7, 1905. The cornea recipient was a blind worker from a small town in the Czech Republic. The patient was able to see again after the transplant.

Zirm became a role model for surgeons all over the world trying to perform organ transplants. However, it took another 50 years for this dream to be realized. In 1954 Joseph Murray transplanted a kidney successfully for the first time. This feat was followed by the first successful pancreas transplant in 1966. Thomas Starzl followed with a liver transplant in 1967. Later in the same year,

Christiaan Barnard performed the first successful heart transplant in South Africa.

An organ transplant is considered a landmark in the field of biology for obvious reasons. Who would have thought in the past that a patient whose kidneys were not functioning could receive a healthy kidney from another person? With the progress in science and technology, it is now possible to transfer an organ from one person to another and save someone's life.

There are at least 100,000 patients in the United States waiting for a suitable organ donor. However, only a few of them are lucky enough to receive an organ from a donor. For example, when Steve Jobs, founder of Apple Inc., was ill, he was lucky to receive a liver from a 23-year-old who had recently died in a car accident. As you can imagine, not everyone is as fortunate as Steve Jobs was. Most patients awaiting an organ do not get a second chance to live. There simply aren't enough organ donors.

Collaboration

Considering the Topic

Answer the following questions with a partner.

1. In what ways have organ transplants changed the way people live?

2. Do you think that some day there will be enough organ donors for patients in need of an organ? Explain.

3. Can you imagine another technological breakthrough in the field of biology that will further change the way we live? Explain.

Internet Connection

Research another landmark in the field of biology, and fill out the section below.

cloning	stem-cell research
genetically modified foods	in vitro fertilization
DNA evidence	plastic surgery

Landmark: _____

Question	*Answer*
When did this landmark become a reality?	
Who was involved in developing this landmark?	
What made this landmark special?	
How did this landmark change the way people live?	

READING

Organ Donation: Don't Let These Myths Confuse You

Reading Selection **3**

Web Article

Preview Questions

MyReadingLab™
Complete this **Exercise**
at **myreadinglab.com**

1. In your opinion, is donating an organ to save someone's life a generous act? If so, would you be willing to donate an organ after you pass away? Why or why not?

2. Approximately 100,000 people are waiting for an organ donation in the United States. However, only a few patients are fortunate enough to find a suitable donor organ. Why do you think there is a scarcity of donor organs in the United States? In other words, why do you think people might not be willing to donate an organ after they pass away?

3. In your opinion, should an organ donor or her or his family members be compensated monetarily for donating an organ? Why or why not?

Collaboration

Pre-Reading Vocabulary: Focus on Some Key Terms

Before beginning the reading selection, it may be helpful to focus on the meaning of some key words in the article. Working with a partner, try to guess the meaning of these words. Then look up the words in a dictionary.

Word Definition	Your Definition	Dictionary Definition
myths		
generous		
transplant		
tabloids		
wiggle		

Organ Donation: Don't Let These Myths Confuse You

By **Mayo Clinic staff**

Unsure about donating organs for transplant? Don't let misinformation keep you from saving lives.

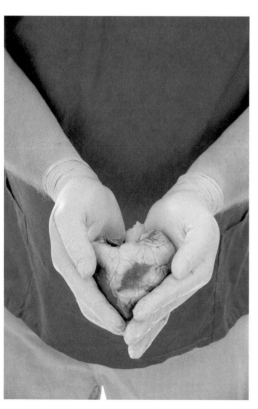

1   Enough people to populate a small city—over 100,000—are waiting for an organ donation in the United States. Unfortunately, thousands never get the call saying that a suitable donor organ—and a second chance at life—has been found.

2   It can be hard to think about what's going to happen to your body after you die, let alone donating your organs and tissue. But being an organ donor is a generous and worthwhile decision that can be a lifesaver.

3   Understanding organ donation can make you feel better about your choice. If you've delayed your decision to be a donor because of possibly inaccurate information, here are answers to some common organ donation myths and concerns.

4   **Myth: If I agree to donate my organs, the hospital staff won't work as hard to save my life.**

Fact: When you go to the hospital for treatment, doctors focus on saving your life—not somebody else's. You'll be seen by a doctor whose specialty most closely matches your particular emergency. The doctor in charge of your care has nothing to do with transplantation.

5 **Myth: Maybe I won't really be dead when they sign my death certificate.**

Fact: Although it's a popular topic in the tabloids, in reality, people don't start to wiggle their toes after they're declared dead. In fact, people who have agreed to organ donation are given more tests (at no charge to their families) to determine that they're truly dead than are those who haven't agreed to organ donation.

6 **Myth: Organ donation is against my religion.**

Fact: Organ donation is consistent with the beliefs of most religions. This includes Catholicism, Protestantism, Islam and most branches of Judaism. If you're unsure of or uncomfortable with your faith's position on donation, ask a member of your clergy. Another option is to check the federal Web site OrganDonor.gov, which provides religious views on organ donation and transplantation by denomination.

7 **Myth: I'm under age 18. I'm too young to make this decision.**

Fact: That's true, in a legal sense. But your parents can authorize this decision. You can express to your parents your wish to donate, and your parents can give their consent knowing that it's what you wanted. Children, too, are in need of organ transplants, and they usually need organs smaller than those an adult can provide.

8 **Myth: An open-casket funeral isn't an option for people who have donated organs or tissues.**

Fact: Organ and tissue donation doesn't interfere with having an open-casket funeral. The donor's body is clothed for burial, so there are no visible signs of organ or tissue donation. For bone donation, a rod is inserted where bone is removed. With skin donation, a very thin layer of skin similar to a sunburn peel is taken from the donor's back. Because the donor is clothed and lying on his or her back in the casket, no one can see any difference.

9 **Myth: I'm too old to donate. Nobody would want my organs.**

Fact: There's no defined cutoff age for donating organs. Organs have been successfully transplanted from donors in their 70s and 80s. The decision to use your organs is based on strict medical criteria, not age. Don't disqualify yourself prematurely. Let the doctors decide at your time of death whether your organs and tissues are suitable for transplantation.

10 **Myth: I'm not in the best of health. Nobody would want my organs or tissues.**

Fact: Very few medical conditions automatically disqualify you from donating organs. The decision to use an organ is based on strict medical criteria. It may turn out that certain organs are not suitable for transplantation, but other organs and tissues may be fine. Don't disqualify yourself prematurely. Only medical professionals at the time of your death can determine whether your organs are suitable for transplantation.

11 **Myth: I'd like to donate one of my kidneys now, but I wouldn't be allowed to do that unless one of my family members is in need.**

Fact: While that used to be the case, it isn't any longer. Whether it's a distant family member, friend or complete stranger you want to help, you can donate a kidney through certain transplant centers. If you decide to become a living donor, you will undergo extensive questioning to ensure that you are aware of the risks and that your decision to donate isn't based on financial gain. You will also undergo testing to determine if your kidneys are in good shape and whether you can live a healthy life with just one kidney.

12 **Myth: Rich and famous people go to the top of the list when they need a donor organ.**

Fact: The rich and famous aren't given priority when it comes to allocating organs. It may seem that way because of the amount of publicity generated when celebrities receive a transplant, but they are treated no differently from anyone else. In fact, the United Network for Organ Sharing (UNOS), the organization responsible for maintaining the national organ transplant network, subjects all celebrity transplants to an internal audit to make sure the organ allocation was appropriate.

13 **Myth: My family will be charged if I donate my organs.**

Fact: The organ donor's family is never charged for donating. The family is charged for the cost of all final efforts to save your life, and those costs are sometimes misinterpreted as costs related to organ donation. Costs for organ removal go to the transplant recipient.

14 **Why you should consider organ donation**

Now that you have the facts, you can see that being an organ donor can make a big difference, and not just to one person. By donating your organs after you die, you can save or improve as many as 50 lives. And many families say that knowing their loved one helped save other lives helped them cope with their loss.

15   It's especially important to consider becoming an organ donor if you belong to an ethnic minority. Minorities including African-Americans, Asians and Pacific Islanders, Native Americans, and Hispanics are more likely than whites to have certain chronic conditions that affect the kidney, heart, lung, pancreas and liver. Certain blood types are more prevalent in ethnic minority populations. Because matching blood type is necessary for transplants, the need for minority donor organs is especially high.

16 **How to donate**

Becoming an organ donor is easy. You can indicate that you want to be a donor in the following ways:

- **Register with your state's donor registry.** Most states have registries. Check the list at OrganDonor.gov.

- **Designate your choice on your driver's license.** Do this when you obtain or renew your license.

- **Sign and carry a donor card.** Cards are available from OrganDonor.gov.

It's also important to tell your family that you want to be a donor. Hospitals seek consent from the next of kin before removing organs, although this is usually not required if you're registered with your state's donor registry. The best way to ensure that your wishes are carried out is to put them in writing. Include your wishes in your living will, as well as on your driver's license. If you have no next of kin or you doubt your family will agree to donate your organs, you can assign durable power of attorney to someone who you know will abide by your wishes. A lawyer can help you prepare this document.

Reading Comprehension Check

MyReadingLab™
Complete this **Exercise**
at **myreadinglab.com**

1. "You will also **undergo** testing to determine if your kidneys are in good shape and whether you can live a healthy life with just one kidney." (para. 11)
   The word *undergo* in the above context means
   a. participate in.
   b. pass up a chance.
   c. avoid a process.
   d. eliminate completely.

2. "It may seem that way because of the amount of publicity generated when **celebrities** receive a transplant, but they are treated no differently from anyone else." (para. 12)
   In the above sentence, the word *celebrities* means
   a. medical practitioners.
   b. patients.
   c. ordinary people.
   d. famous people.

3. "And many families say that knowing their loved one helped save other lives helped them **cope** with their loss."
   The word *cope* in the above sentence means
   a. to make worse.
   b. to handle.
   c. to weaken.
   d. to annoy.

4. The main idea of the article is that
   a. organ donation is a dangerous process, which may cost the donors their lives.
   b. most donors die before donating organs, so organ donation must be avoided.
   c. people should not let myths about organ donation keep them from donating organs.
   d. it is best if the donor's family members decide whether the organ is suitable for donation.

5. The main point of the last paragraph is that
   a. you should prepare a legal document stating clearly that you wish to donate an organ after your death.
   b. you should give your next of kin the authority to remove your organs after your death.
   c. only a lawyer can remove your organs after preparing a legal document.
   d. it is not necessary to prepare a legal document to state that you wish to be an organ donor.

Collaboration

Exploring the Topic

Discuss the following questions to review the content of the article you have just read.

1. According to the article, there are certain myths and concerns about organ donation that keep people from donating an organ. Discuss with your classmates whether some of these concerns are valid. Give specific examples to support your answer.

2. In your opinion, who should be given priority when it comes to providing an organ? In other words, what should be the most important criterion for determining who deserves the organ first?

3. The article suggests that it is important to prepare a legal document including one's wish to donate an organ. Why do you think it is necessary to include this wish in your living will? Give specific reasons to support your answer.

Post-Reading Vocabulary

Without using a dictionary, determine the meaning of the bolded words from the context.

1. "The rich and famous aren't given **priority** when it comes to allocating organs." (para. 12)

   Priority means _____

2. "The family is charged for the cost of all final efforts to save your life, and those costs are sometimes **misinterpreted** as costs related to organ donation." (para. 13)

   Misinterpreted means _____

3. "Hospitals seek **consent** from the next of kin before removing organs, although this is usually not required if you're registered with your state's donor registry." (para. 16)

   Consent means _____

READING

Reading Selection 4

Newspaper Article Excerpt

MyReadingLab™
Complete this **Exercise**
at **myreadinglab.com**

Monkeys Live Longer on Low-Cal Diet; Would Humans?

Preview Questions

1. Do you believe that you have healthy lifestyle habits? In other words, do you eat well, sleep well, and live in a stress-free environment? If you do not have a healthy lifestyle, what changes would you consider making? Be as specific as you can.

2. Despite the fact that aging is a natural process, why do you think most people are so worried about getting old? In other words, why are so many people obsessed with looking young?

3. Some experts believe that the process of aging can be reversed by controlling some of the factors that cause it. Do you agree with this view? If you do, what are some of the factors that can accelerate the aging process?

Pre-Reading Vocabulary: Focus on Some Key Terms

Collaboration

Determine the meaning of these words below with a classmate. Then consult a dictionary to see if your definition was correct or not.

Word	Your Definition	Dictionary Definition
fend off		
deprivation		
striking		
sustain		
caution		

Monkeys Live Longer on Low-Cal Diet; Would Humans?

By Brennan Lingsley, *USA Today,* July 9, 2009

1   WASHINGTON (AP) — Eat less, live longer? It seems to work for monkeys: A 20-year study found cutting calories by almost a third slowed their aging and fended off death. This is not about a quick diet to shed a few pounds. Scientists

have long known they could increase the lifespan of mice and more primitive creatures—worms, flies—with deep, long-term cuts from normal consumption.

2   Now comes the first evidence that such reductions delay the diseases of aging in primates, too—rhesus monkeys living at the Wisconsin National Primate Center. Researchers reported their study Friday in the journal *Science*.

3   What about those other primates, humans? Nobody knows yet if people in a world better known for pigging out could stand the deprivation long enough to make a difference, much less how it would affect their more complex bodies. Still, small attempts to tell are underway.

4   "What we would really like is not so much that people should live longer but that people should live healthier," said Dr. David Finkelstein of the National Institute on Aging. The Wisconsin monkeys seemed to do both.

5   "The fact that there's less disease in these animals is striking," Finkelstein said.

6   The federal government is funding a small study to see if some healthy normal-weight people could sustain a 25% calorie cut for two years and if doing so signals some changes that might, over a long enough time, reduce age-related disease.

7   But NIA's Finkelstein cautions that people shouldn't just try this on their own; cutting out the wrong nutrients could cause more harm than good. Just follow commonsense healthful lifestyle advice, he said.

8   "Everyone's obviously looking for the magic pill," and there's not one, Finkelstein said. "Watch what you eat, keep your mind active, exercise and don't get run over by a car."

The Associated Press, July 9, 2009. Reprinted by permission of the The YGS Group.

Reading Comprehension Check

Now that you have read the article, answer the multiple-choice questions to check your understanding of the article.

1. In the phrase "… such reductions **delay** the diseases of aging," (para. 2) the word *delay* means
   a. speed up.
   b. stop.
   c. concern.
   d. slow down.

2. In the study mentioned, what did the scientists do to slow the aging process in monkeys?
   a. cut their calorie intake by a third
   b. increase their food portions
   c. cut their calorie intake in half
   d. treat them more kindly

3. What is the topic of this article?
   a. monkeys
   b. Humans can possibly slow the aging process
   c. slowing the process of aging by eating less
   d. the similarity of monkeys to humans

4. The main idea of the essay is that
   a. monkeys are a good source for scientific studies on human behavior.
   b. scientists found that there might be a link between calorie reduction and the process of aging.
   c. we cannot assume that what we learn from studies with monkeys will have the same result in humans.
   d. aging is a natural process that cannot be manipulated by science.

5. What is Dr. Finkelstein's main point in the last paragraph of the article?
   a. Scientists may be able to find the magic pill to longevity.
   b. Pay attention when you walk.
   c. Living a longer life involves both maintaining a healthy lifestyle and being lucky.
   d. Unhealthy lifestyle habits play no role in determining how long you will live.

Exploring the Topic

Working in small groups, discuss the following questions.

Collaboration

1. The writer of the article suggests that even if people knew they could delay aging by cutting calories, many couldn't handle the sacrifice. Do you agree with this idea? Explain why or why not.

2. This experiment on delaying the aging process was done on monkeys. Do you think it is ethical for humans to be using other animals for the purpose of medical science? How much faith do you put in the results of numerous medical experiments done on other species?

3. Read Dr. Finkelstein's advice in the last sentence of the article. Do you agree with his philosophy? What advice would you add if you were interviewed on the secrets of longevity?

Post-Reading Vocabulary

Determine the meaning of the bolded words in the following sentences.

1. "This is not about a quick diet to **shed** a few pounds." (para. 1)

   The word *shed* means _____

2. "Still, small attempts to tell are **underway**." (para. 3)

   Underway means _____

3. "Just follow **commonsense** healthful lifestyle advice." (para. 7)

   Commonsense means _____

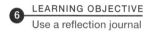

WRITING CONNECTIONS: *Free Writing in a Reflection Journal*

One way to think about reading is as a conversation between the writer and reader of a given text. Every reader brings their own knowledge and personal experience to the table when they read something new. Five people may be reading the same article on athletes and performance enhancement drugs, but based on their life experiences and interests will most likely offer five unique perspectives on the same topic.

Reflection journals give you the opportunity to reflect on readings you found interesting in the chapter and to "free write" on these chosen topic areas. When you free write, you are not being asked to answer a particular question and are not being tested on a particular subject area. You do not have to worry about grammar or mechanics. The idea is to write whatever comes to your mind in relation to a topic you have read about.

Example of a free writing journal entry on human cloning

Date: February 5th

Topic: Human Cloning

    I certainly would not want two me's walking around town. Life is complicated enough with just one of me present. Having a clone would invite dishonest behavior. The original me could be skipping class while the clone is forced to attend. The original me could be relaxing on the beach, while my clone could be spying on my girlfriend. Seriously, I simply would not trust myself to do things in a fully honest way if I knew I had the insurance of a clone to back me up.

    Now, is human cloning really going to happen or is it just science fiction? Well, I know they have cloned a sheep and can clone fruits and vegetables. My guess is that most governments would not allow scientists to go ahead and try to actually clone people. The risks are too high for that.

Okay. Now it is time to get your reflection journal rolling! Purchase a small notebook that you can use throughout the semester as a reflection journal.

Reading passages in this chapter focused on the following topics:

human cloning	how to live longer
how to lose belly fat	corn-based food products
organ donation	human biology and socilogy

If you choose, for example, to focus on the topic of losing weight, you can share your sister's experience of trying to get fit. You could write about your distaste for low-calorie foods and high-energy drinks. You can discuss a TV program you saw about America's obesity crisis. The point is that you are free to explore one or more of the chapter's topics in any way you want! Write as much as you need to write to fully express yourself.

Practice: Choose from the reading topics focused on in this biology chapter, and write a journal entry.

A Field of Corn, from *The Omnivore's Dilemma*

Reading Selection **5**

Nonfiction Book Excerpt

Preview Questions

1. When you buy fruits and vegetables from a supermarket, do you usually care whether they were grown naturally or whether they were genetically modified? In other words, would you rather consume organic food, or genetically modified food?

2. In the book excerpt you are about to read, the author discusses the many food products we eat that are corn-based. Can you think of any food items that you eat that are made of corn?

3. Some experts argue that the world will eventually run out of food if people continue to eat lots of meat. This is because animals are very high on the food chain and need lots of grains to survive. Given this information, would you will be willing to give up meat and become a vegetarian? Why or why not?

MyReadingLab™
Complete this **Exercise** at **myreadinglab.com**

Pre-Reading Vocabulary: Focus on Some Key Terms

As you have done before, try to guess the meaning of these words below with a classmate. Then consult a dictionary to determine how accurate you were.

Collaboration

Word	Your Definition	Dictionary Definition
range		
suspect		
coats		
trace		
prized		

A Field of Corn, from *The Omnivore's Dilemma*

By Michael Pollan

Michael Pollan, one of America's most renowned food writers, discovers in his investigation of the food chain and of what we typically find on the shelves of our supermarkets that it all comes down to one crop and one crop only: corn.

1   The average supermarket doesn't seem much like a field of corn. Take a look around one. What do you see? There's a large, air-conditioned room. There are long aisles and shelves piled high with boxes and cans. There are paper goods and diapers and magazines. But that's not all. Look again. Somewhere behind the brightly colored packaging, underneath the labels covered with information, there is a mountain of corn.

2   You may not be able to see it, but it's there. I'm not talking about the corn in the produce section. That's easy to recognize. In the spring and summer, the green ears of corn sit out in plain view with all the other fruits and vegetables. You can see a stack of ears next to the eggplants, onions, apples, bananas, and potatoes. But that's not a mountain of corn, is it?

3   Keep looking. Go through produce to the back of the supermarket and you'll find the meats. There's corn here too, but it's a little harder to see. Where is it? Here's a hint: What did the cows and pigs and chickens eat before they became cuts of meat? Mainly corn.

4   Go a little further now. There's still a lot of corn hiding in this supermarket. How about those long aisles of soft drinks? Made from corn. That freezer case stuffed with TV dinners? Mostly corn. Those donuts and cookies and chips? They're

made with a whole lot of corn. Supermarkets look like they contain a huge variety of food. The shelves are stuffed with thousands of different items. There are dozens of different soups and salad dressings, cases stuffed with frozen dinners and ice cream and meat. The range of food choices is amazing. Yet if you look a little closer, you begin to discover: It's All Corn.

5   Well, maybe not all corn, but there's still an awful lot of it hiding here—a lot more than you suspect. We think of our supermarkets as offering a huge variety of food. Yet most of that huge variety comes from one single plant. How can this be? Corn is what feeds the steer that becomes your steak. Corn feeds the chicken and the pig. Corn feeds the catfish raised in a fish farm. Corn-fed chickens laid the eggs. Corn feeds the dairy cows that produce the milk, cheese, and ice cream. See those chicken nuggets in the freezer case? They are really corn wrapped up in more corn. The chicken was fed corn. The batter is made from corn flour. The starch that holds it together is corn starch. The oil it was fried in was corn oil.

6   But that's not all. Read the label on any bag of chips, candy bar, or frozen snack. How many ingredients do you recognize? Maltodextrin? Monosodium glutamate? Ascorbic acid? What are those things? What about lecithin and mono-, di-, and triglycerides? They are all made from corn. The golden food coloring? Made from corn. Even the citric acid that keeps the nugget "fresh" is made from corn. If you wash down your chicken nuggets with almost any soft drink, you are drinking corn with your corn. Since the 1980s almost all sodas and most of the fruit drinks sold in the supermarket are sweetened with something called high-fructose corn syrup.

Let's stop reading for a moment and consider what we have just read!

Halfway Comprehension Check

Working in a small group, discuss the first part of the reading and make predictions about the second half.

Collaboration

1. What is this reading about?

2. What is the most interesting part so far? Explain.

3. Choose one quote to focus on and paraphrase what the speaker said.

4. You have only read half of the reading. Try to predict what the second half of the article will discuss.

Now continue with the reading and answer the questions when you get to the end.

---

7   Read the label on any processed food, and corn is what you'll find. Corn is in the non-dairy creamer and the Cheez Whiz, the frozen yogurt and the TV dinner, the canned fruit and the ketchup. It's in the candy, the cake mixes, the mayonnaise, mustard, hot dogs and bologna, the salad dressings and even in some vitamins. (Yes, it's in a Twinkie too.)

8   There are some forty-five thousand items in the average American supermarket and more than a quarter of them now contain corn. This goes for the

non-food items as well—everything from toothpaste and cosmetics to disposable diapers, trash bags, and even batteries.

Hidden Corn

9   Ever look at the ingredient list on a food label and wonder about those strange names? All of these common ingredients and hundreds more are made from corn:

modified starch

unmodified starch

glucose syrup

maltodextrin

ascorbic acid

crystalline fructose

lactic acid

MSG

caramel color

xanthan gum

10   Corn is in places you would never think to look. It's in the wax that coats the other vegetables in the produce section. It goes into the coating that makes the cover of a magazine shine. It's even part of the supermarket building, because the wallboard, the flooring, and many other building materials are made with corn.

11   You are what you eat, it's often said. If this is true, then what we are today is mostly corn. This isn't just me being dramatic—it's something that scientists have been able to prove. How do they do this? By tracing the element carbon as it goes from the atmosphere into plants, then into our food, and finally, into us.

12   You may have heard the expression that humans are a carbon-based life form. (This always seems to come up in science fiction movies, but it's true.) Like hydrogen and oxygen, carbon is an element, one of the basic building blocks of matter. All the molecules that make up our cells—carbohydrates, proteins, and fats—contain the element carbon. All of the carbon in our bodies was originally floating in the air, as part of a carbon dioxide molecule. Plants take the carbon out of carbon dioxide and use it to make food—carbohydrates. They do this through a process called photosynthesis. In photosynthesis, plants use the energy of the sun (*photo* means light) to synthesize (make) food.

13   All of our food, in fact almost all life on earth, can be traced back to photosynthesis in plants. It's more than a figure of speech to say that plants create life out of thin air. So the plants take carbon and make it into food. Then we eat the plants, or we eat animals that have eaten the plants. That's how the carbon winds up in our cells. But not all carbon is the same. Corn uses slightly different types of carbon than other plants. So by looking at the type of carbon in our cells, scientists can tell how much corn we have been eating. Todd Dawson, a biologist at the University of California, Berkeley, has done exactly that kind of research. He says that when you look at the carbon in the average American's cells, "we look like corn chips with legs."

14   Americans don't think of themselves as corn eaters. Our bread is made from wheat flour. We don't eat a lot of corn on the cob. When we think of serious corn eaters, we often think of people in Mexico. About 40 percent of their calories come directly from corn, mostly in the form of corn tortillas. Yet Americans have more corn in their diet than Mexicans. It's just that the corn we eat wears many different disguises.

15   How did corn take over America? It's really a tremendous success story—for corn, anyway. Corn has managed to become the most widely planted crop

in America—more than 80 million acres of farmland are planted with corn every year. Today it covers more acres of the country than any other living species, including human beings. It has pushed other plants and animals off the American farm. It has even managed to push a lot of farmers off the farm. (I'll explain that one later.) Corn is now one of the most successful plants on earth.

16   It's important to remember that while humans use plants and other animals, it's not a one-way street. Plants and animals don't just sit around waiting for human beings to use them—they use us, too. The ones that can adapt use our farms and cities to spread and multiply. Corn became king of the farm and the supermarket because it adapted itself easily to the needs of farmers and food makers. It had qualities that human beings prized. Those qualities allowed it to spread and grow until it worked its way into every corner of our lives—and every cell in our bodies.

Reading Comprehension Check

MyReadingLab™
Complete this Exercise
at myreadinglab.com

1. What is the topic of this reading?
   a. supermarkets
   b. Corn has completely overtaken our diets.
   c. the amount of corn in food products
   d. the business of food

2. The author mentions that corn can be found in many food products, including all of the following except
   a. meat.   c. soda.
   b. candy.   d. fruit.

3. What point does the author make in comparing the diets of Mexicans and Americans?
   a. Americans consume more corn than Mexicans.
   b. Mexicans consume much more corn than Americans.
   c. Americans eat a lot of Mexican food.
   d. Americans and Mexicans do not consume a lot of corn.

4. What is the main point made in the last paragraph of the reading?
   a. The rise of corn as an important crop was a coincidence.
   b. Corn spread because it had qualities prized by humans.
   c. People adapt to crops.
   d. Corn has not been around very long.

5. The main idea of the article is that
   a. corn syrup is found in many soft drinks.
   b. we must be more aware of the unhealthy nature of many food items.
   c. many people do not realize how many everyday food products contain corn.
   d. photosynthesis plays a significant role in how our food is produced.

Collaboration

Exploring the Topic

Discuss the following questions to review the content of the passage you have just read.

1. One of Michael Pollan's goals in writing this book was to wake Americans up to the basic facts surrounding the everyday food choices that they make. Do you think it is true that most Americans are disconnected from information about the food that they eat? Explain your opinion with some examples.

2. The author spends a lot of time in this reading passage making the point that corn is in almost everything we eat these days. Why do you think the author feels that this fact matters and that we should be alarmed by this information?

3. This reading was selected for this particular chapter, which focuses on biology. In your opinion, what is the connection between the topic of this passage and the field of biology? Explain.

Post-Reading Vocabulary

Without using a dictionary, determine the meaning of the bolded words from the context.

1. "Read the label on any **processed** food, and corn is what you'll find." (para. 7)

   The word *processed* means _____

2. "Like hydrogen and oxygen, carbon is an **element**." (para. 11)

   The word *element* means _____

   _____

3. "That's how the carbon **winds up** in our cells." (para. 12)

   The expression *winds up* means _____

TEXTBOOK APPLICATION   **Human Biology, Science, and Society**

Listen to the lecture on biology and take notes for further discussion. You can listen to the lecture by scanning the QR code on the next page with your smart phone. Your professor may also read the selections or play the audio file in class. Make sure that you write down the key points of the lecture.

Collaboration

Group Discussion

As you discuss the following questions with your classmates, refer to the notes you took while listening to the lecture. Your instructor may ask you to share your answers with your classmates. Therefore, it is best to write brief answers to each of the questions below using your own words. After the discussion, you will have an opportunity to share your answers with your peers.

1. In the twenty-first century, much advancement in science and technology has taken place. How do you think these scientific discoveries will influence the human condition?

2. Do you believe that scientists will find a cure for AIDS in your lifetime? In your opinion, what will be the cure for this disease?

3. Some people think that with the aid of medical science, soon parents will be able to select their children's features before they are even born. Do you think this is necessarily a blessing for humans? Why or why not?

4. What do biologists study? What are some other branches of science?

5. Do you agree with the view that humans evolved from single-celled organisms that arose from chemical elements approximately 3.5 billion years ago? Why or why not?

6. In your opinion, why do humans get diseases, and how do they survive them?

7. Do you think that humans influence the destinies of other organisms on earth? If so, how do they affect the lives of other living creatures?

Now that you have discussed the highlights of the lecture with your classmates, read the following selection and answer the multiple-choice questions that follow.

Human Biology, Science, and Society

By Michael D. Johnson

Scan this code using your smart phone to listen to an audio version of this reading

1   You were born into exciting times, when scientific discoveries are happening more rapidly than at any other time in human history. Like the Industrial Revolution of the nineteenth century and the discovery of DNA in the twentieth, today's scientific innovations will change the human condition forever.

2   In your lifetime people may be able to select or modify their children's features before they are born. People may even be able to have clones (copies) made of themselves. At the very least, certain diseases that threaten us now will become curable. Perhaps your grandchildren will not even know what AIDS is because the disease will have disappeared.

3   What you are witnessing is the power of science. Science is the study of the *natural world*, which includes all matter and all energy. Because all living organisms are also made of matter and energy, they are part of the natural world. Biology is one of many branches of science. More specifically, biology (from the Greek words *bios*, life, and *logos*, word or thought) is the study of living organisms and life's processes. It is the study of life. Other branches of science are chemistry, physics, geology, astronomy, and related fields such as medicine.

4   This text is specifically about *human* biology. We will explore what it means to be alive. We will see how the molecules that make up our bodies are created from molecules in the air and in our food and drink. We will learn how our cells grow and divide, and how we evolved from single-celled organisms that arose from non-living chemical elements nearly 3.5 billion years ago. We will explore how our bodies function, why we get diseases, and how we manage to survive them. We will

look at how we develop into adults, reproduce, and influence the destinies of other organisms on Earth.

5   With the power of science comes an awesome responsibility. All of us, individually and collectively, must choose how to use the knowledge that science gives us. Will human cloning be acceptable? Can we prevent global warming? Should your insurance company be able to reject you for coverage because genetic testing shows that you may develop cancer forty years from now?

6   We all have to make responsible decisions concerning not only our own health and well-being but also the long-term well-being of our species. This book considers many aspects of human interaction with the natural world. We'll contemplate human functioning within the environment and the impact of humans on the environment. Along the way we'll confront a variety of social and personal issues and discuss the choices we might make about them. Because biology is the study of life, we begin by defining life itself.

from Michael D. Johnson, *Human Biology: Concepts and Current Issues*, 6e, p. 4

Reading Comprehension Check

1. "You were born into exciting times, when scientific discoveries are happening more **rapidly** than at any other time in human history." (para. 1)
   The word *rapidly* means
   a. gradually.   c. slightly.
   b. slowly.   d. quickly.

2. "Like the Industrial Revolution of the nineteenth century and the discovery of DNA in the twentieth, today's scientific **innovations** will change the human condition forever." (para. 1)
   In the above sentence, the word *innovations* means
   a. interventions.   c. preventions.
   b. inventions.   d. alterations.

3. "At the very least, certain diseases that threaten us now will become **curable**." (para. 2)
   In this context, the word *curable* means
   a. unable to be cured.
   b. unable to be helped.
   c. able to be damaged.
   d. able to be fully healed.

4. "What you are **witnessing** is the power of science." (para. 3)
   The word *witnessing* in the above context means
   a. forgetting.
   b. ignoring.
   c. seeing.
   d. overlooking.

5. "We will learn how our cells grow and divide, and how we **evolved** from single-celled organisms that arose from non-living chemical elements nearly 3.5 billion years ago." (para. 4)
   In the above sentence, the word *evolved* means
   a. reduced.
   b. shrank.
   c. developed.
   d. eliminated.

6. The main point of the first paragraph is that
   a. scientific discoveries made in the twenty-first century will influence humans incredibly.
   b. scientific discoveries made in the twentieth century will influence the human condition forever.
   c. scientific innovations in the nineteenth century will change the human condition forever.
   d. scientific advancements made in the twenty-first century will be disappointing and useless.

7. The main point of the second paragraph is that
   a. humans will be free from diseases in the twenty-first century.
   b. humans will be able to do things they were unable to do in the past.
   c. humans will be unable to do things they were able to do in the past.
   d. humans will suffer miserably because of scientific discoveries in the twenty-first century.

8. The main point of the third paragraph is that
   a. humans are experiencing exciting discoveries in the twenty-first century because of the power of science.
   b. humans experienced exciting discoveries in the twentieth century without the power of science.
   c. biology is the study of life.
   d. biology is one of the branches of science.

9. The main point of the fourth paragraph is that
   a. some non-living chemical elements changed about 3.5 billion years ago.
   b. the text primarily focuses on human biology.
   c. humans were born 3.5 billion years ago.
   d. biology is the study of living and non-living organisms.

10. The main idea of the last paragraph is that
    a. it is not the responsibility of humans to protect their environment.
    b. humans need not worry about their interaction with the natural world
    c. humans are responsible for their health and the well-being of their species.
    d. humans are only responsible for their health.

INTERNET FACT SEARCH

Biology

Using your background knowledge and logic, answer the following data questions. Check your answers with your classmates to discuss the topics further. Then, go online and search for the relevant data. Be sure to write the Web source next to your research finding.

1. What is the leading cause of death in the United States?

   a. cancer
   b. heart disease

   c. diabetes
   d. accidents

   Your guess: _____   Research finding: _____

   Web source: _____

2. What percentage of American adults are obese?

   a. 24%
   b. 31%

   c. 59%
   d. 63%

   Your guess: _____   Research finding: _____

   Web source: _____

3. What is the average life expectancy of an American?

   a. 101 years
   b. 98 years

   c. 77 years
   d. 67 years

   Your guess: _____   Research finding: _____

   Web source: _____

4. How many Americans are waiting for transplant surgeries?

   a. 27,000
   b. 59,000

   c. 91,000
   d. 101,000

   Your guess: _____   Research finding: _____

   Web source: _____

5. According to a recent poll by Harris Interactive, what percentage of Americans are registered organ donors?

   a. 87%
   b. 63%

   c. 50%
   d. 22%

   Your guess: _____   Research finding: _____

   Web source: _____

FORMAL PRESENTATION PROJECTS

You will be given the opportunity to present on a topic of your interest pertinent to one of the text's chapter disciplines. Topics could relate to one of the questions you checked off in the "Follow Your Interests" section at the beginning of the chapter. Your instructor may ask you to browse through the chapters to guide you toward a given discipline focus.

For more help with **Highlighting** and **Identifying Topics and Main Ideas**, go to your learning path in **MyReadingLab.com**.

PERSONAL FINANCE

Learning Objectives

IN THIS CHAPTER, YOU WILL LEARN TO . . .

1. Describe the discipline of personal finance
2. Define key terms in the field of personal finance
3. Effectively annotate a text
4. Communicate with professors
5. Identify key supporting details in a reading

INTRODUCTION TO THE DISCIPLINE OF PERSONAL FINANCE

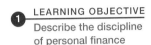

LEARNING OBJECTIVE
Describe the discipline of personal finance

Personal finance is about planning your spending habits, financing, and investing to improve your overall financial situation. You may not realize the importance of personal finance, but it is a fact that the everyday decisions you make about spending your hard-earned money can have a positive or negative effect on your savings and financial health in the long term. This chapter introduces you to the fundamentals of personal finance and touches on topics such as personal savings, using credit cards, tenant protection from foreclosure, online banking, student loan issues, and college and careers. After reading the several different selections in this chapter, you will arrive at a better understanding of how to manage your financial situation well and will hopefully make sound decisions to build a stable financial future.

Reading into a Photo

Collaboration

Working in a small group, examine the following photograph and answer the questions that follow.

1. In your opinion, what do these people seem to be discussing?
2. What message does this image convey to you?

Follow Your Interests

Collaboration

Review the set of questions below that personal finance experts might explore. Check off the three or four questions that are most interesting to you.

1. Why are so many Americans spending more than they earn? What can be done to stop or change this trend?

2. "A penny saved is a penny earned" is old wisdom. Why isn't this common-sense practice more valued by American society?

3. What are some of the important issues a potential homebuyer must take into consideration?

4. How can a homeowner best avoid foreclosure?

5. How can one develop sound credit card spending habits?

6. How do credit card companies determine who is qualified to be a card member?

7. Identity theft is a growing concern among Americans. How can one protect oneself from being a victim of such fraud?

8. In today's competitive world, how can college students afford a decent education and stay afloat financially?

9. How much information must one have in order to file taxes without the help of a certified accountant?

10. There are many wealthy individuals who continue to amass great amounts of money without having to pay their fair share of taxes. How can the government more successfully collect taxes from the rich? Are changes needed to reform America's tax structure?

11. A working individual is expected to buy home insurance, car insurance, life insurance, and health insurance. What types of insurances are really necessary, and which ones should be the responsibility of the government?

12. What types of homework does one need to do to become an informed and successful investor in the stock market?

13. Many people are frustrated by financial wrongdoing on Wall Street. What can the government do to win back the trust of the people in the investment world?

Now, share your choices with a small group of classmates and discuss why these particular questions are most interesting to you. You may wish to discuss these questions with them and ask which questions they found interesting.

Key Terms in the Field of Personal Finance

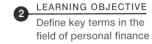

LEARNING OBJECTIVE
2 Define key terms in the field of personal finance

The following key terms are frequently used in the discipline of personal finance. Learning these key terms will be helpful when you take a college-level course in personal finance. Review the words below and answer the multiple-choice questions that follow.

allocation	disability	investing
assessing	estate	managing
assets	financing	mutual funds
bonds	forecasting	planning
budgeting	implement	stocks

EXERCISE 1   Inferring Meaning from Context

Read each sentence below and try to derive the meaning of the italicized key terms from the context. Circle the correct definition of each italicized term.

1. People who understand the importance of personal finance know that *budgeting* for the rainy days is a wise decision.
   a. wasting money on unnecessary things
   b. spending more than you earn every month
   c. setting aside money for specific purposes
   d. not saving enough money for the future

2. Experts in personal finance suggest that people should buy *disability* insurance even if they are perfectly healthy.
   a. having enough power and strength
   b. good physical and mental ability
   c. lack of sufficient power and strength to do things
   d. sufficient power and strength to do things

3. With the increasing popularity of its iPhone and iPad around the world, the *stocks* of Apple Inc. have risen in value.
   a. the shares of a corporation
   b. the mutual funds of a company
   c. a corporation's positive cash flow
   d. the dividends of a company

4. Many people believe that *assessing* your credit from time to time can help you build a good credit score.
   a. ignoring   c. overlooking
   b. not giving importance to   d. estimating the value of

5. Uncle Peter died a poor man and left no *assets* behind.
   a. children   c. property
   b. education   d. birth certificate

6. A good financial adviser recommends that clients invest in government *bonds* for a safe return.
   a. shares of a company
   b. an IOU of the US Treasury
   c. a foreign currency
   d. an amount of money deposited

7. Parents must teach their children that *managing* money is an important part of personal financial planning.
   a. using with good judgment
   b. wasting money all the time
   c. spending money unwisely
   d. throwing money away without much thought

8. Experienced financial advisers know that balanced asset *allocation* is a crucial part of personal financial planning.
   a. putting all your eggs in one basket
   b. not dividing expenses
   c. investing money in different situations
   d. only investing in high-risk stocks

9. Knowing that individual stocks are risky, most senior citizens invest their life-time savings in *mutual funds*, which is a safer, more conservative investment.
   a. risky individual stocks
   b. the shares of a corporation
   c. an investment company that issues shares and has to repurchase them from shareholders on demand
   d. a pension plan for senior citizens

10. If you are young and have a high risk tolerance, *investing* in individual stocks might be a better option for you than investing in mutual funds.
   a. studying   c. doing research
   b. purchasing   d. depositing

11. Mr. Baghdatis, a successful businessman, died a bachelor and left a rich *estate* behind.
   a. property and possessions
   b. many children
   c. a huge debt
   d. many business loans

12. It is not enough to have a personal financial plan. Once you have a plan, you must *implement* it to manage your financial situation well.
   a. not fulfill   c. carry out
   b. fail to perform   d. not put into effect

13. *Financing* a car may save you some money at the time of the purchase, but it will cost you much more than the book value of the vehicle in the long term because of the interest rate.
   a. paying cash upfront for a purchase
   b. lending money for a purchase
   c. borrowing money for a purchase
   d. giving funds for a purchase

14. Because of the bad economy, most middle-class workers are realizing that *planning* for a safe financial future is not an option anymore.
   a. method or scheme for action
   b. acting carelessly without much thought
   c. not saving for the future
   d. having no specific purpose

15. Financial experts are *forecasting* that the economy is going to get even worse in the near future.
   a. thinking about the past
   b. considering the economy in the past
   c. coming up with a poor plan
   d. making a prediction

Collaboration

EXERCISE 2   Creating Meaningful Sentences with the Key Terms

Working with a partner, choose five of the key terms in personal finance and write an original sentence about each one.

1. Word = _____

_____

_____

2. Word = _____

_____

_____

3. Word = _____

_____

_____

4. Word = _____

_____

_____

5. Word = _____

_____

_____

COLLEGE STUDY SKILLS
Making Annotations

3 LEARNING OBJECTIVE
Effectively annotate a text

In the previous chapter, you learned to highlight key terms and concepts. In this chapter, we will examine the critical skill of annotating relevant text. After reading this section, you will understand that active readers make annotations as they read and have an ongoing dialogue with the text.

Introducing the Skill

You may not realize it, but there is a big difference between *taking* notes and *making* notes. When we take notes, the source of information is external. That is to say, when we listen to a lecture given by a speaker, we take notes, making a list of key terms and concepts, interesting ideas, questions to consider later, and so on. However, when we make notes, we respond to a piece of text. It is important to note that while the source of information is still external, the process of making notes is more internal than that of taking notes, as the reader engages herself with the text and formulates questions for further clarification and reflection.

Remember that each reader is different, and that there are many ways one can make annotations. Some readers may underline a piece of text that they find intriguing. Others may circle key terms and unfamiliar vocabulary. Yet others write questions in the margin. Some may choose to paraphrase certain ideas for the purpose of understanding. Other readers may use all of these things and create their own unique way of annotating relevant text. As you practice this skill more often, you will develop your own techniques and become more familiar with the art of making annotations.

You may wish to annotate relevant text as follows:

- Circle key terms, concepts, and unfamiliar vocabulary items.

- Underline important bits and pieces of information such as statistics and specific examples.

- Write pertinent questions that will allow you to understand the main ideas and related points.

- Underline important sentences that will help you understand the reading with relative ease.

Let's look at the following text, which is taken from an introductory personal finance textbook, and see how the reader has annotated the text.

How You Benefit from an Understanding of Personal Finance

By Jeff Madura

1   (Personal finance) (also referred to as (personal financial planning)) is the process of planning your spending, financing, and investing to optimize your financial situation. A personal finance plan specifies your financial goals and describes the spending, financing, and investing plans that are intended to achieve those goals. Although the U.S. is one of the wealthiest countries, many Americans do not manage their financial situations well. Consequently, they tend to rely too much on credit and have excessive debt. Consider these statistics:

How is personal finance relevant to me?

Do I need a personal finance plan?

Why is it that most Americans do not manage their financial situation well?

- More than 1.2 million people filed for personal (bankruptcy) in 2008.

What is bankruptcy?

- The level of savings in the U.S. is only about 1 percent of income earned. (Some investments, including retirement accounts, are not included as savings.)

- About half of all surveyed people in the U.S. who are working full-time state that they live from one paycheck to the next, without a plan for saving money.

- About 40 percent of people who work full-time do not save for retirement. Those who do typically save a relatively small amount of money.

Why don't 40 percent of people save for retirement?

2   The lack of savings is especially problematic given the increasing cost of health care and other necessities. You will have numerous options regarding the choice of bank deposits, credit cards, loans, insurance policies, investments, and retirement plans. With an understanding of personal finance, you will be able to make decisions that can enhance your financial situation.

from Jeff Madura, *Personal Finance*, 4e, p. 4.

Putting the Skill into Action

As mentioned previously, you need to practice annotating relevant text to build your own unique system of conversing with and reflecting on the reading. Now that you have seen an example of how to make annotations, let's practice reading a passage and annotating the text.

Practice: As you reflect on the reading, be creative and do whatever helps you improve your reading comprehension.

Judge the Advice of Financial Advisers

1   The personal financial planning process will enable you to make informed decisions about your spending, saving, financing, and investing. Nevertheless, you may prefer to rely on advice from various types of financial advisers. An understanding of personal finance allows you to judge the guidance of financial advisers and to determine whether their advice is in your best interest (or in their best interest).

2   Example: You want to invest $10,000 of your savings. A financial adviser guarantees that your investment will increase in value by 20 percent (or by $2,000) this year, but he will charge you 4 percent of the investment ($400) for his advice. If you have a background in personal finance, you would know that no investment can be guaranteed to increase in value by 20 percent in one year. Therefore, you would realize that you should not trust this financial adviser. You could either hire a more reputable financial adviser or review investment recommendations made by financial advisers on the Internet (often for free).

from Jeff Madura, *Personal Finance*, 4e, p. 5

After you finish making annotations, share your work with a classmate and answer the following questions:

1. What key terms and concepts did you circle and why?

2. What bits and pieces of information did you underline?

3. What questions did you write to understand the reading?

4. What questions do you still have about the reading?

The Last Word

Active readers do not simply flip through the pages. They annotate the text for various purposes: to determine the main idea, to look for specific examples that support the main idea, and to ask questions for further clarification and reflection. You too can become an active, fluent, and engaged reader by annotating relevant text. Remember that practice makes perfect, and that the more you practice making annotations, the more active a reader you will become.

READINESS FOR COLLEGE SUCCESS
Communicating with Your Professor

LEARNING OBJECTIVE
4 Communicate with professors

Most successful college students are proactive in their approach to their academic studies. They seize every opportunity to enhance their learning and to progress in their academic area. Professors recognize and appreciate those students who are active learners and who are curious about building their knowledge base.

One of the best ways to show your interest in a college course and to clear up any confusion surrounding class lectures and assignments is to make an appointment to speak with your professor one-on-one in his or her office.

A few tips on how best to set up this meeting with your professor might be helpful.

- **Always make an appointment first.** Do not just walk in on your professor. Professors are busy people and most likely will not have the time to speak with you if you do not have an appointment set up in advance.

- **Do not be shy when approaching a professor to schedule an office conference.** Communicating with students during their office hours is part of a professor's job, and most professors appreciate when students make an effort to meet with them.

- **Set up specific questions in advance of your appointment with your professor and bring the appropriate materials.** If you have a question about a recent lecture, bring your lecture notes. If you want to discuss a particular class reading, bring the text with you. Feel free to ask the professor to recommend a book, an article, or a Web site that can help you with a particular project you are working on.

- **Finally, do not be embarrassed to admit that you are "lost" or that you find a certain component of the course confusing.** Making things more clear for students is what professors are being paid for! Do not hesitate!

Preparing for Your Meeting with a Professor

Examine and fill out the chart below in preparation for a conference with your professor. First, check off the appropriate reasons for your intended meeting and proceed to fill out the other sections of the chart. Then, set up an appointment and visit your professor.

Main Reason(s) for Your Appointment	*Materials You Will Bring to Your Professor*	*Specific Questions for Your Professor*
☐ Questions about an assignment / a reading		
☐ Questions about an upcoming exam		
☐ Questions about a grade		
☐ Questions about a lecture / a point made in class		
☐ Seeking a recommendation for a text / Web site, etc. …		
☐ Just want to meet the professor and have a general discussion about course / academic discipline		
☐ Other		

READING

Reading Selection 1

Web Article

MyReadingLab™
Complete this **Exercise**
at **myreadinglab.com**

The Importance of Creating a Savings Account

Preview Questions

1. While the media emphasizes losing weight and living a long and healthy life, why do you think saving money is not given much importance?

2. Do you have a personal savings plan? In other words, do you keep track of how you spend your money to manage your financial situation well? Why or why not?

3. If you were to eliminate some of your everyday expenses, what are some things you could live without? Give specific examples to support your answer.

4. The article you are about to read is written by a banking institution. In writing about the topic of keeping a savings account, what bias do you think a bank would have? Why is it important to keep the source of an article in mind as you read?

Collaboration

Pre-Reading Vocabulary: Focus on Some Key Terms

Before beginning the reading selection, it may be helpful to focus on the meaning of some key words in the article. Working with a partner, try to guess the meaning of these words. Then look up the words in a dictionary.

Word	Your Definition	Dictionary Definition
volatile		
fluctuate		
overwhelmed		
recurring		
frugal		

The Importance of Creating a Savings Account

By Jeremy Vohwinkle

1 Saving money. It's something everyone knows they should do. So why does it seem so difficult to get started? The fact is everyone has to start somewhere, and starting is the hardest part. Having liquid savings is something that might impact you in ways you hadn't thought of.

2 We all know how important having an emergency savings is in an emergency, but think of the decrease in stress when you have some money set aside. Think of the discipline and confidence you'll gain in making a savings plan and sticking to it. If the worst happens and you lose your job, money in the bank is the difference between living off of high-interest credit cards and having a safety net to pay your bills. A savings account is the first step to building a better financial future for you and your loved ones.

Why People Save

3 The uncertainty of living paycheck to paycheck is a real fear that affects millions of Americans, especially with the volatile economy and job market in recent years. Money in the bank is peace of mind, something that won't fluctuate if the market crashes or the economy sours. Whether it's for an emergency fund, saving for a vacation, or buying a home, a savings account should be a priority on everyone's financial "to-do" list. Think of savings as a way of paying yourself first. People are used to paying bills, and a savings account is no different. Think of your monthly savings goal as a bill that has to be paid just like any other. If your cell phone bill is $100/month do you always find a way to pay it? Of course. So if your goal

is to put $100/month into a savings account you should treat it like a bill and make sure it gets paid!

How to Start Saving Money

4   The first step is to set up a savings account. Whether it's online or at a physical bank down the road, don't get overwhelmed with all the options. Pick an account that has minimal fees, no minimum balance, and if possible, a decent interest rate to start. Rates are low right now, so if you find an account that doesn't have fees you're already ahead of the game.

5   Opening up an account with an online bank is usually the quickest and easiest way to get started. The application process can be done 24 hours a day and usually only takes a few minutes. You can usually fund the account with a small opening deposit (usually around $50, though some banks require a little more or less) transferred instantly from your existing checking account. Once your savings account is linked up with one of your existing accounts transferring money is as easy as a click as a mouse. In fact, you can even set up scheduled and recurring deposits so that it's all done automatically. Ally Bank is currently offering one of the highest rates.

6   If you'd prefer to go in person it's still a simple process that should take less than 30 minutes. You can stop into any branch office of your existing bank or a new one and let them know you'd like to open an account. In the end it doesn't matter so much where you bank as it does just setting up an account somewhere and actually putting it to work.

Building Your Savings

7   Once the savings account is set up it's time to start focusing on building your savings. The most intimidating part of beginning to save money usually stems from looking at the big picture before focusing on smaller goals so that you know what you're up against. Financial professionals often recommend having 3 to 6 months of emergency expenses in savings. That's a big chunk of cash and most people are not going to be able to save that kind of money in a short amount of time, and no one expects you to. This is the big picture so don't try to bite it all off at once.

8   Instead, break your goals into smaller, more sizable benchmarks. Try having 10% of your salary direct deposited into your savings account. Direct deposit means you won't see the money hit your checking account first, and therefore will probably be less inclined to spend it. If 10% is too much to start with, begin with 5% and increase the percentage by 1% every three to four months. If you receive your paychecks via paper check, discipline yourself to taking a percentage of that check and physically depositing or transferring the equivalent amount into your savings whenever you get paid.

9   Don't get discouraged in the first few months. Remember, if you're depositing just small amounts and earning little interest it won't seem like you're making progress, but you are! Periodically, check your progress to make sure you've been saving as much as you should. The goal doesn't have to be a dollar amount, but every quarter or every six months, make sure you've been keeping up on your savings plan. This can be as informal as a simple spreadsheet to as detailed as you

want by managing your accounts in something like Quicken. Tweak your progress periodically to reinforce your savings goals or plan for upcoming expenses. If you receive a bonus, put the same percentage straight into your savings account. Remember, pay yourself when you receive income, whether from a gift, a bonus, side income, or tax refund. Continuing to reinforce the pattern of saving only puts you closer and closer to meeting your goals.

Stay on Track Once You Start

10   Keep yourself on track with your saving and the rewards will be tremendous. The biggest thing is to keep from getting discouraged. Most people take years to build up a savings fund, and having a small amount of money in the bank is better than having none at all. It's easy to feel like saving just $20/week or something isn't doing any good, but remember that you're setting a plan in place that will likely take a few years to reach your goals. It's a marathon, not a sprint.

11   Eventually, you'll check your progress and be amazed at how those small steps towards saving have turned into a sizable balance in your savings account. It takes discipline, patience, and maybe even some steps towards more frugal living, but the rewards of building a cash cushion will be well worth it. The peace of mind of having a savings account is, in a word, priceless. So, what are you waiting for?

Reprinted by permission of the author.

Reading Comprehension Check

1. In the sentence, "Having liquid savings is something that might impact you in ways you hadn't thought of," (para. 1) the word *liquid* means
   a. a drink.
   b. cash flow.
   c. wet.
   d. disguised.

2. "Money in the bank is peace of mind, something that won't fluctuate if the market crashes or the economy **sours**." (para. 3) In this sentence, the word *sours* means
   a. smells.
   b. delays.
   c. sweetens.
   d. goes in a bad direction.

3. The main idea of the article is that
   a. it is better to invest in stocks than to keep money in the bank.
   b. a savings plan is only good for college students.
   c. setting up a savings account is easier than most people realize.
   d. spending money is more important than keeping track of one's expenses.

4. Which of the following is offered as an example of a way to make sure you don't spend your paycheck right away?
   a. cashing your work check right away
   b. setting up a direct deposit into your savings account
   c. converting your savings account into a checking account
   d. always using credit cards

5. Which of the following is NOT mentioned as an example of extra income that can be deposited into a savings account?
   a. gift money
   b. a bonus
   c. a tax refund
   d. a weekly paycheck

Collaboration

Exploring the Topic

Discuss the following questions to review the content of the article you have just read.

1. According to the article, what are some reasons why people choose to save some of their income?

2. Why does the author advise the reader to "break your goals into smaller, more sizable benchmarks"?

3. After reading the pro-savings account arguments put forth by a bank, do you agree that keeping a savings account is the best way to go? What other options are out there for building your savings?

Post-Reading Vocabulary

Without using a dictionary, determine the meaning of the bolded words from the context.

1. "A savings account should be a **priority** on everyone's financial 'to-do' list." (para. 3)

   Priority means _____

2. "… so if you find an account that doesn't have fees you're already **ahead of the game.**" (para. 4)

   Ahead of the game means _____

3. "Instead, break your goals into smaller, more sizable **benchmarks**." (para. 8)

   Benchmarks means _____

READING

Reading Selection **2**

Web Article

MyReadingLab™
Complete this **Exercise**
at **myreadinglab.com**

Credit Card Smarts: Take Charge of Your Cards

Preview Questions

1. Could you survive a month without access to a credit card? Explain how the absence of a credit/debit card would change your life.

2. In your opinion, why do so many Americans lose control of their credit card spending? Is there a solution?

3. Are credit card companies partially to blame for college students' credit card debt? Explain.

Pre-Reading Vocabulary: Focus on Some Key Terms

Collaboration

Before beginning the reading selection, it may be helpful to focus on the meaning of some key words in the article. Working with a partner, try to guess the meaning of these words. Then look up the words in a dictionary.

Word	*Your Definition*	*Dictionary Definition*
scenario		
indisputable		
enacted		
promptly		
impulse		

Credit Card Smarts: Take Charge of Your Cards

1   Imagine being 30 years old and still paying off a slice of pizza you bought when you were in college. It may sound crazy, but problems with credit card debt can lead to this scenario.

2   Learning how to use credit cards responsibly now can save you from having to dig yourself out of debt after you graduate. It also helps prevent you from having a bad credit history in the future that will affect other things you want to do.

3   You know that the loans you take out for college need to be paid back once you graduate. If you add a large monthly credit card bill (avoid the temptation to charge your tuition!) to that amount, you may find yourself in a very difficult situation financially.

Credit Cards and College Students

4   Credit cards are an indisputable fact of life and there are many good reasons to have one. They give you protection for your purchases, allow you to shop on-line, and provide a cushion in case of emergencies. The secret is to use the credit card as a tool to help you when you need it, but not to excess. Discuss with your family what kind of expenses it is reasonable to charge.

5   Credit card abuse has become such a problem that, in February 2010, the federal government recognized the importance of protecting college students from the consequences of misusing credit cards. They enacted legislation chang-ing how credit card companies can do business with students. Although the law provides some protection, it's still up to you to manage credit wisely.

6   The law bans credit card companies from issuing cards to people under the age of 18. If you're under 21 years old, you need an adult cosigner to get a card, unless you can prove that you have the financial means to pay your bill. Other pro-visions in the law limit some of the fees credit card companies can charge—and, in response, the companies are raising interest rates to avoid losing income. Any-one without an established credit history may face the highest interest rates—and that group typically includes students.

Credit Card Offers on Campus

7   If you don't already have a card, you'll have plenty of opportunities to ap-ply for one once you hit campus. It shouldn't surprise you that the companies are allowed on campus; many colleges earn money by permitting this practice and from creating affinity cards—credit cards that include the name of your college. The law requires that educational institutions and credit card companies let you know about these agreements, but the messages may be subtle. Learn about fees and interest rates to protect yourself.

Carrying a Balance Can Be Very Expensive

8   Credit cards are actually high-interest loans in disguise. Companies may lend you money, but they get it all back and a lot more by charging you fees. Finance charges on the unpaid portion of your bill can be as much as 25 percent each month, and cash-advance fees have even higher interest rates. Annual fees just to carry the card in your wallet range from $20 to $100; there are also late-payment fees, typically $25–$50.

9   Not paying off the entire amount in your account each month can lead to big finance charges. Take the story of Joe:

10   Joe's average unpaid credit card bill during a year is $500, and his finance charge is 20 percent—so he has to pay $100 in interest for the year. He pays a $20 annual fee per year, plus a $25 late fee one month (he was up late studying and forgot to mail in his check). After a year, Joe ends up owing $145 in interest and fees to his credit card company, and he still hasn't paid for any of his actual purchases!

Credit Report Matters

11   Your college years are an important time to build the good credit history you need after you graduate. You need to provide a credit report to apply for an

apartment or finance a large purchase, such as a car. Employers often review a credit report when they hire and evaluate employees. Problems with credit cards, such as late or missed payments, stay in your credit report for seven years.

Be Credit Smart

12   When you sign up for a credit card, you are responsible for paying the bills. Follow these rules of credit management to lead a financially healthy life:

- Consider using a debit card instead of a credit card. Money is deducted directly from your checking account, so you can't spend more than you actually have.

- Read all application materials carefully—especially the fine print. What happens after the "teaser rate" expires? What happens to your interest rate if you're late with a payment or fail to make a payment? What's the interest rate for a cash advance?

- Pay bills promptly to keep finance and other charges to a minimum; pay the balance off if you can.

- Use credit only if you're certain you are able to repay the debt.

- Avoid impulse shopping on your credit card.

- Save your credit card for a money emergency.

Reading Comprehension Check

1. What is the topic of the article?
   a. Credit cards must be used responsibly and in moderation.
   b. credit cards
   c. credit card usage and students
   d. student finance

2. What is NOT mentioned as a benefit of having a credit card, in para. 4?
   a. Credit cards allow you to shop online.
   b. Credit cards provide a financial cushion.
   c. They give you protection for your purchases.
   d. They guarantee you a debt-free year.

3. In the sentence, "The law requires that educational institutions and credit card companies let you know about these agreements, but the messages may be **subtle**," (para. 7) the word *subtle* could be replaced by _____.
   a. direct   c. indirect
   b. serious   d. singular

4. The rules offered in the final section of the article are
   a. recommendations from the authors.
   b. government laws.
   c. local regulations.
   d. advice from students.

5. What is the main idea of the article?
    a. Students should not own credit cards unless they absolutely need them.
    b. While credit cards have benefits, students should use them responsibly.
    c. students and credit cards
    d. Credit card companies attract vulnerable students and the result is often a disaster.

Collaboration

Exploring the Topic

Discuss the following questions to review the content of the article you have just read.

1. The author argues that "credit cards are actually high-interest loans in disguise" (para. 8). What does he or she mean by this? Do you agree or disagree? Explain your point.

2. The law states that you must be 18 to have a credit card and that you must have a cosigner for your card if you are under 21. Why do you think these laws are in place? Do you think they are fair?

3. According to the article, what are some of the advantages of having a good credit report?

Post-Reading Vocabulary

Without using a dictionary, determine the meaning of the bolded words from the context.

1. "Discuss with your family what kind of expenses it is **reasonable** to charge." (para. 4)

    Reasonable means _____

2. "The law **bans** credit card companies from issuing cards to people under the age of 18." (para. 6)

    Bans means _____

3. "Read all application materials carefully—especially the **fine print**." (para. 12)

    Fine print means _____

Katrina Lin   An Interview with a Student in the Field of Personal Finance

Baruch College

1. How did you find your path to majoring in finance/accounting?

I have passion for math. I thought that instead of majoring in math, maybe accounting would be more interesting because it's not all about math but something else.

2. What is the biggest obstacle you face in your study of finance/accounting?

The biggest obstacle is communication skills. Being a good accounting student, it's not enough to just have good math skills. Sometimes we need to be able to communicate with others about things that we do and be able to explain things. As an ESL student, communication skills are one of the biggest obstacles that I have to face and contend with.

3. What area(s) of finance/accounting in particular do you find most interesting?

I like to record the daily transactions and prepare financial statements at the end of the fiscal year period. I also like

doing the Waren Case that Baruch College required us to do in the course on accounting information systems. I find the Waren Case to be very helpful because it provides a real-world accountant case/data for us to record and prepare a financial statement as all the accountants do in the real world. It gives an opportunity to practice a real case, which is very helpful and very interesting. It also gives us a view of what the accountant job looks like, and many students get to think whether this is a kind of job that they expect to do or not.

4. What specific skills are required of students who study finance/accounting?

As I mentioned, being an accounting student, you need to have good math skills and excellent communication skills.

5. Other than being an accountant, what other career avenues are available for finance/accounting majors?

Other than being an accountant, there are some other career avenues available for an accounting major, such as teacher or professor; we can also pursue careers in areas like taxes, finance, insurance, and banking.

READING

Tenant Protections Facing Foreclosure

Reading Selection **3**

Preview Questions

1. Many Americans have lost their homes during the recent economic crisis. Discuss how these homeowners ended up losing their homes.

2. In your opinion, what can the government and lenders do to help the homeowners who are at risk of losing their homes? Give specific examples to support your answer.

3. If you were a tenant who lived in a house that was about to be foreclosed, what steps would you take to make sure that you stayed in your home?

Collaboration

Pre-Reading Vocabulary: Focus on Some Key Terms

As you have done before, try to guess the meaning of these words below with a classmate. Then consult a dictionary to determine how accurate you were.

Word	Your Definition	Dictionary Definition
auction		
evict		
lease		
jurisdiction		
attorney		

Tenant Protections Facing Foreclosure

By Marie Wolf, contributor, eHow.com (last updated September 27, 2011)

1 While foreclosure can mean financial disaster for your landlord, for you as a tenant it is the uncertainty of dealing with a new property owner. Whether the property sells at auction or the bank retains it, the new owner of your home steps into your landlord's shoes. This may mean that you can stay in your home and pay rent to someone new, or it may mean that the new property owner will ask you to leave. Federal law generally gives you the right to substantial notice after foreclosure before the request to leave your home. In some situations, you may also have recourse against your original landlord.

1. Paying Rent

2 Regardless of the new owner's actions, one of the easiest ways you can protect yourself is to continue paying rent. Before the foreclosure, you owe rent to your original landlord. After the foreclosure sale, the new landlord should send you notice, and you will begin paying rent to him. Failure to pay rent gives your landlord cause to evict you earlier than he otherwise might be able to. If you have trouble contacting your new landlord or are not sure what to do about rent, contact an attorney for advice.

2. Requirement of Notice

3 The federal Protecting Tenants at Foreclosure Act of 2009 establishes rules for the minimum notice a new landlord must give prior to evicting you after foreclosure. If you have a qualifying lease entered into before foreclosure, you are generally entitled to stay in your home for the remainder of your lease term—unless the new owner wants to move into your home. In this case, he must give you 90 days' notice before asking you to leave. If you do not have a lease with a set term, you are a tenant at will. In this situation, you are generally entitled to 90 days' notice before the start of eviction proceedings.

3. Eviction

4 The eviction process itself serves as a protection if you are a tenant facing a landlord's foreclosure. Your new property owner cannot force you out himself or

change the locks on your home. Instead, he has to follow the eviction rules of your local jurisdiction. This involves filing papers in court, giving you time to respond, and having a hearing before a judge. Only after a judge approves an eviction can the new property owner set a date to force you to leave your home.

4. Lawsuit against the Original Landlord

5   If you have a valid lease, but the new owner decides to move into your home and terminate your lease early, you may be able to sue your original landlord. This generally happens in small claims court, where you can request that the judge award you damages for the cost of finding a new place to live, as well as for moving expenses and certain other costs.

5. Considerations

6   The laws concerning eviction and foreclosure vary depending on your location and your specific situation. If you have questions about your rights as a tenant, check with an attorney.

Demand Media.

Reading Comprehension Check

1. In the sentence, "While foreclosure can mean financial **disaster** for your landlord, for you as a tenant it is the uncertainty of dealing with a new property owner," (para. 1) the word *disaster* means
a. a windfall.
b. a blessing in disguise.
c. great hardship.
b. a gift certificate.

2. "Whether the property sells at auction or the bank **retains** it, the new owner of your home steps into your landlord's shoes." (para. 1) In this sentence, the word *retains* means
a. gives as a gift.
b. keeps possession of.
c. demolishes.
d. renovates.

3. The author's main idea is that
a. tenants must stop paying rent if the house they live in is facing foreclosure.
b. foreclosure improves a tenant's credit report.
c. only divorced tenants run the risk of foreclosure.
d. tenants can protect themselves if the house they live in is facing foreclosure.

4. Which of the following examples is NOT offered to support the idea that tenants can protect themselves if the house is facing foreclosure?
a. writing a thank-you letter to the new landlord
b. paying rent
c. requiring a notice from the new landlord
d. filing a lawsuit against the original landlord

5. According to the article, if the tenants wish to stay in their home, which of the following are they NOT allowed to do?
   a. keep paying rent
   b. require a notice from the new homeowner
   c. file a lawsuit against the new homeowner
   d. file a lawsuit against the original homeowner

Exploring the Topic

Discuss the following questions to check your comprehension of the article you have just read.

1. The author states that foreclosure means financial disaster for the landlord? What are some of the reasons that may cause homeowners to lose their homes?

2. What are some of the issues a tenant may face if his or her landlord loses the house to foreclosure? Explain.

3. In addition to the suggestions made by the author, is there anything else that tenants can do to protect their rental homes? Be specific.

Post-Reading Vocabulary

Without using a dictionary, determine the meaning of the bolded words from the context.

1. "In some situations, you may also have **recourse** against your original landlord." (para. 1)

   Recourse means _____

2. "If you have a qualifying lease entered into before foreclosure, you are generally **entitled** to stay in your home for the remainder of your lease term—unless the new owner wants to move into your home." (para. 3)

   Entitled means _____

3. "Only after a judge **approves** an eviction can the new property owner set a date to force you to leave your home." (para. 4)

   Approves means _____

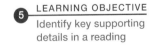

SKILL FOCUS
Supporting Details

LEARNING OBJECTIVE
Identify key supporting details in a reading

In Chapter 2, you learned how to determine the main idea of a reading. This chapter's skill focus is on supporting details. As you can see, these are sentences that support the main idea, and that is why they are called supporting details. In other words, **supporting details** provide more specific information about the main idea. It is important for you to differentiate between the main idea and supporting details. A standardized reading test usually has a main idea question

followed by a few supporting details questions. Knowing the difference between the main idea and supporting details will help you answer these questions
correctly.

It should be noted that an essay usually has one main idea followed by several supporting details. Furthermore, supporting details can be divided into
major details and minor details. Keep in mind that minor details support major
details, and that major details support the main idea. It is important for you to
remember that not all major details are followed by minor details, but that some
major details may be followed by several minor details. Last but not least, while
major details provide additional information about the main idea, minor details
give us more information about the major details. Let's look at the following diagram to understand this clearly.

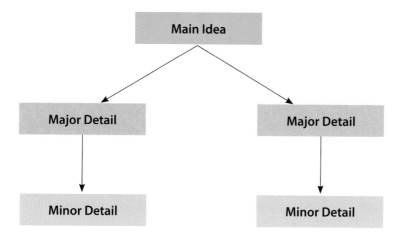

As the diagram shows, the major details support the main idea, and the
minor details provide more information about the major details. Let's read a
short passage now to understand supporting details fully. After you read the passage, try to answer the following questions:

1. What is the main idea of the passage?
2. Which major details support the main idea?
3. Which minor details, if any, provide additional information about the major
   details?

> If you are in an auto accident, contact the police immediately. Request
> information from the other driver(s) in the accident, including their insur-
> ance information. You may also obtain contact information (including license
> plate numbers) from witnesses, just in case they leave before the police ar-
> rive. Make sure that you can validate whatever information other drivers pro-
> vide. Some drivers who believe they are at fault and without insurance may
> attempt to give you a fake name and leave before police arrive. Take pictures
> of any evidence that may prove that you were not at fault. Write down the
> details of how the accident happened while they are fresh in your mind. Ask
> for a copy of the police report.

from Jeff Madura, *Personal Finance*, 4e, p. 317

Did you answer the three questions correctly? Look at the following diagram to understand how the main idea and the major details and the minor details are related.

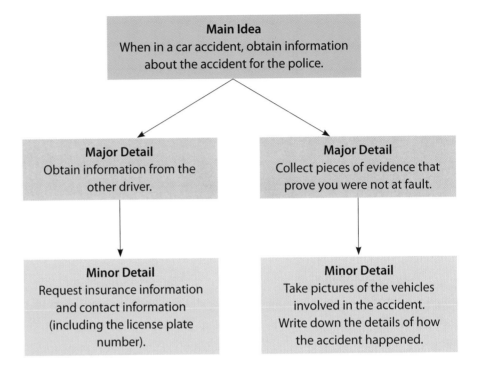

Now that you have read a passage and have answered questions about the main idea, the major details, and the minor details, let's practice identifying supporting details. As you know, practice makes perfect, so let's begin.

EXERCISE 1   Identifying Main Ideas and Details

Read the following passages and complete the diagrams that follow with relevant pieces of information. Before you do the exercise, here are some important points to remember:

- The main idea is usually a statement or a claim or a piece of advice. It is never an example.
- When reading a passage, remember that supporting details answer questions such as *who, what, when, where, why,* and *how.*
- Major details are general examples, reasons, and explanations to support the main idea.
- Minor details are more specific examples that provide additional information about the major details. These specific examples may be the number of people, the percentage of something, and the time and place where something happened.

Passage 1

Your general goals in life influence your financial goals. It takes money to support many of your goals. If you want to have a family, one of your financial goals may be that you and your spouse earn enough income and save enough money over time to financially support a family. If you want to own your own home, one of your financial goals may be that you earn enough income and save enough money over time to make a substantial real estate purchase. If you want to retire by age 55, this will require you to save enough money by then so that you could afford to stop working.

from Jeff Madura, *Personal Finance*, 4e, p. 10

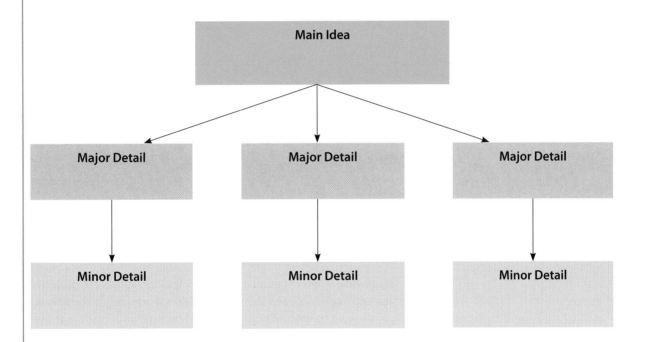

Passage 2

Your career choices also affect your income and potential for spending and saving money. If you become a social worker, you will be in a different financial position than if you choose to work as an electrical engineer. As a social worker, you will need to save a much higher proportion of your income to achieve the same level of savings that you could amass as an electrical engineer. If you choose a career that pays a low income, you will need to set attainable financial goals. Or you may reconsider your choice of a career in pursuit of a higher level of income. However, be realistic. You should not decide to be a doctor just because doctors' salaries are high if you dislike health-related work. You should choose a career that will be enjoyable and will suit your skills. If you like your job, you are more likely to perform well. Since you may be working for 40 years or longer, you should seriously think about the career that will satisfy both your financial and personal needs.

from Jeff Madura, *Personal Finance*, 4e, p. 11

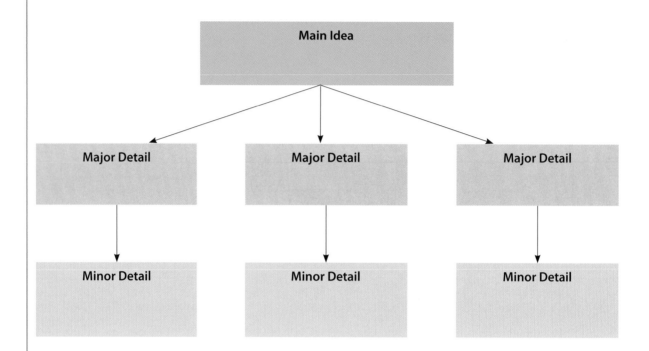

Passage 3

The Internet provides you with valuable information for making financial decisions. Your decision to spend money on a new stereo or to save the money may be dependent on how much you can earn from depositing the money. Your decision of whether to purchase a new car depends on the prices of new cars and financing rates on car loans. Your decision of whether to purchase a home depends on the prices of homes and financing rates on home loans. Your decision of whether to invest in stocks is influenced by the prices of stocks. Your decision of where to purchase insurance may be influenced by the insurance premiums quoted by different insurance agencies. All of these financial decisions require knowledge of prevailing prices or interest rates, which are literally at your fingertips on the Internet.

from Jeff Madura, *Personal Finance*, 4e, p. 14

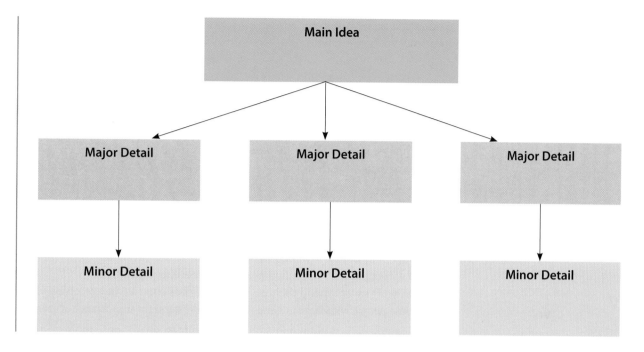

EXERCISE 2 Identifying Supporting Details

By now you should have reached a good understanding of how supporting details, including both major and minor details, elaborate on the main idea. Let's practice reading more passages. Instead of completing a diagram about the passage, this time you will answer multiple-choice questions that follow the passage. Read the following passages and identify the supporting details.

Passage 1

People's consumption behavior varies substantially. At one extreme are people who spend their entire paycheck within a few days of receiving it, regardless of the size of the paycheck. Although this behavior is understandable for people who have low incomes, it is also a common practice for some people who have very large incomes, perhaps because they do not understand the importance of saving for the future. At the other extreme are "big savers" who minimize their spending and focus on saving for the future. Most people's consumption behavior is affected by their income. For example, a two-income household tends to spend more money when both income earners are working full-time.

from Jeff Madura, *Personal Finance*, 4e, p. 32

1. What is the main idea of the passage?
   a. People's consumption behavior is more or less the same regardless of their income.
   b. People spend their entire paycheck as soon as they receive it.
   c. People's spending habits differ from individual to individual.
   d. People do not understand how to save for the future.

2. The first major detail the author provides is that
   a. most people are not in the habit of saving money.
   b. some people spend all of their earnings right after receiving their paycheck.
   c. some people make enormous amounts of money.
   d. there are big savers who spend less and save more for the future.

3. According to the passage, which of the following statements is NOT true?
   a. Only people with low incomes spend their entire paycheck.
   b. Some people with large incomes spend their entire paycheck.
   c. Some people with large incomes do not understand the importance of saving.
   d. Some people with low incomes do not understand the importance of saving.

4. Which of the following statements is true?
   a. Only people with low incomes spend their entire paycheck.
   b. Only people with large incomes spend their entire paycheck.
   c. Only big savers spend their entire paycheck as soon as they receive it.
   d. Some people with large incomes do not understand the importance of saving.

5. The statement "a two-income household tends to spend more money when both income earners are working full-time" is a
   a. topic sentence.   c. major detail.
   b. main idea.   d. minor detail.

Passage 2

You can use a debit card to make purchases that are charged against an existing checking account. If you use a debit card to pay $100 for a car repair, your checking account balance is reduced by $100. Using a debit card has the same result as writing a check from your checking account. Many financial institutions offer debit cards for individuals who find using a debit card more convenient than carrying their checkbook with them. In addition, some merchants will accept a debit card but not a check because they are concerned that a check may bounce. A debit card differs from a credit card in that it does not provide credit. With a debit card, individuals cannot spend more than they have in their checking account.

from Jeff Madura, *Personal Finance*, 4e, p. 126

1. The main idea of the passage is that
   a. it is better to use a credit card than it is to use a debit card.
   b. purchases made by a debit card are debited from a checking account.
   c. if you use a debit card to pay $100, the creditor deposits $100 to your checking account.
   d. most people find carrying their checkbook more convenient than using a debit card.

2. According to the passage, which of the following statements is true?
   a. Using a debit card is different from writing a check.
   b. Some merchants prefer to accept a check.

   c. Carrying a checkbook is more convenient than using a debit card.

   d. Many people find using a debit card is more convenient than carrying a checkbook.

3. The sentence "If you use a debit card to pay $100 for a car repair, your checking account balance is reduced by $100" is offered as an example to
   a. support a major detail.
   b. support the main idea.
   c. elaborate on a minor detail.
   d. give additional information about a major detail.

4. The sentence "In addition, some merchants will accept a debit card but not a check because they are concerned that a check may bounce" is a
   a. topic sentence.   c. major detail.
   b. main idea.   d. minor detail.

5. The sentence "With a debit card, individuals cannot spend more than they have in their checking account" is a
   a. topic sentence.   c. major detail.
   b. main idea.   d. minor detail.

Passage 3

There can be a high cost to using credit. If you borrow too much money, you may have difficulty making your payments. It is easier to obtain credit than to pay it back. And having a credit line can tempt you to make impulse purchases that you cannot afford. College students are carrying credit cards in record numbers. 83 percent of all students have at least one credit card, and almost a third have four or more. The average credit card balance for 21 percent of undergraduates is between $3,000 and $7,000. Many students make minimum payments on their credit cards while in school with the expectation that they will be able to pay off their balance once they graduate and are working full-time. Yet the accumulating interest fees catch many by surprise, and the debt can quickly become difficult to manage. Today's graduating students have an average of $24,567 in combined education loan and credit card balances. If you are unable to repay the credit you receive, you may not be able to obtain credit again or will have to pay a very high interest rate to obtain it.

from Jeff Madura, *Personal Finance*, 4e, p. 173

1. What is the main idea of the above passage?
   a. Using a credit card can be expensive.
   b. There is almost no cost to using a credit card.
   c. Using a credit card is convenient.
   d. It is good that college students are using credit cards.

2. The first major detail is which of the following?
   a. Having a credit card may not force you to buy things you cannot afford.
   b. It is easy to obtain a credit card.
   c. It will be difficult to pay back if you use your credit card too much.
   d. It is much easier to make your payments if you borrow too much money.

3. The sentence "83 percent of all students have at least one credit card, and almost a third have four or more" is a
   a. topic sentence.
   b. main idea.
   c. major detail.
   d. minor detail.

4. The sentence "Many students make minimum payments on their credit cards while in school with the expectation that they will be able to pay off their balance once they graduate and are working full-time" is a
   a. topic sentence.
   b. main idea.
   c. major detail.
   d. minor detail.

5. According to the passage, which of the following statements is true?
   a. College students do not carry enough credit cards.
   b. 21 percent of undergraduates owe between $3,000 and $7,000.
   c. Many students pay off their debt while in college.
   d. Today's graduate students have approximately $25,000 in education loan.

LANDMARK IN THE FIELD OF PERSONAL FINANCE

Online Banking

Just a few decades ago you had to go to a bank location and wait in line for a teller in order to do most banking transactions. Not so today. Online banking, along with the ATM, has changed the way we interact with banks.

Online banking allows individuals to perform many banking applications through the Internet. The common features fall into two categories:

- **Transactional:** You can transfer money from one account to another. You can pay most of your bills online. It is possible to apply for a bank loan. You can also set up a new account online.

- **Non-transactional:** You can check your online statements to find out how much funds you have in a particular account. You can confirm whether a particular transaction went through. This might be a bill payment, a transfer of funds from account to account, a wiring of funds, etc. ...

Online banking services began in New York in 1981. This was when four of the city's major banks offered home banking services using the videotex system. This early effort was a failure as videotex technology never really caught on. In the 1990s the time was ripe for banks to offer their services online. Internet usage was already popular. In 1994, Stanford Federal Credit Union was the first bank to offer Internet banking services to all of its members. The idea was quickly picked up by other banks such as Wells Fargo and Chase Manhattan.

Today there are many banks that are "Internet only" banks. These banks try to differentiate themselves from brick-and-mortar bank branches. They do this by offering better interest rates and convenient online banking features.

Online banking does present some security risk to users. There have been many cases of account theft and even identity theft. The main security method used for online banking is the PIN/TAN system. The PIN represents a password for the login. The TANs are used for one-time passwords to authenticate a transaction.

The inventors of online banking predicted that online banking would soon completely replace traditional banking. The facts prove that this is not what happened. Many customers still prefer visiting their local bank. They distrust any system of money transaction that does not involve face-to-face interaction. This being said, the number of online banking customers has been increasing at a very quick rate. It seems that the younger generation prefers to do its banking transactions from the comfort of home.

Considering the Topic

Answer the following questions with a partner.

1. How has online banking changed the way people interact with their personal savings?

2. Do you think this has been a positive or negative change? Explain.

3. Can you imagine another technological development that could fundamentally change the way we interact with banks? Explain.

Internet Connection

Research another landmark in the field of personal finance, and fill out the section below.

ATMs	craigslist
online trading	credit reports
credit cards	electronic tax filing

Landmark: _____

Question	Answer
When did this landmark become a reality?	
Who was involved in developing this landmark?	
What made this landmark special?	
How did this landmark change the way people interact?	

How to Repay Your Student Loans

Reading Selection **4**

Web Article

Preview Questions

1. Most students who cannot afford a college education apply for a student loan. How much do you think they owe the lender on average after they graduate from college? Take an educated guess.

MyReadingLab™
Complete this Exercise
at **myreadinglab.com**

2. More and more students are finding it difficult to repay their student loans after graduation. In your opinion, what can be done to make the situation more manageable for students? Be specific.

3. Most parents are shocked by the high cost of education these days. What is the best option for them if their children need to apply for a student loan? Give specific examples to support your answer.

Collaboration

Pre-Reading Vocabulary: Focus on Some Key Terms

Determine the meaning of these words below with a classmate. Then consult a dictionary to see if your definition was correct or not.

Word	Your Definition	Dictionary Definition
default		
consequence		
garnish		
circumstance		
defer		

How to Repay Your Student Loans

CBS News, New York, August 18, 2010

1   **(CBS)** A recent report by the Department of Education found that students defaulting on loans are up seven percent.

2   With the average debt upon graduation totaling more than $23,000, what can you do to make the situation more manageable?

3   CBS News Business and Economics Correspondent Rebecca Jarvis shared some useful information on "The Early Show" Wednesday for how students can make their debt more manageable.

4   According to Jarvis, the No. 1 thing to avoid is defaulting on your student loans.

5   "You don't want to default. Being default in student loans means not paying it off for 270 days," she explained. "The reason you don't want to default is there are huge consequences to this. The bank, the lender, can garnish up to 15 percent of your wages. They can take back your tax refunds. They can even keep you from getting new professional licenses and getting work in the future."

6   If you are having difficulty paying back your loans, what should you do?

7   "First thing you want to do is contact the lender. Whether it is a private lender, whether it's the institution where you're attending school, let them know your circumstances. Sometimes they can defer your payment terms for up to three years. Especially when it comes to federal loans."

8   "On top of that, you can change your repayment schedule. Make sure you talk to them about all of those alternatives. Remember, pay off the highest interest rate loans first because those are the ones costing you the most."

9   With loans coming from several different lenders, is it difficult to consolidate loans?

10   "It's actually easier than many people think. It's a very good option for people who just want one payment and they also want to cut their monthly payments," she said. "In many cases consolidating loans can cut your monthly payments up to 50 percent, cut them in half."

11   According to Jarvis, graduates should really consider consolidation.

12   "You want to go to loanconsolidation.ed.gov if they're government loans. With private loans you have to consolidate under a private lender, Wells Fargo and Chase are some of the banks that do it," she added.

13   As lots of kids head off to college, parents are shocked by the cost of education these days. So what's the best thing to do if they need to get a student loan?

14   "First, look at federal loans; generally speaking, the terms are better for the
people who are borrowing: students and their parents. So [apply for] the Stafford
loans, Perkins loans. If you're looking for a private loan, again, finaid.org as well as
bankrate.com talk to students about good places to go," she said.

Reading Comprehension Check

MyReadingLab™
Complete this Exercise
at **myreadinglab.com**

Now that you have read the article, answer the multiple-choice questions to
check your understanding of the article.

1. "The bank, the lender, can garnish up to 15 percent of your **wages**." (para. 4)
   In this sentence, the word *wages* means
   a. money received for work.   c. money received as a gift.
   b. money inherited from parents.   d. money paid to an employer.

2. "On top of that, you can change your repayment schedule. Make sure you
   talk to them about all of those **alternatives**." (para. 7) In this context, the
   word *alternatives* means
   a. no possibility.   c. only two possibilities.
   b. only one possibility.   d. several possible choices.

3. What is the main idea of the article?
   a. Students have no choice but to default on their student loans.
   b. There are several alternatives for repaying student loans.
   c. Defaulting on student loans is in students' best interest.
   d. Students should avoid applying for student loans.

4. Which of the following examples is NOT offered to explain what banks can
   do to students if they default on their loans?
   a. They can garnish students' wages.
   b. They can force students' to resign from their jobs.
   c. They can take back students' tax refunds.
   d. They can keep students from getting new jobs.

5. The author suggests many ways to avoid defaulting on a student loan. If
   students are having difficulty repaying their loans, which of the following
   examples is suggested as a way to cope with the situation?
   a. Students can go overseas to work and pay off their loans.
   b. Students can ask their friends and relatives to pay off their loans.
   c. Students can change their repayment schedule.
   d. Students can go on a payment holiday for an indefinite period.

Exploring the Topic

Working in small groups, discuss the following questions.

Collaboration

1. Why is it that the number of students defaulting on loans is up seven
   percent? Think of all possible reasons that can cause this situation.

2. According to Jarvis, what are the consequences of defaulting on student loans?

3. Jarvis offers many suggestions to cope with the situation if students are having difficulty repaying their loans. Which of the suggestions do you find most practical and why? Are there other ways students can make the debt more manageable? Give specific examples to support your answer.

Post-Reading Vocabulary

Determine the meaning of the bolded words in the following sentences from the context.

1. "Whether it is a private **lender**, whether it's the institution where you're attending school, let them know your circumstances." (para. 7)

Lender means _____

2. "It's actually easier than many people think. It's a very good **option** for people who just want one payment and they also want to cut their monthly payments," she said. (para. 10)

Option means _____

3. "In many cases **consolidating** loans can cut your monthly payments up to 50 percent, cut them in half." (para. 10)

Consolidating means _____

Panel Discussion on the Plight of Homeowners Who Are at Risk of Losing Their Homes

During the recent economic meltdown, many Americans lost their jobs. As a result, they could not make their mortgage payment every month. The lenders are after the homeowners, demanding that the payments be made as soon as possible. As a panelist, participate in a discussion focusing on the housing crisis and offer possible ways to help homeowners avoid foreclosure. Here are some possible profiles for you and your classmates. You are free to choose other profiles that you think are appropriate for the panel discussion.

1. an unemployed homeowner

2. another homeowner who has a job but is not able to pay the mortgage

3. a child of a homeowner

4. a federal government employee

5. a bank officer

6. a lawyer

7. a foreclosure expert

8. a real estate agent

9. a tenant living in a house that is to be foreclosed

10. the district attorney

To help you prepare for the panel discussion, here are some questions you may want to address:

1. How did the homeowners end up in a situation where they could lose their homes?

2. Did the lender act irresponsibly in approving these people's mortgage applications? In other words, did the lender's greed overcome its good sense?

3. Who is a winner and who is a loser in this situation?

4. What can be done to ensure that other people do not become victims of the same misfortune?

As you participate in the panel discussion, try to use examples based on your own experience or on something you read in the newspaper. Be sure to refer to the guidelines that your instructor will provide.

WRITING CONNECTIONS: *Building Your Own Financial Plan*

When thinking about your short-term and long-term goals, it can be very helpful to evaluate both your current financial situation and your future outlook in writing. The following three tables will give you the opportunity to reflect on your financial situation and to map out your longer-term financial goals and strategies.

As information related to personal finance is a private matter, keep in mind that you will not be asked to share this information with your fellow classmates.

Table A Personal Cash Flow Statement

Cash Inflows	*This Month*
Disposable (after tax) income	
Interest on deposits	
Dividend payments (if you own stock)	
Regular gifted income (allowance)	
Other	
Cash Outflows	
Rent/mortgage	
Electricity and water	
Cable TV	
Phone	
Groceries/restaurants	
Transportation (car expenses or mass transit)	
Clothing	
Recreation	
Educational expenses	
Other	
Total Cash Outflows	
Net Cash Flows (the difference between inflows and outflows)	

Note: If you enter your cash flow information in an Excel worksheet, the software will create a pie chart of your cash inflows and outflows.

Table B Personal Financial Goals

Financial Goal	$ Amount Needed to Reach Goal	Priority Level (High/Low/Medium)
Short-term Goals		
1.		
2.		
3.		

Long-term Goals		
1.		
2.		
3.		

Table C Personal Career Goals (You will need to use the Internet to do some research on specific data related to an occupation that interests you).

Personal Career Goals	Career One	Career Two
Job title		
Brief job description		
Skills needed		
Educational requirements		
Job outlook (for next five years)		
Salary range		
Benefits (vacation, etc.)		
Opportunities for advancement in field		

READING

Reading Selection 5

Blog

MyReadingLab™
Complete this **Exercise**
at **myreadinglab.com**

Collaboration

What Is a College Degree Worth?

Preview Questions

1. In terms of long-term financial planning, is going to college a good investment? Is it worth the cost of tuition?

2. Beyond possible financial benefits, are there other advantages of pursuing a college degree?

3. What are the keys to getting a good starting salary once you have graduated from college?

Pre-Reading Vocabulary: Focus on Some Key Terms

Before beginning the reading selection, it may be helpful to focus on the meaning of some key words in the article. Working with a partner, try to guess the meaning of these words. Then look up the words in a dictionary.

Word	Your Definition	Dictionary Definition
consequences		
dampen		
plight		
indictment		
skyrocketed		

What Is a College Degree Worth?

By **Maggie Gallagher**—**Wed., June 27, 2012**

1 What is college really worth?

2 A lot of people are asking that question–and it's the cover story of this month's *Utne Reader* magazine.

3 My older son is 30, and my younger is 17. I'm hoping my two sons escape from the consequences of graduating into this terrible economy, which is going to dampen the value of not only a college degree, but of all those graduate degrees parents are paying for (and students are borrowing on) for decades to come.

4 The companion piece to the *Utne Reader* cover story is called "The Ph.D. Now Comes with Food Stamps." It highlights the plight of adjunct professors who require food stamps to get by. Melissa Bruninga-Matteau, for example, is a 43-year-old white single mother who teaches two courses in humanities at Yavapai College in Prescott Arizona.

5 She never expected to be on food stamps. Somehow she imagined her Ph.D. in medieval history was a guaranteed ticket to the middle class. Another college teacher in Florida is married with two kids. He's a graduate student in film studies at Florida State University.

6 Somehow he hasn't yet processed that a married father of two probably should not be getting an advanced degree in film studies. I'm not sure anybody should, actually.

7 *Utne* sees this as a plea for paying college teachers even more (raising tuition prices even higher). I see it as an indictment of colleges making money by enrolling students for whom there is no plausible career path with borrowed government money.

8 My sons are lucky. We are able to pay for college. By "we" I do not mean just my husband and me, but my husband and me and our parents.

9 My older son graduated with money in the bank, not debt. He spent years as a starving artist, but once he began to make money, his economic situation was quickly transformed into a situation of building capital, human and otherwise, not paying for his college degrees until he's 40.

10 I'm pretty sure that if I could not afford to pay for my children's college, I would advise them to live at home, go to community college for two years and then to two years of state school. Pay tuition as you go. Parents don't charge rent. Mom will throw in doing your laundry, no extra charge.

11 Save the Ivy League dream for graduate school, if you've made the grades to get into an Ivy grad school. (If not, don't go to grad school.)

12 Since both my husband and I are Yale graduates, it's kind of shocking to me that I think this.

13   But the truth is that as loans have become available and every teen is encouraged to borrow money and go to college, the costs of college have skyrocketed out of proportion to the reasonable return.

14   The average cost of room, board and tuition at a public university is seven times what it was when I went to Yale, according to Utne Reader.

15   Yes, a college degree is "worth it" in general terms.

16   It's just not worth going $50,000 into debt at the age of 22 to achieve.

17   There's got to be a better way.

18   The culture of debt being created for college grads will affect them for years to come.

19   Colleges have become complicit in teaching teenagers bad financial lessons that hurt their ability to make it. According to *Utne Reader*, at least 700 colleges have contracts with banks to market credit cards to students. About nine in 10 students use credit cards to help pay their education expenses. The average college student now has 4.6 credit cards.

20   I'm 51 years old and I have two.

21   We are going to see a lot more generational *cris de coeur*, like the hilarious viral YouTube music video "The Ivy League Hustle (I Went to Princeton, B----!),'' youtube.com/watch?v=YDhf9qwiA34. Overlaying its sexual complaint by elite women about the men they have to date, there is an amazing riff on the anomalous position of the overeducated artist, trying to persuade himself or herself that being economically marginal is a sign of moral superiority.

22   Borrowing more to pay for colleges that raise their tuition so they can enroll more film studies majors?

23   That is madness, and it has to stop.

Maggie Gallagher is the founder of the National Organization for Marriage and has been a syndicated columnist for 15 years.

Reading Comprehension Check

1. What is the topic of the article?
   a. the value of going to college
   b. the tuition cost of college
   c. College offers many benefits beyond just economic rewards.
   d. college classes

2. The example of adjunct professors who need food stamps to survive is given to support the idea that
   a. most Ph.D. programs come with food stamps.
   b. adjunct professors cannot afford food stamps.
   c. most universities offer food stamps to Ph.D. candidates.
   d. a Ph.D. no longer guarantees financial security.

3. The author suggests that an advanced degree in film studies
   a. must be pursued by most adjunct professors.
   b. does not ensure a lucrative job.
   c. ensures a job in the film industry.
   d. is the best way to land a decent job

4. The author's son graduated from college with no debt because
   a. he was extremely rich and paid for his education without borrowing.
   b. he went to a state college and did not have to pay tuition.
   c. she and her husband and their parents paid for his education.
   d. her parents paid for their grandson's education.

5. The author predicts that "The culture of debt being created for college grads will affect them for years to come." (para. 17) She means that
   a. the culture of debt is highly effective for college grads.
   b. using credit cards to pay for college is a good strategy.
   c. college students will be struggling to pay debt for several years after they graduate.
   d. college grads must not pay tuition to avoid debt.

Exploring the Topic

Discuss the following questions to review the content of the article you have just read.

1. The title of the article is "What Is a College Degree Worth?". Discuss why many people are wondering if pursuing a college degree is worthwhile. Refer to the article as you answer the question.

2. The author hopes her two sons will escape from the consequences of graduating into this weak economy. What does she mean by the "consequences of graduating into this terrible economy"? Explain.

3. Do you think some people are better off entering the job market without a college degree? Explain.

Post-Reading Vocabulary

Without using a dictionary, determine the meaning of the bolded words from the context.

1. "He spent years as a starving artist, but once he began to make money, his economic situation was quickly **transformed** into a situation of building capital, human and otherwise, not paying for his college degrees until he's 40." (para. 9)

   Transformed means _____

2. "Colleges have become **complicit** in teaching teenagers bad financial lessons that hurt their ability to make it." (para. 10)

   Complicit means _____

3. "Overlaying its sexual complaint by elite women about the men they have to date, there is an amazing riff on the anomalous position of the overeducated artist, trying to persuade himself or herself that being economically **marginal** is a sign of moral superiority." (para. 21)

Marginal means _____

TEXTBOOK APPLICATION   **How You Benefit from an Understanding of Personal Finance**

The purpose of this exercise is to get you acquainted with the type of reading you will be required to do in college. First, listen to the lecture and take notes. You can listen to the lecture by scanning the QR code on the next page with your smart phone. Your professor may also read the selection or play the audio file in class. Make sure that you write down the important points of the lecture.

Collaboration

Group Discussion

Working in small groups of three to four students, answer the following questions. Your instructor may ask you to share your answers with your classmates. As you refer to your notes, it is best to write brief answers to each of the questions below using your own words. After the discussion, you will have an opportunity to share your findings with your peers.

1. According to the lecture, what is the definition of personal finance?
2. What does a personal financial plan include?
3. The lecturer gives four examples to support the claim that many Americans do not manage their financial situations well. What are the examples, and what can be done to change the American people's spending habits?
4. Why is the lack of savings among the American people especially problematic? Give specific reasons to support your answer.
5. The lecturer points out that understanding the fundamentals of personal finance is beneficial in three ways. What are they, and which one is most important to you?
6. What is an opportunity cost? Give an example of your own spending habits to explain the concept.
7. Why does the lecturer advise that following the guidance of financial advisers may or may not be in your best interest?
8. After listening to the lecture, are you interested in considering a career in personal finance? Why or why not?

Now that you have discussed the highlights of the lecture with your classmates, read the following selection and answer the multiple-choice questions that follow.

How You Benefit from an Understanding of Personal Finance

By Jeff Madura

Scan this code using your smart phone to listen to an audio version of this reading

1   Personal finance (also referred to as personal financial planning) is the process of planning your spending, financing, and investing to optimize your financial situation. A personal finance plan specifies your financial goals and describes the spending, financing, and investing plans that are intended to achieve those goals. Although the U.S. is one of the wealthiest countries, many Americans do not manage their financial situations well. Consequently, they tend to rely too much on credit and have excessive debt. Consider these statistics:

- More than 1.2 million people filed for personal bankruptcy in 2008.

- The level of savings in the U.S. is only about 1 percent of income earned. (Some investments, including retirement accounts, are not included as savings.)

- About half of all surveyed people in the U.S. who are working full-time state that they live from one paycheck to the next, without a plan for saving money.

- About 40 percent of people who work full-time do not save for retirement. Those who do typically save a relatively small amount of money.

2   The lack of savings is especially problematic given the increasing cost of health care and other necessities. You will have numerous options regarding the choice of bank deposits, credit cards, loans, insurance policies, investments, and retirement plans. With an understanding of personal finance, you will be able to make decisions that can enhance your financial situation.

3   How much do you know about personal finance? Various government agencies of various countries have attempted to assess financial literacy in recent years. Surveys have documented that people tend to have very limited personal financial skills. In addition, surveys have found that many people who believe they have strong finance skills do not understand some basic personal finance concepts. Even if your knowledge of personal finance is limited, you can substantially increase your knowledge and improve your financial planning skills by reading this text. An understanding of personal finance is beneficial to you in many ways, including the following:

Make Your Own Financial Decisions

4   An understanding of personal finance enables you to make informed decisions about your financial situation. Each of your spending decisions has an opportunity cost, which represents what you give up as a result of that decision. By spending money for a specific purpose, you forgo alternative ways that you could have spent the money and also forgo saving the money for a future purpose. For example, if your decision to use your cell phone costs $100 per month, you have forgone the possibility of using that money to buy concert tickets or to save for a new car. Informed financial decisions increase the amount of money that you accumulate over time and give you more flexibility to purchase the products and services you want in the future.

Judge the Advice of Financial Advisers

5   The personal financial planning process will enable you to make informed decisions about your spending, saving, financing, and investing. Nevertheless, you may prefer to rely on advice from various types of financial advisers. An understanding of personal finance allows you to judge the guidance of financial advisers and to determine whether their advice is in your best interest (or in their best interest).

6   Example: You want to invest $10,000 of your savings. A financial adviser guarantees that your investment will increase in value by 20 percent (or by $2,000) this year, but he will charge you 4 percent of the investment ($400) for his advice. If you have a background in personal finance, you would know that no investment can be guaranteed to increase in value by 20 percent in one year. Therefore, you would realize that you should not trust this financial adviser. You could either hire a more reputable financial adviser or review investment recommendations made by financial advisers on the Internet (often for free).

Become a Financial Adviser

7   An understanding of personal finance may interest you in pursuing a career as a financial adviser. Financial advisers are in demand because many people lack an understanding of personal finance or are not interested in making their own financial decisions. A single course in personal finance is insufficient to start a career as a financial adviser, but it may interest you in taking additional courses to obtain the necessary qualifications.

Jeff Madura, *Personal Finance*, 4e, pp. 4–5.

Reading Comprehension Check

1. In the sentence, "Personal finance (also referred to as personal financial planning) is the process of planning your spending, financing, and investing to **optimize** your financial situation," (para. 1) the word *optimize* means
   a. minimize.
   b. reduce.
   c. execute.
   d. maximize.

2. "A personal finance plan specifies your financial goals and describes the spending, financing, and investing plans that are intended to **achieve** those goals." (para. 1) In this passage, the word *achieve* means
   a. avoid.
   b. ignore.
   c. fail.
   d. reach.

3. In the introductory paragraph, we read, "Although the U.S. is one of the wealthiest countries, many Americans do not manage their financial situations well. Consequently, they tend to rely too much on credit and have **excessive** debt." In this context, the word *excessive* means
   a. sufficient.
   b. insufficient.
   c. too much.
   d. reasonable.

4. In the sentence, "More than 1.2 million people filed for personal **bankruptcy** in 2008," (para. 1) the word *bankruptcy* means
   a. state of being without financial resources.
   b. having robust financial resources.
   c. continuously improving financial resources.
   d. having an abundance of financial resources.

5. "With an understanding of personal finance, you will be able to make decisions that can **enhance** your financial situation." (para. 2) In this sentence, the word *enhance* means
   a. deteriorate.   c. weaken.
   b. improve.   d. worsen.

6. In the sentence, "Various government agencies of various countries have attempted to **assess** financial literacy in recent years," (para. 3) the meaning of the word *assess* is
   a. neglect.   c. determine.
   b. overlook.   d. eliminate.

7. The main idea of the essay is that
   a. most Americans do not understand personal finance is good for the economy.
   b. it is in people's best interest to learn about personal finance.
   c. personal financial planning is only important for financial advisers.
   d. people should never question the investment recommendations made by their financial advisers.

8. Which of the following examples is NOT used to support the idea that most Americans do not manage their financial situations well?
   a. More than 1.2 million people filed for personal bankruptcy in 2008.
   b. The level of savings in the U.S. is only about 1 percent of income earned.
   c. About 40 percent of people who work full-time do not save for retirement.
   d. Rather than going to a bank to deposit or withdraw money, more than 40 percent of the American people prefer on-line banking.

9. According to the lecture, making informed financial decisions is important because
   a. it can help people accumulate more money and spend it wisely in the future.
   b. it can help people spend more than they earn every month.
   c. it can help people file for personal bankruptcy.
   d. it will enable people to trust their financial advisers blindly.

10. Which of the following examples is given to explain the importance of understanding personal financing?
    a. People will not manage their financial situations well.
    b. People can make their own financial decisions.
    c. More people will continue to file for personal bankruptcy.
    d. People will let someone else make crucial financial decisions for them.

The Internet can be a powerful and effective research tool once you have learned how to successfully limit your information searches and have learned how to interpret the results of your search with a critical lens.

Instructions: First try to use logic and background knowledge in guessing the correct answers to the following data questions. Then, go online and search for the relevant data. Be sure to write the web source next to your research finding.

INTERNET FACT
SEARCH

Personal
Finance

1. What percentage of full-time working Americans do <u>not</u> save money for retirement?
   a. 10%   c. 40%
   b. 25%   d. 65%

   Your guess: _____   Research finding: _____

   Web source: _____

2. Home mortgages typically have a maturity of
   a. 5 or 10 years   c. 15 or 30 years
   b. 10 or 20 years   d. 40 or 50 years

   Your guess: _____   Research finding: _____

   Web source: _____

3. The Social Security tax is equal to _____ percent of your salary (up to a maximum level).
   a. 4.3   c. 9.0
   b. 6.2   d. 10

   Your guess: _____   Research finding: _____

   Web source: _____

4. What percentage of Americans receives a high credit rating score (over 700)?
   a. 28%   c. 58%
   b. 38%   d. 75%

   Your guess: _____   Research finding: _____

   Web source: _____

5. The New York Stock Exchange (NYSE) handles transactions for approximately _____ stocks.
   a. 2,800   c. 5,000
   b. 4,200   d. 8,100

   Your guess: _____   Research finding: _____

   Web source: _____

FORMAL PRESENTATION PROJECTS

You will be given the opportunity to present on a topic of your interest pertinent to one of the text's chapter disciplines. Topics could relate to one of the questions you checked off in the "Follow Your Interests" section at the beginning of the chapter. Your instructor may ask you to browse through the chapters to guide you toward a given discipline focus.

MyReadingLab™   For more help with **Annotation** and **Supporting Details**, go to your learning path in **MyReadingLab.com**.

ECONOMICS

Learning Objectives

IN THIS CHAPTER, YOU WILL LEARN TO . . .

1. Describe the discipline of economics
2. Define key terms in the field of economics
3. Write effective lecture notes
4. Collaborate with peers in small groups
5. Make inferences based on facts
6. Effectively paraphrase

INTRODUCTION TO THE DISCIPLINE OF ECONOMICS

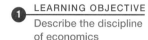

1 **LEARNING OBJECTIVE**
Describe the discipline of economics

You may not know it, but economics has an effect on our everyday life. Economists, experts who study economics, look at what goods and services are offered to meet people's needs. They are also interested in finding out how and why the decisions to make goods and services are made. Soft drinks, fast-food items, and shoes are some examples of goods that people want, and businesses produce them. In this chapter, you will learn about supply and demand, profit and loss, competition and government policy, markets and government, globalization and economic growth, and money. We hope that after reading this chapter, you will understand how economics affects life every day.

Collaboration

Reading into a Photo

Working in a small group, examine the following photograph and answer the questions that follow.

1. In your opinion, what economic issue does this image represent?
2. What message does this image convey to you?

Follow Your Interests

Review the set of questions below that economists might explore. Check off the three or four questions that are most interesting to you.

Collaboration

1. In recent times, there has been an economic crisis affecting the United States and the entire world. In your opinion, what are the causes of the economic downturn?

2. How does an economic crisis affect our daily lives? Give specific examples to support your answer.

3. What can the U.S. president and other global leaders do to improve the world's economy?

4. The fundamentals of economics are based on supply and demand. Do you think that demand can be created by corporations? For example, do you really believe that everyone needs an iPod or can't live without chewing gum?

5. In a fair world, consumers should be given the opportunity to control demand. In other words, they should be able to dictate what companies produce. If consumers had this power, how would it affect America's economy?

6. Why does a can of Coca Cola cost approximately $1, a generic brand of cola $0.75, and a bottle of water $1.50? How are these prices determined?

7. Most people believe that business and ethics cannot coexist. Do you think that a corporation can maximize its profits without compromising its ethics, or do you believe that greed drives the corporate machine?

8. Why is it the case that one employee is paid minimum wage for an hour's work while another employee in the same building might be paid $100 an hour? What causes this wage inequality? Do you think it is fair that a corporate lawyer makes a fortune whereas a janitor can barely scrape by on his or her salary?

9. Most Americans are concerned that many U.S. jobs are being taken away by people in foreign countries who are more than willing to work for much lower pay. Outsourcing, in other words, is seen as a threat to American employment. What is your opinion about outsourcing? Can you blame companies for seeking cheaper labor overseas?

10. Many Americans have lost their jobs during the economic meltdown. Is it the government's responsibility to guarantee job security for Americans? Might there be other institutions that should also play an instrumental role in ensuring employment opportunities for all?

11. On Monday, the price of groceries and the price of gasoline are affordable based on your income. On Friday, with the same salary, you can no longer afford the same amount of gas and food. What do you think causes the price change within a week? What economic factors determine the cost of living, from housing to consumer goods?

12. With all the world's resources and the common knowledge that there is more than enough for every individual, why does poverty continue to exist? In other words, what keeps the poor poor?

13. Should one country have the right to block trade with another country? What might be the motivation behind excluding a country from international trade?

14. Some people argue that capitalism is a cruel economic system that hurts many people. In your opinion, is there a better system that does justice to all in terms of economic fairness?

Now, share your choices with a small group of classmates and discuss why these particular questions are most interesting to you. You may wish to discuss these questions with them and ask which questions they found interesting.

LEARNING OBJECTIVE
2
Define key terms in the field of economics

Key Terms in the Field of Economics

The following key terms are frequently used in the discipline of economics. If you take a college-level course in economics, it will be important for you to remember these words and to use them in your speech and writing. Review the words below and answer the multiple-choice questions that follow.

capitalism	incentive	production
competition	inflation	profit
consumption	loss	recession
demand	policy	scarcity
employment	prediction	supply

EXERCISE 1 **Inferring Meaning from Context**

Read each sentence below and try to derive the meaning of the italicized key terms from the context. Circle the correct definition of each italicized term.

1. The iPad has become so popular worldwide that the company cannot produce enough to meet the increasing *demand*.
   a. a company's inability to produce enough
   b. the consumer's inability to purchase something
   c. the desire to purchase something
   d. a lack of interest in a product

2. When *supply* is larger °than demand, the price of the product usually falls.
   a. the amount available
   b. the inability to satisfy
   c. the ability to produce less
   d. the ability to produce more

3. Most Americans are not spending money on goods and services as much as they used to in the past, and that has made it difficult for businesses to make a *profit*.
   a. the money left after deducting expenses
   b. the money used to pay for expenses
   c. the money needed to produce goods and services
   d. the money used to pay the employees

4. The computer company took a huge *loss* this year because the competitors provided better and cheaper products to the consumers.
   a. the gain to the amount of money invested in a company
   b. a company's revenue exceeding the cost of production
   c. the cost exceeding a company's revenue
   d. demand being more than supply

5. A price war has emerged among computer makers as a result of the severe *competition* to provide the best computer at the most affordable price.
   a. no demand for the best computer
   b. the rivalry between companies
   c. no contest between companies to make the best computer
   d. the most affordable computer

6. Most American companies are finding cheap labor in foreign countries, so there is a *scarcity* of jobs for middle-class workers in the United States.
   a. sufficient number   c. adequate number
   b. ample number   d. insufficient number

7. The drugstore gives its employees a bonus every year in addition to their salaries as an *incentive* to encourage them to perform well.
   a. something that discourages employees from performing well
   b. something that encourages employees to resign
   c. something that encourages employees to make a greater effort
   d. something that scares employees to make a greater effort

8. The Food and Drug Administration (FDA) has warned people that certain types of tuna fish are high in lead and are not suitable for human *consumption*.
   a. the process of catching tuna   c. the purpose of cooking
   b. the art of fishing   d. the act of eating

9. The government is offering many *employment* opportunities to jobless people to improve the economy.
   a. occupations that help people earn a living
   b. an activity that allows people to have fun together
   c. an act of fining middle-class workers
   d. an occupation that seeks volunteers for free work.

10. Even though the unemployment rate has gone down this month, economists believe that the economy is still in a *recession*.
    a. the act of improving the economy
    b. a period of economic prosperity
    c. a long period of robust economic activity
    d. a temporary depression in the economy

11. Most U.S. economists have made a *prediction* that the economy will turn around within the next year.
    a. the act of saying what happened in the past
    b. the act of saying what caused the problem in the past
    c. the act of saying what will happen in the future
    d. the act of saying what happened centuries ago

12. The company's hiring *policy* is to give preference to people who are from a minority group.
    a. a course of action
    b. a preference to offer employment to the rich
    c. an unspoken rule to fire people from a minority group
    d. an action carried out carelessly

13. Individual buyers and sellers dealing with each other in markets, making important economic decisions, are the cornerstone of *capitalism*.
    a. an economic system in which individual buyers and sellers are not allowed to exchange wealth
    b. an economic system in which exchange of wealth is controlled by private individuals
    c. an economic system in which production and distribution are controlled by the government
    d. an economic system in which wealth is equally distributed among the citizens of a country

14. The *production* of personal computers has been hurt by the increasing popularity of the iPad.
    a. discontinuation   c. destruction
    b. manufacture   d. failure

15. Insufficient jobs, the stock market crash, home foreclosures, and the loss of value of currency have resulted in *inflation*.
    a. affordable products
    b. increased value of currency
    c. a rise in prices
    d. more supply than demand

Collaboration

EXERCISE 2   Creating Meaningful Sentences with the Key Terms

Working with a partner, choose five of the key terms in economics and write an original setence about each one.

1. **Word** = _____

_____

_____

2. Word = _____

_____

_____

3. Word = _____

_____

_____

4. Word = _____

_____

_____

5. Word = _____

_____

_____

COLLEGE STUDY SKILLS
Note Taking

 LEARNING OBJECTIVE
Write effective lecture notes

In college, you will have many opportunities to listen to lectures given by professors or a guest speaker. Your professor may ask you to take specific notes on lectures and give you a few questions later to test how much you understood them.

No matter how fast you write, it is difficult to keep up with a lecturer, who is not a tape recorder that you can rewind or fast forward. So, it is important that you write down a lecturer's most important points such as his or her main idea and key major details. Remember that it will not be easy for you to write complete sentences while the lecturer is speaking, so you will need to take quick notes. Everyone works differently, so you too will have to develop your own method of taking notes.

The following are some effective ways to take notes while listening to a lecture. Keep in mind that you do not necessarily have to follow these symbols when you take notes. Be creative, aim high, and make up your own symbols. You should use whatever works for you.

Abbreviations	*Symbols*
US = United States	= equal
inv = investment	+ growth, progress, surplus
Pr = President	– decrease, shortage
econ = economy	$ profit, revenue, money, savings
bus = Business	% percentage
fin = finance	# number
BS = balance sheet	& in addition

Abbreviations	Symbols
FS = financial statement	< less than
emp = employment	> greater than
inf = inflation	
mkt = market	
mgmt = management	
stk = stock	
eqt = equity	
acct = account/accounting	

After you take notes on a lecture, review your notes and listen to the lecture a second time. You will notice that you understand the lecture even more the second time. Go through your notes as you listen to the lecture again and fill in information you missed the first time.

Putting the Skill into Action

Now that you have learned about the importance of writing down pieces of information while listening to a lecture, let's practice taking notes. Your instructor will play you a short lecture "Economics Defined" by Robin Blade and Michael Parkin (or you can play it by scanning the QR code on p. 167). As you listen to the lecture, use abbreviations and symbols from the table above or make up your own symbols and take specific notes. If you wish, listen to the lecture a second time and check your notes to make sure you took down the most important points. Refer to your notes when the professor asks you to answer the questions that follow the lecture. You may want to compare your notes to those of your classmates to answer the questions correctly.

The Last Word

One of the goals of taking notes is to help you improve your understanding of what you listen to. It is our belief that as you practice taking notes, you will improve your ability to follow information related to the lecture. Another benefit of taking notes is that it will improve your writing skill. As you learn to select bits and pieces of information, you will be able to transfer this skill to writing as you write a paragraph. As you can see, there are many benefits to taking notes.

READINESS FOR COLLEGE SUCCESS
Collaborative Learning

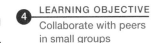

④ LEARNING OBJECTIVE
Collaborate with peers in small groups

As a college student, you will be asked to work in small groups and complete tasks together with your classmates. The professor may ask you to answer questions related to a reading, or he or she may give you a topic and ask you to form a group either arguing for or arguing against the view. Your success in college will depend on how well you work with your classmates, how flexible you are in accepting viewpoints that are different than yours, and how productive you are as a teammate.

What follows are some of the activities you may be required to do while studying in college.

Small Group Discussions

Be prepared to work in small groups and make up questions about a reading. You may have to write short answers to the questions to take part in whole-class discussion. Sometimes the professor may give you study questions to check your understanding of a reading.

Debates

Your professor may break the class up into small groups and have each take a position on a topic such as gun control or making drugs legal. You will need to not only give your best arguments to defend your position but also anticipate arguments made by the other groups and be able to respond to them.

Collaborative Writing

Another activity you might be asked to do is working in small groups to write a summary of a difficult paragraph or passage or write a speech given by a small group of students.

Brainstorming

This is probably one of the most useful activities you will be doing throughout your college career. You will often be asked to work in groups to create ideas for a research paper, make a list of examples to support or challenge a point, and so on.

Joint Research

As members of a group, you may each take responsibility for different parts of a research project and then report to the class.

Role-Playing

In this activity, you can either play the role of a character in a short story or a play, or you can take on real roles such as a discussion leader or tutor in a workshop.

Dramatic Readings

Sometimes you may be asked to work in small groups and write your own scenes for a play using characters from a short story or play you have read. This activity may be followed by discussion of how the new material affects the original work.

Collaboration

Collaborative learning is a powerful way to learn to brainstorm ideas, to ask and respond to questions, and to become an active member of the class. Use the following table to brainstorm with your peers how you will prepare for each of the above activities. The first example is done for you.

Collaborative Learning Activity	*How to Prepare*
small-group discussion	***Read the reading selection beforehand and write questions for class discussion.***
debate	
collaborative writing	
brainstorming	
joint research	
role-playing	
dramatic readings	

READING

Reading Selection **1**

Web Article

Anyone Want a Flu Shot? Supply Grows, But Demand Withers

MyReadingLab™
Complete this **Exercise**
at **myreadinglab.com**

Preview Questions

1. In your opinion, what happens when supply exceeds demand? Likewise, what happens when demand exceeds supply? Be specific.

2. Do you think everyone needs a flu shot every year? Should flu shots be given only when the flu is rampant?

3. If there were a shortage of the flu vaccine, do you think more people would get sick and die?

Pre-Reading Vocabulary: Focus on Some Key Terms

Before beginning the reading selection, it may be helpful to focus on the meaning of some key words in the article. Working with a partner, try to guess the meaning of these words. Then look up the words in a dictionary.

Word	Your Definition	Dictionary Definition
aplenty		
serum		
immunization		
dwindling		
exceed		

Anyone Want a Flu Shot? Supply Grows, But Demand Withers

By Joel Roberts

1   Rod Watson had to cancel 1,000 flu-shot clinics in four states when the national vaccine shortage cut off his supply two months ago. Now Watson has flu shots aplenty—and he can't give them away.

2   "My biggest fear is I'm going to end up with a lot of serum, and there's a national shortage," said Watson, president of Prevention MD, a medical screening and immunization company. He offers $20 flu shots Monday through Friday at his Seattle-area office. Public health officials in California, Colorado and other states have voiced similar fears. Some are relaxing the rules to offer shots to more people.

3   In October and November people stood in line for hours to get one of the precious few flu shots. But now that more vaccine is available—with a few million more doses expected from British and German suppliers—demand is dwindling.

4   "It's one of those things like Beanie Babies or something," said Doug McBride, spokesman for the Texas Department of State Health Services. "If you can't get something, you've got more people wanting them."

5   Supply exceeds demand in some areas, the federal Centers for Disease Control and Prevention acknowledges. In other areas, people are still desperate for the vaccine.

6   So far this year the flu is still not widespread, reports CBS News Early Show Health Correspondent Dr. Emily Senay. There are a few states reporting local and regional flu activity, with the rest of the country still looking pretty good.

7   "But we still have the depths of winter to get through, and the vaccine shortage this year means that many people are not being offered a flu shot unless they're in a high-risk category," Dr. Senay said.

8   The best way to find a flu shot is to call your local health department, the CDC advises. The CDC says 98 million people need the vaccine this winter. About 65 million doses will be available in the United States, including a nasal vaccine that's safe only for healthy people.

9   Public health officials say they hope demand is dwindling because they've reached the people who need flu vaccine the most: babies, the aged and the infirm. But they acknowledge that other factors—from frustration and apathy to simple human nature—might be at work too. When something is scarce, people naturally want it more. Being told they can't get a desired immunization is an unfamiliar and unwelcome sensation for most Americans. "Anytime a commodity is scarce, and it is a desired item, demand will increase," Dr. Louis Manza, psychology professor at Lebanon Valley College in Pennsylvania, said in an e-mail.

10   Some people probably gave up after trying unsuccessfully to get a flu shot, said Mary Selecky, director of the Washington State Health Department and member of a national advisory group on flu vaccine distribution. Recent reports on this flu season's mild start may have convinced others that getting a flu shot wasn't worth the trouble—an impression Selecky is trying to erase.

     "It's a mild flu season up to now, but next week could be another story," Selecky said. "As a society we're driven by what's in front of us. . . . We're having to work a little bit harder so people know that getting a flu vaccine in December and January is still very effective."

11   David Marks was surprised at how easy it was to get vaccinated at a Seattle grocery store last week. The line in the express checkout lane was longer than the line to get flu shots. "I just assumed it was going to be hard," said Marks, 44, whose severe asthma puts him in the high-risk group. "I think people have given up."

12   High-risk groups, as defined by the CDC, are people age 65 and older, adults and children with chronic diseases, babies 6 months to 23 months, pregnant women, nursing home residents, and people who live with children under 6 months of age.

13   Some state officials are expanding eligibility to younger people, those just over 50. The CDC is encouraging state officials to set their own guidelines based on local needs. "They know what's best for their community," CDC spokesman Llelwyn

Grant said. The federal agency is also working with state and local officials to redirect vaccine to areas where it's most needed for high-risk patients.

14   Health officials are worried about elderly and infirm people who don't live in nursing homes and who lack the resources to track down a flu shot. "There are still some real desperate people out there," said Watson, of the Seattle medical company. "We just don't know how to find them."

15   It's still too soon to tell whether more people will get sick and die this year because of the vaccine shortage. Most years, the peak flu month is actually February, according to the CDC. Public health officials say the silver lining may be that the shortage focused more attention on simple, common-sense ways to stop the spread of the virus—washing your hands, staying home from school or work when you're sick, and avoiding touching your nose, eyes and mouth. "At the turn of the 20th century, public health was all about teaching people not to spread disease," Selecky said. "Now at the turn of the 21st century, here we are again."

The Associated Press January 23, 2005. Reprinted by permission of The YGS Group.

Reading Comprehension Check

1. The main idea of the article is that
   a. the demand for flu shots has become increasingly bigger and bigger.
   b. there are not enough flu shots available to meet the demand.
   c. the demand for flu shots has become smaller and smaller as more than sufficient flu shots available.
   d. the demand for flu shots far exceeds its supply.

2. "Some are **relaxing** the rules to offer shots to more people." (para. 2) In this context, the word *relaxing* means
   a. making more strict.   c. making something impossible.
   b. making something difficult.   d. making less strict.

3. The example of people standing in line to get a flu shot in October and November is used to support the fact that
   a. most people get sick in October and November.
   b. when supply of something is limited, more and more people will demand it.
   c. supply usually exceeds demand in the months of October and November.
   d. when supply exceeds demand, people stand in line.

4. "Being told they can't get a desired immunization is an unfamiliar and unwelcome sensation for most Americans." (para. 9) It can be inferred from the above statement that
   a. most Americans do not desire much even when there is a low supply of goods and services.
   b. only when supply exceeds demand, do Americans get desperate.
   c. Americans like to be told that they cannot get something.
   d. when supply of a product or service is limited, Americans want it more.

5. "At the turn of the 20th century, public health was all about teaching people not to spread disease," Selecky said. "Now at the turn of the 21st century, here we are again." (para. 15) Based on the above passage, it can be inferred that
   a. public health has not made sufficient progress in 100 years.
   b. people nowadays are more aware of how not to spread disease than they were 100 years ago.
   c. public health has made significant progress in 100 years.
   d. there is so much medication available that people do not need to know how not to spread disease.

Collaboration

Exploring the Topic

Discuss the following questions to review the content of the article you have just read.

1. Why do you think the flu is widespread in the winter?

2. The CDC says 98 million people will need the flu vaccine this year. How do you think it is determined how many people will need the flu shot? Refer to the article to answer the question.

3. In your opinion, why is it that when supply of a product or service is dwindling, people demand it more and more? Give specific examples to support your answer.

Post-Reading Vocabulary

Without using a dictionary, determine the meaning of the bolded words from the context.

1. "Public health officials in California, Colorado and other states have **voiced** similar fears." (para. 2)

   Voiced means _____

2. "Public health officials say they hope demand is dwindling because they've reached the people who need flu vaccine the most: babies, the aged and the **infirm**." (para. 9)

   Infirm means _____

3. "When something is **scarce**, people naturally want it more." (para. 9)

   Scarce means _____

READING

Reading Selection **2**

Blog

How Mobile Phone Companies Profit from Handset Loss

Preview Questions

1. Have you ever lost a cell phone? If yes, how much did it cost to get a new cell phone? Were you surprised by the amount it cost you to get a replacement?

2. When you signed a cell phone contract with your service provider, did you read all the terms and conditions? Were you aware of all the services for which the service provider was going to charge you?

3. In your opinion, what should the government do when a service provider charges a subscriber too much money in the event that the cell phone was lost or stolen? Be specific.

MyReadingLab™
Complete this **Exercise**
at **myreadinglab.com**

Collaboration

Pre-Reading Vocabulary: Focus on Some Key Terms

Before beginning the reading selection, it may be helpful to focus on the meaning of some key words in the article. Working with a partner, try to guess the meaning of these words. Then look up the words in a dictionary.

Word	Your Definition	Dictionary Definition
absurd		
liability		
astonishing		
detect		
decline		

How Mobile Phone Companies Profit from Handset Loss

By Patrick Collinson, money editor, The *Guardian*
(posted Friday 17 December, 2010)

1   When are mobile phone companies going to address the problem of handset theft and the absurd liability that customers face? Steve Jensen, who was chased for a debt of £7,000 for the last year by Vodafone, would certainly like to know, as would many of other victims of this issue featured in *Guardian Money* over the past few years.

2   Currently, when you take out a mobile phone contract, you sign up for all calls from the handset … until you report it stolen. But if, unknown to you, a thief has

got his hands on your phone and makes endless calls, you will also have to pick up the bill—however large.

3   Thieves, we understand, sell the phones on to backstreet call bureaus who then rent them out to users making international calls. That's why the bills can reach astonishing levels. You may have never called Pakistan, but that will cut no ice with the phone companies if hundreds of calls to Karachi appear on your account in a matter of days: you are liable until the phone is reported missing. In no other area of life are consumers exposed in this way. If your credit card is stolen you have a maximum liability of £50.

4   Why have the banks developed sophisticated systems that detect unusual spending patterns? Because they have to pick up the bill. If the regulator, Ofcom, told the phone companies that an individual's liability is capped at, say, £100, they would soon institute bank-like controls. Vodafone declined to detail the systems it has in place to monitor airtime abuse, and other phone companies have been similarly tight-lipped.

5   In Jensen's case it emerged that a text questioning whether he was making these calls was sent to his handset. Unsurprisingly, the thief failed to respond and the account remained open with the bill mounting up and up.

6   The phone companies have the technology to stamp out this problem but are oddly resistant to using it. It beggars belief that their systems cannot detect unusual calling patterns early on. Of course, consumers need to bear responsibility for looking after their phone—but a bill of £7,000? One can only conclude that the phone companies are profiting from crime.

7   *Guardian Money* has highlighted the absurd cost of calling 118 directory inquiries, and the fact that so-called 0800 free-phone numbers are charged at 40p a minute from a mobile. After years of complaints from consumers, this week Ofcom finally announced it is prepared to tackle this issue. But don't hold your breath. It says it wants 0800 calls from mobiles to be free. It has also called for clearer charging structures to directory inquiries, and other chargeable numbers such as 0845.

8   A consultation has been announced, which is expected to conclude in the summer. As it is fairly straightforward, you would expect changes to come fairly soon. But this is the telecoms market and nothing happens quickly at Ofcom. We've been told not to expect concrete changes for 18 months. In the meantime, phone users will overpay millions of pounds for these services.

MyReadingLab™
Complete this **Exercise**
at **myreadinglab.com**

Reading Comprehension Check

1. "Unsurprisingly, the thief failed to respond and the account remained open with the bill **mounting up** and up." (para. 5) The phrasal verb *mounting up* in this context means

a. decreasing.   c. increasing.

b. declining.   d. deteriorating.

2. The author's main idea is that
   a. cell phone companies replace a lost phone without any charge.
   b. cell phone companies stand to gain every time a subscriber loses his or her phone.
   c. the government does not protect cell phone users when they lose their phones.
   d. cell phone users are generally happy with the cell phone companies.

3. Which of the following statements is NOT true?
   a. Steve Jensen owed Vodafone £7,000.
   b. According to the contract, you must pay for all the calls made from the handset.
   c. You cannot sign a cell phone contract until someone steals it.
   d. It costs to dial a toll-free number from your cell phone.

4. "When are mobile phone companies going to address the problem of handset theft and the absurd liability that customers face? Steve Jensen, who was chased for a debt of £7,000 for the last year by Vodafone, would certainly like to know, as would many of other victims of this issue featured in *Guardian Money* over the past few years." (para. 1) A logical conclusion drawn from the passage is that
   a. Jensen stole money from the cell phone company.
   b. Vodafone lent the money to Steve Jensen and wanted him to repay the loan.
   c. Vodafone wanted to reward Steve Jensen for being a loyal customer.
   d. Steve Jensen lost his phone and wasn't responsible for all the calls made from his handset, so he should not have to pay for them.

5. "The phone companies have the technology to stamp out this problem but are oddly resistant to using it." (para. 6) It can be inferred from the statement that
   a. the phone companies are determined to solve this problem.
   b. it is in the phone companies' best interest not to solve the problem.
   c. the phone companies have used the technology in the past.
   d. the phone companies use the technology only when the amount is an odd number.

Exploring the Topic

Collaboration

Discuss the following questions to review the content of the blog you have just read.

1. Why do you think the phone companies have not addressed the issue of handset theft?

2. Is texting a cell phone subscriber an effective way of letting the customer know that the company has noticed an unusual spending pattern? What other ways can a phone company resolve this issue without hurting the customer? Be specific.

3. In your opinion, why hasn't the British government mandated how much a phone company should charge in case of handset theft? In other words, why are British phone companies given the right to charge their customers large amounts of money when they lose their handsets?

Post-Reading Vocabulary

Without using a dictionary, determine the meaning of the bolded words from the context.

1. "In no other area of life are consumers **exposed** in this way." (para. 3)

   Exposed means _____

2. "Vodafone declined to detail the systems it has in place to monitor airtime abuse, and other phone companies have been similarly **tight-lipped**." (para. 4)

   Tight-lipped means _____

3. "The phone companies have the technology to stamp out this problem but are oddly **resistant** to using it." (para. 6)

   Resistant means _____

Nidhi Shah   An Interview with a Student in the Field of Economics

University of Maryland Baltimore County

1. How did you find your path to majoring in economics?

I was initially a bio major but took introductory economics courses as part of my general requirements. I found the subject very interesting because it allowed me to connect the information to households as well as on a global scale. I particularly became interested in macroeconomics. I did some studying on my own and took a couple more economics classes and knew that this was the right major for me.

2. What is the biggest obstacle you face in your study of economics?

The biggest obstacle I faced in the upper-level courses, I would say, was that none of my professors wanted to use online aids or even the textbook thoroughly. They would just use the board and skipped around from topic to topic, so it became very difficult to understand the material from just attending class. I had to put in a lot of effort outside of class to actually learn the material.

3. What area(s) of economics in particular do you find most interesting?

Macroeconomics is very interesting to me. It lets me analyze the economy as a whole. Keynesian economics is a subject I really like to learn about in particular.

4. What specific skills are required of students who study economics?

I would definitely say that students should be able to analyze graphs, because they are a large part of economics. Students should have problem-solving skills and be able to think things through logically. Students should be able to observe and interpret data as well as be able to connect theories learned to the real world.

5. Other than being an economist, what other career avenues are available for economics majors?

Economics majors can go on to MBA, CPA, and CFA programs. They can become economists as well.

SKILL FOCUS
Making Inferences

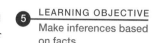

Making an **inference** is about drawing a logical conclusion based on facts. Most of the time, authors drop a hint for the reader to draw a conclusion about. Therefore, it is important to look at the facts and details. Keep in mind that your opinion does not matter at all. You must pay attention to all the facts in a reading passage first. After that, you can make an inference based on those facts and details.

Remember the following points to make an inference in a multiple-choice test correctly:

- You must look at the facts and details in the passage.
- Go through the four choices and look for the three statements that are false.
- Look for the single statement that is true.
- Do not form an opinion that is not stated in the passage.
- Be sure that the inference you are making is logical and is based on facts.

Let's read a passage to understand how inferences are made. Keep all of the above points in mind as you read the following passage. Remind yourself to pay attention to all the facts and details in the passage.

Example

> Because most people want and expect their standard of living to improve continually, economic growth—expansion in the economy's capacity to produce goods and services—is an important objective. If population is increasing, some economic growth is necessary just to maintain the existing standard of material welfare. When a nation's population is stable or is increasing less rapidly than output, economic growth results in more goods and services per person, contributing to a higher standard of living.
>
> from William D. Rohlf, *Introduction to Economic Reasoning*, 8e, pp. 16–17

Which of the following conclusions can be drawn from the passage?

a. When a country's population increases less than its output, the standard of living decreases.

b. When a country's population increases more than its output, the standard of living improves.

c. When a country's population increases less than its output, the standard of living improves.

d. When a country's population remains the same as its output, the standard of living decreases.

Let's read each of the choices carefully. Then determine if each statement is true or false.

a. The passage says that when a country's population increases less rapidly than its output, the standard of living is usually high. **Statement a** says that when the population increases less than its output, the standard of living decreases. It is clearly a false statement.

b. **Statement b** says that when a country's population increases more than its output, then the standard of living improves. This is illogical, because supply will be less than demand. If anything, the standard of living will get worse. This statement is also incorrect.

c. The passage states clearly that when a country's population increases less than its output, the standard of living is usually high. This makes sense, as supply will be more than demand. There will be enough goods and services for the people, so the standard of living will be high; therefore, **statement c** is true.

d. **Statement d** is misleading. If supply and demand are equal, the standard of living is not going to decrease. If anything, the standard of living will remain the same because the population is not increasing more than the country's output. This is a false statement.

As you can see, making an inference is all about drawing a logical conclusion based on facts. Always remember that you should not make an inference based on your opinion.

Now that you have seen one example, let's practice making inferences based on all the facts and details in a passage. As they say, practice makes perfect. The more you practice making an inference, the more comfortable you will feel drawing a conclusion based on facts.

EXERCISE 3   Making Inferences

Read the following passages carefully. In the space provided below each passage, write a logical conclusion.

Passage 1

Because no society can produce everything its members desire, each society must sort through and assess its various wants and then decide which goods and services to produce in what quantities. Deciding the relative value of military products against civilian goods is only one part of the picture because each society must determine precisely which civilian and military products it will produce. For example, it must decide whether to produce clothing or to conserve its scarce resources for some other use. Next, it must decide what types of clothing to produce—how many shirts, dresses, pairs of slacks, overcoats, and so on. Finally, it must decide in what sizes to produce these items of clothing and determine the quantities of each size. Only after considering all such alternatives can a society decide which goods and services to produce.

from William D. Rohlf, *Introduction to Economic Reasoning,* 8e, p. 14

Based on this passage, a logical conclusion that can be drawn is that _____

_____

_____

Passage 2

After deciding which products to produce, each society must also decide what materials and methods to use in their production. In most cases, a given good or service can be produced in more than one way. For instance, a shirt can be made of cotton, wool, or acrylic fibers. It can be sewn entirely by hand, partly by hand, or entirely by machine. It can be packaged in paper, cardboard, plastic, or some combination of materials. It can be shipped by truck, train, boat, or plane. In short, the producer must choose among many options with regard to materials, production methods, and means of shipment.

from William D. Rohlf, *Introduction to Economic Reasoning,* 8e, p. 15

It can be inferred from the above passage that _____

_____

Passage 3

Finally, each society must decide how to distribute or divide up its limited output among those who desire to receive it. Should everyone receive equal shares of society's output? Should those who produce more receive more? What about those who don't produce at all, either because they can't work or because they don't want to work? How much of society's output should they receive? In deciding how to distribute output—how output will be shared—different societies are influenced by their traditions and cultural values.

from William D. Rohlf, *Introduction to Economic Reasoning,* 8e, p. 15

A logical conclusion drawn from the above passage is that _____

_____

_____

EXERCISE 4   Making inferences

Let's take a multiple-choice test now. This time you do not have to write the conclusion. Your task is to read the four choices carefully, eliminate the three statements that are false, and choose one statement that is true. Read the following passages carefully. Then make an inference that is logically drawn from the passage.

Passage 1

People who are both *willing and able* to make purchases are the consumers who determine which products a market economy will produce. When consumers lack either the willingness or the ability to spend, producers do not respond. Thus, the concept of demand includes the willingness and ability of potential buyers to purchase a product. We define **demand** as a schedule (or table) showing the quantities of a good or service that consumers are willing and able to purchase at various prices during a given time period, when all factors other than the product's price remain unchanged.

from William D. Rohlf, *Introduction to Economic Reasoning*, 8e, p. 68

It can be inferred from the above passage that

   a. producers pay attention to those consumers who do not have the ability to spend.

   b. producers respond to those consumers who are only willing to purchase a good or service.

   c. producers listen to those consumers who are willing and have the ability to pay for a good or service.

   d. producers usually avoid responding to those who are willing and able to purchase products.

Passage 2

Suppose that demand is highly elastic, that is, very responsive to price changes. If tuition is increased, the college will receive more money from each student, but it will enroll considerably fewer students; the percentage *reduction* in quantity demanded will be greater than the percentage *increase* in price. As a result, the college will take in less total revenue than it did before the tuition hike. In the face of elastic demand, the logical action for the college to take—assuming there are vacant dormitory rooms and unfilled classes—would be to lower, not raise, tuition. The college will receive less from each student who enrolls, but it will enroll many more students, and total revenue will increase.

from William D. Rohlf, *Introduction to Economic Reasoning*, 8e, p. 114

According to the passage, which of the following conclusions is true?

   a. It is in the college's best interest to increase tuition every year.

   b. The college is better off lowering tuition.

   c. If the college increases tuition, its total revenue will increase.

   d. If the college increases tuition, enrollment will be high.

Passage 3

The role of self-interest in motivating men and women may seem self-evident to you. But the fact is that we sometimes forget this fundamental characteristic of human nature. And forgetting it may cause us to make errors in judgment. Consider, for example, the automobile salesman who promises to be your friend and "give you a good deal." If self-interest is the primary factor motivating salespeople, your first response when confronted by such a pledge should be to question it. After all, a salesperson who is motivated by self-interest won't be concerned about promoting yours—at least no more than the competition demands. And when an advertisement offers "free" products or "unbelievable bargains," don't rush down to the store. Read the fine print; that's where you will generally discover the true cost.

from William D. Rohlf, *Introduction to Economic Reasoning*, 8e, p. 132

Which of the following conclusions can be drawn from the passage?

   a. A car salesman who promises to give you a good deal has your best interest at heart.

   b. Consumers make the right decision when they forget the fundamental characteristics of human nature.

   c. Companies offering "free" products or "unbelievable bargains" have absolutely no self-interest.

   d. Consumers are likely to make the right decision if they remember that self-interest is a part of human nature.

Passage 4

How do individuals pursue their self-interest; how do they make certain that their decisions improve their own well-being? They do so by comparing the costs and benefits of a contemplated action rather than acting impulsively. Consider, for example, the decision that confronts you in the morning when your alarm goes off. Do you get out of bed and go to class or stay in bed and get a couple more hours of sleep? Economists assume that rather than just hitting the alarm and going back to sleep (an impulsive reaction), you weigh the costs and benefits of getting up. In other words, you consider what you would learn in class and the likelihood of a quiz (the benefits of getting up) against the lost sleep (the cost of getting up) and make a decision. If the value of going to class exceeds the cost, you get up. If not, you make the rational decision and stay in bed.

from William D. Rohlf, *Introduction to Economic Reasoning*, 8e, p. 133

A logical conclusion drawn from the above passage is that

   a. most individuals act if the costs far exceed the benefits.

   b. some individuals are not interested in improving their well-being.

   c. individuals act if they believe the benefits exceed the costs in a given situation.

   d. most people protect their self-interest by giving up the benefits of their action.

Passage 5

Sometimes we forget that the true cost of any decision is the opportunity cost, and that can lead to poor decisions. Consider the case of Tom Sanders, a 40-year-old dentist living in College City. Tom recently decided to build a new home, and he stopped by his banker to arrange financing. When the banker asked Tom where he was planning to build, he replied that the location would be at the corner of Main and First Streets, a longtime vacant lot just across the street from

State University. That seemed to the banker an expensive piece of real estate for a single-family home, so she asked Tom why he had chosen that location. Tom's response was, "Because I inherited the land and it won't cost me anything to use it." His answer illustrates a common problem in making decisions—failing to consider opportunity costs. Because Tom was not required to make an explicit dollar payment to buy the land, he assumed that it was free; he ignored the opportunity cost of using it.

from William D. Rohlf, *Introduction to Economic Reasoning*, 8e, p. 136

It can be inferred from the above passage that

    a. we should ignore the opportunity cost of an action.

    b. we ought to remember the opportunity cost of an action we decide to take.

    c. overlooking the opportunity cost of an action is a wise decision.

    d. Tom Sanders made a wise decision by not considering the opportunity cost of building a home on the vacant lot.

LANDMARK IN THE FIELD OF ECONOMICS

The Social Security Act

In the old days, the American people had to work very hard and save for rainy days. Even if they were still in good health in their old age, many people had to keep working to make ends meet. There were no government programs to help them.

That changed on August 14, 1935, when President Roosevelt signed the Social Security Act to help older people economically. The act also gave money to those who had lost their jobs and were having a hard time living a normal life. Some people did not like the idea and said that the act would cause a loss of jobs. However, those who supported the act argued that it would encourage older people to retire and make it easier for younger people to find jobs.

The Social Security program is the largest government program in the world and is right now the largest social program in the United States (37% of the government budget is spent on Social Security benefits). Money is paid every year to older people, to those who have lost their jobs, and to the husbands, wives, and children of workers who have passed away. The program keeps about 40% of the American people who are at least 65 years old out of poverty. The headquarters of the Social Security Administration is based in Woodlawn, Maryland.

In recent years, some people have become worried that when they retire, there will be no Social Security benefits for them. This is a real issue as it is the contributions of younger, current workers into the program that support retirees. As large numbers of baby boomers retire and more young people have difficulty finding work, there will be an increasing imbalance between money coming in and benefits being paid out. There are other factors that harm the Social Security program. These are the rising costs of goods and services and much lower economic growth in the last ten years.

The government is well aware of this problem, and Congress has made some changes in Social Security to make sure that older people will be taken care of when they retire in the future. It is hoped that the government will find a way to keep helping the people who need money for their basic needs.

Collaboration

Considering the Topic

Answer the following questions with a partner.

1. How has the Social Security Act changed the way people live?

2. Do you think that soon the government will run out of money and there will be no financial support for the elderly? In your opinion, what can be done to support retirees and the unemployed?

3. Can you imagine another breakthrough in the field of economics that will further change the way people live? Explain.

Internet Connection

Research another landmark in the field of economics, and fill out the section below.

Game Theory	currency exchange
Karl Marx's Theory of Value	free market economy
capitalism	the stock market

Landmark: _____

Question	Answer
When did this landmark become a reality?	
Who was involved in developing this landmark?	
What made this landmark special?	
How did this landmark change the way people interact?	

READING

Reading Selection **3**

Blog

Capitalism Bites the Carpenters in Vegas

Preview Questions

MyReadingLab™
Complete this **Exercise**
at **myreadinglab.com**

1. Do you believe that illegal immigrants are taking jobs away from the American people? Some believe that this has a direct and negative impact on the economy. Do you agree with this view? Why or why not?

2. Some people believe that capitalism and free markets are best for the robust growth of an economy. Others think that free markets are not necessarily good for the economy. What is your position? Use specific examples to support your answer.

3. In your opinion, how much control should the government have in a free market economy? Are you aware of an economy where the government controls the market and a free market is not allowed to thrive? Be specific.

Collaboration

Pre-Reading Vocabulary: Focus on Some Key Terms

Before beginning the reading selection, it may be helpful to focus on the meaning of some key words in the article. Working with a partner, try to guess the meaning of these words. Then look up the words in a dictionary.

Word	*Your Definition*	*Dictionary Definition*
demise		
boom		
wailing		
pretend		
intervention		

Capitalism Bites the Carpenters in Vegas

By **Charles Trentelman, December 18, 2010**

1   [There is an] interesting story in the *Washington Post* today about the demise of the construction industry in Vegas and what it's doing to the carpenters there.

2   It's an interesting story on the view it gives of carpenters in Vegas who, during the boom, were making Union Scale of $37.50 an hour (dunno if that includes benefits, probably does) and racking it up pretty well. Some describe living in gated communities, shopping at Tiffany's, and buying Jags (albeit used).

3   Of course, now they're all out of work, and in the comment section there are a lot of people wailing about how illegal immigrants are stealing all the existing jobs and how unfair this all is and so on and so forth.

HENDERSON, NV - NOVEMBER 17: Portrait of unemployed carpenters

4   Which led me to put up the following comment:

5   *All you folk screaming about illegals stealing your work—let's pretend you are right (and you may be).*

6   *So, what to do? Who is forcing employers to hire those guys? Who puts a gun to their head? Who screams, "You will hire illegals and pay them less and put Americans out of work!"*

7   *No, don't blame liberals. Most of those business owners/construction contractors are good ol' boy Americans, conservative flag-waving to the core. And THEY are hiring illegals, and sticking it to you, because it's cheaper that way and like most conservatives these days, they firmly believe in capitalism when it pays them too.*

8   *And, guess what? In capitalism at its strongest, the lowest bidder gets the job.*

9   *Got a problem with them hiring illegals (which, by the way, IS illegal), maybe you need to do something about these good old boy flag-waving contractors.*

10   *No, wait, that would involve government intervention, and that would mean a bigger government. Can't have that.*

11   *Sorry, guys, you lose.*

12   Really, it is interesting—people scream for capitalism and free markets right up to the second that capitalism and free markets cost them their jobs. Suddenly they're liberals screaming for protection.

13   Hard truth—we need some of both, but it is also true, as I say, that it is the freest of the free market capitalists who are hiring those cheap workers. You can say "well, unions are making life worse" but unions made it possible for a lot of carpenters (and others) to buy a lot of expensive junk, and if you are in the business of selling junk you may want to think twice about calling for union workers, federal workers and all the rest to have their pay cut.

14   Unions, remember, got their start making sure that workers got living wages in industries where a few people got stinking rich while the people who created that wealth by making stuff got the shaft. Business owners thought the idea of children working on assembly lines at half an adult's pay was a really swell deal, and 6-day weeks, 10- and 12-hour days were only fair.

15   Five-day work weeks were socialistic. Living wages were a threat to America itself. Henry Ford's idea that his workers should be able to buy the cars they made was radically extreme, if not downright socialistic, for his time. More typical was Andrew Carnegie, who hired federal troops to shoot at his striking workers. "We must coddle the rich because they create jobs," although how that theory jibes with the current employment situation, puzzles me.

16   Now, of course, it's all about cutting spending. The pendulum has swung, workers have to take the wage they're offered because that's how it works, supply and demand.

17   I can't wait for the screaming when House Speaker–presumptive John Boehner gets his way and cuts $100 billion out of discretionary federal spending. Look around, folks, at how many companies in Utah's defense-related industries depend on that discretionary spending to make their payrolls. A lot of Utah earmarks are defense-related, and we've already lost the earmarks, or so our Congress people claim.

18   But don't worry, it's all OK because they're going to balance the budget by cutting taxes by $800 billion. Spend 100 less, take in 800 less—that will work.

19   It's like selling nickels for 4 cents each and making your profit on volume.

Standard-Examiner Blogs, posted December 18, 2010. Reprinted by permission.

MyReadingLab™
Complete this **Exercise**
at **myreadinglab.com**

Reading Comprehension Check

1. "Business owners thought the idea of children working on assembly lines at half an adult's pay was a really **swell** deal, and 6-day weeks, 10- and 12-hour days were only fair." (para. 14) In the above context, the word *swell* means
   a. bad.   c. illegal.
   b. poor.   d. great.

2. The main idea of this post is that
   a. capitalism has cost many carpenters in Las Vegas their jobs.
   b. capitalism has provided excellent employment opportunities for the carpenters in Vegas.
   c. free markets have allowed the carpenters in Vegas to keep their jobs.
   d. capitalism has made it easier for the carpenters in Vegas to earn a living.

3. The example of the carpenters in Vegas making $37.50 per hour is given to support the fact that
   a. the carpenters suffered miserably during the economic boom.
   b. the carpenters were not happy with their wages during the economic boom.
   c. the carpenters were better off during the economic boom.
   d. the carpenters did not make enough money during the economic boom.

4. "It's an interesting story on the view it gives of carpenters in Vegas who, during the boom, were making Union Scale of $37.50 an hour (dunno if that includes benefits, probably does) and racking it up pretty well. Some describe living in gated communities, shopping at Tiffany's, and buying Jags (albeit used)." (para. 2) It can be inferred from the above passage that
   a. after the boom, the carpenters continued to live in gated communities and shop at boutique stores.

b. during the boom, the financial condition of the carpenters in Vegas was not as good as it is now.

c. during the boom, the carpenters could not afford used luxury cars.

d. after the boom, the financial condition of the carpenters in Vegas became worse.

5. "Now, of course, it's all about cutting spending. The pendulum has swung, workers have to take the wage they're offered because that's how it works, supply and demand." (para. 16) Based on this passage, a logical conclusion can be drawn that

a. workers are in great demand nowadays.

b. workers are earning high wages because supply is much less than demand.

c. employers prefer cheap labor, so workers are not able to earn high wages as they did in the past.

d. employers are not interested in cutting spending.

Exploring the Topic

Collaboration

Discuss the following questions to review the content of the post you have just read.

1. What is the author's attitude toward illegal immigrants? Do you agree with his view?

2. What does the author think about capitalism and free markets? Do you think he favors socialism?

3. The author seems to be suggesting that the government should have some control over the market. Do you agree with him, or do you think that a free market economy is best served when there is no government involvement? Give specific reasons for your answer.

Post-Reading Vocabulary

Without using a dictionary, determine the meaning of the bolded words from the context.

1. "Unions, remember, got their start making sure that workers got living wages in industries where a few people got stinking rich while the people who created that wealth by making stuff **got the shaft**." (para. 14)

   Got the Shaft means _____

2. "'We must coddle the rich because they create jobs,' although how that theory **jibes** with the current employment situation, puzzles me." (para. 15)

   Jibes means _____

3. "'The pendulum has swung, workers have to take the **wage** they're offered because that's how it works, supply and demand." (para. 16)

   Wage means _____

Reading Selection **4**

Web Article

People Respond to Economic Incentives

MyReadingLab™
Complete this **Exercise**
at **myreadinglab.com**

Preview Questions

1. Experts in economics believe that people with health insurance are more likely to be obese than people without health insurance. Do you agree with this view? Why, or why not?

2. Based on the above claim, is it reasonable to assume that we are likely to find obese people in a robust economy and to see thinner or fewer obese people in a sluggish or weak economy? Use clear examples to support your answer.

3. Other than economic reasons, what factors contribute to obesity? Be specific.

Collaboration

Pre-Reading Vocabulary: Focus on Some Key Terms

Before beginning the reading selection, it may be helpful to focus on the meaning of some key words in the article. Working with a partner, try to guess the meaning of these words. Then look up the words in a dictionary.

Word	Your Definition	Dictionary Definition
potential		
decline		
moderate		
incur		
reimburse		

People Respond to Economic Incentives

By R. Glenn Hubbard and Anthony Patrick O'Brien, 2013

1   Many obese people have several medical conditions. Obesity is an unfortunate medical problem that these obese people cannot control. For some people obesity is the result of diet and lifestyle. Potential explanations for the increase in obesity include eating fast foods, lack of exercise, and a decline in physical activity. The CDC recommends that teenagers get a minimum of 60 minutes of aerobic exercise per day. Only 15 percent of high school students met this standard in 2011. In 1960, 50 percent of jobs in the United States required at least moderate physical activity. By 2010, only 20 percent of jobs did. As a result, the typical worker was burning off about 130 fewer calories per workday.

2   Could health insurance be a cause of obesity? Obese people have many medical problems and incur higher medical costs. Overweight people with health insurance that will reimburse them for only part of their medical bills must pay some

or all of these higher medical bills. Overweight people with health insurance that covers most of their medical bills will not pay a large cost. In other words, by reducing some of the costs of obesity, health insurance may give people an economic incentive to gain weight. At first, this argument may seem illogical. Some people suffer from medical conditions that can make physical activity difficult or that can cause weight gain even with moderate eating. These people may become overweight. Some people are overweight due to poor eating habits. These people don't consider health insurance when deciding whether to have another slice of chocolate cake or to watch television instead of going to the gym. If economists are correct about the importance of economic incentives, then we would expect that people with health insurance will be more likely to be overweight than people without health insurance.

3   Jay Bhattacharya and Kate Bundorf of Stanford University, Noemi Pace of University College London, and Neeraj Sood of the RAND Corporation, a research center, have analyzed the effects of health insurance on weight. Using a sample that followed nearly 80,000 people during the years 1989–2004, they found that after controlling for income, education, race, gender, age, and other factors, people with health insurance are significantly more likely to be overweight than are people without health insurance. Having private health insurance increased BMI by 1.3 points, and having public health insurance, such as Medicaid, which is a program under which the government provides health care to low-income people, increased BMI by 2.3 points. These findings suggest that people respond to economic incentives even when making decisions about what they eat and how much they exercise.

from Glenn R. Hubbard and Anthony P. O'Brien, *Economics*, 4e, pp. 6–7

Reading Comprehension Check

MyReadingLab™
Complete this **Exercise**
at **myreadinglab.com**

1. "Jay Bhattacharya and Kate Bundorf of Stanford University, Noemi Pace of University College London, and Neeraj Sood of the RAND Corporation, a research center, have **analyzed** the effects of health insurance on weight." (para. 3) The word *analyzed* in the above context means
   a. discarded.   c. emptied.
   b. cleaned.   d. examined.

2. The author's main idea is that
   a. health insurance cannot be a cause of obesity.
   b. people without health insurance are more likely to be obese than those who have health insurance.
   c. people with health insurance are more likely to be obese than those who do not have health insurance.
   d. people with health insurance are less likely to be obese than those who do not have health insurance.

3. Which of the following statements is NOT true?
   a. People without health insurance are more likely to be overweight.
   b. Some people become overweight whether they have health insurance or not.
   c. Some people are overweight due to poor eating habits.
   d. Some people watch television instead of going to the gym.

4. "Overweight people with health insurance that will reimburse them for only part of their medical bills or who have no health insurance must pay some or all of these higher medical bills themselves. Overweight people with health insurance that covers most of their medical bills will not suffer as large a monetary cost from being obese." (para. 2) It can be inferred from the above passage that
   a. obese people with health insurance usually incur a heavy cost.
   b. there may be an economic incentive for people with health insurance to gain weight.
   c. people without health insurance have an economic incentive to gain weight.
   d. people do not buy health insurance because they are obese.

5. "Some people suffer from medical conditions that can make physical activity difficult or that can cause weight gain even with moderate eating. These people may become overweight. Some people are overweight due to poor eating habits. These people don't consider health insurance when deciding whether to have another slice of chocolate cake or to watch television instead of going to the gym." (para. 2) A logical conclusion drawn from the above passage is that
   a. people who eat moderately usually have health insurance.
   b. people with poor eating habits do not wish to purchase health insurance.
   c. some people gain weight despite doing physical activity on a regular basis.
   d. some people may not have health insurance in mind when they eat unhealthy foods or live a sedentary life.

Collaboration

Exploring the Topic

Working in small groups, discuss the following questions to review the content of the article you have just read.

1. The article begins with the statement "Many obese people have several medical conditions." Discuss the medical conditions that are caused by obesity.

2. According to the article, how is health insurance a cause of obesity? Refer to the article and find specific reasons to support your answer.

3. The author concludes, "These findings suggest that people respond to economic incentives even when making decisions about what they eat and how much they exercise." Discuss the meaning of this statement.

Post-Reading Vocabulary

Without using a dictionary, determine the meaning of the bolded words from the context.

1. "At first, this argument may seem **illogical**." (para. 2)

   Illogical means _____

2. "In other words, by reducing some of the costs of obesity, health insurance may give people an economic **incentive** to gain weight." (para. 2)

   Incentive means _____

3. "Using a sample that followed nearly 80,000 people during the years 1989–2004, they found that after controlling for income, education, race, gender, age, and other factors, people with health insurance are **significantly** more likely to be overweight than are people without health insurance." (para. 3)

   Significantly means _____

Panel Discussion on China Becoming the World's Second Largest Economy

Recently China surpassed Japan as the world's second largest economy. As you know, the United States still remains the world's largest economy. However, China's amazing economic growth has concerned the United States, Europe, and some other countries in Asia such as Japan and South Korea. As a panelist, participate in a panel discussion and exchange views on how the United States can continue to be the world's largest economy. What follows are some profiles for you and your peers. However, you can create your own profile as long as it is appropriate for the panel discussion.

1. U.S. president
2. chairman of the U.S. Federal Reserve
3. CEO of an American corporation
4. CEO of a Chinese corporation
5. Chinese president
6. Chinese economist
7. U.S. economist
8. member of the European Union
9. South Korean president
10. Asian economist

Use the following questions to prepare for the panel discussion. Keep in mind that you may come up with more questions as you listen to other panelists.

1. How did China become the world's second largest economy so quickly?

2. Is China's economic growth a threat to the United States and Europe? If so, what can the United States do to maintain its supremacy as the world's largest economy?

3. Japan is worried about its economic growth being stifled by that of China. Is this a valid concern? If so, what can Japan do to remain a key player in the global economy?

4. If China continues to grow as an economic power, what other countries or institutions might be affected by its growth?

During the panel discussion, your arguments will be based on your profile. After you choose a profile, be sure to take a position. Then build arguments that strengthen your position. Your instructor will provide you with specific guidelines on how to participate in a panel discussion.

WRITING CONNECTIONS: *Paraphrasing*

6 LEARNING OBJECTIVE
Effectively paraphrase

Paraphrasing is restating an idea written by another author, keeping the important bits and pieces of information from the original text. It is important to note that when you paraphrase an original statement, you must use your own words. The key to paraphrasing is changing the language completely without altering the meaning expressed in the original statement. In college, your professor may ask you to orally paraphrase an original idea to check your understanding. Your professor also may give you a writing assignment that requires you to paraphrase an author's most important ideas.

Let's look at an example to fully understand how to paraphrase an original statement. First, read the original statement made by an author. Then read the four paraphrases carefully. Finally, decide which is the best paraphrase.

Example

The ability to acquire goods at a lower opportunity cost (and thereby increase the total amount of goods and services available for consumption) is why free trade—trade that is not hindered by artificial restrictions or trade barriers—is generally supported by economists (Rolf, 2009, p. 14).

from William D. Rolf, *Introduction to Economic Reasoning*, 8e, 2009, p. 14

1. The ability to acquire goods at a lower opportunity cost is why free trade is generally supported by economists.

2. William Rolf (2009) states that economists support free trade that is not hindered by artificial restrictions or trade barriers.

3. Most economists like the concept of free trade whereby businesses find goods at a lower cost and provide them to consumers at a competitive price.

4. According to William Rolf (2009), most economists like the concept of free trade whereby businesses purchase goods at a lower cost and provide them to consumers at a competitive price.

Let's take a look at each of the paraphrased sentences and determine which is the best paraphrase of the original statement.

1. **This paraphrase is a clear example of plagiarism.** Notice that all the writer has done is simply repeat the original statement word for word. In this case, the writer has committed an academic crime.

2. **This is a slightly better paraphrase than the first one.** However, it is still not acceptable because the writer has copied information from the original statement. The writer does acknowledge the source by saying, "William Rolf (2009) states that …," but the rest of the sentence is copied.

3. **This is probably the best paraphrase so far, but there is a problem.** The writer does not tell the reader who made the original statement. It is clear that the writer changed the language completely without changing the meaning. However, the writer forgot to mention William Rolf, who made the original statement. For this reason, this paraphrase is not acceptable.

4. **We hope you agree that this is the best paraphrase for the following reasons.** First, the writer acknowledges the source. Second, the language of the paraphrase is very different from that of the original statement. Finally, the writer has maintained the idea in the original statement. For all of these reasons, the last paraphrase is the best.

Let's wrap up what you have learned so far. A good paraphrase should

- acknowledge the source (McCormick argues that …);
- use completely different language (use synonyms for the key important points); and
- maintain the idea expressed in the original statement. Keep in mind that while you must use your own words, you cannot change the idea or meaning stated in the original statement.

Last but not least, beware of plagiarism. It is tempting to simply copy words from the original text. As you know, this is plagiarism, an academic crime. Try to use your own words as you paraphrase. If you cannot think of a synonym to replace a word in the original statement, use a thesaurus to find an appropriate synonym. Always remind yourself that a good paraphrase changes the language completely but retains the original idea. The more you practice paraphrasing, the more you will be able to express thoughts using your own words.

EXERCISE 5 Paraphrasing

You have learned about the characteristics of a good paraphrase. It is time now for you to practice writing your own paraphrase. Read the following statement carefully and write a paraphrase. Keep in mind the three key elements of a good paraphrase: source, different language, original meaning.

"Most U.S. businesses, from industrial giants like Ford Motor Company and General Electric to small firms like your neighborhood barbershop or hair salon, are private operations, not government-owned enterprises" (Rolf, 2009, p. 49).

from William D. Rolf, *Introduction to Economic Reasoning*, 8e, 2009, p. 49

Write your paraphrase of this statement here:

_____

_____

_____

_____

After you write the paraphrase, answer the following questions by circling either Yes or No.

1. Do you think you used your own words to restate the original idea? In other words, did you change the language of the original statement completely?

                    Yes   No

2. Does your paraphrased sentence convey the same idea expressed in the original statement?

                    Yes   No

3. Did you acknowledge the source? In other words, did you mention the author of the original statement?

                    Yes   No

If you answered "yes" to all of the above questions, then your paraphrased sentence is a good representation of the idea expressed in the original statement.

Keep practicing paraphrasing, and your ability to restate other people's ideas in writing will improve significantly.

READING

Reading Selection **5**
_____

Web Article

MyReadingLab™
Complete this **Exercise**
at **myreadinglab.com**

Food Prices Rising, but No Shortage in U.S.
Tight Supplies May Ultimately Force Americans to Adjust Diets

---

Preview Questions

1. Have you visited grocery stores in foreign countries? If you have, describe how they are different from the grocery stores in the United States. Be specific.

2. Experts believe that food costs in the United States will continue to climb in the coming years. If this were to be true, what food items would you be willing to sacrifice to use your money wisely?

3. In your opinion, why are food prices rising constantly? Discuss what can be done to keep the food prices steady.

Collaboration

Pre-Reading Vocabulary: Focus on Some Key Terms

Before beginning the reading selection, it may be helpful to focus on the meaning of some key words in the article. Working with a partner, try to guess the meaning of these words. Then look up the words in a dictionary.

Word	Your Definition	Dictionary Definition
hallmark		
abundance		
cattle		
grain		
shortage		

Food Prices Rising, but No Shortage in U.S.
Tight Supplies May Ultimately Force Americans to Adjust Diets

By Allison Linn

Charlie Riedel / AP file

1   Ask a foreigner what's different about the United States, and one of the first things you'll often hear about is our grocery stores—those endlessly long aisles piled high with grains, produce, and meat. For many visitors, it's a hallmark of America's abundance. For us, it's a constant reminder that, whatever problems we may face here, we live in the land of plenty.

2   Now, there is news that some wholesale clubs appear to be seeing a run on food items such as rice. This is raising the question of whether Americans could ever face a situation many of us can't even understand—a shortage of the food we take for granted.

3   The good news: Experts say the short answer is no. "I really don't see any chance of that," said Jerry Bange, chair of the World Agriculture Outlook Board for the Department of Agriculture.

4   Still, that doesn't mean Americans aren't facing any food woes. The price of foods such as corn, wheat and rice have risen in recent years. Also, the cost increases are not expected to go away any time soon. For Americans, that means higher prices for everything from bread to meat, since cattle and other animals are raised on a grain-based diet.

5   Americans also are seeing the tightest supply of wheat since 1946, and soybean supplies also are uncommonly low. Although there is by no means a shortage, the situation could become problematic if weather patterns make for poor crops in the coming seasons.

6   In addition, because of free trade agreements U.S. food prices and supplies are much more dependent on what's going on in the rest of the world. We are affected by a drought in Australia or a weakening of Brazil's currency.

7   Food prices are rising, and supplies are tightening, for a number of reasons. These include a growing middle class in the developing world that is buying more food and an increase in the price of fuel used to produce and transport food. Another factor is a move to plant more crops for ethanol and other biofuels instead of food. Weather also has been a factor, and a weak U.S. dollar has affected the situation.

8   "If you just take one (of these factors) away, we wouldn't have this," said Chris Hurt, agricultural economist with Purdue University. "It's because these things are happening together."

MSNBC.com, April 29, 2008. Copyright © 2008 by MSNBC Interactive News, LLC.

MyReadingLab™
Complete this **Exercise**
at **myreadinglab.com**

Reading Comprehension Check

1. "Ask a foreigner what's different about the United States, and one of the first things you'll often hear about is our grocery stores—those endlessly long aisles **piled** high with grains, produce, and meat." (para. 1) The word *piled* in this context means
   a. discarded.   c. emptied.
   b. cleaned.   d. loaded.

2. The author's main idea is that
   a. food prices are not rising in the United States.
   b. the current increase in food costs has caused a food shortage in the United States.
   c. Americans may eventually be affected by the rising food costs.
   d. food prices are rising worldwide, but America is not affected at all.

3. Which of the following statements is NOT true?
   a. There is a food shortage in the United States.
   b. The price of corn, wheat, and rice has risen in the United States.
   c. Animals are raised on a grain-based diet.
   d. More crops are planted for ethanol and other biofuels.

4. "Now, there is news that some wholesale clubs appear to be seeing a run on food items such as rice. This is raising the question of whether Americans could ever face a situation many of us can't even understand—a shortage of the food we take for granted." (para. 2) It can be inferred from this passage that
   a. regardless of what happens to food prices, there will never be a shortage of food in the United States.
   b. if food prices continue to rise worldwide, there might be a shortage of food in the United States in the future.
   c. Americans do not need to worry about a food shortage because food will always be plentiful.
   d. the price of rice will go down in the near future.

5. "In addition, because of free trade agreements U.S. food prices and supplies are much more dependent on what's going on in the rest of the world. We are affected by a drought in Australia or a weakening of Brazil's currency." (para. 6) A logical conclusion drawn from this passage is that
   a. U.S. food prices will only be affected if there is a drought in Australia.
   b. U.S. food prices will never rise no matter what happens in the rest of the world.
   c. what goes on in the world has no effect on U.S. food prices and supplies.
   d. global factors may affect U.S. food prices and supplies.

Exploring the Topic

Collaboration

Discuss the following questions to review the content of the article you have just read.

1. According to the article, why aren't rising food costs a concern for the United States?

2. How may free trade agreements affect U.S. food costs and supply? Give specific reasons to support your answer.

3. The article mentions that U.S. food prices are rising, and that supplies are limited because of a number of reasons. What are the reasons, and what can be done to avoid a severe food crisis in the United States? Be specific.

Post-Reading Vocabulary

Without using a dictionary, determine the meaning of the bolded words from the context.

1. "For us, it's a constant reminder that, whatever problems we may face here, we live in the land of **plenty**." (para. 1)

   Plenty means _____

2. "Still, that doesn't mean Americans aren't facing any food **woes**." (para. 4)

   Woes means _____

3. "We are **affected** by a drought in Australia or a weakening of Brazil's currency." (para. 6)

   Affected means _____

TEXTBOOK APPLICATION   **Economics Defined**

The purpose of this exercise is to get you acquainted with the type of reading you will be required to do in college. First, listen to the lecture and take notes. You can listen to the lecture by scanning the QR code on the next page with your smart phone. Your professor may also read the selections or play the audio file in class. Make sure that you write down the important points of the lecture.

Collaboration

Group Discussion

Working in small groups of three to four students, answer the following questions. Your instructor may ask you to share your answers with your classmates. As you refer to your notes, it is best to write brief answers to each of the questions below using your own words. After the discussion, you will have an opportunity to share your findings with your peers.

1. What comes to your mind when you hear the word *economics?* Define the term in your own words and give at least one example to support your definition.

2. Discuss how economics influences our lives and give specific examples to support your answer.

3. According to the lecture, what kinds of questions do economists try to answer? Why do you think it is important to address these questions? Explain.

4. Give specific examples of goods and services and tell why they are provided. Consider if all kinds of goods and services are necessary for people. In your opinion, what goods and services are absolutely necessary for people?

5. How is the decision to produce goods and provide services made? What possible changes do you see in the goods and services provided in the near future with the advancements in science and technology? Be specific.

6. In the modern world, technology has made significant progress. In some cases, it has replaced human workers with machines. Do you think that machines will eventually destroy jobs for people, or do you believe that mechanization and technological change are good for humanity? Explain your answer.

7. According to the lecture, Americans earn more than Europeans, and Europeans earn more than Asians and Africans. Similarly, college graduates make more

money than high school graduates. In your opinion, what factors determine the incomes people earn? Give specific examples to support your answer.

Now that you have discussed the highlights of the lecture with your classmates, read the following selection and answer the multiple-choice questions that follow.

Economics Defined

By Robin Blade and Michael Parkin

1   Economics is the social science that studies the choices that individuals, businesses, governments, and entire societies make as they cope with *scarcity*, the *incentives* that influence those choices, and the arrangements that coordinate them.

Scan this code using your smart phone to listen to an audio version of this reading

2   The subject is extremely broad and touches all aspects of our lives. To get beyond this definition of economics, you need to understand the kinds of questions that economists try to answer and the way they think and go about seeking those answers.

3   We begin with some key economic questions. Although the scope of economics is broad and the range of questions that economists address is equally broad, two big questions provide a useful summary of the scope of economics:

- How do choices end up determining *what*, *how*, and for *whom* goods and services get produced?
- When do choices made in the pursuit of *self-interest* also promote the *social interest*?

What, How, and for Whom?

4   Goods and services are the objects and actions that people value and produce to satisfy human wants. Goods are *objects* that satisfy wants. Running shoes and ketchup are examples. Services are *actions* that satisfy wants. Haircuts and rock concerts are examples. We produce a dazzling array of goods and services that range from necessities such as food, houses, and health care to leisure items such as DVD players and roller coaster rides.

What?

5   What determines the quantities of corn we grow, homes we build, and health-care services we produce? Sixty years ago, 25 percent of Americans worked on a farm. That number has shrunk to less than 3 percent today. Over the same period, the number of people who produce goods—in mining, construction, and manufacturing—has also shrunk, from 30 percent to 20 percent. The decrease in farming and the production of goods is matched by an increase in the production of services. How will these quantities change in the future as ongoing changes in technology make an ever-wider array of goods and services available to us?

How?

6   How are goods and services produced? In a vineyard in France, basket-carrying workers pick the annual grape crop by hand. In a vineyard in California, a huge machine and a few workers do the same job that a hundred grape pickers in France do. Look around you and you will see many examples of this phenomenon—the same job being done in different ways. In some stores, check-out clerks key in prices. In others, they use a laser scanner. One farmer keeps track of his livestock feeding schedules and inventories by using paper-and-pencil records, while another uses a personal computer. GM hires workers to weld auto bodies in some of its plants and uses robots to do the job in others.

7   Why do we use machines in some cases and people in others? Do mechaniza-tion and technological change destroy more jobs than they create? Do they make us better off or worse off?

For Whom?

8   For whom are goods and services produced? The answer to this question depends on the incomes that people earn and the prices they pay for the goods and services they buy. At given prices, a person who has a high income is able to buy more goods and services than a person who has a low income. Doctors earn much higher incomes than do nurses and medical assistants, so doctors get more of the goods and services produced than nurses and medical assistants get.

9   You probably know about many other persistent differences in incomes. Men, on the average, earn more than women. Whites, on the average, earn more than minorities. College graduates, on the average, earn more than high school gradu-ates. Americans, on the average, earn more than Europeans, who in turn earn more, on the average, than Asians and Africans. But there are some significant exceptions. The people of Japan and Hong Kong now earn an average income similar to that of Americans. And there is a lot of income inequality throughout the world.

10   What determines the incomes we earn? Why do doctors earn larger incomes than nurses? Why do men earn more, on average, than women? Why do college graduates earn more, on average, than high school graduates? Why do Americans earn more, on average, than Africans?

11   Economics explains how the choices that individuals, businesses, and govern-ments make and the interactions of those choices end up determining what, how, and for whom goods and services get produced. In answering these questions, we have a deeper agenda in mind. We're not interested in just knowing how many DVD players get produced, how they get produced, and who gets to enjoy them. We ultimately want to know the answer to the second big economic question that we'll now explore.

from Robin Bade and Michael Parkin, *Foundations of Microeconomics*, 5e, pp. 3–4.

Reading Comprehension Check

MyReadingLab™
Complete this Exercise
at **myreadinglab.com**

1. As used in the sentence, "Economics is the social science that studies the choices that individuals, businesses, governments, and entire societies make as they **cope** with *scarcity*, the *incentives* that influence those choices, and the arrangements that coordinate them," (para. 1) the word *cope* means
   a. struggle.
   b. entertain.
   c. purchase.
   d. fail.

2. As used in the sentence, "Economics is the social science that studies the choices that individuals, businesses, governments, and entire societies make as they cope with **scarcity**, the *incentives* that influence those choices, and the arrangements that coordinate them," (para. 1) the word *scarcity* means
   a. plentiful.
   b. shortages.
   c. abundance.
   d. sufficient.

3. "Economics is the social science that studies the choices that individuals, businesses, governments, and entire societies make as they cope with *scarcity*, the **incentives** that influence those choices, and the arrangements that coordinate them." (para. 1) In the sentence above, the word *incentives* means
   a. punishment.
   b. discouragement.
   c. disadvantages.
   d. rewards.

4. In the sentence, "The subject is extremely **broad** and touches all aspects of our lives," (para. 2) the word *broad* means
   a. specific.
   b. narrow.
   c. general.
   d. limited.

5. The main idea of the essay is that
   a. economics is the social science that solely focuses on the goods people purchase.
   b. economics studies the choices people, businesses, governments, and societies make about the production of goods and services.
   c. economics is a discipline that is only interested in the goods companies produce.
   d. economics only focuses on the services businesses provide to people in all societies.

6. Which of the following is not used as an example of goods and services produced in the passage?
   a. food
   b. health care
   c. flowers
   d. DVD players

7. According to the passage, which of the following statements is true?
   a. Goods are objects that do not satisfy wants.
   b. Services are actions that do not satisfy wants.
   c. DVD players and roller coaster rides are not produced to satisfy human wants.
   d. Businesses produce goods and services that satisfy human wants.

8. According to the passage, which of the following statements is false?
   a. In a vineyard in France, basket-carrying workers pick the annual grape crop by hand.
   b. In a vineyard in California, a huge machine and a few workers do the same job that a hundred grape pickers in France do.
   c. One farmer keeps track of his livestock feeding schedules and inventories by using paper-and-pencil records, while another uses a personal computer.
   d. All around the world, it takes people the same amount of time and effort to do each every task.

9. "What determines the quantities of corn we grow, homes we build, and health-care services we produce? Sixty years ago, 25 percent of Americans worked on a farm. That number has shrunk to less than 3 percent today. Over the same period, the number of people who produce goods—in mining, construction, and manufacturing—has also shrunk, from 30 percent to 20 percent. The decrease in farming and the production of goods is matched by an increase in the production of services. How will these quantities change in the future as ongoing changes in technology make an ever-wider array of goods and services available to us?" (para. 5) Which of the following conclusions can be drawn from the passage?
   a. Only 25 percent of the American people work on a farm today.
   b. 20 percent of Americans produced goods sixty years ago.
   c. Compared to sixty years ago, more Americans are spending money on services today.
   d. Only 30 percent of Americans produce goods today.

10. "You probably know about many other persistent differences in incomes. Men, on the average, earn more than women. Whites, on the average, earn more than minorities. College graduates, on the average, earn more than high school graduates. Americans, on the average, earn more than Europeans, who in turn earn more, on the average, than Asians and Africans. But there are some significant exceptions. The people of Japan and Hong Kong now earn an average income similar to that of Americans. And there is a lot of income inequality throughout the world." (para. 9) According to the passage, which of the following conclusions cannot be drawn?
   a. Men usually earn more than women.
   b. College graduates usually earn more than high school graduates.
   c. The people of Japan and Hong Kong earn more than Americans.
   d. Asians and Africans earn less than Europeans.

The Internet can be a powerful and effective research tool once you have learned how to successfully limit your information searches and have learned how to interpret the results of your search with a critical lens.

**INTERNET FACT
SEARCH**

Economics

Instructions: First try to use logic and background knowledge in guessing the correct answers to the following data questions. Then, go online and search for the relevant data. Be sure to write the Web source next to your research finding.

1. Which country is the second largest economy in the world?
   a. United States
   b. Japan
   c. Germany
   d. China

   Your guess: _____   Research finding: _____

   Web source: _____

2. Who is the world's largest automobile manufacturer?
   a. General Motors
   b. Tata Motors
   c. Toyota
   d. Volkswagen Group

   Your guess: _____   Research finding: _____

   Web source: _____

3. How many gallons of gasoline and diesel fuel were used by cars and light trucks around the world in 2007?
   a. 150 billion
   b. 260 billion
   c. 300 billion
   d. 350 billion

   Your guess: _____   Research finding: _____

   Web source: _____

4. What percentage of the world's population do the American people make up?
   a. 2
   b. 3.5
   c. 4
   d. 5

   Your guess: _____   Research finding: _____

   Web source: _____

5. What percentage of the world's global energy supply do the American people consume?
   a. 5
   b. 10
   c. 20
   d. 25

   Your guess: _____   Research finding: _____

   Web source: _____

FORMAL PRESENTATION PROJECTS

Choose a topic related to one of the aspects of economics. Then speak to your instructor about whether it is appropriate for a class presentation. Your instructor will give you specific guidelines on how to give a formal presentation. You might want to write your speech and practice it before you present to the class.

MyReadingLab™   For more help with **Note Taking** and **Paraphrasing**, go to your learning path in **MyReadingLab.com**.

LITERATURE

5

Learning Objectives

IN THIS CHAPTER, YOU WILL LEARN TO . . .

1. Describe the discipline of literature
2. Identify fundamental literary terms
3. Avoid plagiarism
4. Write an accurate summary
5. Recognize an author's tone and purpose

INTRODUCTION TO THE DISCIPLINE OF LITERATURE

1 LEARNING OBJECTIVE
Describe the discipline
of literature

Literature depicts life in all its shining colors. Whether we are reading a poem or a play, reading a story or a novel, love and hate, romance and tragedy, jealousy and compassion take center stage and challenge the way we see the world around us. In this chapter, you will have a chance to read some poems, a story, a scene from a play, and a chapter from a great novel. You will also read about how technology, in the form of audio and e-books, is changing the way we interact with literature.

Reading into a Photo

Working in a small group, examine the following photograph and answer the questions that follow.

1. In your opinion, what action is taking place?
2. What message does this image convey to you?

Follow Your Interests

Collaboration

Review the set of questions below that literature majors might explore. Check off the three or four questions that are most interesting to you.

1. Do you have a favorite novel or a favorite author? What book or author would you recommend to a friend, and why?
2. What are the purposes of reading beyond a class assignment or preparing for an exam?

3. Many teachers and parents are concerned that America is becoming a nation of non-readers. Why do you think this is the case?

4. What can be done to inspire more people to read for pleasure?

5. Bookstores across America are worried that traditional printed books are going to disappear because of the increasing popularity of audio and e-books. Do you think paper-based text will become extinct?

6. Given the choice, would you prefer reading a printed book or a technology-based text, such as an audio book, an e-book, or online material? Explain your preference.

7. There are many types of literature: novels, short stories, poetry, plays, etc. If you were required to read a piece of literature and were given a choice, which of the above types would you select? Explain your choice.

8. What literary genres are most interesting to you: romance, horror, mystery, comedy, tragedy, or adventure?

9. The United States is known for honoring freedom of speech, yet there have been multiple cases throughout American history where works of literature have been censored. What would cause an institution, such as a library or a public school, to ban a piece of literature?

10. In many countries where there are stricter limits on people's freedom of expression, certain authors are completely banned from publishing their works. Why is literature sometimes considered "dangerous" to society?

11. A writer composes a short work of fiction, uploads the file, and moments later his or her work is available worldwide. How has the Internet changed the concept of "audience," and how will this affect the way we view literature?

12. If you just completed reading a novel that you enjoyed greatly and then found out that the author plagiarized (stole ideas from) another author, would this matter to you? Would you feel that you have been wronged as a reader?

13. If you were asked to write a creative piece for a literature class, what topics do you think you would write about? Explain your choices.

14. Most writers are influenced by their local environment. For example, a Louisiana native might write about fishing or Hurricane Katrina. Do you think a writer's creative imagination can overcome cultural barriers?

Now, share your choices with a small group of classmates and discuss why these particular questions are most interesting to you. Discuss your answers to the questions you chose and ask your partners which questions they found most interesting.

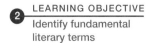

Key Terms in the Field of Literature

The following key terms are frequently used in the discipline of literature. If you take a college-level literature course, it will be important for you to remember these words and to be able to use them in your speech and writing. Review the words below and answer the multiple-choice questions that follow.

alliteration	irony	scene
character	metaphor	setting
conflict	personification	stanza
dialogue	plot	symbolism
foreshadowing	point of view	tone

EXERCISE 1   Inferring Meaning from Context

Read each sentence below and try to derive the meaning of the bolded key terms from the context. Circle the correct definition of each italicized term.

1. An example of a **dialogue** from a William Faulkner story follows:

   " 'I want some poison,' she said to the druggist."

   " 'Yes, Miss Emily. What kind? For rats and such?' "

   A *dialogue* is
   a. a tragedy.
   b. an exchange of words between characters.
   c. a comparison of ideas.
   d. a term used only in poetry.

2. An example of **symbolism** follows: After my girlfriend left, the sky grew dark and cold. *Symbolism* is when
   a. an object or situation charged with meaning suggests another thing.
   b. meaning is lost.
   c. a scene is both tragic and comic.
   d. animals act like people.

3. The new play has three principle **characters.** A *character* is
   a. always evil.
   b. an object of affection.
   c. a setting.
   d. a person (or being) in a literary work.

4. The **plot** of a romantic novel often involves three stages: finding love, enjoying love, and losing love. A *plot* is
   a. the ending of a story.
   b. a particular scene in a story.
   c. the episodes in a narrative work; that is, what happens.
   d. the beginning of a narrative.

5. The novel I am reading is told from the **point of view** of a single mother in New Orleans around the time of Hurricane Katrina. *Point of view* means
   a. opinion.
   b. the perspective from which a story is told.
   c. what can be seen within a certain distance.
   d. a sharp point.

6. The **setting** of his new play is Paris, France, on a rainy winter afternoon. The *setting* is
   a. what happens in a story.
   b. why a character acts the way he or she does.
   c. the time and place of a story, play, or poem.
   d. always dark and rainy.

7. The central **conflict** of the play is that the husband is jealous of his new tenant's sexual appeal. *Conflict* means
   a. a struggle between a character and some obstacle.
   b. a solution to a problem.
   c. a resolution.
   d. the selling point of a work of art.

8. An example of **alliteration** follows: The fruit of the fig tree frequently tastes fabulous. *Alliteration* is when
   a. an object is personified.
   b. consonant sounds are repeated.
   c. rhyming words are repeated.
   d. literature is translated.

9. An example of **irony** follows:

   Bob is tired of all of his neighbors and wants to be left alone. The door rings, he answers it and says to his neighbor Joe, "It is so great to see you!" *Irony* means
   a. anything funny.
   b. predictable behavior in any form.
   c. not believing in anyone or anything.
   d. in verbal form, the contrast between what is said and what is meant.

10. My favorite **scene** in the novel is when Santiago meets the alchemist. *Scene* means
    a. the part of a chapter where the most action happens.
    b. the unit of a play or story in which the setting is unchanged and the time continuous.
    c. a pause from any action or dialogue in a dramatic work of fiction.
    d. a display of emotion which takes place early in a work of fiction and steers the story in one direction or another.

11. Two examples of **metaphor** follow: 1. "That book is garbage." 2. "Her smile lights up the sky." A *metaphor* can be described as
    a. figurative language.
    b. make-believe language.
    c. rhyming slang.
    d. unsubstantiated facts.

12. An example of **foreshadowing** in the play is when Julius Caesar receives the kiss of death in an early scene. *Foreshadowing* means
    a. a suggestion of what is to come.
    b. a killing.
    c. an act of kindness followed by an act of ill will.
    d. a light shining down.

13. I love the third **stanza** of the poem when he writes, "life is the death of life." *Stanza* means
    a. chapter.
    b. the rhyming scheme in a poem.
    c. an instance of plot in poetry.
    d. a group of lines forming a unit in a poem.

14. The following is an example of **personification**: "The trees ached and cried out for love." *Personification* means
    a. when a person is given characteristics of non-living objects.
    b. when an inanimate object, animal, or other non-human is given human traits.
    c. a dialogue between nature and humans.
    d. the exhibition of dialogue between two unrelated characters in a play or other dramatic work.

15. In the Langston Hughes's poem we read in class, the author's **tone** was light-hearted and comical. *Tone* means
    a. attitude or mood.
    b. purpose.
    c. dialogue and setting.
    d. manner of movement.

Collaboration

 **EXERCISE 2**   Creating Meaningful Sentences with the Key Terms

Working with a partner, choose five of the key terms in literature and write an original sentence about each one.

1. Word = _____

_____

_____

2. Word = _____

_____

_____

3. Word = _____

_____

_____

4. Word = _____

_____

_____

5. Word = _____

_____

_____

READINESS FOR COLLEGE SUCCESS
Avoiding Plagiarism

LEARNING OBJECTIVE
3 Avoid plagiarism

As you make your way through your first years of college, it is important to develop the habit of expressing yourself in writing in your own words. Whether you are writing an essay, a research paper, or simply answering homework assignment questions, you need to cite any words, or ideas, borrowed from someone else.

Plagiarism is copying the work of others and turning it in as your own. If you plagiarize, you run a terrible risk of being punished or even expelled from college. Gordon Harvey of Harvard University provides a wonderful analogy to explain the crime of plagiarism. He says that plagiarism is like kidnapping a baby and claiming that you have fathered the child. And the baby is too young to protest or refute the claim.

Many inexperienced college students plagiarize by accident when they fail to cite their sources completely or correctly. Careful note taking and a better understanding of the rules for paraphrasing and direct quotation can help you avoid plagiarism.

Some Quick Tips

1. You do **NOT** have to cite
   - the results of your own research ("My research has shown that …")
   - common knowledge ("Sacramento is the capital of California")
2. You **DO** have to cite
   - others' opinions or arguments (If you are writing a paper on Toni Morrison, and find that someone named Johnson wrote, "Toni Morrison's fiction is full of beautiful shadows and light," you need to cite your source: "According to Johnson (2003) …")
   - statistics and less-known facts ("35% of Americans enjoy their e-readers." Well, where did you get this information?)
3. When you choose to use someone's words directly, use quotation marks.

   Stanley, in her essay entitled "Morrison's Voice," makes the point that, "Toni Morrison's fiction is full of beautiful shadows and light."

- If you choose to paraphrase another's words, you still need to cite your source clearly, so be sure to include an in-text citation.

    Kevin Jones (2007) compares August Wilson's plays to great works of American jazz.

- Be sure to introduce the material you have chosen to quote, paraphrase, or summarize in the first sentence. In other words, make it clear that what comes next is someone else's idea.

    - According to Jones …
    - Cutler says …
    - In his 2006 report, Givens showed …

- Be careful to avoid misplaced citations. If you use a direct quotation or paraphrase, you should place the reference at the very end of all the material cited. Any quoted, paraphrased, or summarized material that comes *after* the reference is plagiarized in that it will appear as your words and not someone else's.

    Example of a misplaced citation: Burrows (2009) argues that "poetry has no place in American schools." Poetry is boring for students and should be left for independent study time.

    Discuss with a classmate: Why is the above an example of plagiarism? How can the reference be made correct?

    _____

    _____

    Let's look at one more example of "accidental plagiarism" and discuss how plagiarism can be avoided.

    Mystery writing is so exciting. It "livens the soul and turns us into detectives."

    _____

    The best advice for avoiding plagiarism is to develop more confidence in your own ideas and your own writing voice. You can still integrate interesting ideas from other writers, but when you do, make sure to give credit where credit is due.

READING

Reading Selection **1**

Short Story

MyReadingLab™
Complete this **Exercise**
at **myreadinglab.com**

Samuel

_____

Preview Questions

1. What are the greatest potential dangers to young children growing up in big cities?

2. What do you think is an appropriate age for parents to permit their children to travel around on mass transit without an adult chaperone? Explain your opinion.

3. The story you are about to read is suspenseful. Do you enjoy suspenseful movies, stories, or TV programs? If yes, share a few examples.

Collaboration

Pre-Reading Vocabulary: Focus on Some Key Terms

Before beginning the reading selection, it may be helpful to focus on the meaning of some key words in the article. Working with a partner, try to guess the meaning of these words. Then look up the words in a dictionary.

Word	Your Definition	Dictionary Definition
accelerate		
blush		
bawling		
hiss		
abandoned		

Collaboration

Pre- and Post-Reading Checklist

Before jumping into the story, it might be helpful to consider the many different ways to interpret a short story. Read through the checklist questions below with a partner. To make sure you fully understand each item, try to rephrase each question in your own words.

After reading the story, you will be asked to go back to the checklist and answer each of the questions.

Responding to Stories

PLOT	☐ Does the plot grow out of the characters, or does it depend on chance or coincidence?
	☐ Does surprise play an important role, or does foreshadowing?
	☐ What conflicts does the story include?
	☐ Are certain episodes narrated out of chronological order?
CHARACTER	☐ Which character chiefly engages your interest?
	☐ What purposes do minor characters serve?
	☐ How does the author reveal character?
	☐ Is the behavior plausible—that is, are the characters well motivated?
	☐ If a character changes, why and how does he or she change?
	☐ Are the characters round or flat?
	☐ How has the author caused you to sympathize with certain characters?
POINT OF VIEW	☐ Who tells the story?
	☐ How does the point of view help shape the theme?
	☐ Does the narrator's language help you to construct a picture of the narrator's character, class, attitude, strengths, and limitations?

SETTING	☐ Do you have a strong sense of time and place?
	☐ What is the relation of the setting to the plot and characters?
SYMBOLISM	☐ Do certain characters seem to you to stand for something in addition to themselves?
	☐ If you do believe that the story has symbolic elements, do you think they are adequately integrated within the story, or do they strike you as being too obviously stuck in?
STYLE	☐ How would you characterize the style?
	☐ How has the point of view shaped or determined the style?
	☐ Do you think the style is consistent?
THEME	☐ Is the title informative?
	☐ Do certain passages—dialogue or description—seem to you to point especially toward the theme?
	☐ Is the meaning of the story embodied in the whole story, or does it seem conveyed chiefly by certain passages of editorializing?
	☐ Suppose someone asked you to state the point—the theme—of the story. Could you?

from Barnet, Burto, and Cain, *An Introduction to Literature*, 16e, pp. 10–11

Samuel

By **Grace Paley** (1968)

Grace Paley (1922–2007) was born in New York City. While raising two children she first focused on writing poetry and later began to write fiction. The main subject of Paley's writing is the life of little people struggling in the big city.

Grace Paley

1   Some boys are very tough. They're afraid of nothing. They are the ones who climb a wall and take a bow at the top. Not only are they brave on the roof, but they make a lot of noise in the darkest part of the cellar where even the super hates to go. They also jiggle and hop on the platform between the locked doors of the subway cars.

2   Four boys are jiggling on the swaying platform. Their names are Alfred, Calvin, Samuel, and Tom. The men and the women in the cars on either side watch them. They don't like them to jiggle or jump but don't want to interfere. Of course some of the men in the cars were once brave boys like these. One of them had ridden the tail of a speeding truck from New York to Rockaway Beach without getting off, without his sore fingers losing hold. Nothing happened to him then or later. He had made a compact with other boys who preferred to watch: Starting at Eighth Avenue and Fifteenth Street, he would get to some specified place, maybe

Twenty-third and the river, by hopping the tops of the moving trucks. This was hard to do when one truck turned a corner in the wrong direction and the nearest truck was a couple of feet too high. He made three or four starts before succeeding. He had gotten his idea from a film at school called *The Romance of Logging*. He had finished high school, married a good friend, was in a responsible job and going to night school.

3   These two men and others looked at the four boys jumping and jiggling on the platform and thought, It must be fun to ride that way, especially now the weather is nice and we're out of the tunnel and way high over the Bronx. Then they thought, These kids do seem to be acting sort of stupid. They *are* little. Then they thought of some of the brave things they had done when they were boys and jiggling didn't seem so risky.

4   The ladies in the car became very angry when they looked at the four boys. Most of them brought their brows together and hoped the boys could see their extreme disapproval. One of the ladies wanted to get up and say, Be careful you dumb kids, get off that platform or I'll call a cop. But three of the boys were Negroes and the fourth was something else she couldn't tell for sure. She was afraid they'd be fresh and laugh at her and embarrass her. She wasn't afraid they'd hit her, but she was afraid of embarrassment. Another lady thought, Their mothers never know where they are. It wasn't true in this particular case. Their mothers all knew that they had gone to see the missile exhibit on Fourteenth Street.

5   Out on the platform, whenever the train accelerated, the boys would raise their hands and point them up to the sky to act like rockets going off, then they rat-tat-tatted the shatterproof glass pane like machine guns, although no machine guns had been exhibited.

6   For some reason known only to the motorman, the train began a sudden slowdown. The lady who was afraid of embarrassment saw the boys jerk forward and backward and grab the swinging guard chains. She had her own boy at home. She stood up with determination and went to the door. She slid it open and said, "You boys will be hurt. You'll be killed. I'm going to call the conductor if you don't just go into the next car and sit down and be quiet." Two of the boys said, "Yes'm," and acted as though they were about to go. Two of them blinked their eyes a couple of times and pressed their lips together. The train resumed its speed. The door slid shut, parting the lady and the boys. She leaned against the side door because she had to get off at the next stop.

7   The boys opened their eyes wide at each other and laughed. The lady blushed. The boys looked at her and laughed harder. They began to pound each other's back. Samuel laughed the hardest and pounded Alfred's back until Alfred coughed and the tears came. Alfred held tight to the chain hook. Samuel pounded him even harder when he saw the tears. He said, "Why you bawling? You a baby, huh?" and laughed. One of the men whose boyhood had been more watchful than brave became angry. He stood up straight and looked at the boys for a couple of seconds. Then he walked in a citizenly way to the end of the car, where he pulled the emergency cord. Almost at once, with a terrible hiss, the pressure of air abandoned the brakes and the wheels were caught and held.

8   People standing in the most secure places fell forward, then backward. Samuel had let go of his hold on the chain so he could pound Tom as well as Alfred. All the passengers in the cars whipped back and forth, but he pitched only forward and fell head first to be crushed and killed between the cars.

9   The train had stopped hard, halfway into the station, and the conductor called at once for the trainmen who knew about this kind of death and how to take the body from the wheels and brakes. There was silence except for passengers from other cars who asked, What happened! What happened! The ladies waited around wondering if he might be an only child. The men recalled other afternoons with very bad endings. The little boys stayed close to each other, leaning and touching shoulders and arms and legs.

10   When the policeman knocked at the door and told her about it, Samuel's mother began to scream. She screamed all day and moaned all night, though the doctors tried to quiet her with pills. Oh, oh, she hopelessly cried. She did not know how she could ever find another boy like that one. However, she was a young woman and she became pregnant. Then for a few months she was hopeful. The child born to her was a boy. They brought him to be seen and nursed. She smiled. But immediately she saw that this baby wasn't Samuel. She and her husband together have had other children, but never again will a boy exactly like Samuel be known.

"Samuel," from *Enormous Changes at the Last Minute*, Grace Paley.
Copyright © 1971, 1974 by Grace Paley. Farrar, Straus and Giroux, LLC.

Now return to the checklist on pages 181–182 and see how many questions about this story you are able to answer.

Reading Comprehension Check

1. Where does this story take place?
   a. in the countryside
   b. in someone's home
   c. on a city subway
   d. on the street

2. Who is the narrator of the story?
   a. one of the boys
   b. The narrator is not a physical character in the story.
   c. one of the older men watching
   d. a woman who felt bad for the victim

3. What do we learn in the second paragraph about some of the older men watching?
   a. They are angry at the boys.
   b. They are jiggling too.
   c. They are listening to music on their headphones.
   d. They used to do similar dangerous things.

4. What caused the accident to happen?
   a. The boys were jumping too heavily.
   b. The embarrassed woman called the cops.
   c. One of the men watching pulled the emergency cord.
   d. The boys got stuck between the train cars.

5. What is the meaning of the last line of the story, "She and her husband together have had other children, but never again will a boy exactly like Samuel be known"?
   a. The mother was able to continue her life by having other children.
   b. A lost child can never be replaced.
   c. The mother was unable to conceive again.
   d. Samuel would one day be forgotten.

Exploring the Topic

Discuss the following questions to review the content of the story you have just read.

Collaboration

1. How does race play a role in this story?

2. The author keeps shifting the focus of who is watching the boys from the older men to the angry women and finally to the embarrassed woman. Why do you think the author tells the story in this way?

3. How do you feel about the way the writer ended the story? Could you think of a more interesting ending?

Post-Reading Vocabulary

Without using a dictionary, determine the meaning of the bolded words from the context.

1. "They also **jiggle** and hop on the platform between the locked doors of the subway cars." (para. 1)

   Jiggle means _____

2. "They don't like them to jiggle or jump but don't want to **interfere**." (para. 2)

   Interfere means _____

3. "Then they thought of some of the brave things they had done when they were boys and jiggling didn't seem so **risky**." (para. 3)

   Risky means _____

COLLEGE STUDY SKILLS
Summarizing

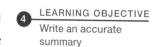
4 LEARNING OBJECTIVE
Write an accurate summary

In college classes, students are often asked to read some material and to write a short summary of what they have read. A **summary** is a way of taking a longer passage and condensing it into one or two paragraphs by focusing in on the author's main ideas and key points and leaving out the minor details.

We practice summary skills often in our daily lives. If you miss a lecture and a classmate asks you what the lecture was about, you are not going to tell them every last detail of the professor's hour-long lecture; this would put your classmate to sleep! No, you are going to summarize the key points of the lecture. If a friend of yours missed the latest episode of his or her favorite TV program and you happened to catch it, he or she might ask you what happened on the show. Again, you are not going to go through every last action that took place in the TV program, but will summarize the most significant events. Your summary, if you wrote it out, might look like this:

> The show began with Jill breaking up with her boyfriend, Ray. Later on, she found a new boyfriend, and days later learned that Ray was spying on her and was clearly jealous that she had moved on to another guy. In fact, Ray was so jealous that when he found Jill with her new boyfriend hugging in his car, he deflated all four of the guy's tires. At the end of the episode, Jill confronted Ray about the incident and they had a big argument.

Guidelines for Effective Summary Writing

Organizing a summary of a college-level text might prove more challenging than providing an oral summary of a favorite TV program, however. Here are some guidelines for effective summary writing.

- **First and foremost, you must take the time to comprehend the whole reading passage:** How can you be expected to extract the main points of a reading if you did not understand what you have read?
- **Include all the main ideas:** Most reading passages contain from one to three key points. As you read, highlight these key points. Only include a supporting detail in your summary if a main idea cannot be understood without it.
- **Paraphrase the author's key points:** In Chapter Four you learned about the critical skill of paraphrasing. Summarizing offers you the opportunity to sharpen your paraphrasing skills. Try to rephrase the key points of the reading without adding any of your own ideas or changing the author's intended meaning.
- **Maintain the author's sequence of ideas:** Do not mix up the order of the author's points. Summarize the author's ideas from beginning to end, in the same order these ideas were presented in the original text.
- **Set up your summary well by providing a context for the original text (imagine that your audience did not read the passage):** If you are summarizing a novel, you might begin, "The novel *The Kite Runner begins in Afghanistan and …*" If you are summarizing a newspaper article, you might begin with the topic, "*The article is about the rise of nuclear power in China.*" If you are summarizing a section of a textbook on nutrition, you might begin, "*The second section of Chapter 3 of* Nutrition and Lifestyle *focuses on three healthy ways we can lose weight.*" Whether you are summarizing a novel, newspaper, magazine, or Web article, be sure to include precise source information; you do not want to be accused of plagiarism.

Putting the Skill into Action

Practice your summary skills by reviewing "Samuel" by Grace Paley and writing a four- to six-sentence summary of the story's plot. Remember to set up your summary well, including source information to avoid plagiarism, and to only include key details of the story.

Summary of "Samuel"

_____

_____

_____

_____

_____

_____

The Last Word

Summarizing is a great way to check your comprehension. If you can write a clear summary of what you have read, then this tells you that you most likely understood the reading. Summarizing incorporates such key academic skills as highlighting, paraphrasing, and identifying key points. If you follow the guidelines laid out above, with a little practice you will be on your way to writing smooth and effective summaries.

Rean Valere   An Interview with a Student in the Field of Literature

LaGuardia Community College

1. How did you find your path to majoring in literature?

I have always loved to read older novels in literature, novels by authors who have been dead for more than 100 years. Not that I was specifically seeking them out. While I was doing my associate's degree at La Guardia Community College, I fell in love with novels such as *Bleak House, Jane Eyre, Robinson Crusoe, Pamela, Tess of the D'Urbervilles,* and many others. I know that these novels are somewhat "long-winded" and "boring" to many students. But, when reading these novels, I look for the realism component of them. In other words, how can I compare this to twenty-first century society. Or even how I can compare this to my daily life? When I came to Queens College, I knew that my major should be without a doubt literature and English along with elementary education. It also helped that my favorite subject in high school and elementary school was English.

2. What is the biggest obstacle you face in your study of literature?

I would say the biggest challenge I faced was not having enough time to really dive into the novels I was currently reading. There was always something to pull me away from my studies. Another obstacle was not finding classes that would do justice to literature. Many of the classes offered were discussing the literary criticism of the novels and not the novels themselves, which every English major fanatic knows is key to the love of literature.

3. What area(s) of literature in particular do you find most interesting?

As mentioned before, I really enjoy reading early Victorian literature. These to me are the foundation of literature and are what inspire modern writers to write.

4. What specific skills are required of students who study literature?

Besides a love of reading, if there is any real "skill" as to studying literature it would probably be reading comprehension and analyzing. You have to understand what you are reading in order to get what you are reading. Once clarification is had, you must be able to analyze what you read. You have to be able to take from what you read and put it in context for a deeper understanding.

(continued)

5. Other than being an English teacher, what other career avenues are available for literature majors?

Absolutely, in fact I posed this question to one of my English professors, and he gave a good size list of careers. For starters, journalism is one of the best careers that can come out of the English major. Another is being a historian, and with this career path you can work in museums, colleges, and more. A lot of companies are looking for people to write proposals and edit their important documents, so there are some choices in editing and writing for bigger companies. If corporate America is not your cup of tea, there are careers in the media such as daily news writer, soap opera writer, newspaper writer and editor, and magazine writer and editor. I may be biased, but I think one of the greatest choices would be being a teacher/college professor because you can help someone realize their dream of becoming an English major.

READING

Reading Selection **2**

Poetry

MyReadingLab™
Complete this **Exercise**
at **myreadinglab.com**

Two Poems

Preview Questions

1. The first poem you are going to read is from the perspective of an immigrant mother. Do you think all immigrant parents want their children to embrace American culture? What might be the cost of their child doing so?

2. The second poem you will read is full of slang speech, or informal expressions. Why would an educated poet use slang in his or her poetry? What effect can this type of language have on the reader?

3. Although you haven't read the two poems yet, how is the process of reading a poem different than reading a short story?

Pre-Reading Vocabulary: Focus on Some Key Terms

Before beginning the reading selection, it may be helpful to focus on the meaning of some key words in the poems. Working with a partner, try to guess the meaning of these words. Then look up the words in a dictionary.

Word	Your Definition	Dictionary Definition
mashed		
cleats		
crystal		
tacks		
bare		

Poem 1: "Immigrants," by Pat Mora

Pat Mora was born in El Paso, Texas, in 1942. She earned a master's degree at the University of Texas at El Paso. She is known for her poems, but has also written books and essays on Chicano culture and is the author of many award-winning books for children. She lives in Sante Fe, New Mexico. This poem was written in 1986.

Pat Mora

wrap their babies in the American flag,
feed them mashed hot dogs and apple pie,
name them Bill and Daisy,
buy them blonde dolls that blink blue
eyes or a football and tiny cleats   5
before the baby can even walk
speak to them in thick English, hallo, babee, hallo,
whisper in Spanish or Polish,
when the babies sleep, whisper
in a dark parent bed, that dark   10
parent fear, "Will they like
our boy, our girl, our fine american
boy, our fine american girl?"

Poem 2: "Mother to Son," by Langston Hughes

Langston Hughes (1902–1967) was a versatile writer: a poet, short story writer, dramatist, essayist, and editor. He was born in Joplin, Missouri, and he grew up in Lawrence, Kansas, and Cleveland, Ohio. He studied at Columbia University in New York City in the early 1920s, but left early to travel around Europe for a few years. Hughes returned to the United States in 1925 and continued his studies at Lincoln University in Pennsylvania.

Hughes had a very successful literary career, drawing upon spirituals, blues, jazz, and folk expression. His poetry is still read widely in American classrooms, from middle school through college. This poem was written in 1992.

Langston Hughes

Well, son, I'll tell you:
Life for me ain't been no crystal stair.
It's had tacks in it,
And splinters,
And boards torn up,   5
And places with no carpet on the floor—

Bare.
But all the time
I'se been a-climbin' on,
And reachin' landin's,   10
And turnin' corners,
And sometimes goin' in the dark
Where there ain't been no light.
So boy, don't you turn back.
Don't you set down on the steps   15
'Cause you finds it's kinder hard.
Don't you fall now—
For I'se still goin', honey,
I'se still climbin',
And life for me ain't been no crystal stair.   20

"Mother to Son" from *The Collected Poems of Langston Hughes*, by Langston Hughes,
edited by Arnold Rampersad with David Roessel, Associate Editor.
Copyright © 1994 by the Estate of Langston Hughes. Alfred A. Knopf,
a division of Random House, Inc. and Harold Ober Associates.

Collaboration

Post-Reading Activity

Discussing poetry demands a close reading and rereading of a poem, line by line.
Working with the following "Responding to Poems" checklist below will guide
you toward a better understanding of the two poems you have just read.

Work with a partner and try to answer the checklist questions about each of
the poems.

Responding to Poems

First Response	☐ What was your response to the poem on first reading?
Speaker and Tone	☐ Who is the speaker?
	☐ Do you think the speaker is fully aware of what he or she is saying, or does the speaker unconsciously reveal his or her personality and values?
	☐ Is the speaker narrating on an earlier experience or attitude?
Audience	☐ To whom is the speaker speaking?
Structure and Form	☐ Does the poem proceed in a straightforward way, or at some point or points does the speaker reverse course, altering his or her tone or perception?
	☐ Is the poem organized into sections?
	☐ What is the effect on you of the form—say quatrains (stanzas of four lines) or blank verse (unrhymed lines of ten syllables of Iambic pentameter)?

Center of Interest and Theme	☐ What is the poem about?
	☐ Is the theme stated explicitly (directly) or implicitly?
Diction	☐ How would you characterize the language?
	☐ Do certain words have rich and relevant associations that relate to other words and help to define the speaker or the theme or both?
	☐ What is the role of figurative language, if any?
	☐ What do you think is to be taken figuratively or symbolically and what literally?

from Barnet, Burto, and Cain, *An Introduction to Literature*, 16e, p. 12

Reading Comprehension Check

MyReadingLab™
Complete this **Exercise**
at **myreadinglab.com**

1. In the poem "Immigrants," what is the purpose of the reference to the names "Bill and Daisy" in line 3?
   a. These are immigrant names.
   b. These are typically American names.
   c. These are symbols of food.
   d. These are the names of the two parents.

2. What language is spoken to the immigrant child in the poem?
   a. English when the child is awake and the parent's native language when the child sleeps
   b. English only
   c. Spanish or Polish
   d. the child's native language usually and some English

3. What is one of the main messages of "Immigrants"?
   a. Immigrants should work hard to keep their own culture.
   b. Immigrant children want only American things.
   c. Immigrants feel pressure to fit in to American culture.
   d. Americans don't like immigrants.

4. What does the mother mean in "Mother to Son" when she says, "Life for me ain't been no crystal stair" (line 2)?
   a. Life is unpredictable.
   b. Life hasn't been easy.
   c. Life is full of stairs to climb.
   d. Her son needs to respect older people.

5. What advice is the mother giving to her son?
   a. He should stop and smell the roses.
   b. He should fight against evil.
   c. He should study hard in school.
   d. He should never give up, no matter how hard life gets.

Collaboration

Exploring the Topic

Discuss the following questions to review the content of the poems you have just read.

1. After reading the poem "Immigrants," what kind of ideas do you think the poet, Pat Mora, had about new immigrants and American culture? Do you agree with her? Explain.

2. Langston Hughes wrote the poem "Mother to Son" in a different time, nearly 90 years ago. Do you think the poem could have been written today? In other words, is life still this hard for some people in America? Explain.

3. Which poem did you enjoy more? What was it that you liked better about this poem?

Post-Reading Vocabulary

Without using a dictionary, determine the meaning of the bolded words from the context.

1. "buy them blonde dolls that *blink* blue" ("Immigrants" line 4)

   Blink means _____

2. "And boards **torn up**" ("Mother to Son" line 5)

   Torn up means _____

3. "Don't you **set down** on the steps" ("Mother to Son" line 15)

   Set down means _____

SKILL FOCUS
Determining an Author's Tone and Purpose

⑤ LEARNING OBJECTIVE
Recognize an author's tone and purpose

Understanding the Author's Tone

What does the term "author's tone" mean? Share a few synonyms for "tone" with another classmate.

Synonyms for tone: _____

The best way to understand a concept is through example and application. There are 1,001 ways to write about *life*. Here are 10 examples. Read each out loud with a partner.

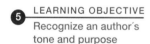

Collaboration

A. **"Life** is great. You work, pay your taxes, and then you die."

B. "In the early years of our **life**, we go through a number of critical developmental stages."

C. **"Life** is a bowl of cherries. Watch out for the pits!"

D. "As we move deeper into the twenty-first century, **life** gets better and better for more people on earth."

E. "In this **life**, we must be open to all peoples and all cultures. We can learn from others."

F. "If I had another **life**, I would go back in time to enjoy the old days when life was less complicated and people were nicer to each other."

G. "It is my belief that there is a better and happier **life** beyond the one I am presently living."

H. "There are people who believe in **life** after death and others who do not."

I. "I am sorry, child, that I didn't give you the **life** you deserved."

J. "If you work hard, you will taste only the sweetness of **life** and everything beautiful will fall into your lap."

When we talk, our tone of voice often signals our attitude toward what we are speaking about. Speakers rely on a number of vocal cues such as volume, pitch, and inflection to convey tone. If a listener is paying attention, it is usually not too difficult to catch a speaker's tone of voice and know whether they are angry, joyful, or sad. If a classmate says to you, "Today's lesson was so interesting," you would probably understand by their tone whether they meant this seriously or were being sarcastic.

It is more challenging to catch an author's tone than a speaker's tone, as writers have to rely on their choice of words to convey their attitude toward a given topic. You cannot see or hear the writer. In trying to determine an author's tone, pay close attention to key words that signal a positive, negative, or neutral attitude. It may be helpful to read the passage out loud and try to sense the tone from the sound and style of the words.

Determining an author's tone is critical to successful reading. If you misunderstand the tone, you can easily misinterpret the author's message. An author might write, "All of the gorillas in the jungle are suicidal these days," and if you missed the humorous tone, you might be left horrified with a terrible image of thousands of apes killing themselves!

As stated above, a good place to start in determining the author's tone for a given reading passage is to first get a clear sense of whether the author's attitude toward the topic is positive, negative, or neutral. We learned in an earlier chapter that most words have a positive or negative connotation, and paying close attention to key signal words in a reading passage will clue you in to the author's overall tone.

Practice 1: Let's revisit our 10 example sentences about life. Read each out loud again with a partner and try to determine if the author's tone is positive, negative, or neutral. Write down one or two signal words that keyed you into the author's attitude. In some cases where the tone is neutral, there may not be a clear signal word. The first example is done for you.

Collaboration

Example Sentences	Author's Attitude	Signal Words
A. "**Life** is great. You work, pay your taxes, and then you die."	Negative	pay taxes/die
B. "In the early years of our **life**, we go through a number of critical developmental stages."		
C. "**Life** is a bowl of cherries. Watch out for the pits."		
D. "As we move deeper into the twenty-first century **life** gets better and better for more people on earth."		
E. "In this **life**, we must be open to all peoples and all cultures. We can learn from others."		
F. "If I had another **life**, I would go back in time to enjoy the old days when life was less complicated and people were nicer to each other."		
G. "It is my belief that there is a better and happier **life** beyond the one I am presently living."		
H. "There are people who believe in **life** after death and others who do not."		
I. "I am sorry, child, that I didn't give you the **life** you deserved."		
J. "If you work hard, you will taste only the sweetness of **life** and everything beautiful will fall into your lap."		

As you can see, it is not too difficult to comprehend whether authors are expressing themselves in a positive, negative, or neutral tone. However, determining the specific words that capture an author's tone is more challenging. There are many adjectives that can describe an author's tone. The list that follows offers you some of the more common adjectives of tone, and it would be helpful to study any of the words that are unfamiliar to you.

Objective Tones

These are often used in textbooks, newspaper and magazine articles, and reference materials.

Neutral	not taking a particular side
Straightforward	simple and easy to understand
Indifferent	not caring; not having any opinions about something
Serious	stated with a sense of importance
Instructional	to give information about how to do something

Emotional Tones

These are used in persuasive writings such as editorials and political writing.

Concerned	worried about something
Sentimental	showing emotions such as love or sadness too strongly
Nostalgic	longing for things or situations in the past
Inspirational	motivating the reader to act
Remorseful	feeling sorry for something you have done
Apologetic	expressing sorrow
Proud	feeling satisfaction over something credited to oneself
Angry	showing anger or resentment
Joyous	full of joy, happy

Disapproving Tones

These may be found in movie and art reviews and editorials.

Critical	severely judging people or things
Pessimistic	having a negative outlook
Intolerant	not willing to accept other ways of thinking
Bitter	a sour reaction
Cruel	mean, heartless
Disappointed	discouraged by the failure of one's hopes or expectations
Doubtful	feeling unsure about something

Supportive Tones

These may be found in reviews and editorials, as well as in inspirational writing.

Encouraging	showing support
Hopeful	believing that things will improve
Optimistic	having a bright view of the future
Sympathetic	understanding of how someone feels
Enthusiastic	showing a lot of interest and excitement about something
Convincing	trying to persuade the reader
Admiring	to regard with wonder and approval
Respectful	showing politeness or deference

Humorous and Sarcastic Tones

These may appear in many kinds of writing, including cartoons, literature and criticism, poetry and newspaper columns.

Ironic	using words that are the opposite of what they mean
Sarcastic	harsh or bitter derision; a cutting remark
Skeptical	doubting or not believing something
Mocking	laughing at something to make it seem silly
Lighthearted	cheerful; not intended to be serious
Comical	funny, especially in a strange and unexpected way

Practice 2: Let's revisit the example sentences describing life one last time (yes, we know you have already read them a few times). This time, for each sentence choose two adjectives of tone from the list on page 195 that fit the author's tone.

Example Sentences	*Author's Tone*
A. "Life is great."	*pessimistic/sarcastic*
B. "In the early years…"	
C. "Life is a bowl…"	
D. "As we move…"	
E. "In this life…"	
F. "If I had…"	
G. "It is my belief…"	
H. "There are people…"	
I. "I am sorry…"	
J. "If you work hard…"	

Now that you have a better understanding of how to determine an author's tone, let's move from the sentence level to the stanza level and onward to longer reading passages.

Practice 3: Read the following examples from literary works and try to determine the author's tone.

1. A limerick entitled "There Was a Young Fellow of Riga" (anonymous)

> There was a young fellow of Riga,
> Who smiled as he rode on a tiger.
> They returned from the ride,
> With the fellow inside,
> And the smile on the face of the tiger.

The author's tone is _____

a. angry

b. serious

c. humorous

d. neutral

Justify your answer: I chose answer _____ because _____

_____

2. A poem entitled "To My Dear and Loving Husband" by Anne Bradstreet

> If ever two were one, then surely we.
> If ever man were lov'd by wife, than thee;
> If ever wife was happy in a man,
> Compare with me ye women if you can.
> I prize my love more than whole mines of gold,   5
> Or all the riches that the East doth hold.

My love is such that rivers cannot quench,
Nor ought but love from thee, give recompense
Thy love is such I can no way repay,
The heavens reward thee manifold I pray.   10
Then while we live, in love let's so persevere,
That when we live no more, we may live ever.

The author's tone is _____

a. joyous   c. disappointed
b. pessimistic   d. objective

Justify your answer: I chose answer _____ because _____

_____

3. From a poem entitled "Do Not Go Gentle Into That Good Night" by Dylan
   Thomas

   Do not go gentle into that good night
   Old age should burn and rave at close of day
   Rage, rage against the dying of the light.

   > From "Do Not Go Gentle Into That Good Night" by Dylan Thomas,
   > from *The Poems of Dylan Thomas*, copyright © 1952 by Dylan Thomas.
   > Reprinted by permission of New Directions Publishing Corp.

The author's tone is _____

a. glad   c. apologetic
b. angry   d. neutral

Justify your answer: I chose answer _____ because _____

_____

4. From a poem entitled "On the Amtrak from Boston to New York City" by
   Sherman Alexie

   The white woman across the aisle from me says, "Look,
   look at all the history, that house
   on the hill there is over two hundred years old,"
   as she points out the window past me   4

   into what she has been taught. I have learned
   little more about American history during my few days
   back East than what I expected and far less
   of what we should all know of the tribal stories   8

   whose architecture is 15,000 years older
   than the corners of the house that sits
   museumed on the hill. "Walden Pond,"
   the woman on the train asks, "Did you see Walden Pond?" 12

   and I don't have a cruel enough heart to break
   her own by telling her there are five Walden Ponds
   on my little reservation out West
   and at least a hundred more surrounding Spokane,   16

   > Reprinted from *First Indian on the Moon* © 1993 by Sherman Alexie,
   > by permission of Hanging Loose Press.

Sherman Alexie

The author's tone is _____

a. enthusiastic   c. bitter

b. neutral   d. sarcastic

Justify your answer: I chose answer _____ because _____

_____

Let's practice some more with the critical skill of determining an author's tone. Keep in mind these questions as you read both the author's choice of words and choice of writing style: Is the tone negative or positive or neutral? Is the style formal, informal, serious, or lighthearted?

Practice 4: Read the following passages taken from works of literature and choose at least two adjectives of tone to describe each author's voice.

1. From a short story entitled "Cathedral" by Raymond Carver

    This blind man, an old friend of my wife's, he was on the way to spend the night. His wife had died. So he was visiting the dead wife's relatives in Connecticut. He called my wife from his in-laws'. Arrangements were made. He would come by train, a five-hour trip, and my wife would meet him at the station. She hadn't seen him since she worked for him one summer in Seattle ten years ago. But she and the blind man had kept in touch. They made tapes and mailed them back and forth. I wasn't enthusiastic about his visit. He was no one I knew. And his being blind bothered me. My idea of blindness came from the movies. In the movies, the blind moved slowly and never laughed. Sometimes they were led by seeing-eye dogs. A blind man in my house was not something I looked forward to.

    From "Cathedral," from *Cathedral* by Raymond Carver, copyright © 1981, 1982, 1983 by Raymond Carver. Alfred A. Knopf, a division of Random House, Inc.

    The author's tone is _____

    Justify your answer: _____

    _____

2. From a poem entitled "For a Lady I Know" by Countee Cullen

    She even thinks that up in heaven
    Her class lies late and snores
    While poor black cherubs rise at seven
    To do celestial chores.

    From "For a Lady I Know" published in *Color*, © 1925 by Harper & Bros., NY.

    The author's tone is _____

    Justify your answer: _____

    _____

3. From a novel entitled *Harry Potter and the Deathly Hallows* by J.K. Rowling

    Harry was bleeding. Clutching his right hand in his left and swearing under his breath, he shouldered open his bedroom door. There was a crunch of breaking china: He had trodden on a cup of cold tea that had been sitting on the floor outside his bedroom door.

J. K. Rowling

"What the__?"

He looked around; the landing of number four, Privet Drive, was deserted.

© 2007 by J.K. Rowling, published by Arthur A. Levine Books,
an imprint of Scholastic, Inc.

The author's tone is _____

Justify your answer: _____

_____

4. From a poem entitled "Hay for the Horses" by Gary Snyder

He had driven half the night
From far down San Joaquin
Through Mariposa, up the
Dangerous mountain roads
And pulled in at eight a.m.
With his big truckload of hay
    Behind the barn.
With winch and ropes and hooks
We stacked the bales up clean
To splintery redwood rafters
High in the dark, flecks of alfalfa
Whirling through shingle-cracks of light

Copyright © 2009 by Gary Snyder from *Riprap and Cold Mountain Poems*.
Reprinted by permission of Counterpoint.

The author's tone is _____

Justify your answer: _____

_____

Identifying the Author's Purpose

An author's **purpose** is his or her reason for writing whatever it is he or she has
written. Authors don't just sit down and begin writing for no particular reason.
When we are reading, sometimes we forget that a real person, with a specific purpose in mind, sat down and wrote what is now in front of us. Authors write with
an intended audience in mind. For instance, a literature professor writing a textbook is writing for an audience of college students. A fashion magazine journalist
has an audience of readers who have an interest in the world of fashion. A technical writer developing a new Toyota car manual has an audience of car owners.

Examine the chart below, which lists the four most common purposes for
writing and the "genres" (or types) often associated with each purpose.

Purpose	*Genre*
• to Inform	newspaper articles, textbooks, legal documents, reference materials
• to Persuade/Convince	advertising, editorials, music/art criticism, political speeches
• to Instruct	how-to manuals, technical guides, math/ computer-related textbooks
• to Entertain	novels, poems, jokes, gossip columns

Practice 5: Imagine authors in the following scenarios getting ready to begin writing. Can you guess their mostly likely purposes?

a. A *New York Times* reporter stationed in Paris writing an article about the European economy.

Most likely purpose: _____

b. A technical writer for Apple Inc. composing a manual for the latest iPod.

Most likely purpose: _____

c. A romance novelist starting her latest novel about a rich woman's many lovers.

Most likely purpose: _____

d. A presidential hopeful's speechwriter composing an election-year speech.

Most likely purpose: _____

Author's Purpose Clues You into an Author's Tone

If you understand an author's purpose, it is much easier then to identify the author's tone. This is because HOW (tone) authors express themselves in writing is very much connected to WHY (purpose) they are writing in the first place. So, for example, if an author's purpose is to entertain, then perhaps the tone will be humorous, sad, or exciting. If an author's purpose is to inform, then most likely the tone will be more unemotional: neutral or objective. Finally, if an author's goal is to make you believe his or her ideas, then the tone would be convincing, admiring, or pessimistic.

Let's make this connection between author's purpose and author's tone more clear with the following exercise.

Practice 6: Read each of the following passages and try to determine both the author's purpose and tone.

a. If you pay close attention to William Faulkner's words and ideas, you will understand that it is not true that he was a racist as many have said, but on the contrary, he had great respect for black culture. There is much evidence to prove this point correct.

Author's purpose: _____

Author's tone: _____

Explain your answer choices. _____

_____

b. Sherman Joseph Alexie, Jr. is a writer, poet, filmmaker, and comedian. His writing is influenced by his experiences as a Native American. Three of Alexie's best-known works are *The Lone Ranger and Tonto Fistfight in Heaven* (1994), a book of short stories and the movie, *Smoke Signals*.

Author's purpose: _____

Author's tone: _____

Explain your answer choices. _____

_____

c. When you read a newspaper or magazine, it is best to first skim through its many articles and to select a few that are of interest to you. If you do not have time, you should skip longer pieces, such as short stories or editorials. You can also cut out articles that look interesting and save for later review.

Author's purpose: _____

Author's tone: _____

Explain your answer choices. _____

_____

d. It is not just her emerald eyes that shine / Nor is it the waves of silky black coming in waves / A smile to tame a warlord burns the disappointment from my expression

Author's purpose: _____

Author's tone: _____

Explain your answer choices. _____

_____

e. Detective fiction is a genre of crime fiction where a detective, either professional or amateur, investigates a crime, often a homicide. This type of fiction, made popular by both the Sherlock Holmes series and the many works of Agatha Christie, has become even more popular today, with many titles found on the best-sellers lists.

Author's purpose: _____

Author's tone: _____

Explain your answer choices. _____

_____

LANDMARK IN THE FIELD OF LITERATURE

Audio Books

If William Shakespeare came back to life four hundred years after writing some of his best plays, he would be shocked to learn that some of his current fans are listening to his plays alone in their cars on the way to work! Yes, the age of the audio book has arrived.

Many people believe that audio books are a recent invention because of the technical terms mentioned when discussing them. These include CDs, downloadable digital formats, MP3s and PDAs. But, in fact, recording of books in audio formats has been around for a long time. In 1933 anthropologist J. P. Harrington drove through the country recording oral histories of Native American tribes on aluminum discs. The Library of Congress made recordings of literary works for use by the blind more than fifty years ago.

The transition of the recording of books into audio-cassette tapes happened in the late 1970s. Yet, it wasn't until the invention of CD technology that the concept of audio books really took off. Now audio book technology has joined the digital age with downloadable formats that can be heard on your computer. Audio files of text can be transferred to a portable audio player or burned to a CD.

In the 1980s a major effort was made by large publishing houses to attract book retailers to the concept of the audio book. As more and more publishers entered the world of spoken-word publishing, audio books appeared on retail bookstore bookshelves. In 2005 cassette-tape sales were 16% of the audio book market, with CD sales accounting for 74% of the market. Downloadable audio books accounted for about 9%.

The future looks bright for audio books. In the age of multitasking, today's audio books allow readers to listen to a romance novel while cooking, or to enjoy detective fiction (or a Shakespeare tragedy) on their way to work.

Collaboration

Considering the Topic

Answer the following questions with a partner.

1. Have you ever listened to a reading on an audio book? How was the experience different than reading a printed book? If you have not yet listened to an audio book, would you like to try it? Why or why not?

2. According to the reading, who were the main consumers of early audio recordings of literature?

3. How do audio books speak to the younger generation's multitasking lifestyle? Explain.

Internet Connection

Research another landmark in the field of literature, and fill out the section below.

lending libraries	Shakespeare's plays
e-readers	science fiction
comic books	Braille

Landmark: _____

Question	Answer
When did this landmark become a reality?	
Who was involved in developing this landmark?	
What made this landmark special?	
How did this landmark change the way people interact?	

Chapter One from *Lucy*

Preview Questions

1. Does a book or story always catch your attention from the first page? How many pages of reading a book does it take for you to know whether or not it is a book that interests you?

2. The story you are about to read is about a young woman who has just arrived in New York City from a poor country in the Caribbean. The woman describes her first days working for a wealthy white family in Manhattan. From this short description, can you guess what kinds of tensions and/or problems the young woman will deal with?

3. What rights do poor, undocumented house servants working for rich families have in this country? Are they protected under the law? Explain.

MyReadingLab™
Complete this Exercise
at myreadinglab.com

Pre-Reading Vocabulary: Focus on Some Key Terms

Before beginning the reading selection, it may be helpful to focus on the meaning of some key words in the story. Working with a partner, try to guess the meaning of these words. Then look up the words in a dictionary.

Collaboration

Word	Your Definition	Dictionary Definition
bout		
sensation		
gesture		
cargo		
linger		

Chapter One from *Lucy*

By Jamaica Kincaid

Jamaica Kincaid

1   IT WAS MY FIRST DAY. I had come the night before, a gray-black and cold night before—as it was expected to be in the middle of January, though I didn't know that at the time—and I could not see anything clearly on the way in from the airport, even though there were lights everywhere. As we drove along, someone would single out to me a famous building, an important street, a park, a bridge that when built was thought to be a spectacle. In a daydream I used to have, all these places were points of happiness to me; all these places were lifeboats to my small drowning soul, for I would imagine myself entering and leaving them, and just that—entering and leaving over and over again—would see me through a bad feeling I did not have a name for. I only knew it felt a little like sadness but heavier than that. Now that I saw these places, they looked ordinary, dirty, worn down by so many people entering and leaving them in real life, and it occurred to me that I could not be the only person in the world for whom they were a fixture of fantasy. It was not my first bout with the disappointment of reality and it would not be my last. The undergarments that I wore were all new, bought for my journey, and as I sat in the car, twisting this way and that to get a good view of the sights before me, I was reminded of how uncomfortable the new can make you feel.

2   I got into an elevator, something I had never done before, and then I was in an apartment and seated at a table, eating food just taken from a refrigerator. In the place I had just come from, I always lived in a house, and my house did not have a refrigerator in it. Everything I was experiencing—the ride in the elevator, being in an apartment, eating day-old food that had been stored in a refrigerator—was such a good idea that I could imagine I would grow used to it and like it very much, but at

first it was all so new that I had to smile with my mouth turned down at the corners. I slept soundly that night, but it wasn't because I was happy and comfortable—quite the opposite; it was because I didn't want to take in anything else.

3   That morning, the morning of my first day, the morning that followed my first night, was a sunny morning. It was not the sort of bright sun-yellow making everything curl at the edges, almost in fright, that I was used to, but a pale-yellow sun, as if the sun had grown weak from trying too hard to shine; but still it was sunny, and that was nice and made me miss my home less. And so, seeing the sun, I got up and put on a dress, a gay dress made out of madras cloth—the same sort of dress that I would wear if I were at home and setting out for a day in the country. It was all wrong. The sun was shining but the air was cold. It was the middle of January, after all. But I did not know that the sun could shine and the air remain cold; no one had ever told me. What a feeling that was! How can I explain? Something I had always known—the way I knew my skin was the color brown of a nut rubbed repeatedly with a soft cloth, or the way I knew my own name—something I took completely for granted, "the sun is shining, the air is warm," was not so. I was no longer in a tropical zone, and this realization now entered my life like a flow of water dividing formerly dry and solid ground, creating two banks, one of which was my past—so familiar and predictable that even my unhappiness then made me happy now just to think of it—the other my future, a gray blank, an overcast seascape on which rain was falling and no boats were in sight. I was no longer in a tropical zone and I felt cold inside and out, the first time such a sensation had come over me.

4   In books I had read—from time to time, when the plot called for it—someone would suffer from homesickness. A person would leave a not very nice situation and go somewhere else, somewhere a lot better, and then long to go back where it was not very nice. How impatient I would become with such a person, for I would feel that I was in a not very nice situation myself, and how I wanted to go somewhere else. But now I, too, felt that I wanted to be back where I came from. I understood it, I knew where I stood there. If I had had to draw a picture of my future then, it would have been a large gray patch surrounded by black, blacker, blackest.

5   What a surprise this was to me, that I longed to be back in the place that I came from, that I longed to sleep in a bed I had outgrown, that I longed to be with people whose smallest, most natural gesture would call up in me such a rage that I longed to see them all dead at my feet. Oh, I had imagined that with my one swift act—leaving home and coming to this new place—I could leave behind me, as if it were an old garment never to be worn again, my sad thoughts, my sad feelings, and my discontent with life in general as it presented itself to me. In the past, the thought of being in my present situation had been a comfort, but now I did not even have this to look forward to, and so I lay down on my bed and dreamt I was eating a bowl of pink mullet and green figs cooked in coconut milk, and it had been cooked by my grandmother, which was why the taste of it pleased me so, for she was the person I liked best in all the world and those were the things I liked best to eat also.

6   The room in which I lay was a small room just off the kitchen—the maid's room. I was used to a small room, but this was a different sort of small room. The ceiling was very high and the walls went all the way up to the ceiling, enclosing the

room like a box—a box in which cargo traveling a long way should be shipped. But I was not cargo. I was only an unhappy young woman living in a maid's room, and I was not even the maid. I was the young girl who watches over the children and goes to school at night. How nice everyone was to me, though, saying that I should regard them as my family and make myself at home. I believed them to be sincere, for I knew that such a thing would not be said to a member of their real family. After all, aren't family the people who become the millstone around your life's neck? On the last day I spent at home, my cousin—a girl I had known all my life, an unpleasant person even before her parents forced her to become a Seventh-Day Adventist—made a farewell present to me of her own Bible, and with it she made a little speech about God and goodness and blessings. Now it sat before me on a dresser, and I remembered how when we were children we would sit under my house and terrify and torment each other by reading out loud passages from the Book of Revelation, and I wondered if ever in my whole life a day would go by when these people I had left behind, my own family, would not appear before me in one way or another.

7   There was also a small radio on this dresser and I had turned it on. At that moment, almost as if to sum up how I was feeling, a song came on, some of the words of which were "Put yourself in my place, if only for a day; see if you can stand the awful emptiness inside." I sang these words to myself over and over, as if they were a lullaby, and I fell asleep again. I dreamt then that I was holding in my hands one of my old cotton-flannel nightgowns, and it was printed with beautiful scenes of children playing with Christmas-tree decorations. The scenes printed on my nightgown were so real that I could actually hear the children laughing. I felt compelled to know where this nightgown came from, and I started to examine it furiously, looking for the label. I found it just where a label usually is, in the back, and it read "Made in Australia." I was awakened from this dream by the actual maid, a woman who had let me know right away, on meeting me, that she did not like me, and gave as her reason the way I talked. I thought it was because of something else, but I did not know what. As I opened my eyes, the word "Australia" stood between our faces, and I remembered then that Australia was settled as a prison for bad people, people so bad that they couldn't be put in a prison in their own country.

8   My waking hours soon took on a routine. I walked four small girls to their school, and when they returned at midday I gave them a lunch of soup from a tin, and sandwiches. In the afternoon, I read to them and played with them. When they were away, I studied my books, and at night I went to school. I was unhappy. I looked at a map. An ocean stood between me and the place I came from, but would it have made a difference if it had been a teacup of water? I could not go back.

9   Outside, always it was cold, and everyone said that it was the coldest winter they had ever experienced; but the way they said it made me think they said this every time winter came around. And I couldn't blame them for not really remembering each year how unpleasant, how unfriendly winter weather could be. The trees with their bare, still limbs looked dead, and as if someone had just placed them there and planned to come back and get them later; all the windows of the houses were shut tight, the way windows are shut up when a house will be empty for a long time; when people walked on the streets they did it quickly, as if they were doing something behind someone's back, as if they didn't want to draw attention to themselves, as if being out in the cold too long would cause them to dissolve. How I longed to see someone *lingering* on a corner, trying to draw my

attention to him, trying to engage me in conversation, someone complaining to himself in a voice I could overhear about a God whose love and mercy fell on the just and the unjust.

10   I wrote home to say how lovely everything was, and I used flourishing words and phrases, as if I were living life in a greeting card—the kind that has a satin ribbon on it, and quilted hearts and roses, and is expected to be so precious to the person receiving it that the manufacturer has placed a leaf of plastic on the front to protect it. Everyone I wrote to said how nice it was to hear from me, how nice it was to know that I was doing well, that I was very much missed, and that they couldn't wait until the day came when I returned.

11   One day the maid who said she did not like me because of the way I talked told me that she was sure I could not dance. She said that I spoke like a nun, I walked like one also, and that everything about me was so pious it made her feel at once sick to her stomach and sick with pity just to look at me. And so, perhaps giving way to the latter feeling, she said that we should dance, even though she was quite sure I didn't know how. There was a little portable record-player in my room, the kind that when closed up looked like a ladies' vanity case, and she put on a record she had bought earlier that day. It was a song that was very popular at the time—three girls, not older than I was, singing in harmony and in a very insincere and artificial way about love and so on. It was very beautiful all the same, and it was beautiful because it was so insincere and artificial. She enjoyed this song, singing at the top of her voice, and she was a wonderful dancer—it amazed me to see the way in which she moved. I could not join her and I told her why: the melodies of her song were so shallow, and the words, to me, were meaningless. From her face, I could see she had only one feeling about me: how sick to her stomach I made her. And so I said that I knew songs, too, and I burst into a calypso about a girl who ran away to Port Spain, Trinidad, and had a good time, with no regrets.

12   The household in which I lived was made up of a husband, a wife, and the four girl children. The husband and wife looked alike and their four children looked just like them. In photographs of themselves, which they placed all over the house, their six yellow-haired heads of various sizes were bunched as if they were a bouquet of flowers tied together by an unseen string. In the pictures, they smiled out at the world, giving the impression that they found everything in it unbearably wonderful. And it was not a farce, their smiles. From wherever they had gone, and they seemed to have been all over the world, they brought back some tiny memento, and they could each recite its history from its very beginnings. Even when a little rain fell, they would admire the way it streaked through the blank air.

13   At dinner, when we sat down at the table—and did not have to say grace (such a relief; as if they believed in a God that did not have to be thanked every time you turned around)—they said such nice things to each other, and the children were so happy. They would spill their food, or not eat any of it at all, or make up rhymes about it that would end with the words "smelt bad." How they made me laugh, and I wondered what sort of parents I must have had, for even to think of such words in their presence I would have been scolded severely, and I vowed that if I ever had children I would make sure that the first words out of their mouths were bad ones.

14   It was at dinner one night not long after I began to live with them that they began to call me the Visitor. They said I seemed not to be a part of things, as if I didn't live in their house with them, as if they weren't like a family to me, as if I were just passing through, just saying one long Hallo!, and soon would be saying a quick

Goodbye! So long! It was very nice! For look at the way I stared at them as they ate, Lewis said. Had I never seen anyone put a forkful of French-cut green beans in his mouth before? This made Mariah laugh, but almost everything Lewis said made Mariah happy and so she would laugh. I didn't laugh, though, and Lewis looked at me, concern on his face. He said, "Poor Visitor, poor Visitor," over and over, a sympathetic tone to his voice, and then he told me a story about an uncle he had who had gone to Canada and raised monkeys, and of how after a while the uncle loved monkeys so much and was so used to being around them that he found actual human beings hard to take. He had told me this story about his uncle before, and while he was telling it to me this time I was remembering a dream I had had about them: Lewis was chasing me around the house. I wasn't wearing any clothes. The ground on which I was running was yellow, as if it had been paved with cornmeal. Lewis was chasing me around and around the house, and though he came close he could never catch up with me. Mariah stood at the open windows saying, Catch her, Lewis, catch her. Eventually I fell down a hole, at the bottom of which were some silver and blue snakes.

15   When Lewis finished telling his story, I told them my dream. When I finished, they both fell silent. Then they looked at me and Mariah cleared her throat, but it was obvious from the way she did it that her throat did not need clearing at all. Their two yellow heads swam toward each other and, in unison, bobbed up and down. Lewis made a clucking noise, then said, Poor, poor Visitor. And Mariah said, Dr. Freud for Visitor, and I wondered why she said that, for I did not know who Dr. Freud was. Then they laughed in a soft, kind way. I had meant by telling them my dream that I had taken them in, because only people who were very important to me had ever shown up in my dreams. I did not know if they understood that.

From *Lucy* by Jamaica Kincaid. Copyright © 1990 by Jamaica Kincaid. Farrar, Straus and Giroux, LLC.

Reading Comprehension Check

1. In describing the family Lucy lived with in New York, Kincaid writes, "In the pictures, they smiled out at the world, giving the impression that they found everything in it unbearably wonderful." (para. 12) What is the author's tone here?
   a. joyous
   b. mocking
   c. serious
   d. objective

2. How does the family maid treat Lucy?
   a. with respect
   b. fairly
   c. poorly
   d. violently

3. We can infer from Lucy's description of life back home that her life there was
   a. relaxed and easy.
   b. sunny and pleasant.
   c. full of family love.
   d. troubled.

4. What is the main idea of this passage?

   "I wrote home to say how lovely everything was, and I used flourishing words and phrases, as if I were living life in a greeting card—the kind that has a satin ribbon on it, and quilted hearts and roses, and is expected to be so precious to the person receiving it that the manufacturer has placed a leaf of plastic on the front to protect it. Everyone I wrote to said how nice it was to hear from me, how nice it was to know that I was doing well, that I was very much missed, and that they couldn't wait until the day came when I returned." (para. 10)

   a. Lucy and her family are pretending that everything is fine.

   b. Lucy is having a great experience in America, and her family do not miss her.

   c. Everyone misses Lucy.

   d. Lucy wants her family to visit her.

5. Why did the New York family begin to call Lucy "the Visitor"?

   a. She was visiting their city.

   b. She seemed distant and not part of the family.

   c. They respected her as a guest in their home.

   d. They didn't want her to be in any way part of the family.

6. What was the significance of Lucy's dream?

   a. She didn't feel comfortable with these people.

   b. She was finally accepting this family into her heart.

   c. She acted like a famous psychologist.

   d. She was homesick.

Exploring the Topic

Collaboration

Discuss the following questions to review the content of the text you have just read.

1. How does the weather in New York City affect Lucy's mood?

2. What kinds of things were new to Lucy in her New York residence? How did she feel about all of it?

3. In paragraph 8, Lucy says, "An ocean stood between me and the place I came from, but would it have made a difference if it had been a teacup of water? I could not go back." Explain Lucy's idea.

Post-Reading Vocabulary

Without using a dictionary, determine the meaning of the bolded words from the context.

1. "I wrote home to say how lovely everything was, and I used **flourishing** words and phrases, as if I were living life in a greeting card." (para. 10)

   Flourishing means _____

2. "From wherever they had gone, and they seemed to have been all over the world, they brought back some tiny **memento**, and they could each recite its history from its very beginnings." (para. 12)

   Memento means _____

3. "... for even to think of such words in their presence I would have been **scolded** severely." (para. 13)

   Scolded means _____

Reading Selection **4**

Play

August Wilson

Collaboration

A Scene from *The Piano Lesson*

August Wilson is one of America's most celebrated playwrights. He was born in 1945 and grew up in the Hill District of Pittsburgh, Pennsylvania. His childhood experiences in this poor black community would later influence his dramatic writings. Wilson set the goal of writing a ten-play cycle that captured each decade of the black experience in the twentieth century. The Piano Lesson *takes place in the 1930s. Wilson completed his goal with the opening of his final theater work,* Radio Golf, *in April of 2005. Two months later, he was diagnosed with liver cancer, and on October 2, 2005, August Wilson passed away at the age of 60.*

Preview Questions

1. Consider how "reading" a play might differ from "seeing" a play. How would the experience be different?

2. The play begins with some guests showing up at a home without notice. What kinds of tensions might "unexpected guests" present to a host?

3. One of the themes of *The Piano Lesson* deals with the responsibility siblings hold for each other. Does a brother or sister have to stand by their sibling, even if their sibling means trouble? Share your view.

Pre-Reading Vocabulary: Focus on Some Key Terms

Before beginning the reading selection, it may be helpful to focus on the meaning of some key words in the article. Working with a partner, try to guess the meaning of these words. Then look up the words in a dictionary.

Word	Your Definition	Dictionary Definition
sparsely		
portent		
apt		
brash		
haul		

A Scene from *The Piano Lesson*

By August Wilson

The Setting: The action of the play takes place in the kitchen and parlor of the house where DOAKER CHARLES lives with his niece, BERNIECE, and her eleven-year-old daughter, MARETHA. The house is sparsely furnished, and although there is evidence of a woman's touch, there is a lack of warmth and vigor. BERNIECE AND MARETHA occupy the upstairs rooms. DOAKER'S room is prominent and opens onto the kitchen. Dominating the parlor is an old upright piano. On the legs of the piano, carved in the manner of African sculpture, are mask-like figures resembling totems. The carvings are rendered with a grace and power of invention that lifts them out of the realm of craftsmanship and into the realm of art. At left is a staircase leading to the upstairs.

ACT ONE

(The lights come up on the Charles household. It is five o'clock in the morning. The dawn is beginning to announce itself, but there is something in the air that belongs to the night. A stillness that is a portent, a gathering, a coming together of something akin to a storm. There is a loud knock at the door.)

BOY WILLIE: (Off stage, calling.) Hey, Doaker … Doaker! (He knocks again and calls.) Hey, Doaker! Hey, Berniece! Berniece!

(DOAKER enters from his room. He is a tall, thin man of forty-seven, with severe features, who has for all intents and purposes retired from the world though he works full-time as a railroad cook.)

DOAKER: Who is it?

BOY WILLIE: Open the door, nigger! It's me … Boy Willie!

DOAKER: Who?

BOY WILLIE: Boy Willie! Open the door!

(DOAKER opens the door and BOY WILLIE and LYMON enter. BOY WILLIE is thirty years old. He has an infectious grin and a boyishness that is apt for his name. He is brash and impulsive, talkative and somewhat crude in speech and manner. LYMON is twenty-nine. BOY WILLIE's partner, he talks little, and then with a straightforwardness that is often disarming.)

DOAKER: What you doing up here?

BOY WILLIE: I told you, Lymon. Lymon talking about you might be sleep. This is Lymon. You remember Lymon Jackson from down home? This my Uncle Doaker.

DOAKER: What you doing up here? I couldn't figure out who that was. I thought you was still down in Mississippi.

BOY WILLIE: Me and Lymon selling watermelons. We got a truck out there. Got a whole truckload of watermelons. We brought them up here to sell. Where's Berniece? (Calls.)

Hey, Berniece!

DOAKER: Berniece up there sleep.

BOY WILLIE: Well, let her get up. (Calls.)

Hey, Berniece!

DOAKER: She got to go to work in the morning.

BOY WILLIE: Well she can get up and say hi. It's been three years since I seen her.

(Calls.)

Hey, Berniece! It's me ... Boy Willie.

DOAKER: Berniece don't like all that hollering now. She got to work in the morning.

BOY WILLIE: She can go on back to bed. Me and Lymon been riding two days in that truck ... the least she can do is get up and say hi.

DOAKER: (Looking out the window.) Where you all get that truck from?

BOY WILLIE: It's Lymon's. I told him let's get a load of watermelons and bring them up here.

LYMON: Boy Willie say he going back, but I'm gonna stay. See what it's like up here.

BOY WILLIE: You gonna carry me down there first.

LYMON: I told you I ain't going back down there and take a chance on that truck breaking down again. You can take the train. Hey, tell him Doaker, he can take the train back. After we sell them watermelons he have enough money he can buy him a whole railroad car.

DOAKER: You got all them watermelons stacked up there no wonder the truck broke down. I'm surprised you made it this far with a load like that. Where you break down at?

BOY WILLIE: We broke down three times! It took us two and a half days to get here. It's a good thing we picked them watermelons fresh.

LYMON: We broke down twice in West Virginia. The first time was just as soon as we got out of Sunflower. About forty miles out she broke down. We got it going and got all the way to West Virginia before she broke down again.

BOY WILLIE: We had to walk about five miles for some water.

LYMON: It got a hole in the radiator but it runs pretty good. You have to pump the brakes sometime before they catch. Boy Willie have his door open and be ready to jump when that happens.

BOY WILLIE: Lymon think that's funny. I told the nigger I give him ten dollars to get the brakes fixed. But he thinks that funny.

LYMON: They don't need fixing. All you got to do is pump them till they catch.

(BERNIECE enters on the stairs. Thirty-five years old, with an eleven-year-old daughter, she is still in mourning for her husband after three years.)

BERNIECE: What you doing all that hollering for?

BOY WILLIE: Hey, Berniece. Doaker said you was sleep. I said at least you could get up and say hi.

BERNIECE: It's five o'clock in the morning and you come in here with all this noise. You can't come like normal folks. You got to bring all that noise with you.

BOY WILLIE: Hell, I ain't done nothing but come in and say hi. I ain't got in the house good.

BERNIECE: That's what I'm talking about. You start all that hollering and carry on as soon as you hit the door.

BOY WILLIE: Aw hell, woman, I was glad to see Doaker. You ain't had to come down if you didn't want to. I come eighteen hundred miles to see my sister I figure she might want to get up and say hi. Other than that you can go back upstairs. What you got, Doaker? Where your bottle? Me and Lymon want a drink.

(To BERNIECE.)

This is Lymon. You remember Lymon Jackson from down home.

LYMON: How you doing, Berniece. You look just like I thought you looked.

BERNIECE: Why you all got to come in hollering and carrying on? Waking the neighbors with all that noise.

BOY WILLIE: They can come over and join the party. We fixing to have a party. Doaker, where your bottle? Me and Lymon celebrating. The Ghosts of the Yellow Dog got Sutter.

BERNIECE: Say what?

BOY WILLIE: Ask Lymon, they found him the next morning. Say he drowned in his well.

DOAKER: When this happen, Boy Willie?

BOY WILLIE: About three weeks ago. Me and Lymon was over in Stoner County when we heard about it. We laughed. We thought it was funny. A great big old three hundred-and-forty-pound man gonna fall down his well.

LYMON: It remind me of Humpty Dumpty.

BOY WILLIE: Everybody say the Ghosts of the Yellow Dog pushed him.

BERNIECE: I don't want to hear that nonsense. Somebody down there pushing them people in their wells.

DOAKER: What was you and Lymon doing over in Stoner County?

BOY WILLIE: We was down there working. Lymon got some people down there.

LYMON: My cousin got some land down there. We was helping him.

BOY WILLIE: Got near about a hundred acres. He got it set up real nice. Me and Lymon was down there chopping down trees. We was using Lymon's truck to haul the wood. Me and Lymon used to haul wood all around them parts.

(To BERNIECE.)

Me and Lymon got a truckload of watermelons out there.

(BERNIECE crosses to the window to the parlor.)

Doaker, where your bottle? I know you got a bottle stuck up in your room. Come on, me and Lymon want a drink.

(DOAKER exits into his room.)

BERNIECE: Where you all get that truck from?

BOY WILLIE: I told you it's Lymon's.

BERNIECE: Where you get the truck from, Lymon?

LYMON: I bought it.

BERNIECE: Where he get that truck from, Boy Willie?

BOY WILLIE: He told you he bought it. Bought it for a hundred and twenty dollars. I can't say where he got that hundred and twenty dollars from … but he bought that old piece of truck from Henry Porter. (To LYMON.) Where you get that hundred and twenty dollars from, nigger?

LYMON: I got it like you get yours. I know how to take care of money.

(DOAKER brings a bottle and sets it on the table.)

BOY WILLIE: Aw hell, Doaker got some of that good whiskey. Don't give Lymon none of that. He ain't used to good whiskey. He liable to get sick.

LYMON: I done had good whiskey before.

BOY WILLIE: Lymon bought that truck so he have him a place to sleep. He down there wasn't doing no work or nothing. Sheriff looking for him. He bought that truck to keep away from the sheriff. Got Stovall looking for him too. He down there sleeping in that truck ducking and dodging both of them. I told him come on let's go up and see my sister.

BERNIECE: What the sheriff looking for you for, Lymon?

BOY WILLIE: The man don't want you to know all his business. He's my company. He ain't asking you no questions.

LYMON: It wasn't nothing. It was just a misunderstanding.

BERNIECE: He in my house. You say the sheriff looking for him, I wanna know what he looking for him for. Otherwise you all can go back out there and be where nobody don't have to ask you nothing.

LYMON: It was just a misunderstanding. Sometimes me and the sheriff we don't think alike. So we just got crossed on each other.

BERNIECE: Might be looking for him about that truck. He might have stole that truck.

BOY WILLIE: We ain't stole no truck, woman. I told you Lymon bought it.

DOAKER: Boy Willie and Lymon got more sense than to ride all the way up here in a stolen truck with a load of watermelons. Now they might have stole them watermelons but I don't believe they stole that truck.

BOY WILLIE: You don't even know the man good and you calling him a thief. And we ain't stole them watermelons either. Them old man Pitterford's watermelons. He give me and Lymon all we could load for ten dollars.

DOAKER: No wonder you got them stacked up out there. You must have five hundred watermelons stacked up out there.

BERNIECE: Boy Willie, when you and Lymon planning on going back?

BOY WILLIE: Lymon say he staying. As soon as we sell them watermelons I'm going on back.

BERNIECE: (Starts to exit up the stairs.) That's what you need to do. And you need to do it quick. Come in here disrupting the house. I don't want all that loud carrying on around here. I'm surprised you ain't woke Maretha up.

BOY WILLIE: I was fixing to get her now. (Calls.)

Hey, Maretha!

DOAKER: Berniece don't like all that hollering now.

BERNIECE: Don't you wake that child up!

BOY WILLIE: You going up there … wake her up and tell her her uncle's here. I ain't seen her in three years. Wake her up and send her down here. She can go back to bed.

BERNICE: I ain't waking that child up … and don't you be making all of that noise. You and Lymon need to sell those watermelons and go on back.

(BERNIECE exits up the stairs.)

From *The Piano Lesson* by August Wilson, copyright © 1988, 1990 by August Wilson. Used by permission of Dutton Signet, a division of Penguin Group (USA) Inc.

Reading Comprehension Check

MyReadingLab™
Complete this Exercise
at **myreadinglab.com**

1. What is Doaker's first feeling when Boy Willie comes knocking on his door?
   a. happiness
   b. surprise
   c. sadness
   d. disgust

2. Where did the two guests, Boy Willie and Lymon, begin their journey?
   a. in West Virginia
   b. in Pittsburgh
   c. in Mississippi
   d. in New York City

3. Why is Berniece upset with her brother?
   a. He came unexpectedly.
   b. He is making too much noise.
   c. because he bought the watermelons
   d. She doesn't get along with him.

4. We can infer that Berniece asks twice about where they got the truck
   a. because she is hard of hearing.
   b. because the boys are making too much noise.
   c. because she wants to buy it from them.
   d. because she fears that they stole it.

5. What is the tone of this play scene?
   a. tense and suspicious
   b. serious and pessimistic
   c. light and joyous
   d. objective

Exploring the Topic

Discuss the following questions to review the content of the play excerpt you have just read.

Collaboration

1. From what you know about Boy Willie and Lymon from this scene, do you trust these guys? Why or why not?

2. Why did the two men come north from Mississippi?

3. What predictions can you make about what will happen in later acts of this play?

Post-Reading Vocabulary

Without using a dictionary, determine the meaning of the bolded words from the context.

1. " … a coming together of something **akin** to a storm."

   Akin means _____

2. "She is still **in mourning** for her husband after three years."

   In mourning means _____

3. "He **liable** to get sick."

   Liable means _____

Panel Discussion on the Future of Lending Libraries

With the advent of e-readers, audio books, and the popularity of online reading, some believe that lending libraries should adapt and get rid of the great majority of their paper-based book collection. This panel discussion is on the question of whether libraries should protect their book stock or do away with them.

Here are some possible profiles for you and your classmates. You are free to choose other profiles that you think are appropriate for the panel discussion.

1. a library director who has been working with a paper-based book collection for over forty years
2. a new librarian whose specialty is digital book and online reading education
3. a national book publisher who supplies libraries with many books
4. a senior citizen member of the community who reads a lot, but has little or no computer skills
5. a college student who does a lot of research in the library
6. a representative from a national maker of e-readers
7. a local author who respects only paper-based books
8. a local city council member who is looking to save money on the library budget

To help you prepare for the panel discussion, here are some questions you may want to address:

1. What kinds of changes will help the local library save money?
2. Senior citizens tend to be very active library users. How will these proposed changes affect them?
3. The publishing industry also wants a voice in the direction libraries are going. What do they stand to gain or lose with the elimination of paper-based materials?

4. In the end, who really will control the fate of the library's collection? In other words, who holds the strings: the library users, politicians, the librarians, or the publishing industry?

As you participate in the panel discussion, try to use examples based on your own experience or on something you read in the newspaper. Be sure to refer to the guidelines that your instructor will provide.

WRITING CONNECTIONS: *Writing a Critique of a Literary Work*

If you pick up a daily newspaper or read a magazine focusing on popular culture, you will find critiques, or reviews, of many cultural forms, from new movies to theater, from world premiere television programs to music concerts and new disc recordings. You will also find book reviews of new works of fiction and nonfiction.

However, critiquing works of literature is not limited to the work of journalists. Students in introductory English classes are often asked to write a critique of a piece of literature they have read in class. While this is a challenging task, it can also be an enjoyable one as you have the opportunity to express what you like and dislike about something you have read.

Before discussing some guidelines for critiquing literature, let's look at an example of a short review of a story you read earlier in the chapter. The following is a critique of the short story "Samuel," found on page 180 of the chapter.

Critique of "Samuel," by Grace Paley

"Samuel," a short story written by Grace Paley in 1968, places the reader immediately on a moving subway car in New York City. Four teenage boys are jumping around and playing. The author successfully takes us into the minds of the older seated men and women who are watching the boys taking part in their risky escapades. We learn that some of the older men remember playing similar games when they were younger. We understand that some of the older women are angered by the actions of these young teens. There is a sense of building tension as the train moves forward, a feeling that something tragic is going to happen, and it does.

Paley's story twists unexpectedly forward, and it is easy to miss the message of racism implied in the tale. A white male, frustrated by the antics of black teens on the subway car, pulls the emergency cord, thereby killing an innocent black boy.

"Samuel" is a beautifully told, exciting story which ends with the memorable line, "… but never again will a boy exactly like Samuel be known." I can add to this, never again will a story stay in my mind as long as this one has.

Some Guidelines for Writing a Short Critique of a Work of Literature

Guideline #1: Offer key background information and a short summary of the piece in the first paragraph.
- State the name of the piece, the author, the genre (a poem, a novel, a short story) and the setting (time and place in which the story takes place).

Guideline #2: Focus on what you feel are the strengths and weaknesses of the work.
- Use subjective adjectives to key the reader into your feelings *(beautiful/exciting/ effective/boring/slow-moving/etc.)*.
- Be specific about which parts of the story/poem work and which parts do not (and explain why!).

Guideline #3: Give your verdict on the value of the piece: Would you recommend reading it or not?
- Readers want to know whether or not the piece is worth reading.

Your Turn: Reread the first chapter of *Lucy*, by Jamaica Kincaid, on pages 204–208. Follow the guidelines above and offer a short review of the chapter.

Critique of Chapter One of Lucy, *by Jamaica Kincaid*

_____

_____

_____

_____

_____

_____

_____

_____

_____

_____

_____

_____

Read your review out loud with a small group of classmates and compare your critiques. How are your reviews different from one another?

Are Real Books Nearing the End of Their Shelf Life?

Preview Questions

MyReadingLab™
Complete this Exercise
at **myreadinglab.com**

1. The author of the article you are about to read says that "one thing is certain: eBooks are cool, and fashionable." Would you agree with him? Among your friends, are e-books thought of as "cool"?

2. What are the advantages of saying goodbye to paper books, magazines, and newspapers and reading everything online or on e-readers? Are there any disadvantages?

3. This article was written by a British "insider" in the publishing world. A chief concern in the publishing industry, of course, is making money. Do you think book publishers will see higher or lower profits if more readers switch from paper-based reading to digital? Explain how you think these changes will affect their business.

Pre-Reading Vocabulary: Focus on Some Key Terms

Collaboration

Before beginning the reading selection, it may be helpful to focus on the meaning of some key words in the article. Working with a partner, try to guess the meaning of these words. Then look up the words in a dictionary.

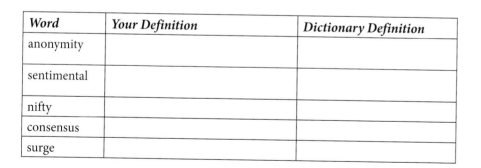

Word	Your Definition	Dictionary Definition
anonymity		
sentimental		
nifty		
consensus		
surge		

Are Real Books Nearing the End of Their Shelf Life?

By Robert McCrum in *The Observer*

Published February 8, 2009

1   Last week, I sent three questions to a selection of insiders from the world of books (publishers, literary agents, editors, and booksellers). Promising anonymity, I asked: 1. Do you have a Sony Reader (or Amazon Kindle)? 2. If so, how do you rate it? And 3. Is your library becoming digital?

2   The answers I received strongly suggest that, although the sales of Kindles and Sony eReaders are statistically insignificant, the age of the ebook has arrived. Just as telling, it has arrived barely six months after the launch of the first ebooks in the UK (about a year in the United States).

3   One independent publisher reported that he was "reading increasingly more on my iPhone" and that he had just read "an entire book on my Sony Reader over Christmas" and had "found the experience surprisingly enjoyable." Book lovers traditionally express a sentimental attachment to ink and paper, fonts and bindings. The next generation seems to be developing a love affair with pixels. "For me," rites one book trade veteran, "it's the text that counts."

4   Another executive from Penguin Books, a company that has issued Sony Readers to all its editors, described hers as a godsend. "I now download virtually all my submissions on to my eReader. In some cases, it means the script is never printed out. The agent emails it and I download it." Inevitably, there's a degree of culture shock. A third senior editor reports: "I can't say I enjoy it very much. Using it at home feels too much like looking at a computer screen."

5   Within the industry, several people declared that, whatever the merits of the eReader as a nifty device for coping with the incessant flow of electronic material, they would emphatically not use an eReader for books on which they were

working with one of their authors. "I can't imagine not annotating a text as I read it," said one literary agent.

6   Obviously, these are specialised responses. Reading for pleasure and the eReader do not seem to go well together. For several correspondents, one forthcoming test will be the restrictions of holiday baggage. "This year," wrote one, "I want to load up my Reader and see how that works for me." To which the traditional book reader will simply respond with three short words: sand, water, power. The meanest paperback will always be a better "delivery system" than a Kindle that's clogged with Ambre Solaire.

7   And yet, looking to a greener future, the consensus from this straw poll was that digital devices would probably make significant inroads into traditional book sales during the next five years. All the major publishers have now set up digital departments to prepare for a decisive shift in reading habits. At the same time, as one put it: "Printed books will continue to be manufactured, bought and cherished for many years to come, if not always." Another wrote: "My work is digital, but my library is 20th century."

8   Today, innovation diffusion is accelerated. Some say that "electronic time" is faster than real time. In other words, that the book is about to become engulfed by an "iPod moment" for literature, analogous to the transformation wrought on the music industry by the download revolution.

9   Who knows? Music and text are fundamentally different. But one thing is certain: ebooks are cool, and fashionable. In the US, Oprah has declared the Kindle her "favourite new gadget." Trend-savvy authors, who used to hesitate before leasing the electronic rights to their work, are coming round to a changed market. According to the *New York Times*, both John Grisham and Danielle Steel are expected soon to be adding their titles to the ebook catalogue.

10   It's already happening here. I have just received a report from a very traditional publisher announcing a surge in e-book sales for one of its authors. The name of this geeky new writer? PD James, the queen of crime, aged 88.

Reading Comprehension Check

MyReadingLab™
Complete this Exercise
at **myreadinglab.com**

1. What is the author's tone?
   a. pessimistic
   b. tolerant and balanced
   c. sad
   d. sarcastic

2. The author believes
   a. paper books are dead.
   b. e-readers have no future.
   c. readers don't care much about how what they read is presented to them.
   d. e-readers have a strong future.

3. From the choice of the author's words in paragraph 7, "And yet, looking to a greener future…", it can be inferred that the author makes the connection between
   a. paper-based books and environmental harm.
   b. e-readers and speed.
   c. colors and reading.
   d. e-readers and their harm to the earth.

4. Why does the author mention music downloads in paragraph 8?
    a. He thinks it is unethical to steal either books or songs from the Internet.
    b. He is comparing the effects of the digital revolution on the music and publishing industries.
    c. He wants readers to see the advantage of free downloads.
    d. There is no relation at all in this section to the world of books.

5. What is the main idea of the article?
    a. Writers feel threatened by new technology.
    b. Things always evolve and transform themselves.
    c. Digital readers will increase in popularity in the coming years.
    d. The author did a survey of people in the publishing world and found most enjoyed their e-readers.

Collaboration

Exploring the Topic

Discuss the following questions to review the content of the article you have just read.

1. In paragraph 3, we learn that one book veteran stated, "For me, it's the text that counts." What do you think he meant with this statement?

2. The author discusses travel reading and makes the point, "The meanest paperback will always be a better 'delivery system' than a Kindle." (para. 6) What advantage of paper books is he referring to here? Do you agree with his claim? Explain.

3. Why is the final sentence reference to the author P. D. James and e-readers a comical one?

Post-Reading Vocabulary

Without using a dictionary, determine the meaning of the bolded words from the context.

1. "Another executive from Penguin Books, a company that has issued Sony Readers to all its editors, described hers as a **godsend**." (para. 4)

   Godsend means _____

2. "In other words, that the book is about to become **engulfed** by an 'iPod moment' for literature." (para. 8)

   Engulfed means _____

3. "In the US, Oprah has declared the Kindle her 'favourite new **gadget**." (para. 9)

   Gadget means _____

An Introduction to Literature

The purpose of this exercise is to get you acquainted with the type of reading you will be required to do in college. First, listen to the lecture and take notes. You can listen to the lecture by scanning the QR code below with your smart phone. Your professor may also read the selections or play the audio file in class. Make sure that you write down the important points of the lecture.

Group Discussion

Collaboration

Working in small groups of three to four students, answer the following questions. Your instructor may ask you to share your answers with your classmates. As you refer to your notes, it is best to write brief answers to each of the questions below using your own words. After the discussion, you will have an opportunity to share your findings with your peers.

1. In the lecture we hear the quote from the writer Ezra Pound, who wrote, "Literature is news that stays news." What do you think he meant by this?

2. What ideas are offered about good writers?

3. What is the topic of the interview excerpt from Ernest Hemingway?

4. What do Jamaica Kincaid and Joseph Conrad think are the aims of writers of literature?

5. The authors ask, "Why not just let people read in their own way, for fun?" They then answer their own question. What do they say?

6. What connections do the authors make between reading literature and watching baseball?

Now that you have discussed the highlights of the lecture with your classmates, read the following selection and answer the multiple-choice questions that follow.

An Introduction to Literature

By **Barnet, Burto, and Cain**

Scan this code using your smart phone to listen to an audio version of this reading

1   Good writers are good readers, careful readers: they know that they must read and reread their own drafts at least as carefully as they read published writing. They know that not until they put words down can they know what they think—and then they usually see that the thoughts are not quite good enough, that the words they put down need to be revised, and revised again. Hemingway, in an interview, commented on this business of writing and revising a couple of more times:

> I always rewrite each day up to the point where I stopped. When it is all finished, naturally you go over it. You get another chance to correct and rewrite when someone else types it, and you see it in clean type. The last chance is in the proofs. You're grateful for these different chances. (*Writers at Work: The Paris Review Interviews, Second Series,* p. 222)

There is a lesson here for all of us, even though our own writing probably is of a humbler sort.

2   What are the aims of the writers of literature? Well, one of our authors, Jamaica Kincaid, in various interviews mentions her "insistence on truth," even if—especially if—the truth is painful. It is not unusual for writers to insist that in their fictions they present truths, they tell it as it is, they wake us up, they seek to make us take off our rose-colored glasses, and to make us see and feel reality. Joseph Conrad, for example, said: "My task ... is by the power of the written word to make you hear, to make you feel—it is, before all, tc make you see."

3   The truth that a writer makes us see is the "news that stays news" that Ezra Pound spoke of. Here is Hemingway talking about the writer's work:

> All good books are alike in that they are truer than if they had really happened and after you are finished reading one you will feel that all that happened to you and afterwards it all belongs to you; the good and the bad, the ecstasy, the remorse, and sorrow, the people and the places and how the weather was. (*Esquire,* December 1934, p. 68)

You may perhaps regard this as Good News and Bad News—Good that you will encounter new literature, not so good (maybe even Bad) that we will be encouraging you to tead analytically, critically, thoughtfully, and to write essays in the same spirit.

4   Why not leave well-enough alone, and just let people read in their own way, for fun? Why this business about analysis? Because some works of literature are deep, and they deserve to be read attentively, seriously, analytically. When you think about it for a moment, you will recall that *thinking* can heighten your daily experience, can increase your enjoyment. Take, for instance, attendance at spectator sports. The person who knows something about baseball surely enjoys the game more than the person who knows almost nothing and who attends the game chiefly to be in the fresh air and to eat a couple of hot dogs. Experienced viewers, for instance, find themselves thinking, "He'll probably bunt," or "Now is the time for the hit and run." Knowing the records of the players and thinking about the players in a specific context heightens—perhaps we can even say "deepens"—one's interest and one's enjoyment in the game.

5   Somewhat similarly, experienced readers of, say, novels by Toni Morrison, get more out of a new book by Morrison than readers who have read very few novels and who now pick up their first Morrison. Yes, of course inexperienced readers can enjoy the book, but, again, experienced readers will see more, hear more, *enjoy more*, because they know what to look for, know (so to speak) *how* to read.

From Barnet et al., *An Introduction to Literature,* 6e, pp. 1, 2, and 4

Reading Comprehension Check

1. The authors make the point that good writers are good readers because
   a. all readers write a lot.
   b. writers must be careful readers of their own work.
   c. reading and writing are the same thing.
   d. reading is more pleasurable than writing.

2. The authors write, "The words they put down need to be **revised**, and revised again." The word *revised* means
   a. erased.
   b. added.
   c. rewritten.
   d. left out.

3. What is the tone of this reading?
   a. angry   c. stubborn
   b. pessimistic   d. enthusiastic

4. What, according to Hemingway, was he grateful for?
   a. the freedom to read
   b. the freedom to correct and rewrite his work
   c. the pressure to write
   d. the beauty of reading novels

5. What topic do the writers Jamaica Kincaid and Joseph Conrad share their views on?
   a. the goals of writers of literature   c. making people hear and feel
   b. waking up   d. the insistence of truth

6. Hemingway argues that after you read a book you can take the emotions into yourself, emotions such as
   a. remorse.   c. ecstasy.
   b. sorrow.   d. all of the above

7. "When you think about it for a moment, you will recall that thinking can **heighten** your daily experience." (para. 4) The word *heighten* means
   a. decrease.   c. neutralize.
   b. intensify.   d. concur with.

8. According to the writers, why is it not enough for readers to read books just for fun?
   a. Books are not written for entertainment.
   b. Fun is something we experience when we are not reading.
   c. A deeper understanding of books can only be found through analysis.
   d. When we read thoughtfully, we can find more success in our lives.

9. The authors discuss the close attention many baseball fans pay to the game to make the point that
   a. baseball players get paid too much money.
   b. reading closely is like catching a ball.
   c. playing baseball and reading literature are very similar activities.
   d. a heightened interest in something deepens the enjoyment of it.

10. The authors' purpose in writing this introduction to literature is to
   a. persuade readers that the study of literature is an enriching experience.
   b. convince the readers to play physical sports and to read.
   c. inform readers of things Ernest Hemingway said.
   d. entertain the readers with quotes from great writers.

Instructions: First try to use logic and background knowledge in guessing the correct answers to the following data questions. Then, go online and search for the relevant data. Be sure to write the Web source next to your research finding.

INTERNET FACT
SEARCH

Literature

1. How long ago did William Shakespeare live?
   a. about four hundred years ago   c. fifty years ago
   b. about two hundred years back   d. He is still alive.

Your guess: _____   Research finding: _____

Web source: _____

2. Who is the best-selling English language writer in history?
   a. William Shakespeare   c. Agatha Christie
   b. Dan Brown   d. John Grisham

   Your guess: _____   Research finding: _____

   Web source: _____

3. How many poems did Emily Dickinson write in her lifetime?
   a. 10   c. none
   b. 180   d. 1,800

   Your guess: _____   Research finding: _____

   Web source: _____

Collaboration

4. Who was America's first great writer of horror?
   a. Stephen King   c. Benjamin Franklin
   b. Edgar Allan Poe   d. Jane Austen

   Your guess: _____   Research finding: _____

   Web source: _____

5. Who dreamed up the character of Harry Potter?
   a. Ernest Hemingway   c. F. Scott Fitzgerald
   b. Nora Roberts   d. J. K. Rowling

   Your guess: _____   Research finding: _____

   Web source: _____

FORMAL PRESENTATION PROJECTS

Students will be given the opportunity to present on a topic of their interest pertinent to one of the text's chapter disciplines. Topics could relate to one of the questions a student has checked off in the "Follow Your Interests" section at the beginning of the chapter. Instructors can have students browse through the chapters to guide them toward a given discipline focus.

MyReadingLab™   For more help with **Writing Summaries** and **Identifying Tone and Purpose**, go to your learning path in **MyReadingLab.com**.

Learning Objectives

IN THIS CHAPTER, YOU WILL LEARN TO . . .

1. Describe the discipline of mathematics
2. Identify key terms in the field of mathematics
3. Read word problems in math effectively
4. Improve your time-management skills
5. Recognize different logical patterns of organization in a text

INTRODUCTION TO THE DISCIPLINE OF MATHEMATICS

1 **LEARNING OBJECTIVE**
Describe the discipline
of mathematics

Arthur Michelson, the author of the first reading selection in the chapter (p. 238) believes that mathematics is not just important for practical reasons. He argues that math knowledge can open our minds to logic and beauty as well. In this chapter, you will have the opportunity to consider how important math is in your own lives. You will read about the nature of coincidence. What are the chances of a mother having seven girls in a row? You can study some humorous math formulas that can be used to help you find the right marriage partner. You will read about how basic calculators evolved into the high-tech scientific calculators that we use in most math and science courses today. One reading will explore how best to calculate your real hourly wage (taking into account your transportation costs, food costs, etc.). Finally, the chapter will also focus on both how to analyze graphs and how to create graphs using Microsoft Excel.

Collaboration

Reading into a Photo

Working in a small group, examine the following photograph and answer the questions that follow.

1. What message does this image convey to you?
2. How has the way we do math in our daily lives changed in the last hundred years?

Collaboration

Follow Your Interests

Review the set of questions below that mathematics experts might explore. Check off the three or four questions that are most interesting to you.

1. In what ways do you use math in your everyday life? Give some examples.
2. Most students in America study math every year of their K–12 studies. Would you say that your experience with math was mostly positive or negative? Explain why.

3. It is common knowledge that math is often disliked by both high school and college students. Why do you think this is the case?

4. If you were chair of a math department, how could you make math more appealing to more students?

5. What, in your opinion, is the most challenging aspect of studying math?

6. What advantages does being a good math student offer someone?

7. Other then teaching, what career opportunities exist for someone with a strong math background?

8. There are many superstitions surrounding numbers, such as the dangers of Friday the 13th and the number 666, as well as the positive attributes of the number 7. In your opinion, how did numbers and superstitions get linked in the first place? Do different numbers have positive or negative associations in your view? Explain.

9. The explosion of digital technology in the world of electronics (cameras, smartphones, MP3 players, etc.) has more and more young people thinking about the importance of size, space, and speed in their usage of these products. Why are these everyday applications of math more appealing to the younger generation? Do you think these changes in technology will make students better appreciate the study of math? Explain.

10. Are some people naturally good at adding, subtracting, multiplying, and dividing numbers, or is it because they have received better instruction than the rest of us? Explain.

11. Survey data is often published in newspapers and magazines. When you read survey results—such as, "73% of men think that high-speed Internet is a necessity," or "women are 18% more likely than men to be concerned about their weight"—do you always trust this information? Why or why not? What factors might skew the results of a survey?

12. Are you a "time conscious" person? In other words, when you have an appointment in 45 minutes, do you play out how much time it will take to get from where you are to where you need to be in order to not show up late ("I will have to wait approximately 10 minutes for the bus, then spend 20 minutes on the bus, and then walk 15 minutes from the bus …")? What is the relationship between mathematics and time?

Now, share your choices with a small group of classmates and discuss why these particular questions are most interesting to you. You may wish to discuss these questions with them and ask which questions they found interesting.

Key Terms in the Field of Mathematics

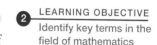

LEARNING OBJECTIVE
Identify key terms in the field of mathematics

The following key terms are frequently used in the discipline of mathematics. If you take a college-level course in mathematics, it will be important for you to remember these words and to use them in your speech and writing. Review the words below and answer the multiple-choice questions that follow.

correlation	graph	probability
deduce	inductive	sequence
equation	inverse	statistics
estimate	logical	subset
factoring	parallel	volume

EXERCISE 1   **Inferring Meaning from Context**

Read each sentence below and try to derive the meaning of the italicized key terms from the context. Circle the correct definition of each italicized term.

1. To figure out which path to take to solve a math equation, one has to use *logical* problem-solving skills.
   a. valid reasoning
   b. random
   c. guessing
   d. math logo

2. When taking a multiple-choice exam, you can often *deduce* the answer by ruling out the incorrect choices.
   a. follow your original guess
   b. figure out from known information
   c. cross out
   d. push forward

3. The student tried and tried, but could not figure out how to make the *equation* work.
   a. the only solution
   b. a figure which is not in balance
   c. a graph showing unequal parts
   d. an expression asserting the equality of two quantities

4. To understand the formula, the teacher began by *factoring* out each part of the equation.
   a. crossing out unnecessary parts
   b. separating an equation, formula, etc., into its component parts
   c. putting all of the parts of a math problem back together
   d. paying debts on time so there are no interest fees

5. What is the *probability* of a woman giving birth to six girls in a row?
   a. most likely outcome of an action
   b. lack of trust in something
   c. the relative possibility that an event will occur
   d. the positive consequences of a combination of actions

6. Scientists found a *correlation* between smoking and the chances of getting lung cancer.
   a. angle
   b. negative consequence
   c. compromise or negotiation
   d. mutual relation of two or more things

7. The zoologist used *inductive* reasoning by first laying out his claim that birds always come back to their original nests.
   a. illogical
   b. working from general to specific through investigation
   c. reasoning from detailed facts to general principles
   d. process of elimination

8. To solve a multi-step problem, one should consider the *sequence* of steps.
   a. order of succession
   b. the relationship of
   c. the fashion involved
   d. the necessary technology

9. First you must *estimate* the distance between point A and point B.
   a. find the exact distance
   b. form an approximate judgment
   c. figure out through logical problem-solving
   d. negate

10. Set A is a *subset* of set B if every element in set A is also in set B.
    a. a set within a smaller set
    b. a set within a larger set
    c. a set with no relationship to any other set
    d. a programmed set

11. The bar *graph* showed how women have passed men in educational achievement.
    a. any information showing the relationship between multiple objects
    b. a drawing depicting the relation between certain sets of numbers or quantities
    c. information focusing on gender comparison
    d. pie chart

12. In class today we measured the *volume* of a cone with a radius of 4 inches and a height of 6 inches.
    a. the audio loudness
    b. a certain amount of business
    c. the full radius of a given object considering all sides
    d. the amount of space that an object or substance occupies

13. If we keep walking on Broadway we will never get to Main Street because the two streets run *parallel* with each other.
    a. intersecting
    b. being of equal lengths and similar trajectories
    c. lying in the same plane but never meeting no matter how far extended
    d. being the same relative distance from one point to the next

14. The newspaper is full of *statistics* about crime in this city.
   a. numerical facts or data
   b. increasing numbers
   c. true numbers
   d. graphs and charts

15. There is an *inverse* relationship between increasing the amount of exercise you do and gaining weight.
   a. parallel
   b. direct
   c. bearing upon other facts
   d. reversed in direction or tendency

Collaboration

EXERCISE 2   Creating Meaningful Sentences with the Key Terms

Working with a partner, choose five of the key terms in mathematics and write an original sentence about each one.

1. **Word =** _____

   _____

   _____

2. **Word =** _____

   _____

   _____

3. **Word =** _____

   _____

   _____

4. **Word =** _____

   _____

   _____

5. **Word =** _____

   _____

   _____

COLLEGE STUDY SKILLS
Effective Ways of Reading and Solving Math Word Problems

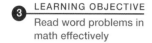

LEARNING OBJECTIVE
Read word problems in math effectively

Strong word problem skills are critical in both the study of math and in business classes as well. To solve math word problems you must first translate ordinary English sentences into the language of algebraic equations.

Strategy for Solving Word Problems

Read the problem carefully several times until you can state in your own words what is given and what the problem is looking for. There is no substitute for careful reading. If you rush it, you may misinterpret the focus of the problem. The following 5 steps will help you solve the problem with ease.

Step 1. Underline key terms and numbers that you think you will make use of in formulating a solution.

Step 2. Let x (or any variable) represent one of the unknown quantities in the problem. If necessary, write expressions for any other unknown quantities in the problem in terms of x.

Step 3. Write an equation in x that models the verbal conditions of the problem.

Step 4. Solve the equation and answer the problem's question.

Step 5. Check the solution in the original wording of the problem, not in the equation obtained from the words.

Let's look at an example word problem and see how we can translate words into equations. You will see how following the 5 steps above will lead you to the correct solution.

> **Example**: Your local computer store is having a terrific sale on digital cameras. After a 40% price reduction, you purchase a digital camera for $276. What was the camera's price before the reduction?
>
> adapted from Blitzer, *Thinking Mathematically*, 5e, pp. 336–337

Step 1. Let x represent one of the unknown quantities. We will let x = the original price of the digital camera prior to the reduction.

Step 2. Represent other unknown quantities in terms of x. There are no other unknown quantities to find, so we can skip this step.

Step 3. Write an equation in x that models the conditions. The camera's original price minus the 40% reduction is the reduced price, $276.

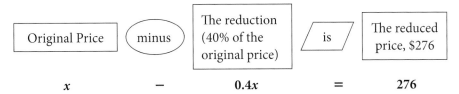

$$x \quad - \quad 0.4x \quad = \quad 276$$

Step 4. Solve the equation and answer the question.

$x - 0.4x = 276$ This is the equation that models the problem's conditions.

$0.6x = 276$ Combine like terms $x - 0.4x = 1x - 0.4x = 0.6x$

$\dfrac{0.6x}{0.6} \quad \dfrac{276}{0.6}$ $x = 460$

       Divide both terms by 0.6

       Simplify 0.6 $\dfrac{460}{276}$

The digital camera's price before the reduction was $460.

Step 5.   Check the proposed solution in the original wording of the problem.
The price before the reduction, $460 minus the 40% reduction, should equal the reduced price in the original wording, $276.
$$460 - 40\% \text{ of } 460 = 460 - 0.4(460) = 460 - 184 = 276$$

from Blitzer, *Thinking Mathematically*, 5e, pp. 336–337

You may find the table below of algebraic translations of English phrases useful in working with word problems.

TABLE 6.1 Algebraic Translations of English Phrases

English Phrase	Algebraic Expression
Addition	
The sum of a number and 7	$x + 7$
Five more than a number; a number plus 5	$x + 5$
A number increased by 6; 6 added to a number	$x + 6$
Subtraction	
A number minus 4	$x - 4$
A number decreased by 5	$x - 5$
A number subtracted from 8	$8 - x$
The difference between a number and 6	$x - 6$
The difference between 6 and a number	$6 - x$
Seven less than a number	$x - 7$
Seven minus a number	$7 - x$
Nine fewer than a number	$x - 9$
Multiplication	
Five times a number	$5x$
The product of 3 and a number	$3x$
Two-thirds of a number (used with fractions)	$\frac{2}{3}x$
Seventy-five percent of a number (used with decimals)	$0.75x$
Thirteen multiplied by a number	$13x$
A number multiplied by 13	$13x$
Twice a number	$2x$
Division	
A number divided by 3	$\frac{x}{3}$
The quotient of 7 and a number	$\frac{7}{x}$
The quotient of a number and 7	$\frac{x}{7}$
The reciprocal of a number	$\frac{1}{x}$
More than one operation	
The sum of twice a number and 7	$2x + 7$
Twice the sum of a number and 7	$2(x + 7)$
Three times the sum of 1 and twice a number	$3(1 + 2x)$
Nine subtracted from 8 times a number	$8x - 9$
Twenty-five percent of the sum of 3 times a number and 14	$0.25(3x + 14)$
Seven times a number, increased by 24	$7x + 24$
Seven times the sum of a number and 24	$7(x + 24)$

from Blitzer, *Thinking Mathematically*, 5e, p. 332.

Putting the Skill into Action

Here are a few more tips you might find helpful in working with math word problems.

- **Learn unfamiliar terminology:** If you find a key vocabulary term that you are unfamiliar with (integer, mean, etc.) try to figure out the meaning from context, and if you cannot, look it up in either a dictionary, or better, in the glossary of your math textbook. Glossaries are found in the back of the text.

- **Ask yourself if you've seen a problem similar to this one.** If so, what is similar about it? What did you need to do?

- **Think about what facts are you given.** What do you need to find out?

- **Work backward:** In some cases you can work backward by guessing a possible solution and seeing if this solution leads to a logical fit with the facts given in the problem.

- **Reflect:** After solving the problem, look over your solution carefully. Does your answer seem probable? Does it make sense?

Now work with a partner to solve a few word problems. Follow the five steps outlined on page 233, and be sure to read the problems multiple times, underlining key terms and numbers.

Collaboration

Word Problem 1

You are choosing between two long-distance telephone plans. Plan A has a monthly fee of $20 with a charge of $0.05 per minute for all long-distance calls. Plan B has a monthly fee of $5 with a charge of $0.10 per minute for all long-distance calls. For how many minutes of long-distance calls will the costs of the two plans be the same?   from Blitzer, *Thinking Mathematically,* 5e, pp. 335–336

Word Problem 2

In a film the actor Charles Coburn plays an elderly "uncle" character criticized for marrying a woman when he is three times her age. He wittily replies, "Ah, but in 20 years time I shall only be twice her age." How old are the "uncle" and the woman?

from Blitzer, *Thinking Mathematically,* 5e, p. 341

Word Problem 3

A thief steals a number of rare plants from a nursery. On the way out, the thief meets three security guards, one after another. To each security guard, the thief is forced to give one-half the plants that he still has, plus two more. Finally the thief leaves the nursery with 1 lone palm. How many plants were originally stolen?

from Blitzer, *Thinking Mathematically,* 5e, p. 341

The Last Word

While word problems can sometimes be tricky, they can also be fun. The key is to read the problem very carefully, underline key terms and numbers, and take the time to understand clearly what you are being asked to do. If you pay close attention to what you are doing and follow the necessary steps, you will find that with more practice the patterns become clear and the solutions much easier to find.

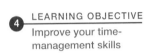

READINESS FOR COLLEGE SUCCESS
Time-Management Skills

LEARNING OBJECTIVE
4
Improve your time-management skills

Do you regularly sit down with a weekly planner and map out your study plan for the week? Do you work with a semester calendar to plan ahead for heavy study periods? Building solid time-management skills yields positive results. Students who don't think ahead and push through the semester procrastinating day in day out end up wildly stressed out with little to show in the way of quality academic work and course grades. If you fit the mold of a "time-wasting student," it is time that you break old habits that don't work for you and build new ones!

Remember, you are the captain of your own ship, and you have 168 hours a week to navigate (24 hours a day, seven days a week). A first step would be to think about the activities you do each week and to estimate how much time you generally spend on each.

Activity: Estimate how much time you spend per week on the following activities:

Number of hours

_____ In-class time

_____ Studying (Most colleges suggest 2–3 hours for every class hour.)

_____ Commuting/transportation time

_____ Job

_____ Co-curricular activities (college clubs/community involvement)

_____ Physical fitness/athletics

_____ Socializing with friends and leisure activities (watching TV, etc.)

_____ Sleeping

_____ Eating meals

_____ Personal hygiene (bathing/hair/shaving/make-up/etc.)

_____ Family responsibilities (cleaning/shopping/spending time with relatives, etc.)

_____ Other activities: _____

Now add up the total number of hours you estimated for all of the activities above that make up your "typical" week.

Total hours from list above = _____

If the total is less than 168 hours, great news! You have more time on your hands than you thought you did. Instead of wasting this precious extra time, build in some more study time.

If your total is more than 168 hours, you will need to rethink how you divide up your time and cut back on certain activities. Perhaps you are spending too much time doing leisure activities such as texting your friends or playing video games. If you make some personal sacrifices, you can free up some more time for studying (and you will see the positive results shortly after you do so).

If you aren't already working with a weekly planner, go out and buy one today. And don't just purchase a planner, use it!

Why Math Always Counts: It Can Open Our Minds to Logic and Beauty

Preview Questions

1. The author of the article you are about to read makes the argument that math really matters and adds beauty to our lives. Would you say that you agree with this idea? Why or why not?

2. Can you think of any professions for which no knowledge of math is necessary? Explain.

3. A number of academics have made arguments in the past that men are generally stronger in math and the hard sciences than women. Do you believe this is the case? How would you go about proving or disproving this argument?

MyReadingLab™
Complete this **Exercise**
at **myreadinglab.com**

Pre-Reading Vocabulary: Focus on Some Key Terms

Collaboration

Before beginning the reading selection, it may be helpful to focus on the meaning of some key words in the article. Working with a partner, try to guess the meaning of these words. Then look up the words in a dictionary.

Word	*Your Definition*	*Dictionary Definition*
counterparts		
implicit		
meticulous		
distinguish		
overstate		

Why Math Always Counts: It Can Open Our Minds to Logic and Beauty

By Arthur Michelson
Los Angeles Times, December 26, 2004

Arthur Michelson teaches at the Beechwood School in Menlo Park, Calif.

1 American middle school students don't much care that they're worse at math than their counterparts in Hong Kong or Finland. "I don't need it," my students say. "I'm gonna be a basketball star." Or a beautician, or a car mechanic, or a singer.

2 It's also hard to get much of a rise out of adults over the fact, released earlier this year, that the United States ranked 28th out of 41 countries whose middle school students' math skills were tested by the Organization for Economic Cooperation and Development. So what if we're tied with Latvia, while nations like Japan and South Korea leave us in the dust? After all, when was the last time you used algebra?

3 But math is not just about computing quadratic equations, knowing geometric proofs or balancing a checkbook. And it's not just about training Americans to become scientists.

4 It has implicit value. It is about discipline, precision, thoroughness and meticulous analysis. It helps you see patterns, develops your logic skills, teaches you to concentrate and to separate truth from falsehood. These are abilities and qualities that distinguish successful people.

5 Math helps you make wise financial decisions, but also informs you so you can avoid false claims from advertisers, politicians and others. It helps you determine risk. Some examples:

- If a fair coin is tossed and eight heads come up in a row, most adults would gamble that the next toss would come up tails. But a coin has no memory. There is always a 50–50 chance. See you at the casino?

- If you have no sense of big numbers, you can't evaluate the consequences of how government spends your money. Why should we worry? Let our kids deal with it . . .

- Enormous amounts of money are spent on quack medicine. Many people will reject sound scientific studies on drugs or nutrition if the results don't fit their preconceived notions, yet they might leap to action after reading news stories on the results of small, inconclusive or poorly run studies.

- After an airplane crash, studies show that people are more likely to drive than take a plane despite the fact that they are much more likely to be killed or injured while driving. Planes are not like copycat criminals. A plane is not more likely to crash just because another recently did. In fact, the most dangerous time to drive is probably right after a plane crash because so many more people are on the road.

6 The precision of math, like poetry, gets to the heart of things. It can increase our awareness.

7 Consider the Fibonacci series, in which each number is the sum of the preceding two, (0, 1, 1, 2, 3, 5, 8, 13 …). Comparing each successive pair yields a relationship known as the Golden Ratio, which often shows up in nature and art. It's the mathematical underpinning of what we consider beautiful. You'll find it in the design of the Parthenon and the Mona Lisa, as well as in human proportion;

for instance, in the size of the hand compared to the forearm and the forearm to the entire arm. Stephen Hawking's editor warned him that for every mathematical formula he wrote in a book, he would lose a big part of his audience. Yet more than a little is lost by dumbing things down.

8   It is not possible to really understand science and the scientific method without understanding math. A rainbow is even more beautiful and amazing when we understand it. So is a lightning bolt, an ant or ourselves.

9   Math gives us a powerful tool to understand our universe. I don't wish to overstate: Poetry, music, literature and the fine and performing arts are also gateways to beauty. Nothing we study is a waste. But the precision of math helps refine how we think in a very special way.

10   How do we revitalize the learning of math? I don't have the big answer. I teach middle school and try to find an answer one child at a time. When I can get one to say, "Wow, that's tight," I feel the joy of a small victory.

Courtesy of Arthur Michelson

Reading Comprehension Check

MyReadingLab™
Complete this **Exercise**
at **myreadinglab.com**

1. What was the author's purpose in writing this article?
   a. to entertain readers with humorous stories
   b. to inform readers about Americans' love of math
   c. to convince readers that math is relevant in our lives
   d. to offer readers information about the state of mathematics in American schools

2. What is the main idea of the article's first two paragraphs?
   a. Most young students and older adults don't seem to care much that America's level of math skills is very low in comparison with many other countries.
   b. Students in Hong Kong surpass American students in math scores.
   c. People generally do not use algebra in their daily lives.
   d. Knowledge of math widens our world and adds beauty to our lives.

3. We can infer from the article that the author most likely believes that
   a. taking a plane always involves significant risk.
   b. math leads us toward informed decisions and away from irrational thinking.
   c. knowledge of math guides us toward more profitable results when we gamble.
   d. young kids should spend most of their free time studying math.

4. As a teacher, what solution does the author offer to increase students' desire to learn math?
   a. more financial motivations
   b. to make math classes more interactive
   c. to hold more hours of math class each day
   d. to work on one student at a time

5. What is the author's tone?
   a. informative
   b. encouraging
   c. pessimistic
   d. angry

Collaboration

Exploring the Topic

Discuss the following questions to review the content of the article you have just read.

1. What does the author mean when he writes in the fourth paragraph, math "has implicit value"?

2. The author shares a number of examples of how mathematical thinking helps us better understand the world around us. Which example, in your opinion, is the most interesting? Why?

3. Near the end of the article, the author makes the claim that "nothing we study is a waste." (para. 4) Would you agree with his point? Why or why not?

Post-Reading Vocabulary

Without using a dictionary, determine the meaning of the bolded words from the context.

1. "It is about discipline, **precision**, thoroughness and meticulous analysis." (para. 4)

   Precision means _____

2. "Enormous amounts of money are spent on **quack** medicine." (para. 8)

   Quack means _____

3. "Consider the Fibonacci series, in which each number is the sum of the **preceding** two." (para. 11)

   Preceding means _____

READING

Reading Selection **2**

Book Excerpt

MyReadingLab™
Complete this **Exercise**
at **myreadinglab.com**

Coincidences and Probability

Preview Questions

1. Do you believe in coincidences, or do you think all things happen for a reason? Explain. Can you justify your position with hard evidence?

2. Can you remember a recent coincidence that you found particularly surprising (bumping into someone you haven't seen for a long time, thinking of someone who then magically appears, etc.)? Share a story involving coincidence.

3. What is the relationship between mathematics and the topic of "coincidences"?

Pre-Reading Vocabulary: Focus on Some Key Terms

Collaboration

Before beginning the reading selection, it may be helpful to focus on the meaning of some key words in the article. Working with a partner, try to guess the meaning of these words. Then look up the words in a dictionary.

Word	Your Definition	Dictionary Definition
mystical		
bound		
outcome		
calculate		
in succession		

Coincidences and Probability

By Robert F. Blitzer

Coincidences

1   The phone rings and it is the friend you were just thinking of. You're driving down the road and a song you were humming in your head comes on the radio. Although these coincidences seem strange, perhaps even mystical, they're not.

2   Coincidences are bound to happen. Ours is a world in which there are a great many potential coincidences, each with a low probability of occurring. When these surprising coincidences happen, we are amazed and remember them. However, we pay little attention to the countless number of non-coincidences. How often do you think of your friend and she doesn't call? How often does she call when you're not thinking about her? By noticing the hits and ignoring the misses, we incorrectly perceive that there is a relationship between the occurrence of two independent events.

3   Another problem is that we often underestimate the probabilities of coincidences in certain situations, acting with more surprise than we should when they occur. For example, in a group of only 23 people, the probability that two individuals share a birthday (same month and day) is greater than ½. Above 50 people, the probability of any two people sharing a birthday approaches certainly.

4   Consider tossing a fair coin two times in succession. The outcome of the first toss, heads or tails, does not affect what happens when you toss the coin a second time. For example, the occurrence of tails on the first toss does not make tails more likely or less likely to occur on the second toss. The repeated toss of a coin produces independent events because the outcome of one toss does not affect the outcome of others.

5   *INDEPENDENT EVENTS: Two events are independent events if the occurrence of either of them has no effect on the probability of the other.*

6   When a fair coin is tossed two times in succession, the set of equally likely outcomes is:

{heads, heads; heads, tails; tails, heads; tails, tails}

7   We can use this set to find the probability of getting heads on the first toss and heads on the second toss:

$$P \text{ (heads and heads)} = \frac{\text{number of ways two heads can occur}}{\text{total number of possible outcomes}} = \frac{1}{4}$$

8   We can also determine the probability of two heads, 1/4, without having to list all the equally likely outcomes. The probability of heads on the first toss is ½. The probability of heads on the second toss is also ½. The product of these probabilities, ½ × ½, results in the probability of two heads, namely 1/4. Thus,

$$P \text{ (heads and heads)} = P \text{ (heads)} \times P \text{ (heads)}.$$

9   In general if two events are independent, we can calculate the probability of the first occurring and the second occurring by multiplying their probabilities.

Probabilities with Independent Events:

If A and B are independent events, then:

$$P(A \text{ and } B) = P \text{ (A)} \times P \text{ (B)}.$$

Example 1: Independent Events on a Roulette Wheel

10 Figure A shows a U.S. roulette wheel that has 38 numbered slots (1 through 36, 0, and 00). Of the 38 compartments, 18 are black, 18 are red, and 2 are green. A play has the dealer spin the wheel and a small ball in opposite directions. As the ball slows to a stop, it can land with equal probability on any one of the 38 numbered slots. Find the probability of red occurring on two consecutive plays.

Figure A

11   **Solution:** The wheel has 38 equally likely outcomes and 18 are red. Thus, the probability of red occurring on a play is 18/38, or 9/19. The result that occurs on each play is independent of all previous results. Thus,

$$P \text{ (red and red)} = P \text{ (red)} \times P \text{ (red)} = 9/19 \times 9/19 = 81/361 = 0.224$$

12   The probability of red occurring on two consecutive plays is 81/361.

13   Some roulette players incorrectly believe that if red occurs on two consecutive plays, then another color is "due." Because the events are independent, the outcomes of previous spins have no effect on any other spins.

14   **Problem:** Find the probability of green occurring on two consecutive plays on a roulette wheel.

15   The rule for independent events can be extended to cover three or more independent events. Thus, if A, B, and C are independent events, then

$$P(A \text{ and } B \text{ and } C) = P(A) \times P(B) \times P(C).$$

Example 2: Independent Events in a Family

16 The picture on the right shows a family that had nine girls in a row. Find the probability of this occurrence.

17   **Solution:** If two or more events are independent, we can find the probability of them all occurring by multiplying their probabilities. The probability of a baby girl is 1/2, so the probability of nine girls in a row is used as a factor nine times.

$$P(\text{nine girls in a row}) = \tfrac{1}{2} \times \tfrac{1}{2} \times \tfrac{1}{2} \times \tfrac{1}{2} \times \tfrac{1}{2} \times \tfrac{1}{2} \times \tfrac{1}{2} \times \tfrac{1}{2} \times \tfrac{1}{2}$$
$$= \frac{1}{2}$$

18   The probability of a run of nine girls in a row is 1/512. (If another child is born into the family, this event is independent of the other nine and the probability of a girl is still ½.)

from Blitzer, *Thinking Mathematically*, 5e, pp. 653, 648–649

Reading Comprehension Check

1. The examples of the phone call from a friend and the song you were humming coming on the radio are given to demonstrate that
   a. these types of coincidences are very rare.
   b. while these coincidences might seem strange, they are not.
   c. coincidences never happen.
   d. coincidences only happen to certain people on certain days.

2. What does the author mean when he talks about "noticing the hits and ignoring the misses"? (para. 2)
   a. We often miss our friends when we are not thinking about them.
   b. We do not pay enough attention to all of the coincidences happening around us.
   c. We tend to pay much more attention when coincidences occur than when they do not.
   d. People notice when they are being hit.

3. What is the main idea of the third paragraph?
   a. We are frequently surprised by situations that, in fact, are more likely to occur than we think.
   b. Two individuals sharing a birthday is not as likely as we may imagine.
   c. The nature of a coincidence depends on the likelihood of its occurrence.
   d. In some cases, we should be more surprised by coincidences.

4. In the section on "Probabilities," an "independent event" is defined as one
   a. where the outcome of an event directly plays on the outcome of another.
   b. when an event is less likely to happen based on another event.
   c. when an event is more likely to happen based on another event.
   d. where the outcome of one event does not affect the outcome of others.

5. Following the example of a family having nine girls in a row, what is the probability of a family having four boys in a row?
   a. 1/264   c. 1/16
   b. 1/2   d. 1/8

Collaboration

Exploring the Topic

Discuss the following questions to review the content of the textbook section you have just read.

1. The author makes the point that we are often surprised by occurrences that should not be considered surprising. The example of someone in your class sharing the same birthday is looked at as a wondrous coincidence, but is really not. Why do you think people act so surprised at relatively common events? Can you think of another example of an occurrence that might be looked at as a great coincidence that is not much of a coincidence at all?

2. If a coin lands on heads three times in a row, why do many people believe that the fourth coin toss will surely land on tails? Is this type of thinking logical? What would the author argue?

3. It is fun to invent probability scenarios. In the reading, you have looked at the probability of a coin landing on heads two times in a row, the probability of the ball landing on certain places on a roulette wheel, and of a family having multiple children of the same gender.

   Create your probability scenario and share it with the class.

   Question: *What is the probability of* _____?

Post-Reading Vocabulary

Without using a dictionary, determine the meaning of the bolded words from the context.

1. "For example, the **occurrence** of tails on the first toss …" (para. 4)

   Occurrence means _____

2. "Find the probability of red occurring on two **consecutive** plays." (para. 10)

   Consecutive means _____

3. "Ours is a world in which there are a great many **potential** coincidences." (para. 2)

   Potential means _____

Rebecca Martin   An Interview with a Student in the Field of Mathematics

Michigan State University

1. How did you find your path to majoring in math?

I chose math as my major because it is at the core of everything. I found that in order to fundamentally understand a subject such as chemistry or physics, I needed to know math, so I decided to devote my studies to the subject.

2. What is the biggest obstacle you face in your study of math?

One obstacle I faced was being a female math major; in most of my classes I am the only girl and as antiquated as it sounds, some people doubt my capability in math because of my gender.

3. What area(s) of mathematics in particular do you find most interesting?

I really enjoy differential equations because of all the real-world applications it possesses.

4. What specific skills are required of students who study math?

To study math, you must be able to think logically and creatively. As you progress in math, solutions become less cut and dry, so you need to think about the problem in multiple ways and you must have perseverance to find the solution, if the problem has one.

5. Other than being a mathematician, what other career avenues are available for math majors?

Math majors can go into a variety of fields including financial analysis, statistical analysis, and biological and physical science modeling.

"Marriage Equations," from *Geek Logic*

Preview Questions

1. Would you describe yourself as a "risk-taker," or someone who makes decisions more cautiously? Explain.

2. When we make big life decisions (whether to marry someone, to move to another state, to have children, etc.), we look at the probability of our choice working out by considering all the factors involved. Do you believe life is generally predictable and that we can see the road ahead, or is life unpredictable and thus not worth too much pre-planning? Discuss your view.

3. Mathematical formulas are often used in business to pinpoint the exact probability of a certain outcome (especially in the world of insurance). Can we write mathematical equations to guide us toward a better understanding of our own personal future? Why or why not?

MyReadingLab™
Complete this **Exercise**
at **myreadinglab.com**

Pre-Reading Vocabulary: Focus on Some Key Terms

Before beginning the reading selection, it may be helpful to focus on the meaning of some key words in the article. Working with a partner, try to guess the meaning of these words. Then look up the words in a dictionary.

Word	Your Definition	Dictionary Definition
intrigue		
statistics		
hindsight		
aversion		
tantrum		

"Marriage Equations," from *Geek Logic*

By Garth Sundem

Garth Sundem is the author of the popular math/humor gift book entitled Geek Logik, *from which this reading is taken. First, read a little about Garth's story. Then investigate a few of his comical math equations.*

Garth Sundem

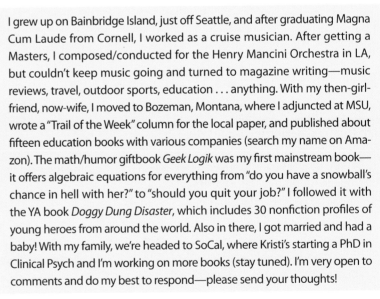

I grew up on Bainbridge Island, just off Seattle, and after graduating Magna Cum Laude from Cornell, I worked as a cruise musician. After getting a Masters, I composed/conducted for the Henry Mancini Orchestra in LA, but couldn't keep music going and turned to magazine writing—music reviews, travel, outdoor sports, education . . . anything. With my then-girlfriend, now-wife, I moved to Bozeman, Montana, where I adjuncted at MSU, wrote a "Trail of the Week" column for the local paper, and published about fifteen education books with various companies (search my name on Amazon). The math/humor giftbook *Geek Logik* was my first mainstream book—it offers algebraic equations for everything from "do you have a snowball's chance in hell with her?" to "should you quit your job?" I followed it with the YA book *Doggy Dung Disaster*, which includes 30 nonfiction profiles of young heroes from around the world. Also in there, I got married and had a baby! With my family, we're headed to SoCal, where Kristi's starting a PhD in Clinical Psych and I'm working on more books (stay tuned). I'm very open to comments and do my best to respond—please send your thoughts!

1   It's been just over two years since I got married, and I remember thinking that it would be wonderful to finally be free forever from the intrigue and confusion of dating.

2   You can't fault the optimism.

3   Now, through the lens of hindsight, I realize that I should have known that dating and even cohabitating were only warm-ups for the big dance.

4   I thought I would look at some more fundamental equations that govern marriage. In the equations below, the first is based on solid statistics—an 11,000-person study by the CDC that explored factors that help and hurt a marriage's chances of working. For example, they found that if a woman is married before age 24, her chances of staying married for 15 years decreased by 30%. These statistics were easy to write in math terms, and the equation does fairly accurately predict your chances of being married at time "T." Granted there are other factors that might help or hurt your specific marriage, but the CDC study found that, for most people, these are the biggest factors. Remember that the average for all marriages is only about 50% and if you get a low number, please accept my very best wishes in bucking the odds.

5   The other two ("should we get married" and "how many kids should we have") are a bit more shoot-from-the-hip. With this kind of equation, I try to make the math match common sense. If you put in honest numbers, they return honest answers, but they're not quite as scientific as the first.

6   So, good luck, have fun, and check out posts deeper in the blog for additional marriage-relevant equations.

7   **What are the chances my marriage will last?**

$$100\left(\frac{A + E}{34}\right)\left(\frac{2K + R + 6}{2D + 10}\right)\left(\frac{100}{102 + 2P}\right)^{2T} = H_{.E.A.}$$

A = Her age at time of marriage
E = Current combined years of post-high-school education
K = Number of kids from this marriage
R = How religious is the couple (1–10 with 10 being "the Pope")
D = Combined number of divorces of couple's parents
P = Combined previous marriages
T = Years at which you are computing the chances

H.e.a. stands for "Happily Ever After" and is the percent chance you will still be married at time "T"

8   **Should we get married?**

$$\left(\frac{S}{A}\right) = \left(\frac{L}{D + 1}\right) + \frac{T}{3(C + 1)} = T_{tk}$$

T = How many years have you been dating?
L = The number of times per day that something makes you think of this person
C = If your families got together for a holiday dinner, the estimated number of times there would be uncomfortable friction
S = How many shared interests and/or goals do you two have?
A = How many individual or conflicting interests and/or goals do you two have?
D = The average number of disagreements you have with this person in a month

If Ttk is above one, you should tie the knot

9 **How many kids should you have?**

$$\sqrt[3]{\left(\frac{S - 30,000}{5,000}\right)} + \frac{K + 11 - E}{\frac{T}{20} + A} = K_{ids}$$

S = Your combined household salary

K = Combined, how many brothers and sisters do you and your spouse have (include yourselves in this number)

T = Combined hours per week you and your significant other work outside the house

A = On a scale from 1–10, the highest level of aversion you have to any of the following: Changing diapers, sleep deprivation, visiting in-laws, tantrums

E = On a scale from 1–10, how concerned are you about global over population

Kids, of course, is the number of kids that your lifestyle supports

Excerpt from geeklogik.blogspot.com.

© Garth Sundem. Garth Sundem is the author of books including *Brain Trust* and *The Geeks' Guide to World Domination*. Reprinted by permission.

MyReadingLab™
Complete this **Exercise**
at **myreadinglab.com**

Reading Comprehension Check

1. The purpose of the author's self-introduction is to
   a. show how important he is in the world.
   b. focus primarily on his *Geek Logik* work.
   c. offer some background about his life and his other projects.
   d. give detailed algebraic equations about real-life questions.

2. What does the author mean when he writes, "I realize that I should have known that dating and even cohabitating were only warm-ups for the big dance"? (para. 3)
   a. Dancing is harder than cohabitating.
   b. Marriage is tougher than just dating or living together.
   c. Dating is a good practice for living together.
   d. Nothing is more challenging than dating.

3. In the first equation, what does 2K + R represent? (para. 7)
   a. two times the number of kids a couple has plus how religious they are
   b. how religious a couple's children are times two
   c. the chances of a marriage succeeding
   d. the number of kids a couple has times two

4. In the second equation (para. 8) what does $\frac{S}{A}$ stand for?
   a. shared interests over artificial obstacles
   b. the number of conflicting goals a couple has over their shared interests
   c. a couple's individual interests in relation to their shared interests
   d. the number of shared interests a couple has over the number of conflicting goals/interests they have

5. What is the main idea behind Garth's life situation equations?
   a. Math can be funny and entertaining.
   b. We can better understand the probability of a life choice working out if we analyze a number of the key factors involved.
   c. Marriage and choosing whether to have children are very big decisions.
   d. Couples that are religious are less likely to get divorced.

Exploring the Topic

Collaboration

Discuss the following questions to review the content of the blog you have just read.

1. After reading Garth's short profile of himself, what did you find most interesting about his story?

2. What statistic does the author cite about couples who marry before the age of 24? Are you surprised by this statistic? Explain.

3. Reexamine the second equation offered above ("Should we get married?"). Think about what is missing from this formula and add some more variables to the equation. Share your creation with your class partner(s).

Post-Reading Vocabulary

Without using a dictionary, determine the meaning of the bolded words from the context.

1. "You can't **fault** the optimism." (para. 3)

   Fault means _____

2. "I thought I would look at some more **fundamental** equations that govern marriage." (para. 5)

   Fundamental means _____

3. "**Granted** there are other factors that might help or hurt your specific marriage." (para. 5)

   Granted means _____

SKILL FOCUS
Logical Relationships

⑤ LEARNING OBJECTIVE
Recognize different logical patterns of organization in a text

For the purpose of gaining a clearer understanding of what they are reading, good readers recognize logical relationships between ideas by focusing on both transition words and patterns of organization. In this section we will primarily examine key transition words. For a detailed discussion of the different types of patterns of organization, see the skill focus section in Chapter 8.

Five Common Logical Relationships

While there are many types of logical relationships, for the scope of this chapter, we are going to learn about five of the most frequently used types of transitions.

They are as follows:

- Addition
- Illustration
- Comparison and contrast
- Cause and effect
- Time

Before we take a closer look at each of the logical relationships listed above, let's see how well you can recognize each category in the examples below.

Practice 1: Connecting Logical Relationships to Examples

Work with a partner to connect the logical relationships to the example text.

Collaboration

Logical Relationships	Examples
____ **Addition**	a. A bar graph has a mostly vertical focus, whereas a pie chart is circular.
____ **Illustration/ example**	b. If you drive 10 miles per hour faster than the car next to you, after 15 minutes you will only be 2.5 miles ahead.
____ **Comparison and contrast**	c. For example, one type of triangle is the right triangle where all three angles measure 90 degrees.
____ **Cause and effect**	d. To better understand our savings plan formula, open up an account with a $50 deposit. Furthermore, you will need to spend some time reading the enclosed customer service booklet.
____ **Time**	e. Just now I am sending you the magazines you requested, but I am not able to find the short stories. Please read the magazine articles for now. Meanwhile, I will look for the stories.

Tips for Identifying Logical Relationships

- **Recognize the topic and the main idea of a reading first.** You cannot zero in on the logical structure of a text if you do not first have a sense of what the reading is about and what the main point is.
- **Consider the author's purpose.** If you understand the author's goal in writing a text, it will be much easier to follow his or her logic in organizing the text.
- **Familiarize yourself with key transitional phrases associated with each pattern.** Sentence transitions, such as some of the key words used in Practice One (*first, whereas, for example*), key you into the text's logical organization.
- **Highlight all of the signal words.** To gain a better understanding of the author's key points, use a highlighter to help you zero in on these key transition terms.

A. Addition

When a writer has an idea and wants to continue in the same direction with another idea, she or he often connects the two ideas with a transition word such as *also, furthermore,* or *in addition*.

> **Example:** The United States has a progressive income tax. **In addition**, the US offers tax credits to married couples.

The following table shows how the two ideas in the above sentence are connected through the use of a transition word.

Initial Idea	Addition	Transition
The United States has a progressive income tax.	The US offers tax credits to married couples	In addition

Here are some transition words that writers commonly use to convey the idea of addition:

Transition Words for Addition				
furthermore	moreover	also	in addition	for one thing
first of all	secondly	next	another	finally

Practice 2: Identifying Ideas Connected by Addition Transitions

Read the following sentences with a partner. Identity both the initial idea and the additional one that follows it. Underline and identify the key connecting transition as well.

Collaboration

1. Many surveyed middle school students report that Algebra is their toughest course. Furthermore, studies show that a high percentage of students must repeat this course.

Initial Idea	Addition	Transition

2. With the continued reliance on calculators, studies show a decline in the ability of math students to show their work on paper. Moreover, studies show that memory skills have also declined.

Initial Idea	Addition	Transition

3. First of all, you need to identify the type of triangle displayed. Secondly, you should figure out the exact measurement of its angles.

Initial Idea	Addition	Transition

B. Illustration/Example

To illustrate, or explain, an important point or an unfamiliar concept, your teacher might provide a clear example. Writers do the same thing, and it is your job as a reader to connect the example offered with the main point or concept being explained.

> **Example:** Overall the old treatment had a higher cure rate, despite the fact that the new treatment had a higher rate for both mild and severe acne cases. **This example illustrates** that it is possible for a set of data to give different results in each of several groups than it does when the groups are taken together. This situation is an **example** of Simpson's paradox.
>
> from Bennett and Briggs, *Using and Understanding Mathematics*, 5e, p. 184

The table below shows how the author uses the illustration/example pattern to explain a concept.

Point/concept being explained	Example offered	Key word/transition
Simpson's paradox	"... the old treatment had a higher cure rate, despite the fact that the new treatment had a higher rate for both mild and severe acne cases."	"This example illustrates ..."

Here is a list of common transition words that signal an illustration/example logical relationship

Transition Words/Phrases for Illustration and Example				
for example	for instance	as an illustration	to be specific	to illustrate

Practice 3: Identifying Examples/Illustrations

Collaboration

Read the following sentences with a partner. Identify the point being explained, the example offered, and the transition words that clue you in to the illustration/example pattern. Underline any transition words as you read.

1. For data that vary continuously across geographical areas, a contour map is more convenient (see Figure 6-1, p. 253). In this kind of map each of the contours connects locations with the same temperature. For example, the temperature is 50°F everywhere along the contour labeled 50°F and 60°F everywhere along the contour labeled 60°F.

   from Bennett and Briggs, *Using and Understanding Mathematics*, 5e, pp. 338–339

Figure 6-1

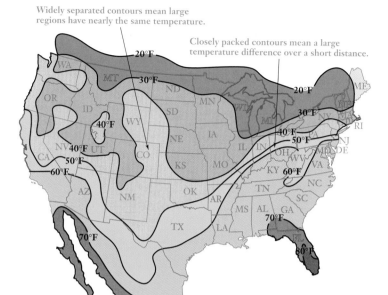

Widely separated contours mean large
regions have nearly the same temperature.

Closely packed contours mean a large
temperature difference over a short distance.

Point/concept being explained	Example offered	Key word/transition

2. An *x*-variable can have a positive, neutral or negative value. An illustration
of each can be found on page 192 in your algebra text.

Point/concept being explained	Example offered	Key word/transition

3. The rate of inflation refers to the relative change in the CPI (consumer price
index) from one year to the next. For example, the inflation rate from 1980
to 1981 was the relative increase in the CPI between those two years.

from Bennett and Briggs, *Using and Understanding Mathematics*, 5e, p. 176

Point/concept being explained	Example offered	Key word/transition

C. Comparison/Contrast

Comparing and contrasting different phenomena is at the basis of academic
learning. Much of your college reading will involve comparison. How are men
and women similar to each other? What are the differences between them? What
characteristics do the circulatory system and the respiratory system have in
common? How are the rules for international adoption different from those for

domestic adoption? As a reader, it is critical to both recognize *what* items are being compared and *how* they are compared, so pay attention to transition words that signal contrast or similarity.

> **Example:** Credit card loans are **different from** installment loans in that you are not required to pay off your balance in any set period of time. **Instead,** you are required to make only a minimum monthly payment that generally covers all the interest but very little principal.
>
> from Bennett and Briggs, *Using and Understanding Mathematics*, 5e, p. 253

The table below shows how the author uses the comparison/contrast pattern to compare concepts.

Concepts being compared	How are they compared?	Key word(s)/transition
credit card loans AND installment loans	they have different rules for paying off balances	different from/instead

Here are some transition words that writers use to signal they are comparing or contrasting items:

Transition Words for Compare and Contrast				
however	on the other hand	in contrast	whereas	conversely
similarly	likewise	just as	both	in the same way

Collaboration

Practice 4: Identifying Comparisons and Contrasts

Read the following sentences with a partner. Identity the concepts being compared, how they are being compared, and the key words and transitions that key the reader in. Underline any transition words as you read.

1. Linear growth occurs when a quantity grows by the same absolute amount in each unit of time. In contrast, exponential growth occurs when a quantity grows by the same relative amount, that is, by the same percentage in each unit of time.

   from Bennett and Briggs, *Using and Understanding Mathematics*, 5e, p. 473

Concepts being compared	How are they compared?	Key word(s)/transition

2. This type of argument, in which the conclusion is formed by generalizing from more specific premises, is called an inductive argument. In contrast, argument 2 is called a deductive argument because it allows us to deduce a specific conclusion from more general premises.

   from Bennett and Briggs, *Using and Understanding Mathematics*, 5e, p. 51

Concepts being compared	How are they compared?	Key word(s)/transition

3. Latitude measures positions north and south of the equator; whereas, longitude measures east-west position.

adapted from Bennett and Briggs, *Using and Understanding Mathematics*, 5e, p. 568

Concepts being compared	How are they compared?	Key word(s)/transition

D. Cause and Effect

This type of relationship focuses on the consequences, or results, of a given action. If the price of gasoline goes up, more people might leave their cars at home. If too many students are failing the math midterm, the professor might make the exam a little easier.

Collaboration

> **Example: When** a jury does not come to a unanimous decision, the judge generally declares a mistrial.
>
> adapted from Bennett and Briggs, *Using and Understanding Mathematics*, 5e, p. 630

The table below shows how the author uses the cause and effect pattern to show how one event causes another to occur.

Cause	Effect	Key word(s)/transition
jury does not come to a unanimous decision	the judge declares a mistrial	When

Here are some transition words that writers use to convey a cause/effect logical relation.

Transition Words for Cause and Effect					
therefore	as a result	consequently	if/then	thereby	because

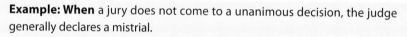

Practice 5: Identifying Causes and Effects

Read the following sentences with a partner. Identity both the cause and the effect. Underline any signal words as you read.

Collaboration

1. One possibility is to award the governorship to the person who received the most votes, called a plurality of the vote. Wilson has the greatest percentage and becomes governor if we decide this election by plurality.

from Bennett and Briggs, *Using and Understanding Mathematics*, 5e, p. 631

Cause	Effect	Key word(s)/transition

2. The equation leaves out some key variables. Therefore, it cannot be solved.

Cause	Effect	Key word(s)/transition

3. In another of his works, al-Khwarizmi described the numerical system developed by Hindu mathematicians, thereby popularizing the decimal system and the use of the numerical zero.

from Bennett and Briggs, *Using and Understanding Mathematics*, 5e, p. 530

Cause	Effect	Key word(s)/transition

E. Time

Collaboration

Another pattern of organization writers' often employ is putting information in proper time sequence. If you were telling a story about the invention of the scientific calculator (see the "Landmark in the Discipline" just ahead on p. 259), you would logically begin with the invention of the basic adding machine many centuries earlier before describing the introduction of the scientific calculator in the 1960s. In other words, you would give the information in consistent time order, or chronological order, so as not to confuse your reader. In the field of mathematics, chronological order is particularly important, as many math formulas can only be solved using the proper order of specific steps.

> **Example: When** the link between cell phones and accidents was first discovered, many people thought that the problem could be solved by mandating that only hands-free cell phones be allowed in cars. However, **more recent studies** show that hands-free systems are nearly as dangerous as regular cell phones.
>
> adapted from Bennett and Briggs, *Using and Understanding Mathematics*, 5e, p. 296

The table below shows how the author uses the chronological order pattern to show the order of events.

What events/steps are being organized in time sequence?	Keyword(s)/transitions/ time references
ideas about cell phone use in cars	when/more recent studies

Here are some transition words that writers use to signal a time relation:

Transition Words for Time Order					
before	after	meanwhile	when	once	then
while	previously	first	secondly	finally	

Practice 6: Identifying Time Order

Read the following sentences with a partner. Identity what events or steps are being organized chronologically. Underline key transition words that clue you into the time ordering.

Collaboration

1. **Working with Units**

    Step One: Identify the units involved in the problem.

    Step Two: Perform any operations on both the numbers and their associated units.

    Step Three: When you complete your calculations, make sure your answer has the units you expected.

    adapted from Bennett and Briggs, *Using and Understanding Mathematics*, 5e, p. 89

What events/steps are being organized in a time sequence?	*Keyword(s)/transitions/ time references*

2. The first permanent standardization of length began when English King Henry I (1100–1135) set the yard as the measurement from the tip of his nose to the tip of his thumb of his outstretched arm. A few centuries later, the English brought their units to the American colonies, and they have since undergone further modification and standardization. Today, all lengths in the US customary system are based on the inch.

    adapted from Bennett and Briggs, *Using and Understanding Mathematics*, 5e, p. 97

What events/steps are being organized in a time sequence?	*Keyword(s)/transitions/ time references*

3. **Calculating the Standard Deviation (Step 1)**

    First compute the mean of the data set. Then, find the deviation from the mean for every data value by subtracting the mean from the data value.

    adapted from Bennett and Briggs, *Using and Understanding Mathematics*, 5e, p. 386

What events/steps are being organized in a time sequence?	*Keyword(s)/transitions/ time references*

LANDMARK IN THE FIELD OF MATHEMATICS

Scientific Calculator

A scientific calculator is used mostly in solving problems in the math field. It has special features that make number crunching much easier. One key feature is the floating point in arithmetic. It also offers some basic functions in trigonometry.

Imagine trying to solve math problems without using a scientific calculator! The very first calculator was an adding and subtracting machine. Pascal invented it in 1642. Not much has changed over the years in terms of how numbers are calculated. However, there is one main difference. The evolution has come in the speed and variety of calculations that can be completed using a scientific calculator.

The modern age of calculators began in the nineteenth century. Early inventors faced many limitations in making better calculators. These challenges resulted in many early calculators not functioning correctly, if at all. However, with the birth of the twentieth century, reliable mechanical calculators began to be built and

operated. Some of the milestones in calculator technology included the following:

- In 1901, Hopkins developed the standard calculator by utilizing two rows of five buttons, representing the digits 0 through 9.
- In 1911, a Swede named Sundstrand designed the standard ten-digit keyboard we are familiar with today.
- In 1914, the first commercial calculators entered the business world. After this, the use of calculators became commonplace.

Calculator technology continued to improve through the twentieth century. The first scientific calculator, the Hewlett-Packard HP-9100A, came out in 1968. The HP-35, introduced in 1972, was the world's first handheld scientific calculator. It cost $395 and was considered very expensive for its time. Since then, the price of scientific calculators has decreased. This is due to competition among the makers.

Scientific calculators are often required for math classes from the middle school level through college. They are generally required on many standardized tests covering math and science subjects. As a result, many are sold into educational markets.

Collaboration

Considering the Topic

Answer the following questions with a partner.

1. As you learned in the reading, the ten-digit standard calculator many use today was invented about one hundred years ago. What types of math problems would be challenging to solve if calculator technology had not evolved since then? In other words, what types of math problems can a standard calculator not compute?

2. What facts do we learn from the reading about the first handheld scientific calculator?

3. The scientific calculator dramatically changed the way we go about solving many math and science calculations. Imagining the world a hundred years from now, can you think of a possible invention that would transform our relationship with math? Share your ideas.

Internet Connection

Research another landmark in the field of mathematics, and fill out the section below.

abacus	Pythagorean theorem	algebra
the concept of zero	game theory	speedometer

Landmark: _____

Question	Answer
When did this landmark become a reality?	
Who was involved in developing this landmark?	
What made this landmark special?	
How did this landmark change the way people interact?	

A Key to Critical Thinking: Understanding All of the Options

Reading Selection **4**

Book Excerpt

Preview Questions

1. Can you think of some examples of how a simple math equation might help you make a decision in your daily life?

2. When you are planning a trip and considering all of the costs involved, would you most likely do the math in your head, on paper, or would you use a calculator? Explain your preferred method.

3. When you get a medical bill, a credit card bill, or a monthly car payment notice, do you always read all of the fine print? Why is it sometimes important to pay attention to this additional information?

MyReadingLab™
Complete this Exercise
at **myreadinglab.com**

Pre-Reading Vocabulary: Focus on Some Key Terms

Collaboration

Before beginning the reading selection, it may be helpful to focus on the meaning of some key words in the article. Working with a partner, try to guess the meaning of these words. Then look up the words in a dictionary.

Word	Your Definition	Dictionary Definition
foresee		
termination		
comply		
forfeit		
imposed		

A Key to Critical Thinking:
Understanding All of the Options

By Jeffrey O. Bennett and William L. Briggs

Review the example below of how to use logical reasoning to choose the best airplane ticket. Then, try to solve some "logic in everyday life" problems in the Reading Comprehension Check that follows.

1   **Hint 4: Understand All the Options**

We regularly make decisions in situations where we have several options. For example, we face decisions about which insurance policy to choose, which auto loan to take, or which model of new computer to buy. The key to such decisions is making sure that you understand how each option would affect you.

2   **Example 4: Which Airline Ticket to Buy?**

Airlines typically offer many different prices for the same trip. Suppose you are planning a trip six months in advance and discover that you have two choices in purchasing an airline ticket:

A. The lowest fare is $400, but 25% of the fare is nonrefundable if you change or cancel the ticket.

B. A fully refundable ticket is available for $800.

Analyze the situation.

3   **Solution**

We can think of each of the two options as a pair of conditional propositions. Under option A, you will lose 25% of $400, or $100, if you cancel your trip. Thus, option A represents the following pair of conditional propositions:

(1A) If you purchase ticket A and *go* on the trip, then you will pay $400.
(2A) If you purchase ticket A and *cancel* the trip, then you will pay $100.

Similarly, option B represents the following pair of conditional propositions:

(1B) If you purchase ticket B and *go* on the trip, then you will pay $800.
(2B) If you purchase ticket B and *cancel* the trip, then you will pay $0.

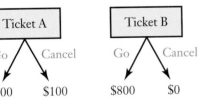

Figure A

4   Figure A represents the four possibilities. Clearly, option A is the better buy if you go on the trip, and option B is the better buy if you end up canceling your trip. However, because you are planning six months in advance, it's impossible to foresee all the circumstances that might lead you to cancel your trip. Therefore,

you might want to analyze the *difference* between the two tickets under the two possibilities (going on the trip or canceling).

If you go on the trip: ticket B costs $400 more than ticket A.
If you cancel the trip: ticket A costs $100 more than ticket B.

5   In effect, you must decide which ticket to purchase by balancing the risk of spending an extra $400 if you go on the trip against spending an extra $100 if you cancel. How would *you* decide?

from Bennett and Briggs, *Using and Understanding Mathematics*, 5e, p. 68

Reading Comprehension Check

1. **Reading a Lease.** Consider the following excerpt from the contract for the lease of an apartment: Landlord shall return the security deposit to resident within one month after termination of this lease or surrender and acceptance of the premises, whichever occurs first. Suppose your lease terminates on June 30.

   Question: If you move out on June 5, the landlord must return your security deposit by which date to comply with the terms of the lease?
   a. June 28
   b. July 5
   c. June 30
   d. June 6
   Explain your choice: _____

2. **Airline Options**. In planning a trip to New Zealand six months in advance, you find that an airline offers two options: **Plan A**, which allows you to buy a fully refundable ticket for $1,000, or **Plan B**, which allows you to buy a ticket for $900, but states that you forfeit 25% of the price if the ticket is changed or canceled. Describe your options in the events that you do and do not make the trip. How would you decide which ticket to buy?

   Question: If you choose Plan B and later have to change the date of your flight, how much extra will you have to pay?
   a. no extra cost
   b. $100
   c. $225
   d. $450
   Explain your choice: _____

3. **Buy vs. Lease**. You are deciding whether to buy a car for $18,000 or to accept a lease agreement. The lease entails a $1000 initiation fee plus monthly payments of $240 for 36 months. Under the lease agreement, you are responsible for service on the car and insurance. At the end of the lease, you may purchase the car for $9,000.

   Question: What is NOT a possible advantage of leasing the car?
   a. You first have a chance to get to know the car before deciding whether to purchase it when the lease runs out.
   b. The installment plan allows to you pay just $240 a month.
   c. You only have to put $1,000 down up front.
   d. You don't have to worry about service charges to your vehicle.
   Explain your choice: _____

4. **Did You Win?** You receive the following e-mail notification: "Through a random selection from more than 20 million e-mail addresses, you've been selected as the winner of our grand prize—a two-week vacation in the Bahamas. To claim your prize, please call our toll free number. Have your credit card ready for identification and a small processing fee."

Question: Why might this e-mail message make you suspicious?
   a. There is no reason to be suspicious. The offer sounds legitimate.
   b. They ask you to call their toll-free number.
   c. There is a mention of a "small processing fee."
   d. The fact that the vacation is for two weeks in the Bahamas.

   Explain your choice: _____

5. **Credit Card Agreement**. The following rules are among the many provisions of a particular credit card agreement:

   [1]For the regular plan, the minimum payment due is the greater of $10 or 5% of the new balance shown on your statement (rounded to the nearest $1) plus any unpaid late fees and returned check fees, and any amounts shown as past due on your statement. [2]If you make a purchase under a regular plan, no finance charges will be imposed in any billing period in which (i) there is no previous balance or (ii) payments received and credits issued by the payment due date, which is 25 days after the statement closing date shown on your last statement, equal or exceed the previous balance. [3]If the new balance is not satisfied in full by the payment due date shown on your last statement, there will be a finance charge on each purchase from the date of purchase.

   Question: Suppose you have a previous balance of $150 and you pay $200 one month after the statement closing date. Will you be assessed a finance charge? The information needed to answer this question can be found in which sentence(s) of the credit card agreement?
   a. sentence 3   c. sentence 2
   b. sentence 1   d. sentences 2 and 3

   Explain your choice: _____

from Bennett and Briggs, Using and Understanding Mathematics, 5e, pp. 73–74

Collaboration

Exploring the Topic

Discuss the following questions to review the content of the book excerpt you have just read.

1. There are so many special discount offers in the marketplace, some of which can be quite tricky to fully understand. What advice would you give someone who is trying to make sense of a discounted plane ticket or a special offer on a new car? How can you guide them toward making a sound decision?

2. All credit card bills, whether in hard copy or online, should be itemized for you. That is, each purchase you have made should be listed. Do you always check the math each time you get a credit card bill? What can you do if the credit card company's math is off?

3. In terms of cost, is it better to buy or lease a car? Prove your point mathematically.

Post-Reading Vocabulary

Without using a dictionary, determine the meaning of the bolded words from the context.

1. "Landlord shall return the security deposit to resident within one month after termination of this lease or surrender and acceptance of the **premises**, whichever occurs first."

   Premises means _____

2. "The lease **entails** a $1000 initiation fee plus monthly payments of $240 for 36 months."

   Entails means _____

3. "Through a **random** selection from more than 20 million e-mail addresses, you've been selected as the winner of our grand prize—a two-week vacation in the Bahamas."

   Random means _____

How to Calculate Your Real Hourly Wage

Reading Selection **5**

Web Article

Preview Questions

1. What are some "hidden costs" that bring down the real salary of most workers?
2. Do you believe the minimum wage is too high or too low? Explain.
3. What percentage of a high school teacher's $50,000 a year salary goes to the IRS? Can you take a guess? Should taxes be lower, higher, or is the current rate reasonable? Explain.

MyReadingLab™
Complete this **Exercise** at **myreadinglab.com**

Pre-Reading Vocabulary: Focus on Some Key Terms

Collaboration

Before beginning the reading selection, it may be helpful to focus on the meaning of some key words in the article. Working with a partner, try to guess the meaning of these words. Then look up the words in a dictionary.

Word	*Your Definition*	*Dictionary Definition*
prospective		
liability		
subsidized		
nominal		
splurge		

How to Calculate Your Real Hourly Wage

www.wikihow.com/Calculate-Your-Real-Hourly-Wage

How much are you really paid?

1 We don't earn as much as we think we do. You may be paid $15 an hour, but your real hourly wage is less than that. Possibly much less. Let's say we have a friend named Joe and that he's a plumber making about $48,000 a year for a 40-hour workweek. His nominal wage is approximately $24 per hour. Ah, but it's not that simple. Joe's *real* hourly wage isn't $24—it's something lower, when you account for the hidden expenses associated with the job. Not only is knowing your real hourly wage useful in terms of budgeting both your time and money, but it's also a great tool for comparing prospective jobs. Even two jobs that offer the same salary in different neighborhoods and cities can have big differences in terms of real hourly wage.

1. Quantify all of the expenses and time associated with your job.

2 Think of all the things you do and the money you spend that you wouldn't if you did not work. What is the *difference*? How long does it take to drive to work? How much does the gas cost? Does your job require that you buy a suit or a uniform? Do you have to take vacations to cope with the stress in your career? Let's continue with the plumber example:

3 • **Taxes**—Federal income taxes will be taking a large share of the income. Most often, this tax is withheld from his paycheck in an amount that should be a close estimate to his anticipated liability. A rough estimate is around 25% of his income of $48,000 a year, or about $5.75 from each hour. Social Security taxes will take an additional 6%, or roughly another $1.40 per hour. If Joe works and lives in a state with a state income tax, this amount will be deducted in addition. There are also payroll income taxes in certain cities that would need to be deducted.

4 • **Commuting**—Joe's office is 20 miles from his home. Every day, he spends an hour commuting to and from work in his 2000 Ford Focus, which costs about 38 cents per mile to operate. His weekly commute costs 5 hours and $76 (38 cents times 200 miles). If Joe's employer is a large plumbing company, he will likely not have to absorb the substantial cost of getting himself and his tools from customer to customer or to the job site. More employers are asking their employees to use their personal vehicle for job-related duties, to run errands, make deliveries, or make bank deposits. If his employer does not pay a mileage reimbursement or only pays for fuel costs, Joe would need to cover the additional costs incurred of using his personal vehicle such as insurance, maintenance, brakes, accelerated vehicle value depreciation and increased wear and tear on his personal vehicle. These additional costs are often difficult to calculate and often grossly underestimated by the employee. Using his personal vehicle for duties related to his job, outside of standard commuting expenses, can substantially impact the amount of money Joe actually is left with as earnings.

5 • **Child Care**—Joe will not be home with his child, and his partner also works a full-time 40-hour workweek. For Joe to make himself available for the job, he will not be able to effectively monitor his child. His solution is to drop the child off at a day care center. The weekly cost of this supervision for the child varies greatly, but Joe's cost is about $600 a month. This means that he will need to deduct about $3.50 per hour from his $24 per hour in order to be relieved of parental duty for such time as is required for employment. If making this calculation for more than one adult in the same family, remember to deduct this cost from only one worker—generally the one who would otherwise be the primary caregiver—or divide the cost between them.

6 • **Clothing**—It doesn't take Joe extra time to get dressed in his work clothes each morning, but it does cost him a little extra money. Several times each year, he has to buy new work clothes because the old ones wear out. Let's suppose he spends $300 more per year doing this than he would by buying only casual clothes.

7 • **Food**—Joe might take a sack lunch if he were on his own, but he works with a partner who prefers fast food. Joe likes McDonald's and Subway, too, so he's happy to go along for the ride. Each day, Joe spends about $5 and one hour for lunch. If Joe and his partner are too tired after work to make dinner, and must go out to eat, the extra expense of driving there and paying for restaurant service must be added in, as well.

8 • **Taxes,** commuting, child care, clothing, and food together cost him about 10 hours per week (or 500 hours per year) and about $107. We'll round it down to $100 per week, so that's about $5,000 each year.

9 **2. Subtract your work-related expenses from your annual salary to find your actual earnings.** Using our earlier figures, Joe the Plumber's actual salary would be $43,000 per year ($48,000 base minus $5,000 for commuting, clothing, and food).

10 **3. Divide your actual earnings by the total number of hours you spend each year on work-related tasks (including business trips, office social events, commuting, etc.).** Joe leaves the house at 6:30 in the morning, and does not return until 4:30 in the afternoon, which means he's devoting 50 hours per week—or about 2,500 hours per year — to his job. Joe is spending about 2,500 hours per year to earn $43,000. His real hourly wage is $17.20. Not bad, but still much lower than the $24 per hour he thinks he's earning.

11 **4. Think about how much time your expenditures are really costing you.** Remember that time is money. Based on a nominal hourly wage, if Joe the plumber decides to buy an iPod Nano ($150), he thinks he's exchanging about six hours of his time for it (6 hours worked × $24 per hour = $144 total wages, which is close enough). But based on his real hourly wage, it would take Joe nearly nine hours to earn the same amount. To earn the money for anything he wants to purchase, Joe has to spend 40% more time working than he thinks he does.

12 Let's say you're spending a lot of money on comic books. After you calculate your real hourly wage and apply the number to your expenses, you'll be

able to see how much time each book is costing you. Was it really worth three hours of your life to buy a collection of Aquaman stories you'll probably never read? If the answer was "no," you'll be more motivated to reduce your spending, especially if there are other things you could be doing with your time.

13   **5.   Add in the benefits.** Are you getting health insurance? Life insurance? Dental and vision? Discounted gym memberships? Free or subsidized computer or cell phone? How much would you pay for these items on your own? Does your employer match your 401(k) contribution (free money!) or provide other retirement benefits? You should also estimate the value of any expected bonuses, stock options, accumulated sick or vacation time, and free training.

14   • When comparing prospective jobs, this exercise helps you remember to take taxes and living expenses into account.

15   • An important job-related expense for many people is the money and time they spend to "unwind" or to reward themselves after a hard day's work. If Joe's plumbing job is so stressful that every night he comes home and spends 2 hours vegging in front of the TV with a beer, then he uses (loses!) an additional 10 hours a week, and whatever he pays for beer. Or if Jill the plumber relaxes on weekends by hitting up the mall because hey, she works hard for her money and deserves some nice clothes, then she also loses time and money. In this sense, it may be perfectly reasonable to take a less stressful, lower paying job that doesn't lead you to splurge regularly, if your real hourly wage ends up being higher.

16   • Medical and childcare flexible spending plans are also a cost savings to you, if you plan well; these increase your spending ability and can be considered part of your "income". However, their savings is in reducing your taxable income, so if you already account for that with accurate tax figures, don't double-count it by adding it to your benefits.

17   • Things like changing to a 4-day week, carpooling or taking mass transit so you can work or read while you're commuting, can all add a few extra dollars to that real hourly wage.

source: wikiHow. Reprinted with permission.

MyReadingLab™
Complete this **Exercise**
at **myreadinglab.com**

Reading Comprehension Check

1. If we review the first paragraph of the reading, what pattern of organization is the author making use of?

    "We don't earn as much as we think we do. You may be paid $15 an hour, but your real hourly wage is less than that. Possibly much less. Let's say we have a friend named Joe and that he's a plumber making about $48,000 a year for a 40-hour workweek. His nominal wage is approximately $24 per hour. Ah, but it's not that simple. Joe's *real* hourly wage isn't $24—it's something lower, when you account for the hidden expenses associated with the job."

    a. compare and contrast   c. cause and effect
    b. illustration and example   d. chronological ordering

2. According to the author, why is it important to know your "real" hourly wage?
   a. for both budgeting and comparing prospective jobs
   b. for budgeting purposes
   c. to get a sense of how much you will lose on taxes
   d. so you can tell your boss what you are really making

3. If we review the example of the plumber's salary, what percentage of his income will go to federal income tax?
   a. 15%   c. 25%
   b. 33%   d. 50%

4. How much will child care cost Joe a month?
   a. The amount is not mentioned in the reading.
   b. $7 an hour
   c. It depends on how often he works.
   d. about $600 a month

5. Why is stress mentioned as a cause for more hidden expenses?
   a. Stress costs could lead to higher medical bills.
   b. Work-related stress might result in more beer drinking and trips to the mall.
   c. Stress could lead you to take more days off.
   d. none of the above

6. What is the central point of the reading?
   a. You should not only consider the costs, but the added benefits of your job.
   b. One hidden cost is the price of take-out meals.
   c. When considering your salary, you have to take into account many hidden costs.
   d. work and hidden expenses

Exploring the Topic

Discuss the following questions to review the content of the Web article you have just read.

Collaboration

1. The author seems to believe that many people do not subtract the hidden costs from their income. Do you agree? Why would someone forget to consider this?

2. According to the author, what is the most expensive hidden cost?

3. In the end, the author states, "Things like changing to a 4-day week, carpooling or taking mass transit so you can work or read while you're commuting, can all add a few extra dollars to that real hourly wage." (para. 17) In your own experience, which of these cost-saving items seem most realistic to you? Explain.

Post-Reading Vocabulary

Without using a dictionary, determine the meaning of the bolded words from the context.

1. "If his employer does not pay a mileage **reimbursement** or only pays for fuel costs, Joe would need to cover the additional costs incurred of using his personal vehicle…" (para. 4)

   Reimbursement means _____

2. "Joe would need to cover the additional costs incurred of using his personal vehicle such as insurance, maintenance, brakes, accelerated vehicle value depreciation and increased **wear and tear** on his personal vehicle." (para. 4)

   Wear and tear means _____

3. "For Joe to make himself available for the job, he will not be able to effectively **monitor** his child." (para. 5)

   Monitor means _____

Collaboration

Panel Discussion on What Should We Cut?

Your locality is faced with a serious budget crisis. The mayor's committee has declared that $100,000 must be cut from the local middle school budget, and the town would be in better financial condition if $200,000 were cut.

You are going to take part in a panel discussion to figure out what would be most fair to cut, and using **mathematical reasoning**, how much should be cut from the following possible sources:

Goal of Cutting between $100,000 and $200,000 from
Local Middle School Budget: Mayor's Committee List of
Possible Spending Cut Sources

Resource	*Savings*
1. Laying off 2–4 teachers	$50,000 a teacher
2. Closing down swimming pool	$20,000 a year
3. Reducing arts supplies	$10,000 a year
4. Getting rid of school lunch program	$90,000 a year
5. No more class textbook sets	$50,000 a year
6. Laying off parent–teacher coordinator	$40,000 a year
7. Laying off some class tutors (6 total)	$20,000 each for a year
8. Canceling after-school programs	$60,000 a year
9. Canceling all free school trips	$15,000 a year
10. No more sports teams	$15,000 a year

Divide yourselves into four groups. Each group will have 15 minutes to organize their plan on what should be cut and what should be maintained in the school. After your planning time is over, you can begin your panel discussion by having each group present their plan. Once each group has been heard, you can have a lively debate on the topic.

WRITING CONNECTIONS: *Using Excel to Organize Data and Create Graphs*

Statistical information can be organized in a number of ways, and Microsoft Excel is a relatively easy program to work with. You can create tables and also convert these tables into bar graphs and pie charts. If you are writing up a report based on your research, graphs and charts are more attractive and often easier to interpret than basic tables.

If we can examine a frequency table, we can see how useful charts and graphs can be.

> **Example:** Imagine a teacher makes the following list of grades she gave to her 25 students on an essay:
>
> A C C B C D C C F D C C C B B A B D B A A B F C B
>
> adapted from Bennett and Briggs, *Using and Understanding Mathematics*, 5e, p. 320

This list contains all of the data, but isn't easy to read. A better way to display these data is with a frequency table, as shown in Figure 6-2.

Figure 6-2: Frequency Table for Grades

Grade	Frequency
A	4
B	7
C	9
D	3
F	2
Total	25

A more descriptive frequency table can be organized with just a few steps.

Organizing Excel Charts from a Set of Statistical Information

Excel is easy to use for statistical tables and calculations. The following steps show how you can create the frequency table for Figure 6-2: Figure 6-3 shows the Excel table with the formulas, and Figure 6-4 shows the results of the formulas.

1. Create columns for the grade and frequency data, which you must type in manually; the screenshots show these data in columns B and C. At the bottom of column C, use the SUM function to compute the total frequency in cell C8.

2. Compute the relative frequency (column D) by dividing each frequency in column C by the total frequency from cell C8. You can enter the formula for the first row (= C3/$C$8) and then use the "fill down" editing option to put the correct formulas in the remaining

rows. Note: When using the "fill down" option, you must include the dollar signs in front of C and 8 to make the reference to cell C8 an "absolute cell reference." Without these dollar signs, the "fill down" option would make the cell reference shift down (becoming C9, C10, etc.) in each row, which would be incorrect in this case.

3. Cumulative frequency (column E) is the total of all the frequencies up to a given category. The first row shows "= C3" because cell C3 contains the frequency for A grades. The next row (= E3+C4) starts with the value in the prior row (cell E3) and adds the frequency for B grades (cell C4), The pattern continues for the remaining rows, which you can fill with the "fill down" option.

Figure 6-3: Excel Table with Formulas

◇ A	B	C	D	E
1				
2	Grade	Frequency	Relative Frequency	Cumulative Frequency
3	A	4	=C3/$C$8	=C3
4	B	7	=C4/$C$8	=E3+C4
5	C	9	=C5/$C$8	=E4+C5
6	D	3	=C6/$C$8	=E5+C6
7	F	2	=C7/$C$8	=E6+C7
8	Total	=SUM(C3:C7)	=SUM(D3:D7)	=C8

Figure 6-4: Excel Table Showing Results of Formulas

◇ A	B	C	D	E
1				
2	Grade	Frequency	Relative Frequency	Cumulative Frequency
3	A	4	16%	4
4	B	7	28%	11
5	C	9	36%	20
6	D	3	12%	23
7	F	2	8%	25
8	Total	25	100%	25

from Bennett and Briggs, *Using and Understanding Mathematics*, 5e, p. 321

Yet we can display the above information in other ways as well. For students who have little or no experience with Excel, it is recommended that you seek guidance on these steps with a computer lab tutor or with a more experienced classmate.

Using Excel to Create Statistical Graphs

Excel can make many types of statistical graphs. Let's start by making a bar graph for the grade data in Figure 6-2. The basic process requires the following steps, though the details vary significantly with different versions of Excel.

1. Beginning with the frequency table created in Figure 6-3, select the grade letters (column B) and the frequencies (column C).

2. Choose the type of chart you want from the Insert menu: here, we choose a 2-D "column" chart, which is Excel's name for a bar graph. The screen shot below (Figure 6-5) shows the process and the resulting graph created in Excel 2007 for Windows. The process is similar with other versions of Excel.

3. You can customize the labels on the bar graph. The procedure differs for different versions of Excel, but in most versions a right-click will allow you to change the axes and other labels; some versions also offer dialog boxes for changing the labels.

Figure 6-5: Process for Creating Graph in Excel

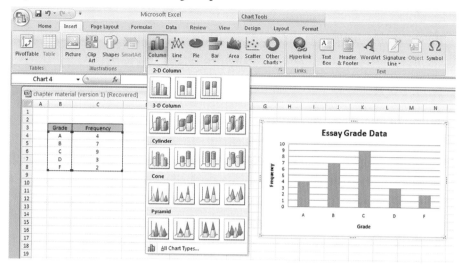

Making a pie chart is similar except for a couple of things:

- For a pie chart, you will probably want to select the relative frequencies rather than the frequencies (though both will work); it may be helpful to cut and paste these data so that they are next to the letter grades.

- Choose a pie chart rather than a column chart from the Insert menu.

- The labeling process is different from that for bar graphs, as are the options for colors and other decorative features. The screen shot below (Figure 6-6) shows some of the options available in Excel 2007 for Windows; other versions of Excel have similar tools.

Figure 6-6: Options for Creating Pie Graphs in Excel

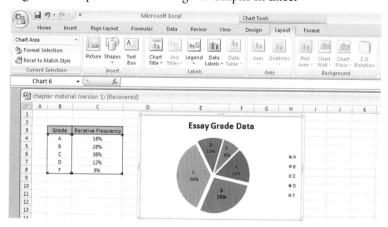

Because the various versions of Excel offer so many options, you should experiment with the different features to learn about the charting possibilities available in Excel.

adapted from Flowtown/Demandforce.

Practice: Now, let's try to create a pie chart from some statistical information.

Example: Cell phone use among teenagers aged 12–17

Statistical Information:

a. 11% send more than 200 texts a day.
b. 25% do not own cell phones.
c. 33% of teens send more than 100 texts a day.
d. 75% own cell phones.
e. 72% are text messagers.
f. 54% of teens text daily.

Using Excel, work with a partner to create a pie chart displaying the above information.

Adapted from Flowtown/Demandforce.

Reading Selection **6**

Graphs

Graphic Analysis

MyReadingLab™
Complete this **Exercise**
at **myreadinglab.com**

Preview Questions

1. Can you think of particular work or educational contexts where you might be asked to interpret a pie chart or a bar graph? Give a few examples of occupational areas and college classes where you might be involved with graphic analysis.

2. In the "Writing Connections" section of this chapter, you were given the task of organizing statistical information into graphic form, using Microsoft Excel. How is the task of organizing this type of data into graphs different from interpreting information from a given graph?

3. Some students shy away from graphic information. They say they are more comfortable with information organized in traditional text format. What are some reasons why these students might be intimidated by charts and graphs? How can they overcome this obstacle?

Collaboration

Pre-Reading Vocabulary: Focus on Some Key Terms

Before beginning the reading selection, it may be helpful to focus on the meaning of some key words. Working with a partner, try to guess the meaning of these words. Then look up the words in a dictionary.

Word	Your Definition	Dictionary Definition
estimated		
commuter		
median		
correlation		
inverse		

Graphic Analysis

1   Whether you are majoring in a health-related field, a social science, law or business, you will interact regularly with graphic information and be expected to show a high level of competence in quickly and accurately interpreting graphs and charts. Understanding graphic information is a form of reading, just as reading texts, Internet blogs, novels, newspaper articles and magazines are forms of information literacy.

2   When we look at a bar graph or a pie chart, we need to take the time to carefully review the visual information as it is all too easy to misinterpret the information represented and to draw false conclusions.

3   Let's take a look at a multiple bar graph, Figure 6-7, examine the data, and see if we can figure out the key message that the graph displays.

Figure 6-7: Income and Employment

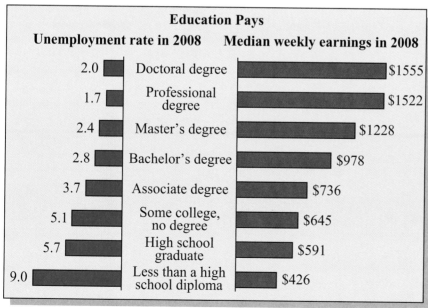

Source: Bureau of Labor Statistics.

Interpreting the graph: You first notice the title of the graph at the top center, "Education Pays." This title keys you into the graph's message. You can see from the text vertically presented in the center of the graph that the categories are levels of education, from "Doctoral degree" going down to "Less than a high school diploma" at the bottom. The two sets of bars represent two sets of measures of how education affects employment: the unemployment rate and weekly earnings.

A. **Larger Message:** Here, we are looking at the big picture; what is the relationship between greater levels of education and employment? Is there a positive or negative correlation?

What do you think? _____

Answer: The data clearly shows that the greater your level of education, the less likely you are to be unemployed and the more you are likely to earn, a positive correlation. In other words, there is an inverse relationship between higher level of education and unemployment.

B. **The Details:** It is also important to pay attention to the many details that a graph offers. On a given college exam, you might be asked to focus on one particular statistic or graphic relation displayed in a graph.

With a partner, try to locate the following information in Figure 6-7:

1. What was the unemployment rate in 2008 for people with a master's degree? _____

2. What was the median weekly earning for high school graduates? _____

3. How much more was the median weekly earning for those with bachelor's degrees over those with associate's degrees? _____

Great! The best way to improve your skills in graphic analysis is through practice. In the reading comprehension check on the following pages, carefully examine the graphs and then answer the multiple-choice questions that follow each one.

_____

Reading Comprehension Check

Graph 1: Undergraduate Budgets

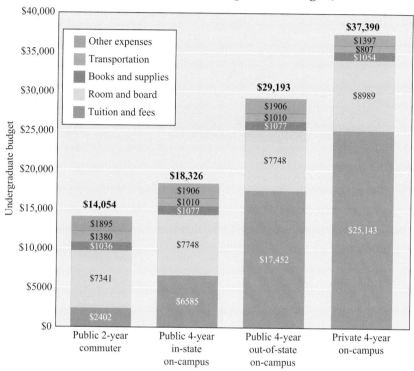

Average Estimated Undergraduate Budgets, 2008–09

Legend:
- Other expenses
- Transportation
- Books and supplies
- Room and board
- Tuition and fees

Y-axis: Undergraduate budget
- $40,000
- $35,000
- $30,000
- $25,000
- $20,000
- $15,000
- $10,000
- $5000
- $0

Public 2-year commuter — $14,054
- $1895
- $1380
- $1036
- $7341
- $2402

Public 4-year in-state on-campus — $18,326
- $1906
- $1010
- $1077
- $7748
- $6585

Public 4-year out-of-state on-campus — $29,193
- $1906
- $1010
- $1077
- $7748
- $17,452

Private 4-year on-campus — $37,390
- $1397
- $807
- $1054
- $8989
- $25,143

This graph uses stacked bars to show the breakdown by category (tuition and fees, room and board, books and supplies, transportation, other) of average student budgets at different types of institutions.

Source: From Trends in College Pricing. Copyright © 2008. The College Board www.collegeboard.org. Reproduced with permission.

1. According to the graph, what was the average cost of books and supplies for students at public 2-year commuter colleges?
   a. $14,054
   b. $1,036
   c. $1,077
   d. $2,100

2. What is the difference in the average cost of tuition and fees for public 4-year in-state students compared with that of private 4-year college students?
   a. $6,585
   b. $25,143
   c. over $18,000
   d. under $7,000

Graph 2: Death Rates from Diseases

Death Rates for Various Diseases: 1900–2004

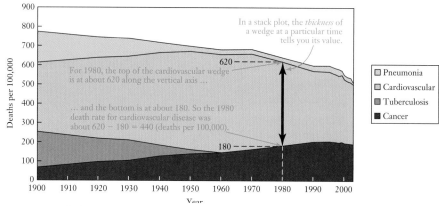

A graph showing trends in death rates from four diseases.
Source: Centers for Disease Control and Prevention.

3. Following the logic of the graph, what was the 1900 death rate for pneumonia?
   a. about 700 deaths per 100,000
   b. just under 800 deaths per 100,000
   c. about 600 deaths per 100,000
   d. none of the above

Graph 3: U.S. Age Distribution

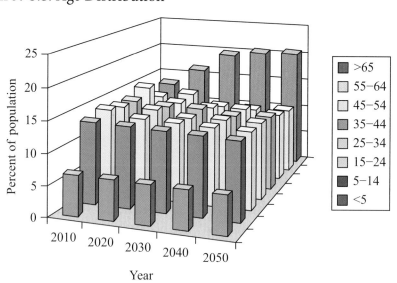

3D graph shows projections of the age distribution of the U.S. population from 2010 through 2050.

from Bennett and Briggs, *Using and Understanding Mathematics*, 5e, p. 348

4. According to the graph, which age group will see the largest increase between 2010 and 2050?
   a. 5–14
   b. 55–64
   c. >65
   d. 15–24

5. What do we learn about growth projections for children under 5?
   a. This population will increase tremendously from 2010 to 2050.
   b. The population of young children will show a significant decrease.
   c. Young children will remain about 10% of the overall population.
   d. This population will remain steady from 2010 through 2050.

Exploring the Topic

Collaboration

Discuss the following questions to review the content of the book excerpt you have just read.

1. You had the chance to examine four graphs focusing on different themes. Which graph did you find the most interesting? Explain your choice.

2. If we revisit the graph focusing on undergraduate tuition, what can be said about the difference in costs for in-state versus out-of-state public 4-year colleges? Why do you think this is the case?

3. Consider the information we learn about population growth from the final graph. Why do you think it is predicted that the largest growth will come for the 65+ age bracket? What factors might contribute to this increase in the number of older people?

Post-Reading Vocabulary

Without using a dictionary, determine the meaning of the bolded words from the context.

1. "Whether you are majoring in a health-related field, a social science, law or business, you will interact regularly with graphic information and be expected to show a high-level of **competence** in quickly and accurately interpreting graphs and charts." (para. 1)

   Competence means_____

2. "We need to take the time to carefully review the visual information as it is all too easy to misinterpret the information represented and to draw false **conclusions.**" (para. 2)

   Conclusions means _____

3. "3D graph shows **projections** of the age distribution of the US population from 2010 to 2050." (Graph 3)

   Projection means _____

TEXTBOOK APPLICATION   **Misconceptions about Math**

MyReadingLab™
Complete this **Exercise**
at **myreadinglab.com**

As you did in each previous chapter, first listen to the lecture on the study of mathematics and take notes for further discussion. You can listen to the lecture by scanning the QR code below with your smart phone. Your professor may also read the selections or play the audio file in class. Make sure that you write down the key points of the lecture.

Group Discussion

After listening to the lecture, work in small groups of three to four students and answer the following questions. Your instructor may ask you to share your answers with your classmates. As you refer to your notes, it is best to write brief answers to each of the questions below using your own words. After the discussion, you will have an opportunity to share your findings with your peers.

1. The lecture began with the term "math phobia." What does this term mean? Do you know anyone who suffers from "math phobia"?

2. According to the authors, what is the first misconception about math? Do you agree that this idea is a misconception, or do you think this idea makes sense? Explain.

3. How is math perceived differently in other countries, in the authors' view?

4. Why do the authors compare studying math with studying law or music?

5. The authors believe there is beauty in math. Do you agree? Explain.

6. What is the final misconception about math? What is your opinion on this question?

7. What is the authors' opinion about the relationship between math and creativity?

Now that you have discussed the highlights of the lecture with your classmates, read the following selection and answer the multiple-choice questions that follow.

Misconceptions about Math

By Jeffrey O. Bennett and William L. Briggs

Scan this code using your smart phone to listen to an audio version of this reading

1   Do you consider yourself to have "math phobia" (fear of mathematics) or "math loathing" (dislike of mathematics)? We hope not, but if you do you aren't alone. Many adults harbor fear or loathing of mathematics, and unfortunately these attitudes are often reinforced by classes that present mathematics as an obscure and sterile subject.

2   In reality mathematics is not nearly as dry as it sometimes seems in school. Indeed, attitudes toward mathematics are often directed not at what mathematics

really is but at some common misconceptions about mathematics. Let's investigate a few of these misconceptions and the reality behind them.

Misconception One: Math Requires a Special Brain

3   One of the most pervasive misconceptions is that some people just aren't good at mathematics because learning mathematics requires special or rare abilities. The reality is that nearly everyone can do mathematics. All it takes is self-confidence and hard work—the same qualities needed to learn to read, to master a musical instrument, or to become skilled at a sport. Indeed, the belief that mathematics requires special talent found in a few elite people is peculiar to the United States. In other countries, particularly in Europe and Asia, all students are expected to become proficient in mathematics.

4   Of course, different people learn mathematics at different rates and in different ways. For example, some people learn by concentrating on concrete problems, others by thinking visually, and still others by thinking abstractly. No matter what type of thinking style you prefer, you can succeed in mathematics.

Misconception Two: The Math in Modern Issues Is Too Complex

5   Some people claim that the advanced mathematical concepts underlying many modern issues are too complex for the average person to understand. It is true that only a few people receive the training needed to work with or discover advanced mathematical concepts. However, most people are capable of understanding enough about the mathematical basis of important issues to develop informed and reasoned opinions.

6   The situation is similar in other fields. For example, years of study and practice are required to become a proficient, professional writer, but most people can read a book. It takes hard work and a law degree to become a lawyer, but most people can understand how the law affects them. And though few have the musical talent of Mozart, anyone can learn to appreciate his music. Mathematics is no different. If you've made it this far in school, you can understand enough mathematics to succeed as an individual and a concerned citizen. Don't let anyone tell you otherwise!

Misconception Three: Math Makes You Less Sensitive

7   Some people believe that learning mathematics will somehow make them less sensitive to the romantic and aesthetic aspects of life. In fact, understanding the mathematics that explains the colors of a sunset or the geometric beauty in a work of art can only enhance aesthetic appreciation. Furthermore, many people find beauty and elegance in mathematics itself. It's no accident that people trained in mathematics have made important contributions in art, music, and many other fields.

Misconception Four: Math Makes No Allowance for Creativity

8   The "turn the crank" nature of the problems in many textbooks may give the impression that mathematics stifles creativity. Some of the facts, formalisms, and skills required for mathematical proficiency are fairly cut and dry, but using those mathematical tools takes creativity. Consider designing and building a home. The task demands specific skills to build the foundation, frame in the structure, install plumbing and wiring, and paint walls. But building the home involves much more. Creativity is needed to develop the architectural design, respond to on-the-spot problems

during construction, and factor in constraints based on budgets and building codes. The mathematical skills you learned in school are like the skills learned in carpentry or plumbing. Applying mathematics is like the creative process of building a home.

from Bennett and Briggs, *Using and Understanding Mathematics*, 5e, pp. 5–7

MyReadingLab™
Complete this **Exercise**
at **myreadinglab.com**

Reading Comprehension Check

1. "Many adults harbor fear or loathing of mathematics, and unfortunately these attitudes are often reinforced by classes that present mathematics as an obscure and sterile subject." (para. 1) In this sentence, which pattern of organization is being employed?
   a. chronological ordering
   b. classification
   c. comparison and contrast
   d. cause and effect

2. In discussing the first misconception, the authors compare studying math with learning a musical instrument and practicing a sport to make the point that
   a. math has a musical feel to it.
   b. math is like an exercise that makes you sweat.
   c. hard work and self-confidence are the keys to success for each.
   d. math can be creative and fun like sports and music.

3. In the third paragraph, the authors write, "Indeed, the belief that mathematics requires special talent found in a few elite people is peculiar to the United States. In other countries, particularly in Europe and Asia, all students are expected to become proficient in mathematics." Which pattern of organization is being employed?
   a. listing
   b. definition/example
   c. comparison and contrast
   d. chronological ordering

4. When the authors write, "Don't let anyone tell you otherwise!" (para. 6) in discussing the second "misconception" about math, they are trying to encourage students to
   a. understand that math is too complex for most people.
   b. understand that with hard work, anyone can build a strong foundation in math.
   c. major in an academic area related to the study of mathematics.
   d. keep the idea in their head that math will make them more complex people.

5. We can infer from this reading that the authors believe that
   a. good math skills require a special kind of brain.
   b. math is not for creative people.
   c. studying math is very similar to studying law.
   d. math is useful for everyone.

6. How do the authors compare building a home to working with math?
   a. Both depend on specific skills and benefit from creativity.
   b. Both need a deep sense of creativity more than any particular skill set.
   c. You have to work hard for both.
   d. There is no relation between building math skills and home building.

7. What purpose did the authors have in writing this piece?
   a. to inform
   b. to persuade students to study high levels of mathematics
   c. to entertain readers
   d. to help clear up any false ideas students might have about the study of math

8. "In fact, understanding the mathematics that explains the colors of a sunset or the geometric beauty in a work of art can only enhance aesthetic appreciation. Furthermore, many people find beauty and elegance in mathematics itself." (para. 7) What logical relationship connects the second sentence to the first?
   a. addition
   b. contrast
   c. cause and effect
   d. example

9. What is the authors' tone in this reading?
   a. angry
   b. encouraging
   c. objective
   d. nostalgic

10. What is the main idea of the reading?
    a. If you work hard, you can have a career involving advanced math skills.
    b. Students need not be intimidated by the study of math, because building strong math skills is mostly a matter of self-confidence and hard work.
    c. Math is not for everyone.
    d. Even though many do not believe so, math involves a lot of creative thinking.

Instructions: First try to use logic and background knowledge in guessing the correct answers to the following data questions. Then, go online and search for the relevant data. Be sure to write the Web source next to your research finding.

INTERNET FACT
SEARCH

Mathematics

1. What Greek math whiz noticed that the morning star and evening star were one and the same, in 530 BCE?
   a. Calculus
   b. Pythagoras
   c. Charles Darwin
   d. Socrates

   Your guess: ——————— Research finding: ———————

   Web source: ————————————————————

2. What do mathematicians call a regular polygon with eight sides?
   a. a rectangle
   b. a hexagon
   c. an octagon
   d. a septagon

   Your guess: ——————— Research finding: ———————

   Web source: ————————————————————

3. A half of a sphere is called what?
   a. multisphere
   b. hemisphere
   c. countersphere
   d. atmosphere

   Your guess: _____   Research finding: _____

   Web source: _____

4. How many faces does a cube have?
   a. 4
   b. 2
   c. none
   d. 6

   Your guess: _____   Research finding: _____

   Web source: _____

FORMAL PRESENTATION PROJECTS

Students will be given the opportunity to present on a topic of their interest pertinent to one of the text's chapter disciplines. Topics could relate to one of the questions a student has checked off in the "Follow Your Interests" section at the beginning of the chapter. Instructors can have students browse through the chapters to guide them toward a given discipline focus.

MyReadingLab™   For more help with **Patterns of Organization,** go to your learning path in **MyReadingLab.com**.

ARCHITECTURE

7

Ellis Island

Learning Objectives

IN THIS CHAPTER, YOU WILL LEARN TO . . .

1. Describe the discipline of architecture
2. Define key terms in the discipline of architecture
3. Answer multiple-choice questions
4. Build computer literacy
5. Recognize the differences between facts and opinion

INTRODUCTION TO THE DISCIPLINE OF ARCHITECTURE

1 LEARNING OBJECTIVE
Describe the discipline
of architecture

Architecture is a field that focuses on designing buildings, both private and commercial, communities, and artificial constructions. It often includes designs of furnishings and decorations, and the restoration and renovation of older buildings. In this chapter, you will come across reading selections that touch upon various aspects of architecture, such as the prairie style created by the legendary American architect Frank Lloyd Wright; Scandinavian architecture; earthquake-proof homes; connecting the urban, suburban, and rural environments; and design students participating in city planning. We hope that this chapter will help you understand the interplay between humans and nature in the field of architecture.

Collaboration

Reading into a Photo

Working in a small group, examine the following photograph and answer the questions that follow.

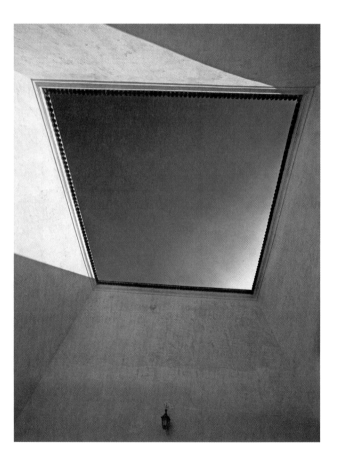

1. In your opinion, what is this place?
2. What message does this image convey to you?

Follow Your Interests

Review the set of questions below that architects might explore. Check off the three or four questions that are most interesting to you.

Collaboration

1. What are some of the most important factors an architect must consider before designing a home?

2. In your opinion, how should homes be built in harmony with nature? In other words, what is the relationship between the natural land and human design?

3. Think about the place where you grew up. Describe a building that you liked most and explain why.

4. What types of architectural structures, such as homes, commercial buildings, or public parks, do you find attractive? Which ones do you find an eyesore?

5. Different cultures have different architectural designs. For example, a Chinese house does not look the same as a house in India or in the United States. How can we account for the differences in the design of these houses? Be specific.

6. What is the role of the environment in the field of architecture? Do you believe that an architect should design a private house or a commercial building that is in harmony with the environment? Why or why not?

7. Feng shui creates harmony in a house by arranging furniture so as not to block a flow of positive energy. Do you agree with the view that space has energy? Give specific reasons to support your answer.

8. The "American dream" usually involves owning a house with a backyard. However, some people find it more desirable to live in condominiums or cooperative apartments. What are the advantages of each choice? Which do you prefer and why?

9. Many people complain that commercial space all over America looks the same due to the rise of chain stores. They say that one could be in a commercial zone and not know if one is in Alaska or in California. What could be done to create unique designs that are more representative of their region?

10. One big problem American cities often face is a lack of green, public space. At the same time, skyscrapers keep rising. What can city governments do to promote the expansion of public parks in urban areas? What can cities do if there is no more space available for these green projects?

11. In some countries, like the Netherlands, most people are not worried about neighbors seeing the interiors of their homes from the outside. In other countries, people are more concerned about keeping their homes private. In your opinion, what causes the difference in their attitude, and which approach fits your personal taste?

12. In some cultures, people prefer open space in their homes and a minimal amount of furniture to allow a smooth flow of energy. Other cultures try to maximize the use of space by filling the rooms in their homes with furniture and artifacts. Which style do you prefer and why?

13. What personality traits are typical of a good architect? In other words, what type of person is best suited for a rewarding career in architecture? Explain.

14. Would you consider choosing a career in architecture? If yes, what would attract you to this field? If not, what would discourage you from pursuing this discipline?

Now, share your choices with a small group of classmates and discuss why these particular questions are most interesting to you. You may wish to discuss these questions with them and ask which questions they found interesting.

Key Terms in the Field of Architecture

② **LEARNING OBJECTIVE**
Define key terms in the discipline of architecture

The following key terms are frequently used in the field of architecture. If you take a college-level course in architecture, it will be important for you to remember these words and to use them in your speech and writing. Review the words below and answer the multiple-choice questions that follow.

appliances	decorative	patios
attic	design	preservation
basement	flooring	renovate
cabinets	furnishings	roofing
decks	interior	woodwork

EXERCISE 1   Inferring Meaning from Context

Read each sentence below and try to derive the meaning of the italicized key terms from the context. Circle the correct definition of each italicized term.

1. Even though Strauss first proposed the Golden Gate Bridge, many architects and engineers worked together to *design* the suspension bridge.
   a. write stories about
   b. paint signboards
   c. plan the form and structure
   d. choose the color of the paint

2. The *interior* of a house can tell you much about the owner.
   a. the front yard of a house
   b. the backyard of a house
   c. the roof of a house
   d. the inside of a house

3. The *furnishings* in a house can help us learn about the taste of the people who live in it.
   - a. furniture only
   - b. furniture, carpets, and curtains
   - c. kitchen accessories
   - d. fireplace

4. The study of *decorative* arts can offer a more detailed view of the objects within interiors.
   - a. serving to adorn
   - b. providing a meaningful experience
   - c. making the interiors less attractive
   - d. serving to confuse the viewers

5. The white marbles of the Taj Mahal are getting yellow because of air pollution, and activists are urging the Indian government to take *preservation* measures.
   - a. preserve fruits and vegetables
   - b. build an area to protect fish
   - c. destruction of a landmark
   - d. protection of a landmark

6. The recent hurricane did not damage Mr. Smith's house, but his *basement* was completely flooded.
   - a. the attic of a house
   - b. the front yard of a house
   - c. the part of a house directly under the roof
   - d. the underground portion of a house

7. A house with an *attic* usually costs more because it allows the owner to store things directly under the roof.
   - a. the basement of a house
   - b. the living room
   - c. the part of a house directly under the roof
   - d. the backyard of a house

8. A modern kitchen comes with many *cabinets* to store cooking accessories such as spoons, forks, knives, etc.
   - a. a piece of furniture with shelves and drawers
   - b. carpets and curtains
   - c. ceramic tiles
   - d. a large bathroom with a Jacuzzi

9. The architect came up with an inexpensive *flooring* plan that saved the owner thousands of dollars.
   - a. the roof of a single-family house
   - b. the roof of a commercial building
   - c. laying a floor
   - d. a special bank for homeowners

10. The tornado damaged Ms. Wilkinson's house so badly that she had to hire a company that specialized in *roofing*.
    - a. the act of covering with a roof
    - b. the underground part of a house
    - c. a machine to detect a tornado
    - d. a company that causes tornadoes

11. The *woodwork* in Mr. Sharma's house, such as doors and staircases, was made of cherry.
    a. the attic of a house
    b. the interior wooden fittings
    c. fittings made of metal
    d. metal doors and stairways

12. Most electronics stores in the United States have a separate section for *appliances* such as refrigerators and washing machines.
    a. rugs and carpets for the floor
    b. tools for gardening
    c. equipment, usually electric, used for domestic purposes
    d. drapes and curtains

13. Most homebuyers prefer *patios* where they can have dinner with friends and family in the summer.
    a. areas in front of a house to play sports
    b. separate areas in the living room to relax
    c. specific areas in the attic to read bedtime stories
    d. areas attached to a house for outdoor dining

14. Houses that come with *decks* appeal more to homebuyers because they can relax with their family members in the open.
    a. open platforms extending from a house
    b. staircases leading to the roof
    c. basement dens
    d. second living rooms

15. The Smiths bought an old house in the heart of the city, but it cost them a large amount of money to *renovate* it.
    a. cause damage to an old house
    b. restore a house to good condition
    c. buy an old house from a bank
    d. sell a house to a private investor

Collaboration

EXERCISE 2   Creating Meaningful Sentences with the Key Terms

Working with a partner, choose five of the key terms in architecture and write an original sentence about each one.

1. Word = _____

   _____

   _____

2. Word = _____

   _____

   _____

3. Word = _____

_____

_____

4. Word = _____

_____

_____

5. Word = _____

_____

_____

COLLEGE STUDY SKILLS
Answering Multiple-Choice Questions

③ LEARNING OBJECTIVE
Answer multiple-choice questions

Most colleges in the United States require students to show their ability to read a selection and understand the content. Students are often asked to read a short essay or article and answer multiple-choice questions about it, choosing one of four answers. In this section, you will learn how to answer multiple-choice questions correctly.

When asked to choose the correct answer from four possible choices, most students tend to look for the right answer first. Sometimes this can be problematic, as usually more than one answer seems to be correct. To avoid this confusion, we suggest that you try to eliminate the incorrect answers first. Begin to cross out the wrong answers mentally, and you will notice that choosing the right answer becomes relatively easier. As you reduce the number of possible choices, you are increasing your chances of choosing the correct answer.

Another useful strategy is to think of the possible choices as true/false statements. It is clear that only one of four answers is correct or a true statement. This means that three choices are incorrect or false statements. Let us say that you are asked to identify the main idea of a passage you have just read. You are now faced with the task of choosing the correct main idea. Since you have four choices, the other three main ideas must be incorrect or misleading. This is especially true of main idea, as a reading selection usually has only one main idea.

Here are some tips to help you succeed in answering multiple-choice questions:

- **Read the directions carefully.**
- **Read the selection slowly and carefully.** It is important that you take time to read the passage.
- **Read the multiple-choice questions.** This will give you a good sense of the answers you should look for.
- **Reread the selection, but this time read with the multiple-choice questions in mind.** You will notice that some answers are becoming clear to you as you read the passage a second time.

- **Do not spend too much time on one question.** If you find a specific question to be difficult or confusing, skip it and move on to the next question. Remember that you will always have a chance to go back to the question you skipped.

- **First, eliminate at least two wrong choices.** If you are left with two seemingly similar answers, reread the passage to find the correct answer and eliminate the other choice. This will leave you with the only possible answer.

- **Remember that your gut feeling is right most of the time.** So, try not to second-guess yourself and change an answer.

- **Review your answers one last time before you hand in the test.** You will need at least five to ten minutes to review your answers.

Let's look at the following passage to fully understand how to choose the right answer by eliminating the wrong answers first.

> In 70 CE the Roman emperor Vespasian built a huge amphitheater in Rome to satisfy the Roman people's fascination with violent shows. The Colosseum was big enough to accommodate hundreds of fighters, animals, and victims. In a single day, as many as 50 pairs of gladiators and 200 animals were killed as 50,000 Romans watched in excitement. The emperor who organized more successful games was more popular among the Roman people.

The author's primary purpose is
  a. to convince the reader to participate in violent games killing animals.
  b. to entertain the reader with an imaginary tale.
  c. to inform the reader why the Colosseum was built in Rome.
  d. to persuade the reader to enjoy violent games.

Nowhere in the passage does the author ask the reader to do anything. Therefore, **Choice a** is not possible, because the author's purpose is not to convince the reader. **Choice b** is also incorrect, as there is nothing funny or entertaining about killing 50 or more humans. **Choice d** cannot be the correct answer since "convince" and "persuade" are more or less similar. The passage does not suggest that the reader should enjoy watching violent games. If you eliminated Choice a, b, and d first, you would be left with only one choice, which is **Choice c**. In the above passage, the author simply presents information about the Colosseum in Rome. For this reason, Choice c is the correct answer.

Putting the Skill into Action

Practice makes perfect, so you will need to practice answering multiple-choice questions. This book gives you many opportunities to use the above strategies as you answer the multiple-choice questions that follow each of the reading selections, which will help you do well on this type of reading test. When in doubt, always ask your instructor for clarification.

The Last Word

One last thing to remember when answering multiple-choice questions is that each question focuses on a particular college-reading skill. It will be important for you to recognize whether you are being asked to guess meaning from context, or to determine the main idea, or to make an inference. Your ability to recognize the particular reading skill being tested will help you a great deal with choosing the right answer. Throughout this book, you will have a chance to improve your college-reading skills. So, keep on practicing reading the selections and answering the questions that follow them.

READINESS FOR COLLEGE SUCCESS
Building Computer Literacy

4 LEARNING OBJECTIVE
Build computer literacy

Regardless of the course you take in college, your professor is likely to give you several writing assignments in a semester. In addition, you may be required to communicate with your classmates via e-mail, use Blackboard to submit your papers digitally, or even create an ePortfolio for yourself. It is necessary for you to be computer literate: You need to have some basic computer skills to be a successful college student. What follows is a brief description of the types of computer skills you will need to succeed in college.

Using a Word Processor

As mentioned previously, your professor may ask you to write an academic essay. You will need to know how to type on a word processor using double spacing. In addition, you will also need to look for grammar and spelling errors after you have typed your paper. Most colleges in the United States have a computer center where students can take free tutorials on using the QWERTY keyboard with relative ease without having to look at the keys.

E-mailing a Professor

There are certain rules of communication college students must follow when e-mailing a professor. You must begin with a salutation such as "Dear Professor Construct" or "Hello Professor Scaffolding." Then you must state the purpose of your e-mail. You may even want to thank the professor for his or her time and effort in replying to your message. Finally, sign off by saying "Sincerely" or "Best regards."

E-mailing a Peer

You are not required to observe the same rules of communication when writing to your classmates. Your tone can be casual if you are writing a classmate; for example, you may not need to say "Sincerely" or "Best wishes" when signing off.

Attaching a Document to an E-mail Message

Most e-mail programs allow the user to attach a text file, an image, or a video file to an e-mail message. As a college student, you may need to send your professor a writing assignment. If you are collaborating with your peers on a project, you may have to share documents with them or send them pictures or video files.

Preparing a Visual Presentation

It is common for college students to give presentations to their instructors and classmates. Several software programs make it possible for you to create slides with text and images. How many presentations you give in one semester will depend on the course you are taking.

Surfing the Internet

The Internet, or "Information Highway," has become a common place for college students. You can perform a variety of tasks on the Internet, such as looking up your library resources and doing some basic research to find information from secondary sources.

Creating a Spreadsheet

In architectural courses, you may have to create a spreadsheet showing numbers. If you do not know how to do this, there is no need to get nervous. There are many software programs that make it easy to create a spreadsheet. Furthermore, you can always get help from the computer center at your college.

Creating a Graph

Graphic analysis has become an integral part of most college courses. Some standardized writing tests even ask students to interpret a graph and write a response to the information in it. Your architecture professor may ask you to collect data on the different types of commercial buildings in a city and create a graph showing the different designs. As you can see, it is important for you to learn how to create a graph to be a successful college student.

The pen-and-paper era in which your grandparents studied is gone. Technology has improved in leaps and bounds since those days. Digital technology has revolutionized how we teach and learn. The following practice will help you become more familiar with the different computer skills and their purposes.

Collaboration

Practice: For each skill in the left column, write some rules you should observe when using them. Use the first example as a model to do the rest with your classmates.

Computer Skill	*Purpose/Some Rules to Observe*
Using a word processor	*For a writing assignment. Double-space, use font size 12, include course title, date, your name, and professor's name*
E-mailing a professor	
E-mailing a peer	
Attaching a document to an e-mail message	
Preparing a visual presentation	
Surfing the Internet	
Creating a spreadsheet	
Creating a graph	

Frank Lloyd Wright: Prairie Style

Preview Questions

1. Have you heard Frank Lloyd Wright's name before? Given that the chapter's focus is architecture, what can you tell about this person? Why do you think he was chosen for the first reading selection in this chapter?

2. Some people believe that modern architects do not pay attention to the landscape when they build a building. In your opinion, how can an architect strike a balance between the building and the landscape? Be specific.

3. If you were an architect, would you consider the exterior or the interior of the house more important? Give specific reasons to support your answer.

MyReadingLab™
Complete this Exercise
at **myreadinglab.com**

Pre-Reading Vocabulary: Focus on Some Key Terms

Before beginning the reading selection, it may be helpful to focus on the meaning of some key words in the article. Working with a partner, try to guess the meaning of these words. Then look up the words in a dictionary.

Word	*Your Definition*	*Dictionary Definition*
landscape		
evolving		
foreshadowed		
chimney		
interior		

Frank Lloyd Wright: Prairie Style

"The good building is not one that hurts the landscape, but one which makes the landscape more beautiful than it was before the building was built." —FLW

1   Through the turn of the [twentieth] century, Wright's distinctively personal style was evolving, and his work in these years foreshadowed his so-called "prairie style," a term deriving from the publication in 1901 of "A Home in a Prairie Town" which he designed for the *Ladies' Home Journal.*

2   Prairie houses were characterized by low, horizontal lines that were meant to blend with the flat landscape around them. Typically, these structures were built around a central chimney, consisted of broad open spaces instead of strictly defined rooms, and deliberately blurred the distinction between interior space and the surrounding terrain. Wright acclaimed "the new reality that is space

Frank Lloyd Wright

Frederick C. Robie House (1909), Chicago, Illinois,
Wright's masterpiece of the prairie style.

Fallingwater (1935), Bear Run, Ohiopyle, Pennsylvania

instead of matter" and, about architectural interiors, said that the "reality of a building is not the container but the space within." The W. W. Willits house, built in Highland Park, Illinois, in 1902, was the first house that embodied all the elements of the prairie style. His masterpiece of the prairie style is the Robie House, built in Chicago in 1909.

3   Wright did not aspire simply to design a house, but to create a complete environment, and he often dictated the details of the interior. He designed stained glass, fabrics, furniture, carpet and the accessories of the house. Legend has it that, in at least one case, he even designed the gowns of his client's wife. The controlling factor was seldom the wishes of the individual client, but Wright's belief that buildings strongly influence the people who inhabit them. He believed that "the architect is a molder of men, whether or not he consciously assumes the responsibility."

Wright on the Web
http://www.delmars.com/wright/flw2.htm
Reprinted by permission.

Reading Comprehension Check

1. "He designed stained glass, fabrics, furniture, carpet and the **accessories** of the house." (para. 3) In this context, the word *accessories* means
   a. the exterior of the house.
   b. the interior of the house.
   c. additional decorative and convenience items.
   d. gloves and earrings.

2. The main idea of the passage is that
   a. Frank Lloyd Wright, the European architect, studied architecture in Paris.
   b. Frank Lloyd Wright, the American architect, is known for his famous prairie style.
   c. all his life, Frank Lloyd Wright aspired simply to design houses.
   d. Frank Lloyd Wright designed the gowns of his client's wife.

3. Which of the following is a statement of fact?
   a. Prairie houses were meant to blend with the flat landscape around them.
   b. Frank Lloyd Wright was the most brilliant American architect.
   c. European architects paled in comparison to Frank Lloyd Wright.
   d. Frank Lloyd Wright was attracted to his client's wife and designed many gowns for her.

4. "Prairie houses were characterized by low, horizontal lines that were meant to blend with the flat landscape around them. Typically, these structures were built around a central chimney, consisted of broad open spaces instead of strictly defined rooms, and deliberately blurred the distinction between interior space and the surrounding terrain." (para. 2) The author's primary purpose in this passage is to
   a. entertain.   c. inform.
   b. persuade.   d. convince.

5. "The W. W. Willits house, built in Highland Park, Illinois, in 1902, was the first house that embodied all the elements of the prairie style. His masterpiece of the prairie style is the Robie House, built in Chicago in 1909." (para. 2) The overall tone of the passage is
   a. sarcastic.   c. critical.
   b. objective.   d. melancholic.

Exploring the Topic

Collaboration

Discuss the following questions to review the content of the article you have just read.

1. The article begins with a direct quote from Frank Lloyd Wright. Explain what Wright meant by a good building not hurting the landscape.

2. Frank Lloyd Wright emphasized "the new reality that is space instead of matter" and believed that the "reality of a building is not the container but the space within." (para. 2) Do you agree with his view? Why or why not?

3. In 1991 the American Institute of Architects recognized Wright as the greatest American architect of all time. Why do you think the institute considered him the greatest American architect?

Post-Reading Vocabulary

Without using a dictionary, determine the meaning of the bolded words from the context.

1. "Wright acclaimed 'the new reality that is space instead of matter' and, about architectural interiors, said that the 'reality of a building is not the **container** but the space within.'" (para. 2)

   Container means _____

2. "The W. W. Willits house, built in Highland Park, Illinois, in 1902, was the first house that **embodied** all the elements of the prairie style." (para. 2)

   Embodied means _____

3. "Wright did not aspire simply to design a house, but to create a complete environment, and he often **dictated** the details of the interior." (para. 3)

   Dictated means _____

READING

Reading Selection **2**

Blog

MyReadingLab™
Complete this **Exercise**
at **myreadinglab.com**

Collaboration

Scandinavian Architecture: From the Country to the City

Preview Questions

1. You have read about Frank Lloyd Wright's famous prairie style. How do you think Scandinavian architecture is different from Wright's prairie style?

2. Read the title of the reading selection carefully. What do you think the title means?

3. Contrast the differences between urban architecture and rural architecture, and explain how they are different. Be sure to use specific examples to support your answer.

Pre-Reading Vocabulary: Focus on Some Key Terms

Before beginning the reading selection, it may be helpful to focus on the meaning of some key words in the article. Working with a partner, try to guess the meaning of these words. Then look up the words in a dictionary.

Word	Your Definition	Dictionary Definition
countryside		
tame		
Art Nouveau		
inspired		
fascinating		

Scandinavian Architecture: From the Country to the City

Posted on February 25, 2011

1 Life in the country. A walk inside Seurasaari, Helsinki's open air museum is a step back in time, although many of these simple buildings still exist in the countryside today. The squirrels are extremely tame here, they run up to boldly eat nuts from your hands and yell at you if you are empty handed. It is also a wonderful place to pack a picnic, should you find yourself visiting Finland.

Art Nouveau style

Jugendstil

Jugendstil

Jugendstil

Art Nouveau

2   The most popular form of architecture seen throughout the city is inspired by a style called Art Nouveau. Some of the most fascinating examples of Art Nouveau architecture is a style that evolved from Germany called "Jugendstil." These structures look like castles from the pages of a fairy tale book. Some are built with dark rough hewn stones and medieval gargoyle creatures climbing from their edifices, while others are painted in pastels of peach with turrets, soaring minarets and wispy wrought iron. Buildings are mostly painted in white or pale yellow. When snow comes, the city looks starkly pure.

Text and photos from blog entitled "Scandinavian Architecture: From Country to City."

MyReadingLab™
Complete this Exercise
at myreadinglab.com

Reading Comprehension Check

1. "A walk inside Seurasaari, Helsinki's open air museum is a step back in time, although many of these simple buildings still **exist** in the countryside today." (para. 1) The word *exist* in this context means
   a. to stop living.
   b. to continue to be.
   c. to have no life.
   d. to cease from being.

2. "Some are built with dark rough hewn stones and medieval gargoyle creatures climbing from their **edifices**, while others are painted in pastels of peach with turrets, soaring minarets and wispy wrought iron." (para. 2) In this context, the word *edifices* means
   a. small organizations.
   b. easy systems.
   c. large buildings.
   d. small buildings.

3. What is the main idea of the reading selection?
   a. Scandinavian architecture is least influenced by Art Nouveau.
   b. Scandinavian architecture is extremely critical of Art Nouveau.
   c. Scandinavian architecture invented Art Nouveau in the nineteenth century.
   d. Scandinavian architecture is greatly influenced by Art Nouveau.

4. "Life in the country. A walk inside Seurasaari, Helsinki's open air museum is a step back in time, although many of these simple buildings still exist in the countryside today. The squirrels are extremely tame here, they run up to

boldly eat nuts from your hands and yell at you if you are empty handed. It is also a wonderful place to pack a picnic, should you find yourself visiting Finland." (para. 1) The primary purpose of the passage is to
a. to amuse the reader.
b. persuade the reader to visit Finland.
c. warn the reader against the dangers of visiting Finland.
d. contrast the differences between Scandinavian architecture and Finnish architecture.

5. "The most popular form of architecture seen throughout the city is inspired by a style called Art Nouveau. Some of the most fascinating examples of Art Nouveau architecture is a style that evolved from Germany called "Jugendstil". These structures look like castles from the pages of a fairy tale book. Some are built with dark rough hewn stones and medieval gargoyle creatures climbing from their edifices, while others are painted in pastels of peach with turrets, soaring minarets and wispy wrought iron. Buildings are mostly painted in white or pale yellow. When snow comes, the city looks starkly pure." (para. 2) What is the author's primary purpose in this passage?
a. to persuade the reader to visit Finland
b. to give misinformation about the influence of Art Nouveau on Scandinavian architecture
c. to discourage the reader from visiting Finland
d. to inform the reader about the influence of Art Nouveau on Scandinavian architecture

Exploring the Topic

Discuss the following questions to review the content of the blog you have just read.

Collaboration

1. The author says that if you do not feed the squirrels in Finland, they will yell at you. In your opinion, what is the author's primary purpose in writing that?

2. In your opinion, why do you think that the most popular form of architecture seen throughout the city of Helsinki is inspired by Art Nouveau architecture, derived from the Jugendstil style of Germany?

3. The author notes that "when snow comes, the city looks starkly pure." (para. 2) What can we infer from the statement about the city of Helsinki in the summer?

Post-Reading Vocabulary

Without using a dictionary, determine the meaning of the highlighted words from the context.

1. "Some of the most fascinating examples of Art Nouveau architecture is a style that **evolved** from Germany called 'Jugendstil.'" (para. 2)

   Evolved means _____

2. "Some are built with dark rough hewn stones and medieval gargoyle creatures climbing from their edifices, while others are painted in pastels of peach with turrets, soaring minarets and **wispy** wrought iron." (para. 2)

Wispy means _____

3. "When snow comes, the city looks **starkly** pure." (para. 2)

Starkly means _____

Jamie Chow   An Interview with a Student in the Field of Architecture

Cornell University

1. How did you find your path to majoring in architecture?

Unlike some people in my major, I never knew I wanted to be an architect since I was young. I always enjoyed drawing and art at an early age. In high school, I took many math and science classes but still kept doing art as an elective program. Only during my senior year of high school did I realize that architecture was the best combination of math, science, and design. Being solely an art major seemed too self-consuming, and would not provide the same feeling of fulfillment that architecture gives me. Architecture, being components of art and science, allows me to have the best of both worlds.

2. What is the biggest obstacle you face in your study of architecture?

My biggest obstacle is time management. Architects are infamous for pulling all-nighters, and I am no exception to that. In design, there is no fixed method or solution (unlike in a math problem). I could simply work on the project endlessly, depending on how much effort I wish to put in. In architecture, changes can be made to the design up till the last minute before the final submission because you only want to submit the best possible design … and the possibilities are endless. Working on a design is like making an abstract expressionist painting. It is tricky because it is hard to tell when to stop, hard to tell when it is REALLY finished.

3. What area(s) of architecture in particular do you find most interesting?

In architecture, you are limited to building requirements and the client's needs. However, the interesting part is to get creative within these boundaries. And even within these rules, I can create something that surpasses the norm. Architecture is connected to every single aspect of life. A building serves us in ways that we often overlook. It is shelter, protection, public, private, hidden, exposed, religious, etc. It is the most basic creation of humans to serve humans. The architect has a responsibility that goes beyond the building's site—the architect has a social and cultural responsibility as well.

Particularly now that we have acquired more advanced technology, architecture is beginning to take new forms and to give back to the environment. Sustainable architecture has become commonplace, and even a necessity today.

4. What specific skills are required of students who study architecture?

Students need to constantly keep up with new computer programs. Currently, the most common programs used to create computer drawings and 3D modeling are AutoCAD, Revit, Grasshopper, and Rhinoceros. Renderings can be done with V-Ray, Photoshop, Piranesi, etc. It is our responsibility to keep up with them and explore these programs.

Students should have a keen sense of design as well. Architects can be classified on a spectrum. On one end are the ones with a background in art while the other end is technical students that are more inclined to formulas and engineering.

5. Other than being an architect, what other career avenues are available for architecture majors?

Architecture students can venture into the field of interior design, engineering, or even the housing and construction industry. With their exposure to computer programs, architects can go into animation, industrial design, media, etc.

Japan Quake Aftermath: How to Earthquake-Proof Your House

Preview Questions

1. Do you know if the house you live in is earthquake-proof? In other words, if an earthquake happened in your area, do you think your house would survive?

2. Why do you think people choose to live in earthquake-prone areas despite knowing that their lives might be in danger?

3. How do you think homes should be built to withstand an earthquake? Be specific.

Collaboration

Pre-Reading Vocabulary: Focus on Some Key Terms

Before beginning the reading selection, it may be helpful to focus on the meaning of some key words in the article. Working with a partner, try to guess the meaning of these words. Then look up the words in a dictionary.

Word	Your Definition	Dictionary Definition
massive		
wobble		
tremor		
sturdy		
prevent		

Japan Quake Aftermath: How to Earthquake-Proof Your House

By William Browning

Sunday, March 13, 2011

1   Japan's massive earthquake rocked the northern part of the country with an 8.9 magnitude quake and then a 30-foot tall tsunami wave. The quake has damaged buildings, flooded away homes, and thousands of people are feared missing. Added to the problem is a possible nuclear meltdown at two sites.

2   How do residents in earthquake-prone areas make their homes earthquake-proof? Large skyscrapers are made to wobble and bend with the ground's waves, but what about single-family units? California is the most prominent place in America where deadly quakes happen even though tremors occur in the central United States as well.

3   Here are some tips to make your home sturdier during an earthquake.

Inside

4   The key to safeguarding inside your home is to prevent furniture from falling over and cabinets from spilling their contents when tremors happen. The *Los Angeles Times* reports tall furniture like bookshelves and china cabinets should be bolted into the wall with braces so they don't tip over. Anti-slip mats for objects on top of slick surfaces such as mantels are recommended so nothing slides off.

5   Items on the wall should either be anchored to studs in the wall or be light-weight so they don't injure anyone. Loose connections for gas appliances are also recommended instead of stiff pipes to prevent cracking and buckling.

Structure

6   The key to keeping your house upright in a huge earthquake is to bolt it to the foundation. Older homes such as those built before 1940 may not have sill bolts in place.

7   Sill bolts are placed into concrete foundations every 4 feet. They are required to be five-eighths of an inch in diameter and usually bore as much as 7 inches into the foundation through a wooden plank. They help keep your house on the foundation in a major tremor.

New Building

8   When constructing a new house, it is important to take earthquake-proof construction into consideration. Providing sill bolts and sill plates is one way to make your structure safer in a quake. Another method of construction to consider is to use insulated concrete forms. The forms are able to withstand 600 mph winds and are earthquake resistant. Insulated concrete forms are already attached to the foundation by steel-reinforced concrete so you don't have to have sill bolts in the construction of your exterior walls.

9   Newer construction methods for windows include rounding off window glass in the corners of the frame to prevent breakage. Having a rounded corner is less rigid than a 90-degree angle. Scientists and engineers have also experimented with leaving gaps near window frames to help the structures move more fluidly in an earthquake so they don't shatter glass.

10   Californians are well aware of earthquake-proof homes. However, in light of recent earthquakes in the middle of the United States and the major tremor in Japan, it may be time to consider stronger houses and structures everywhere.

Reprinted with permission from Yahoo! Inc.

Reading Comprehension Check

1. "Having a rounded corner is less **rigid** than a 90-degree angle." (para. 9) In this context, the word *rigid* means
   a. stiff.
   b. yielding.
   c. flexible.
   d. soft.

2. The main idea of the passage is that
   a. it is impossible to make homes earthquake-proof.
   b. people who live in earthquake-prone areas should consider moving.
   c. a massive earthquake in Japan damaged several buildings.
   d. there are ways to make homes earthquake-proof.

3. The article mentions that the earthquake in Japan damaged many buildings, flooded away homes, and took many lives. These examples are offered to support the fact that
   a. the earthquake in Japan was rather mild.
   b. Japan was least affected by the earthquake.
   c. the earthquake in Japan was massive.
   d. the earthquake did not cause damage to Japan.

4. "Californians are well aware of earthquake-proof homes. However, in light of recent earthquakes in the middle of the United States and the major tremor in Japan, it may be time to consider stronger houses and structures everywhere." (para. 10) It can be inferred from this passage that
   a. earthquakes mostly happen in the United States and Japan.
   b. earthquakes may happen anywhere.
   c. Californians do not need to build earthquake-proof homes.
   d. Japan and the United States are not aware of earthquake-proof homes.

5. "Californians are well aware of earthquake-proof homes. However, in light of recent earthquakes in the middle of the United States and the major tremor in Japan, it may be time to consider stronger houses and structures everywhere." (para. 10) The author's primary purpose in this passage is to
   a. contrast the differences between homes in Japan and homes in the United States.
   b. entertain the reader by telling humorous stories about earthquakes in California.
   c. persuade the reader that earthquake-proof homes should be built everywhere.
   d. convince the reader to move from earthquake-prone areas.

Exploring the Topic

Collaboration

Discuss the following questions to review the content of the article you have just read.

1. The article mentions that the earthquake damaged many buildings in Japan and took the lives of thousands of people. In your opinion, what could have been done to prevent the damage to the buildings and the loss of lives?

2. According to the article, how do people make their homes earthquake-proof? Refer to the article and give specific examples to answer the question.

3. What is the most prominent place in the United States where deadly earthquakes happen? Name other countries where earthquakes happen frequently.

Post-Reading Vocabulary

Without using a dictionary, determine the meaning of the highlighted words from the context.

1. "The key to safeguarding inside your home is to prevent furniture from falling over and cabinets from **spilling** their contents when tremors happen." (para. 4)

    Spilling means _____

2. "Anti-slip mats for objects on top of **slick** surfaces such as mantels are recommended so nothing slides off." (para. 4)

    Slick means _____

3. "Loose connections for gas appliances are also recommended instead of **stiff** pipes to prevent cracking and buckling." (para. 5)

    Stiff means _____

SKILL FOCUS
Facts and Opinions

⑤ LEARNING OBJECTIVE
Recognize the differences
between facts and opinion

One of the important reading skills you will need to learn is to differentiate between a fact and an opinion. As you know, authors write for different reasons. Some authors write because they have important bits and pieces of information to share with the reader. They usually present facts and remain objective. Other authors write to convince the reader that their opinion is right. In this case, they do not offer many facts, but they express their personal opinion. To make the distinction between a fact and an opinion simple, here is an explanation.

A fact is a statement or a claim that can be proven. If the statement cannot be verified, it is not considered a fact. Let's look at an example:

> Frank Lloyd Wright was born on June 8, 1867, in Wisconsin.

This is a statement of fact, because we can check his birth certificate and verify his date of birth. In contrast, an opinion is a statement that is a personal belief. It cannot be proven, so it remains an opinion, not a fact. Consider the following:

> Frank Lloyd Wright was the most brilliant American architect ever.

Those who know anything about architecture will readily admit that Frank Lloyd Wright was a creative architect. However, whether or not he was the most brilliant architect is debatable. This statement, therefore, is an opinion.

When determining whether or not a statement is a fact or an opinion, ask yourself these questions:

- Can the statement be proven?
- Is the statement just someone's belief?
- Has the author provided evidence to support the opinion?

It is important to keep in mind that sometimes a statement can be both a fact and an opinion. If you come across a statement that seems to be a fact and an opinion, be sure to choose opinion in a multiple-choice test. If you see an option "fact and opinion," choose that. Look at the following example to understand this clearly.

> In 1991, the American Institute of Architects recognized Frank Lloyd Wright as "the greatest American architect of all time."

It is a fact that the American Institute of Architects called Frank Lloyd Wright "the greatest American architect of all time." However, that is the opinion of just one institute. Also, the statement was made in 1991, which was 22 years ago. It is not clear if he is still the greatest American architect. The above statement is a combination of a fact and an opinion.

Last but not least, pay attention to facts and opinions offered in a passage. If a passage only states facts, then there is a good chance that the author's purpose is to inform the reader. If, however, you see many opinions in the passage, then you can conclude that the author's purpose is to persuade or convince the reader. As you can see, facts and opinions offered in a passage can tell you about the author's purpose as well.

Let's read the following passages to recognize facts and opinion. Ask yourself the questions on page 304 and determine whether the author uses facts or opinions.

Practice 1: Identifying Facts and Opinions

> The temple of Angkor Wat in Cambodia draws tourists from all over the world. The temple is built on a site that covers 400 square kilometers. There are several towers, and the central tower of the temple rises to a height of 213 feet. To get to the temple, tourists walk through a stone causeway that is lined with stone figures. The towers represent the spiritual world and mountain homes of the gods. Some artifacts taken from the temple were exhibited in Paris in 1867. The purpose of the exhibit was to show the world a great and unknown civilization.

Let's read each statement carefully and determine whether it is a statement of a fact or an opinion.

1. "The temple of Angkor Wat in Cambodia draws tourists from all over the world."

   It is a fact, because the statement is provable. All one needs to do is collect data from the Department of Tourism in Cambodia to verify this information.

2. "The temple is built on a site that covers 400 square kilometers."

   This statement can also be proven easily.

3. "There are several towers, and the central tower of the temple rises to a height of 213 feet."

   This is a statement of fact, because the height of the temple can be measured.

4. "To get to the temple, tourists walk through a stone causeway that is lined with stone figures."

   This is a fact, because it can be proven.

5. "The towers represent the spiritual world and mountain homes of the gods."

   This is a statement of opinion. Whether or not "the towers represent the spiritual world" is open to debate. It is clear that this statement is a matter of belief.

6. "Some artifacts taken from the temple were exhibited in Paris in 1867."

   This information is verifiable, so it is a fact.

7. "The purpose of the exhibit was to show the world a great and unknown civilization."

   This statement is a fact, because that was the purpose of the exhibit.

Practice 2: Differentiating Between Facts and Opinions

> Whoever said that modern architecture meant ugly buildings? It seems that nowadays architects have forgotten how to design beautiful commercial buildings. All one has to do is to go downtown and look around. One sees a concrete jungle full of eyesores. Most of the buildings are downright ugly and unpleasant. Whatever happened to the beautiful, magnificent, and lovely marvels of architecture of the past? It is about time we demolish all the ugly buildings and make downtown an eye-pleasing experience. Modern architects should create beautiful designs.

Let's read each statement carefully to practice differentiating between a fact and an opinion.

1. "Whoever said that modern architecture meant ugly buildings?"

   We do not know if modern architecture means ugly buildings. This statement is an opinion.

2. "It seems that nowadays architects have forgotten how to design beautiful commercial buildings."

   Again, we do not know if this is true. There is no evidence to support the opinion that modern architects do not design beautiful buildings.

3. "All one has to do is to go downtown and look around. One sees a concrete jungle full of eyesores."

   The author expresses an opinion that all the buildings in downtown are ugly. The opinion is not provable.

4. "Most of the buildings are downright ugly and unpleasant."

   Is this statement provable? Can we prove that most of the buildings are ugly and unpleasant? The answer is no. Therefore, this is a statement of opinion.

5. "Whatever happened to the beautiful, magnificent, and lovely marvels of architecture of the past? It is about time we demolish all the ugly buildings and make downtown an eye-pleasing experience."

   The author is trying to convince us that we should tear down the ugly buildings in downtown. This is not a fact. It is clearly an opinion.

6. "Modern architects should create beautiful designs."

   This statement assumes that modern architects do not create beautiful designs. That is just the author's opinion. How do we determine what is beautiful?

Practice 3: Identifying Facts and Opinions

> If birds and animals could speak our language, they would tell us how we are making them homeless. We humans love to build houses, mansions, apartment complexes, commercial buildings, and museums. However, many

people do not think twice about cutting down trees for wood. If someone were to drive us out of our homes, we would get very angry. We do not even realize that we are doing the same to hundreds of thousands of birds and animals when we cut down their real estate. If we could only listen to birds and animals, we would hear their cries: "Hey, get out of my living room." "Hey, humans, would you please stay out of my storage?" or even "How dare you enter my bedroom without my permission?"

Read the statements carefully and decide if they are facts or opinions. Write your answers below with a brief explanation of why you think each statement is a fact, an opinion, or both.

1. "If birds and animals could speak our language, they would tell us how we are making them homeless."

   _____

   _____

2. "We humans love to build houses, mansions, apartment complexes, commercial buildings, and museums."

   _____

3. "However, many people do not think twice about cutting down trees for wood."

   _____

4. "If someone were to drive us out of our homes, we would get very angry."

   _____

   _____

5. "We do not even realize that we are doing the same to hundreds of thousands of birds and animals when we cut down their real estate."

   _____

   _____

   _____

6. "If we could only listen to birds and animals, we would hear their cries: 'Hey, get out of my living room.' 'Hey, humans, would you please stay out of my storage?' or even 'How dare you enter my bedroom without my permission?'"

   _____

Let's now practice reading three passages. Your goal is to determine whether the passages offer facts or opinion or both.

EXERCISE 1   Distinguishing Facts from Opinions

Read the following passages carefully. Then determine whether a statement is a fact or an opinion. In the space provided below each statement, write the answer using your own words.

Passage 1

Americans tend to love everything big, and architecture is no exception. Our houses are huge, and we really do not know what to do with the space we have everywhere. As a result, we waste space when it comes to building houses. We ought to learn a lesson from the Japanese, who build small houses in harmony with the environment. In contrast, we build massive buildings, private and commercial. At this pace, we are going to run out of space very soon. We should wake up and smell the coffee before it is too late.

1. "Americans tend to love everything big, and architecture is no exception."

   _____

2. "Our houses are huge, and we really do not know what to do with the space we have everywhere."

   _____

3. "As a result, we waste space when it comes to building houses."

   _____

4. "We ought to learn a lesson from the Japanese, who build small houses in harmony with the environment."

   _____

5. "In contrast, we build massive buildings, private and commercial."

   _____

6. "At this pace, we are going to run out of space very soon."

   _____

7. "We should wake up and smell the coffee before it is too late."

   _____

Passage 2

The Taj Mahal is situated on the River Jamuna in Agra, India. The mausoleum was built by the Mogul emperor Shah Jahan. The emperor built it to commemorate his wife, Mumtaz Mahal. Her tomb is in the basement of the mausoleum. The building is surrounded by the mosque, hall, and gateway. The Taj Mahal is a classic example of Islamic architecture. Islam rejects representative images, so you will not find pictures of Shah Jahan or Mumtaz Mahal in the building. Islamic architecture was brought to India by the Persian invaders of the eleventh and twelfth centuries.

1. "The Taj Mahal is situated on the River Jamuna in Agra, India."

   _____

2. "The mausoleum was built by the Mogul emperor Shah Jahan."

   _____

3. "The emperor built it to commemorate his wife, Mumtaz Mahal."

_____

4. "Her tomb is in the basement of the mausoleum."

_____

5. "The building is surrounded by the mosque, hall, and gateway."

_____

6. "The Taj Mahal is a classic example of Islamic architecture."

_____

7. "Islam rejects representative images, so you will not find pictures of Shah Jahan or Mumtaz Mahal in the building."

_____

8. "Islamic architecture was brought to India by the Persian invaders of the eleventh and twelfth centuries."

_____

Passage 3

Architecture and Interior Design from the 19th Century: An Integrated History by Buie Harwood, Bridget May, and Curt Sherman is a useful textbook for students of architecture. It provides a survey of architecture, interiors, furniture, and decorative arts furniture from the nineteenth century to the present. The study of architecture focuses on buildings. The study of interiors deals with areas within the building. Finally, the study of furniture and decorative arts gives us a more detailed view of the objects within a building.

1. "_Architecture and Interior Design from the 19th Century: An Integrated History_ by Buie Harwood, Bridget May, and Curt Sherman is a useful textbook for students of architecture."

_____

2. "It provides a survey of architecture, interiors, furniture, and decorative arts furniture from the nineteenth century to the present."

_____

3. "The study of architecture focuses on buildings."

_____

4. "The study of interiors deals with areas within the building."

_____

5. "Finally, the study of furniture and decorative arts gives us a more detailed view of the objects within a building."

_____

EXERCISE 2   Identifying Facts and Opinions

You have practiced determining whether a statement is a fact, an opinion, or both. Read the following passages carefully, and find statements of facts and opinion. Look for clues you learned earlier to choose the right answer.

Passage 1

The most durable and finest pieces of furniture were manufactured during the Industrial Revolution. The workers were skilled and made furniture at customers' requests. Manufacturers created their finest pieces for exhibits. Many people went to these exhibits to see the latest styles of furniture. Alas, the modern world has seen a decline in both the quality and style of furniture. Machines have replaced humans. Most of the products are not durable, and we have lost the creativity that was a hallmark of the Industrial Revolution. The twenty-first-century furniture manufacturers should learn a lesson or two from the manufacturers belonging to the Industrial Revolution.

What statements of fact and opinion are offered in the above passage?

Facts

1. _____
   _____

2. _____

3. _____

4. _____

5. _____

Opinions

1. _____

2. _____
   _____

3. _____
   _____

Passage 2

The Alhambra palace in Granada is a reminder of the Moors' conquest of Spain. The Alhambra (1238–1358) represents the grace of Moorish culture. The palace has royal apartments, and is surrounded by beautiful courtyard gardens. After the Moors were expelled from Spain, Isabella of Castile (1451–1504) and Ferdinand of

Aragon (1452–1516) lived in the palace briefly. The Alhambra retains its charm with its exquisite apartments and detailed colonnades.

What statements of fact and opinion are offered in the above passage?

Facts

1. _____
2. _____
3. _____
4. _____

_____

Opinion

1. _____

Passage 3

The early settlers built wooden houses in the United States. These exceptionally intelligent settlers conveniently forgot that these houses could catch fire easily. This is not to mention that these wooden homes have contributed to a rise in deforestation. Is there no decency left in the world? We should build houses the way they used to be built in the good old days. If we keep building wooden houses, an entire township can turn into an inferno.

What statements of fact and opinion are offered in the above passage?

Facts

1. _____
2. _____

Opinions

1. _____

_____

2. _____
3. _____
4. _____

Passage 4

The Potala Palace in Lhasa represents the politics, religion, and history of Tibet. The palace is 1,312 feet long and 13 stories high. It has the White Palace (1645–90), which was built by the fifth Dalai Lama. It also has the Red Palace (1690–94), which was built after his death in 1682. The White Palace has dormitories and palace apartments. The Red Palace contains holy tombs. Potala Palace is a reminder of the Chinese invasion of Tibet in 1950 and the exile of the fourteenth Dalai Lama in 1959.

What statements of fact and opinion are offered in the above passage?

Facts

1. _____
2. _____
3. _____
4. _____
5. _____
6. _____
7. _____
    _____

Opinion

1. _____
2. _____

Passage 5

The Empire State Building (1929–31) in New York was designed by R. H. Shreeve, T. Lamb, and A. L. Harmon. It is 1,250 feet tall and has 102 stories. It was the world's tallest building in 1931. This title was previously held by the nearby Chrysler Building, which is 1,046 feet tall. Midtown New York was growing fast, and the property value of buildings in the city was also rising. The Empire State Building was completed during the Great Depression. It remained empty for many years.

What statements of fact and opinion are offered in the above passage?

Facts

1. _____
    _____
2. _____
3. _____
4. _____
5. _____
    _____
6. _____
7. _____

Opinion

1. _____
2. _____

LANDMARK IN THE FIELD OF ARCHITECTURE

The Golden Gate Bridge in San Francisco

It is said that a trip to San Francisco is not complete without seeing the breathtaking Golden Gate Bridge. When it was completed in 1937, it was the longest suspension bridge in the world. The bridge connects San Francisco to Marin County. The Golden Gate Bridge is seen around the world as a symbol of San Francisco, California, the United States of America. The American Society of Civil Engineers has called the Golden Gate Bridge one of the modern Wonders of the World.

In 1916, an engineering student, James Wilkins, offered a proposal to build the bridge. At that time, people used to take a ferry to go from San Francisco to Marin County. The trip cost $1.00 and took 20 minutes. At first, some people did not like the idea of building the bridge. However, car manufacturers saw a great opportunity to sell more cars and supported the proposal. In 1917, M. M. O'Shaughnessy, city engineer of San Francisco, called the bridge the Golden Gate Bridge.

Many engineers were responsible for the huge project. Joseph Strauss, Irving Morrow, Charles Alton Ellis, and Leon Moisseiff designed the bridge together. However, it was Strauss who got credit for designing the Golden

Gate Bridge. It was not until 2007 that the Golden Gate Bridge District gave credit to Ellis for the design of the bridge.

Work on the bridge started on January 5, 1933. It cost more than $35 million to build the bridge. Strauss remained in charge of the project. During construction, eleven workers were killed. Nineteen workers who fell from the bridge were saved by a net. The Golden Gate Bridge was finished in April 1937.

After much waiting, the bridge was opened on May 27, 1937. Celebrations lasted one week. Before cars were allowed to cross the bridge, about 200,000 people crossed the bridge by foot. A song, "There's a Silver Moon on the Golden Gate," was played to mark the occasion. On May 28, 1937, President Roosevelt pushed a button in Washington, D.C. to start vehicle traffic over the bridge officially. Since its opening, the Golden Gate Bridge has appeared in books, films, documentaries, musical shows, and television series. According to the Frommer's travel guide, it is "possibly the most beautiful, certainly the most photographed bridge in the world."

Considering the Topic

Answer the following questions with a partner.

Collaboration

1. The Golden Gate Bridge is not the only suspension bridge in the world. In fact, there are other suspension bridges that are much longer than the Golden Gate Bridge. Why, in your opinion, does it continue to be a symbol of the United States of America all over the world?

2. Many engineers were responsible for designing and building the bridge. Still, only Strauss, and later Ellis, got credit for designing the bridge. Why do you think this happened?

3. In your opinion, how does the Golden Gate Bridge affect the lives of those living in San Francisco and Marin County? Be specific.

Internet Connection

Research another landmark in the field of architecture, and fill out the section below.

Great Wall of China	green buildings
skyscrapers	Grand Canyon Skywalk
Egyptian pyramids	shopping malls

Landmark: _____

Question	Answer
When did this landmark become a reality?	
Who was involved in developing this landmark?	
What made this landmark special?	
How did this landmark change the way people view architecture?	

READING

Reading Selection **4**

Blog

MyReadingLab™
Complete this **Exercise**
at **myreadinglab.com**

Adapted from "Urban vs. Suburban"

Preview Questions

1. Do you like to live in an urban area, or would you prefer to live in the suburbs? Explain your choice with specific reasons.

2. Most people tend to live in an urban area. Why do you think they gravitated toward a city?

3. With over-urbanization and overpopulation, it is becoming more and more difficult to live in a city. As a result, some people live in the suburbs and commute to the city every day. In your opinion, what can be done to connect the urban, suburban, and rural environments?

Collaboration

Pre-Reading Vocabulary: Focus on Some Key Terms

Before beginning the reading selection, it may be helpful to focus on the meaning of some key words in the blog. Working with a partner, try to guess the meaning of these words. Then look up the words in a dictionary.

Word	Your Definition	Dictionary Definition
controversial		
urban		
suburban		
rural		
retreat		

Adapted from "Urban vs. Suburban"

Posted on 02/22/2011 *by* Jeremiah Russell

1   In my Twitter posts, I get into controversial topics related to architecture. I recently had a discussion about the future of our urban and suburban environments. I suggested that the suburbs wouldn't die until Americans changed their "bigger is better" mentality. A friend said that it was not about bigger is better. He suggested that some people like the peace and quiet of suburbs. I asked myself if we really wanted to retreat to the solitude of the suburbs while watching the *Real Housewives of Orange County* and *Jersey Shore* on flat-screen TVs in our minivans? Then I wondered if most people preferred more dense urban lifestyles?

2   Personally, I think it's both. There is a market for everyone. There are those who prefer the quiet suburbs, but then there are those who prefer the hustle and bustle of dense urban metropolis. The real issue is how do we connect all these different "islands" of development? How do we create vibrant and interconnected cities that include urban, suburban and rural neighborhoods?

3   The simple answer is public transit. We need a combination of rail and bus lines that works with roadway networks. In my opinion, this is the future of "city life." You'll be able to live in a rural neighborhood and work in the city as a stockbroker or an architect. You drive to a transit hub, park your car and take a train into the city. The same would be true of living in a suburban area. And then going the other direction, living in the urban core it would be possible to take transit out to the suburban and rural areas. You could then rent a car and go hiking, fishing, river rafting, whatever.

4   I think we're getting close to a time where the old ideas of city planning are going to come true. Whether this happens in the next 5 years or 20 is anyone's guess. What is clear is that we cannot continue as we have. Our total dependence on the single-user auto is ending. Suburban sprawl has failed. Our urban centers struggle to survive. However, if we connect the urban, suburban and rural environments by efficient public transit, success will be much more attainable. What is more, we will not have to give up our diverse lifestyle options.

R|One Studio Architecture, LLC Reprinted by permission.

Reading Comprehension Check

MyReadingLab™
Complete this Exercise
at **myreadinglab.com**

1. "I asked myself if we really wanted to retreat to the **solitude** of the suburbs while watching the *Real Housewives of Orange County* and *Jersey Shore* on flat-screen TVs in our minivans?" (para. 1) The word *solitude* in this context means
a. a lonely place.
b. a hustling bustling place.
c. a crowded place.
d. a noisy place.

2. The main idea of the blog is that
   a. the urban and suburban environments should be isolated from each other.
   b. only the suburban and rural environments need to be connected.
   c. public transit is not needed to connect the three struggling environments.
   d. public transit is needed to connect the urban, suburban, and rural environments.

3. Which of the following statements is NOT a fact?
   a. "I recently had a discussion about the future of our urban and suburban environments."
   b. "He suggested that some people like the peace and quiet of suburbs."
   c. "I think we're getting close to a time where the old ideas of city planning are going to come true."
   d. "There are those who prefer the quiet suburbs, but then there are those who prefer the hustle and bustle of dense urban metropolis."

4. "The simple answer is public transit. We need a combination of rail and bus lines that works with roadway networks. In my opinion, this is the future of 'city life'. You'll be able to live in a rural neighborhood and work in the city as a stockbroker or an architect. You drive to a transit hub, park your car and take a train into the city. The same would be true of living in a suburban area. And then going the other direction, living in the urban core it would be possible to take transit out to the suburban and rural areas. You can then rent a car and go hiking, fishing, river rafting, whatever." The author's primary purpose in the passage is to
   a. entertain.   c. amuse.
   b. persuade.   d. inform.

5. Which sentence is a statement of fact?
   a. "I think we're getting close to a time where the old ideas of city planning are going to come true."
   b. "Whether this happens in the next 5 years or 20 is anyone's guess."
   c. "What is clear is that we cannot continue as we have."
   d. "Our total dependence on the single-user auto is ending."

Collaboration

Exploring the Topic

Discuss the following questions to review the content of the blog post you have just read.

1. In the blog post, the author refers to the American "bigger is better" mentality. Discuss how this mentality contributes to the process of over-urbanization.

2. What does the author recommend to connect the urban, suburban, and rural environments? Do you agree with his proposal? Why or why not? Please give specific reasons to support your answer.

3. Why does the author call the urban, suburban, and rural environments "struggling" entities? Based on the post, why are they struggling?

Post-Reading Vocabulary

Without using a dictionary, determine the meaning of the bolded words from the context.

1. "There are those who prefer the quiet suburbs, but then there are those who prefer the **hustle and bustle** of dense urban metropolis." (para. 2)

   Hustle and bustle means _____

2. "How do we create **vibrant** and interconnected cities that include urban, suburban and rural neighborhoods?" (para. 2)

   Vibrant means _____

3. "However, if we connect the urban, suburban and rural environments by efficient public transit, success will be much more **attainable**." (para. 4)

   Attainable means _____

Panel Discussion on Building a Shopping Mall in the Small Town of Tranquility

Collaboration

You live in the small town of Tranquility with a population of only 250 people. Recently, Builders for Bucks Inc., an architecture company, has approached your mayor with a proposal to build a huge shopping mall in the heart of Tranquility. This may or may not be in your interest, as Tranquility is known for its peace and serenity. Most of the townspeople are worried that the shopping mall will disturb the peaceful environment of Tranquility. They are also concerned that the rate of crime will increase when the shopping mall opens. Your mayor has asked you to participate in a panel discussion to express your opinion about the proposed shopping mall. Keep in mind that the CEO of Builders for Bucks, Mr. Benjamin Smith, will first do a presentation. He will try to convince people that the shopping mall is good for the town. To help you participate in the panel discussion, here are some profiles of the town. You may want to write your speech and present your strongest arguments to support or oppose the shopping mall.

1. farmer

2. owner of a day-care center

3. café owner

4. minister

5. police chief

6. environmentalist

7. high school teacher

8. Internet developer

9. landscape architect

10. real estate consultant

11. florist

12. restaurant owner

Feel free to create more profiles that are appropriate for the topic of the panel discussion. You may use the following questions to prepare for the panel discussion. In addition, you can come up with your own questions for the panel discussion.

1. Why does Builders for Bucks Inc. want to build the shopping mall in Tranquility? In other words, why did the architecture company choose such a small town as Tranquility for the shopping mall?

2. What effects will the shopping mall have on the townspeople's lifestyle?

3. Is the shopping mall in the townspeople's best interest? If not, what can the townspeople do to keep the company from building the shopping mall?

4. What can Builders for Bucks do to ensure the safety of the townspeople after the shopping mall is built?

5. How would the shopping mall look architecturally? Would it be a typical ugly-looking shopping mall, or would it be a gorgeous, state-of-the-art glass structure, or would it be a Frank Lloyd Wright-like building nestled into the natural surroundings?

Whether you support or oppose the shopping mall will depend on the profile you choose. For example, if you are a landscape architect, you will have a chance to work for Builders for Bucks Inc. However, if you are a small restaurant owner, then you ought to worry about the modern food court in the shopping mall driving you out of business. Once you choose a profile, build your arguments that strengthen your position. Be sure to listen to your townspeople's arguments carefully and respond accordingly.

WRITING CONNECTIONS: *Building Your Dream Home*

Imagine that you are a successful architect. You have accomplished a great deal in your professional career. In the process, you have saved up a substantial amount of money. You have always wanted to live in your dream home. Now that you are going to be retiring soon, you are considering building your dream home. Here are some of the factors you may want to consider before you start building your dream home.

Location
Based on the kind of person you are, your dream home may be up in the mountains, or it may be near a lake or a river or a beach. You may want to live in the woods, or you may prefer to live in the city. In other words, the design of your dream home will depend, a great deal, on the surrounding environment. Write the location of your dream home here:

_____

_____

Costs
Since you are extremely wealthy, money is not a concern for you. This means that you do not need to cut corners to build your dream home. You can use the best quality of building materials for your home. In the space provided below, make a list of things you want for your dream home.

_____

_____

Architecture

What will be the design of your dream home? You may get some ideas about design from this chapter. However, you may need to do some basic research on the Internet to choose a specific design. Write the design here:

_____

_____

_____

Make a list of materials for the exteriors. For example, write down the types of windows, doors, knobs, etc., you want for your dream home. Use your notebook if you need more space.

1. _____

2. _____

3. _____

4. _____

5. _____

6. _____

7. _____

Interiors

Write a brief description of the interiors of your dream home. Keep in mind that interiors include everything from types of rooms (kitchen, bathroom, bedroom) to lights, appliances, and electrical sockets. Again, you may want to do some research on the Internet to get an idea of interiors.

_____

_____

_____

_____

_____

_____

Furniture and Decorative Arts

Make a list of furniture items and decorative arts for the inside of your dream home. Furniture includes sofas, chairs, tables, beds, and so on, and decorative arts are paintings, wall hangings, rugs, and carpets.

1. _____

2. _____

3. _____

4. _____

5. _____

6. _____

7. _____

8. _____

9. _____

10. _____

Blueprints

Create a blueprint (a map) of your house in the box below. You may want to do some research on the Internet to see some sample blueprints. A blueprint shows how the interior of a house is laid out. The blueprint clearly indicates the location of the bedrooms (including length and width), the kitchen, the bathrooms, and so on. Draw your blueprint here:

Exterior

In the box below, draw a sketch of your dream home. What will it look like from the outside? The good news is that you are the boss, so you can design your dream home however you wish. The sky is the limit. If you know the architecture software AutoCAD, feel free to use it on a separate page.

A Description of Your Dream Home

Last but not least, write a brief description of your dream home in a paragraph or two. It is true that your dream house is not for sale, so you will not write the description to attract potential buyers. However, it wouldn't hurt to describe your dream home to impress people. Be creative, and write a nice description of your dream home. If you wish, you can submit your paragraph(s) to your instructor for feedback on content and form.

My Dream Home

_____

_____

_____

_____

_____

_____

_____

_____

_____

_____

READING

Reading Selection **5**

Article

OU Design Students Hope to Play a Role in Revitalizing North Tulsa

MyReadingLab™
Complete this **Exercise**
at **myreadinglab.com**

Preview Questions

1. Do you think that design students can play an important role in city planning, or do you feel that this job should be left for experienced architects only?

2. In your opinion, should the community get involved in developing design concepts for the city? Also, how does the architect determine what the community needs?

3. Would you feel comfortable or safe living in a city that was designed by students? Why or why not?

Collaboration

Pre-Reading Vocabulary:
Focus on Some Key Terms

Before beginning the reading selection, it may be helpful to focus on the meaning of some key words in the article. Working with a partner, try to guess the meaning of these words. Then look up the words in a dictionary.

Word	Your Definition	Dictionary Definition
revitalize		
outreach		
potential		
turf		
catalyst		

OU Design Students Hope to Play a Role in Revitalizing North Tulsa

By Kevin Canfield, World Staff Writer
Published 4/9/2011

1   **A group of graduate students at the University of Oklahoma Urban Design Studio is hoping to play a small role in revitalizing a north Tulsa community.**

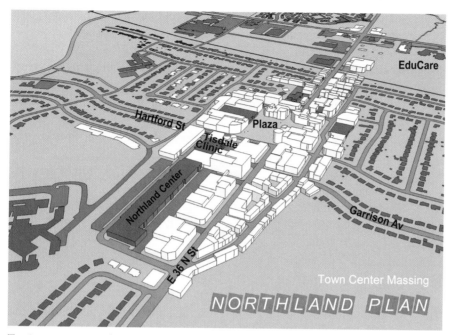

Tan images are actual structures that are either under construction or completed. White images are meant to illustrate possible future development, according to the OU Urban Design Studio.

2   On Saturday, the students will share with the public what they have in mind during an open house.

3   "The purpose of the open house is to invite people in the Northland community and elsewhere to come by and visit with them (the students) and see what they have been working on," said Shawn Schaefer, director of the Urban Design Studio.

4   The Northland Plan—named after the area near the old Northland Shopping Center on 36th Street North and Hartford Avenue—is the students' community-outreach project this year.

5   "The best way to learn is to actually get their hands dirty," Schaefer said.

6   Students have been meeting with local residents for months to identify community needs and potential development concepts.

7   The open house "is just a way of asking them if they would like to come visit us on our turf," Schaefer said.

8   With OU's Wayman Tisdale Specialty Clinic scheduled to open in the neighborhood next summer, taking a broader look at development possibilities in the area made sense, Schaefer said.

9   "We knew there was some change coming, and it would be possible that some of the things we proposed might actually occur," he said.

10 Another catalyst for the project was PlaniTulsa, the city's recently completed effort to update its comprehensive plan.

11 The new comprehensive plan identified the need to develop north Tulsa and encouraged the use of small area plans as a development tool.

12   "What I would hope is that the city would continue these small area plans, so there might be six or eight of these plans and they might end up as a cohesive whole for the area," he said.

13   Schaefer stressed that ultimately the Northland Plan belongs to the community, not to the students.

14   "A lot will depend on the property owners," Schaefer said. "The idea is we are going to try to create a report that can move forward."

15   Before a small area plan can go into effect, it must be approved by the City Council.

16   State Rep. Jabar Shumate, D-Tulsa, encouraged Tulsans to stop by Saturday and give their opinions.

17   "Saturday is sort of the vision part, the beginning of the process," he said.

MyReadingLab™
Complete this **Exercise**
at **myreadinglab.com**

Reading Comprehension Check

1. "'We knew there was some change coming and it would be possible that some of the things we **proposed** might actually occur,' he said." (para. 9) In this context, the word *proposed* means
   a. offered.
   b. rejected.
   c. disagreed.
   d. denied.

2. The main idea of the article is that
   a. the architecture professors at the University of Oklahoma Urban Design Studio have turned down a proposal offered by their students.
   b. a group of design students have proposed a plan to bring a north Tulsa community back to life.
   c. the north Tulsa community has protested the proposal offered by the design students.
   d. Shawn Schaefer, director of the Urban Design Studio, believes that only students with dirty hands should participate in the project.

3. "'A lot will depend on the property owners,' Schaefer said. 'The idea is we are going to try to create a report that can move forward.'" (para. 14) It can be inferred from this statement that
   a. the design students will decide how the community should be developed.
   b. the property owners are extremely upset that they were not consulted before the design students proposed the project.
   c. it is really up to the community whether the city should move forward with the development project.
   d. Shawn Schaefer, director of the Urban Design Studio, will make the final decision on the development project.

4. Which of the following sentences is a statement of opinion?
   a. "A group of graduate students at the University of Oklahoma Urban Design Studio is hoping to play a small role in revitalizing a north Tulsa community."
   b. "On Saturday, the students will share with the public what they have in mind during an open house."

c. "What I would hope is that the city would continue these small area plans, so there might be six or eight of these plans and they might end up as a cohesive whole for the area."

d. "Before a small area plan can go into effect, it must be approved by the City Council."

5. The overall tone of the passage is

a. optimistic.

b. pessimistic.

c. sentimental.

d. straightforward.

Exploring the Topic

Collaboration

Discuss the following questions to review the content of the article you have just read.

1. What do you think will happen on Saturday when the design students share their proposed project with the community? Will the community accept the proposal, or will it reject it?

2. The article mentions that students have been meeting with local residents for months to determine their needs and potential development concepts. Discuss why it is necessary to speak to the local residents before starting the project.

3. Shawn Schaefer, director of the Urban Design Studio, believes that "the best way to learn is to actually get their hands dirty." (para. 5) What does he mean by that? Give specific examples to support your answer.

Post-Reading Vocabulary

Without using a dictionary, determine the meaning of the bolded words from the context.

1. "Another catalyst for the project was PlaniTulsa, the city's recently completed effort to **update** its comprehensive plan." (para. 10)

   Update means _____

2. "What I would hope is that the city would continue these small area plans, so there might be six or eight of these plans and they might end up as a **cohesive** whole for the area, he said." (para. 12)

   Cohesive means _____

3. "Schaefer **stressed** that ultimately the Northland Plan belongs to the community, not to the students." (para. 13)

   Stressed means _____

Approaches to Design History   **TEXTBOOK APPLICATION**

The purpose of this exercise is to get you acquainted with the type of reading you will be required to do in college. First, listen to the lecture and take notes. You can listen to the lecture by scanning the QR code on page 326 with your smart phone. Your professor may also read the selections or play the audio file in class. Make sure that you write down the important points of the lecture.

Collaboration

Group Discussion

Working in small groups of three to four students, answer the following questions. Your instructor may ask you to share your answers with your classmates. As you refer to your notes, it is best to write brief answers to each of the questions below using your own words. After the discussion, you will have an opportunity to share your findings with your peers.

1. What are the different approaches to design history? Think of architecture, interior design, and furniture to answer this question. Be specific.

2. Do you believe that we can examine paintings, furniture, and metals to study the past? Explain how.

3. Some people think that we can learn a great deal about a society or a group of people by studying their buildings. Do you agree with this view? Why or why not?

4. In your opinion, why is it that man-made objects such as pots, vases, and tools differ from society to society?

5. What role does the environment play in design? In other words, what environmental factors does an architect need to take into consideration before designing a commercial building?

6. Do you think that buildings, interior design, furnishings, and decorative arts represent the values and beliefs of a society or an individual? Explain.

7. Do you prefer older architectural styles, or do you like modern architectural styles? Explain your preference with specific examples.

Now that you have discussed the highlights of the lecture with your classmates, read the following selection and answer the multiple-choice questions that follow.

Approaches to Design History

By **Buie Harwood, Bridget May, and Curt Sherman**

Scan this code using your smart phone to listen to an audio version of this reading

1   There are various approaches to the study of design history, whether architecture, interior design and furniture, or a combination. Art history uses works of art such as painting, sculpture, architecture, furniture, ceramics, and metals to study the past. Its formalistic method follows chronology and stylistic development to grasp the meaning of works of art, and, by extension, a society or people. Architectural history follows a similar pattern through its study of buildings. Its method specifically addresses buildings primarily through their individual histories, functions, owners, architects, styles, sitings, materials, construction methods, and contextual environments. Material culture looks specifically at man-made objects as transmitters of ideas and values of a society or group. Objects made and used by a society may include tools, furniture, textiles, and lighting that may be high style or vernacular. Design history studies artifacts and their contexts with a focus on their design and designers, materials, form, and function. Interior design historians bring a unique approach to design history by integrating the relationship of architecture

and interiors in the context of history and design analysis. To accomplish this, the art history, architectural history, material culture, and design history approaches are merged and used as they relate to considerations of research, programming, concept, function, overall aesthetic, principles, and elements, as well as meaning and intent. As interior design educators, we have taken this last approach.

2   A stylistic approach to design identifies forms, function, and visual features. This method, which is typically chronological, can be as simple as codifying visual characteristics with little definition of the roles of form and/or function. In a broader view, such as that of art history, or material culture, style can assume that groups of people during particular times prefer particular forms and motifs as a reflection of their cultural and social qualities or particular design theories, as in the case of many modern designers. Therefore, objects, such as architecture, interiors, furnishings, and decorative arts can embody the values and/or beliefs of a society, group, or individual. In this sense, objects become historical documents or visual records. As primary documents, they can tell us much about an individual or group. Objects survive much longer than written records and often derive from a broader spectrum of society. But the most complete picture exists when objects and written records are integrated.

3   Styles evolve from social, cultural, economic, and/or political factors of a given time. Available materials, climate, location, technology, and historical events affect the visual image. Until the middle of the 19th century, styles originate with political or religious leaders, the wealthy, other important people, or the design elite, and then filter to the middle class through an increasing range of media as time passes. Mass production and communication make it possible for many to emulate high-style design. Style or movement beginnings and endings vary. Consequently, dates provided herein should be considered guidelines because resources deviate in identifying exact dates, and transitions are common as stylistic periods change. Additionally, personal preferences affect or determine the form and appearance of buildings and objects. Some people choose older styles over newer ones, especially in early periods when fashion is less important and visual resources, such as books, periodicals, or photographs, are limited.

from Buie et al., *Architecture and Interior Design from the 19th Century*, pp. xii–xiii

Reading Comprehension Check

MyReadingLab™
Complete this **Exercise**
at **myreadinglab.com**

1. "There are various **approaches** to the study of design history, whether architecture, interior design and furniture, or a combination." (para. 1) In this context, the word *approaches* means
   a. different types of furniture.
   b. the methods used.
   c. interior design.
   d. roofing and lighting.

2. "Its formalistic method follows **chronology** and stylistic development to grasp the meaning of works of art, and, by extension, a society or people." (para. 1) The word *chronology* in this context means
   a. the dates of events.
   b. a group of people.
   c. a particular society.
   d. the names of the artists.

3. "Material culture looks specifically at man-made objects as **transmitters** of ideas and values of a society or group." (para. 1) In this context, the word *transmitters* means
   a. ancient tools.   c. things that convey.
   b. old furniture.   d. primitive weapons.

4. The main idea of the essay is that
   a. there is only one way to study design history.
   b. there is no effective way to study design history.
   c. there are many ineffective ways to study design history.
   d. there are different approaches to study design history.

5. In the first paragraph, the examples of man-made objects such as tools, furniture, textiles, and lighting are offered to support the idea that
   a. these objects were of inferior quality.
   b. people in the past did not know how to make good quality tools and furniture.
   c. one can examine these objects to study the values of a society.
   d. these objects were made by women.

6. Which sentence best states the main idea of the passage?
   a. Interior design historians bring a unique approach to design history by integrating the relationship of architecture and interiors in the context of history and design analysis.
   b. Architects only consider architecture to understand design history.
   c. Experts find it more important to examine man-made objects than to look at interior design.
   d. Design history can be fully understood only if interior design is completely ignored.

7. "Interior design historians bring a unique approach to design history by integrating the relationship of architecture and interiors in the context of history and design analysis. To accomplish this, the art history, architectural history material culture, and design history approaches are merged and used as they relate to considerations of research, programming, concept, function, overall aesthetic, principles, and elements, as well as meaning and intent." (para. 1) It can be inferred from this passage that
   a. interior design historians are more knowledgeable than architects are.
   b. design history is too complex to be understood by a single approach.
   c. interior design historians do not merge architectural history, material culture, and design history approaches.
   d. the integration of architecture and interiors is unnecessary to study design history.

8. "Objects survive much longer than written records and often derive from a broader spectrum of society. But the most complete picture exists when objects and written records are integrated." (para. 2) A logical conclusion drawn from this passage is that
   a. objects alone are sufficient to study the past.
   b. man-made objects are a reliable way to study the values of a society.
   c. experts studying man-made objects should first take pictures.
   d. Written records improve the reliability of objects as sources of information about the past.

9. The overall tone of the passage is
   a. sardonic.
   b. objective.
   c. amusing.
   d. sarcastic.

10. The author's purpose is to
   a. persuade the reader.
   b. inform the reader.
   c. convince the reader.
   d. amuse the reader.

The Internet can be a powerful and effective research tool once you have learned how to successfully limit your information searches and have learned how to interpret the results of your search with a critical lens.

INTERNET FACT SEARCH

Architecture

Instructions: First, try to use logic and background knowledge in guessing the correct answers to the following data questions. Then, go online and search for the relevant data. Be sure to write the Web source next to your research finding.

1. The world's tallest building is
   a. Burj Khalifa in Dubai, United Arab Emirates.
   b. Taipei 101 in Taipei City, Taiwan.
   c. Petronas Tower 1 in Kuala Lumpur, Malaysia.
   d. Petronas Tower 2 in Kuala Lumpur, Malaysia.

   Your guess: _____ Research finding: _____

   Web source: _____

2. The world's longest bridge over sea is
   a. Qingdao Trans-Oceanic Bridge in China.
   b. Hangzhou Bay Bridge in China.
   c. Lake Pontchartrain Causeway in the USA.
   d. Donghai Bridge in China.

   Your guess: _____ Research finding: _____

   Web source: _____

3. The longest suspension bridge in the world is
   a. Golden Gate Bridge in the USA.
   b. Verrazano-Narrows Bridge in the USA.
   c. Tsing Ma Bridge in Hong Kong.
   d. Akashi Kaikyo Bridge in Japan.

   Your guess: _____ Research finding: _____

   Web source: _____

4. The world's longest underwater tunnel currently is
   a. the Gotthard Base Tunnel in Switzerland.
   b. the Lotschberg Base Tunnel in Switzerland.
   c. the Seikan Tunnel in Japan.
   d. the Channel Tunnel in the United Kingdom.

   Your guess: _____   Research finding: _____

   Web source: _____

5. The world's largest shopping mall is
   a. Mall of America in Bloomington, USA.
   b. the Dubai Mall in Dubai, United Arab Emirates.
   c. South China Mall in Dongguan, China.
   d. King of Prussia in Pennsylvania, USA.

   Your guess: _____   Research finding: _____

   Web source: _____

FORMAL PRESENTATION PROJECTS

You will have the opportunity to present on one of the topics pertinent to this chapter's discipline. Topics could relate to one of the questions you have checked off in the "Follow Your Interests" section at the beginning of the chapter. If you wish, your instructor can help you browse through the chapter and choose an appropriate topic related to architecture. What follows are some suggested topics for your presentation:

1. Over-urbanization and overpopulation
2. Harmony between the building and the landscape
3. Feng shui
4. Frank Lloyd Wright
5. Le Corbusier
6. Contextualism
7. Scandinavian architecture
8. Nature and architecture
9. Urban architecture versus suburban architecture
10. Interior design

 For more help with **Test-Taking** and **Distinguishing Between Fact and Opinion**, go to your learning path in **MyReadingLab.com**.

OCCUPATIONAL THERAPY

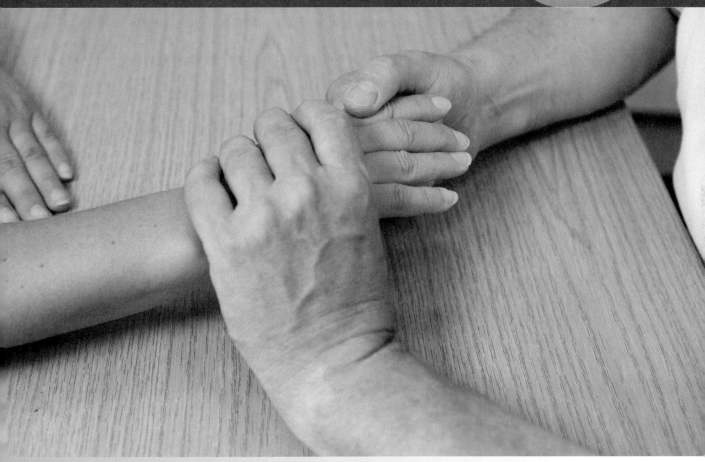

Learning Objectives

IN THIS CHAPTER, YOU WILL LEARN TO . . .

1. Describe the discipline of occupational therapy

2. Identify key terms in the field of occupational therapy

3. Read for meaning

4. Use critical thinking skills

5. Recognize patterns of organization and the transitional words related to each

6. Keep a weekly reading guide

INTRODUCTION TO THE DISCIPLINE OF OCCUPATIONAL THERAPY

LEARNING OBJECTIVE
1 Describe the discipline of occupational therapy

Occupational therapy focuses on the health and well-being of individuals, especially children and adolescents. Occupational therapists and occupational therapy assistants provide services to individuals and address their mental and physical condition related to their occupations. In this chapter, you will read selections on how to use an artificial limb, autism, repetitive motion injuries, rehabilitating veterans returning from war, and the legal rights of the disabled. Reading and discussing the subject matter of these selections will help you understand the importance of occupation for the physical and mental health of individuals.

Reading into a Photo

Working in a small group, examine the following photograph and answer the questions that follow.

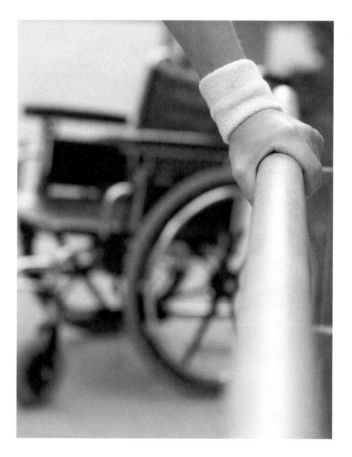

1. In your opinion, what might this person be doing?
2. What message does this image convey to you?

Follow Your Interests

Collaboration

Review the set of questions below that occupational therapy experts might explore. Check off the three or four questions that are most interesting to you.

1. Occupational therapy is a relatively new field, which focuses on the healing powers of work, leisure, daily living, and occupations. In the past, medical science only concentrated on sickness and disease. What do you think made medical experts aware of the fact that other factors such as work and lifestyles also contributed to an individual's health?

2. How does a person's occupation affect her or his physical and mental health? In other words, how does an athlete's profession (tennis, football, etc.) impact his or her health? Give specific examples to support your answer.

3. If you were an occupational therapist, what would you do to help a person with an artificial limb, an arm or a leg, reintegrate into society and become a productive member?

4. Autism is a developmental disorder that affects children's ability to communicate with others. In your opinion, is autism a social disorder? Discuss how you view people with autism.

5. Children born with cerebral palsy have difficulty controlling their hands, arms, legs, or entire body. What can be done to help children with autism develop motor skills, the ability to tie shoes, write, walk, and play soccer? Be specific.

6. Soldiers returning from war with stress, injuries, or an artificial limb often find it difficult to regain their health. What is the role of an occupational therapist in helping these soldiers rehabilitate? Give specific examples.

7. Repetitive motion injuries happen when a person repeats the same movements during work or athletic activities such as typing or swinging a bat. Discuss the body parts that may be injured by making repetitive movements in a certain profession such as education, sports, or nursing, and how people in this profession can avoid these injuries.

8. In the past, most residential and commercial buildings were designed for people who did not have difficulty walking. Nowadays, architects are required by law to design buildings for individuals with a disability. Why, in your opinion, did some architects ignore these people in the past? Discuss why at the present there is increased awareness of the need to accommodate people with disabilities. Be specific.

9. What is the role of parents, school, and society in helping children who are faced with psychological, emotional, and behavioral challenges? As you answer the question, consider your role as a member of society.

10. What would an occupational therapist recommend people with disabilities do so that they can play, enjoy leisure, and participate in social gatherings such as parties, picnics, and trips? Be specific.

11. Some children and even adolescents have difficulty thinking logically, which affects their learning. In your opinion, what kind of therapy may be effective for these children and adolescents?

12. Some people argue that children with attention deficit disorder and learning disabilities should not be allowed to study with other children and that there should be special classes for them. Do you agree or disagree with this view? Support your position with specific examples.

13. Discuss the role of occupational therapists and occupational therapy assistants working with children and adolescents in various settings such as hospitals, houses, prisons, clinics, preschools, elementary schools, and high schools. How do you think they approach their clients in these different settings, and how does the setting influence the relationship between the occupational therapist and the client?

14. Would you consider pursuing a career in occupational therapy? Why or why not? Give specific reasons to support your answer.

Now, share your choices with a small group of classmates and discuss why these particular questions are most interesting to you. You may wish to discuss these questions with them and ask which questions they found interesting.

Key Terms in the Field of Occupational Therapy

② LEARNING OBJECTIVE
Identify key terms in the field of occupational therapy

The following key terms are frequently used in the discipline of occupational therapy. If you take a college-level course in occupational therapy, it will be important for you to remember these words and to use them in your speech and writing. Review the words below and answer the multiple-choice questions that follow.

behavior	disability	outcome
client	ethics	rehabilitation
cognitive	evaluation	sensory
context	intervention	theory
developmental	occupation	therapy

EXERCISE 1 Inferring Meaning from Context

Read each sentence below and try to derive the meaning of the italicized key terms from the context. Circle the correct definition of each italicized term.

1. Occupational therapists provide services to individuals whose health is affected by their *occupation*.
   a. integration
   b. profession
   c. coordination
   d. satisfaction

2. Children with learning disabilities show progress after receiving *therapy* from specialists.
    a. increased power
    b. misguided behavior
    c. treatment
    d. shock

3. An occupational therapist must keep the personal information of a *client* confidential.
    a. a person who refers to another person
    b. a person who provides professional advice
    c. a person who uses professional advice
    d. a person who does not seek professional advice

4. Bandura's *theory* of social learning explains how people behave in a social context.
    a. the well-being of children and adolescents
    b. a center for occupational therapy
    c. a group of professionals
    d. an explanation of certain phenomena

5. Occupational therapists slowly increase the *cognitive* load as they treat their clients during therapy sessions.
    a. pertaining to the processes of judgment and reasoning
    b. pertaining to emotional processes
    c. pertaining to eating processed foods
    d. pertaining to moving body parts

6. The initial diagnosis of the health and well-being of an individual must include a careful examination of the entire *context*.
    a. the client's bank balance
    b. the circumstances or facts
    c. the occupational therapist's educational background
    d. the occupational therapy assistant's educational background

7. The treatment of a child's learning disabilities often depends on a thorough *evaluation*.
    a. the cost of consulting with an occupational therapist
    b. teaching children with learning disabilities separately
    c. eating nutritious meals every day
    d. a diagnosis of a physical or mental condition

8. When people have repetitive motion injuries, some sort of *intervention* is necessary to help them recover.
    a. the act of making an offer
    b. the act of receiving an offer
    c. the act of growing
    d. the act of altering a situation

9. If an occupational therapist fails to produce a favorable *outcome* after several sessions, the client should seek a second opinion.
    a. therapy-related expenses
    b. a final product or result
    c. a series of reading tests
    d. a series of writing tests

10. If parents notice that their child has *developmental* issues, they should see an occupational therapist immediately.
   a. related to growth and progress
   b. a field of science
   c. the part of a composition
   d. a large group of schools

11. The *ethics* of a culture that ignores a fair and equal treatment of children with autism must be questioned.
   a. driving rules
   b. favorite sports
   c. eating habits
   d. moral principles

12. Many people believe that children with learning disabilities may have serious *behavior* issues.
   a. learned from instructors
   b. learned from parents
   c. manner of acting
   d. early education

13. The *rehabilitation* of injured soldiers returning from war is a country's moral responsibility.
   a. to organize social events such as picnics and trips
   b. to renovate old single-family houses
   c. to restore to good health and the ability to work
   d. to publish articles of bravery in leading newspapers

14. In some cultures, people with a *disability* are considered inferior to others.
   a. a physical or mental handicap
   b. a lack of money or resources
   c. an abundance of power and strength
   d. a full and normal life

15. Some children are born with a lack of ability to control their *sensory* organs.
   a. being sensitive to people's needs
   b. related to the senses
   c. being insensitive to others
   d. being affected by insensitive people

Collaboration

EXERCISE 2   Creating Meaningful Sentences with the Key Terms

Working with a partner, choose five of the key terms in occupational therapy and write an original sentence about each one.

1. Word = _____

   _____

   _____

2. Word = _____

   _____

   _____

3. Word = _____

_____

_____

4. Word = _____

_____

_____

5. Word = _____

_____

_____

COLLEGE STUDY SKILLS
Reading for Meaning

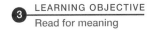

3 LEARNING OBJECTIVE
Read for meaning

Fluent readers read for meaning and have an awareness of what they are about to read. They skim a reading selection quickly and briefly note the first sentence of every paragraph. In other words, they do not necessarily read each and every sentence of the paragraph. They quickly read the conclusion and reflect on the reading by thinking about their expectations of the selection. In this section, you will learn how to use effective strategies to read for meaning.

It is important for you to realize that reading for class is different than reading for pleasure. When most people read a novel or a short story for pleasure, they usually skim the introduction, the body paragraphs, and the conclusion. However, when your professor gives you a reading assignment, you need to do a close reading and pay attention to the details. It is by having a constant dialogue with the text that you begin to understand the author's intended meaning and purpose.

There are many ways in which you can read for meaning by using effective strategies, and one of them is to make annotations. Here are some examples of how to annotate that will help you follow an author's thoughts easily:

- Underline sentences that contain key ideas.
- Circle unfamiliar words.
- Write open-ended questions in the margins.
- Number the major points (the most important point #1, the second most important point #2, and so on)
- Draw arrows, lines, and symbols to connect related ideas.

Putting the Skill into Action

As you annotate a text, you will realize that most reading assignments require you to understand meaning. Throughout this book, you have the opportunity to interact with reading selections. The more you annotate the selections, the more you will understand the authors' main idea, purpose, tone, and patterns of organization. Your annotations will also help you participate in discussions actively, as you can raise questions about the ideas you underlined or highlighted.

The Last Word

When reading for meaning, it is worthwhile to be mindful of the different patterns of organization (see "Skill Focus" on p. 351 for more details). For example, it will be important for you to recognize if an author has used the cause and effect or comparison/contrast pattern of organization. Your ability to annotate a selection and recognize its pattern of organization will improve your reading comprehension.

LEARNING OBJECTIVE
Use critical thinking skills

READINESS FOR COLLEGE SUCCESS
Thinking Critically

As a college student, you have to think critically as you take credit-bearing courses. Regardless of the subject matter, your professor will expect you to be able to read, comprehend, and respond to text both in speech and writing. It is important that you acquire three types of skills that are pivotal to thinking critically: *observation, evaluation,* and *response.* Remember that critical thinking is a process of thinking about an idea from several different angles. Thinking critically involves a series of questions that you apply to the idea being examined as follows.

1. Observation Skills
Asking observation questions will help you understand an author's main idea and build your own reasoning. It should be noted that this is only the first step toward thinking critically. Therefore, you should not respond to the text with your own points of view. In other words, you simply observe the author's reasoning, evidence, and conclusions.

2. Evaluation Skills
When you ask evaluation questions, you evaluate text in relation to the ideas and beliefs expressed by the author. Here you question the author's underlying assumptions and look for supporting evidence for his or her ideas. These questions will lead you to think critically.

3. Response Skills
After you ask the observation and evaluation questions, your task is to get involved personally and ask response questions. It is important to use logic and evidence-based critical thinking at this stage and not jump to conclusions. It is after asking these three types of questions and have an inner dialogue with yourself that you will become a critical thinker.

Choose a reading selection in this chapter and read it carefully. As you read the selection, ask the following questions and think critically about the text.

Observation Questions

1. What is the author's main point?
2. What evidence does the author give to support the main point?

Evaluation Questions

3. Does the evidence make sense to me? Why or why not?
4. Does the evidence match the conclusions?
5. Can I draw conclusions other than the ones drawn by the author?
6. Has the author purposely left out evidence that could have changed the meaning of the text?

Response Questions

7. What is it about this selection that piques my interest?
8. Do I agree or disagree with the author's assertions? What is the specific claim or assertion I agree or disagree with?
9. What do I stand to gain or lose by blindly accepting the author's conclusions?
10. Do the author's values and beliefs match my own?

As you can notice, the observation, evaluation, and response questions are open-ended, higher-order thinking questions. In general, they ask "why" questions and help you become a critical thinker so that you do not accept things at their face value.

Portraits in Post-Humanity: Aimee Mullins

Preview Questions

1. When you come across a person who has a prosthetic (artificial) leg, what is your immediate reaction? Does this person scare you, or do you feel sorry for this individual? Be specific.
2. How do you think a man with a prosthetic leg feels about himself? Similarly, how does a woman with an artificial leg feel about herself?
3. How does a person who has lost a body part, especially an arm or a leg, regain self-confidence? In your opinion, can a person with a prosthetic leg reintegrate into society, become a productive member, and make meaningful contributions to humanity? Give specific reasons to support your answer.

Pre-Reading Vocabulary:
Focus on Some Key Terms

Before beginning the reading selection, it may be helpful to focus on the meaning of some key words in the article. Working with a partner, try to guess the meaning of these words. Then look up the words in a dictionary.

Word	Your Definition	Dictionary Definition
athlete		
activist		
fibulae		
prognosis		
amputate		

Portraits in Post-Humanity: Aimee Mullins

By Annalee Newitz

A one-time intelligence analyst with the Pentagon, Aimee Mullins is an athlete, model, and activist. And she does it all using a collection of experimental prosthetic legs. She says her special "cheetah" legs give her superpowers. On her Web site, Mullins gives a quick background on how she got where she is today.

1   Born without fibulae in both legs, Aimee's medical prognosis was bleak; she would never walk and indeed would spend the rest of her life using a wheelchair. In an attempt for an outside chance at independent mobility, doctors amputated both her legs below the knee on her first birthday. The decision paid off. By age two, she had learned to walk on prosthetic legs, and spent her childhood doing the usual athletic activities of her peers: swimming, biking, softball, soccer, and skiing, always alongside "able-bodied" kids.

2   When Mullins was in college at Georgetown, she set her sights on making the US Team for the 1996 Atlanta Games. She enlisted the expertise of

Frank Gagliano, one of the country's most respected track coaches. Through this partnership, she became the first woman with a "disability" to compete in the NCAA, doing so on Georgetown's nationally ranked Division I track team. Outfitted with woven carbon-fiber prostheses that were modeled after the hind legs of a cheetah, she went on to set World Records in the 100 meter, the 200 meter, and the long jump, sparking a frenzy over the radical design of her prototype sprinting legs.

3   Several other athletes have used the legs developed for Mullins, and they have set a new standard for prosthetic legs that allow the wearer to participate in sports.

4   What makes Mullins post-human is her attitude toward her prosthetics. She doesn't view them as "fixing" something, but rather as augmentations. She wants them to be beautiful, to give her superpowers, to be parts of her body that people look at with admiration. With her public speaking and athletics, Mullins has popularized the idea that synthetic body parts are something to show off, rather than hide.

"Portraits in Posthumanity: Aimee Mullins"
by Annalee Newitz, i.o9.com, May 10, 2010.
Reprinted by permission.

Reading Comprehension Check

MyReadingLab™
Complete this **Exercise**
at **myreadinglab.com**

1. "Born without fibulae in both legs, Aimee's medical prognosis was **bleak**; she would never walk and indeed would spend the rest of her life using a wheelchair." (para. 1) In the above context, the word *bleak* means
   a. hopeless.   c. promising.
   b. encouraging.   d. positive.

2. The main idea of the passage is that
   a. individuals with a prosthetic leg are unable to change their identities.
   b. disabled people can write the script of their own lives.
   c. people with an artificial leg lack the power to create.
   d. children are frightened of people with a prosthetic leg.

3. The author's primary purpose in the above passage is to
   a. persuade.   c. inform.
   b. entertain.   d. amuse.

4. "Outfitted with woven carbon-fiber prostheses that were modeled after the hind legs of a cheetah, she went on to set World Records in the 100 meter, the 200 meter, and the long jump, sparking a frenzy over the radical design of her prototype sprinting legs." (para. 2) It can be inferred from this passage that
   a. cheetahs have set World Records in the 100 meter and the 200 meter.
   b. cheetahs wear prosthetic legs.
   c. a cheetah is a lazy creature.
   d. a cheetah must be a fast animal.

5. "What makes Mullins post-human is her attitude toward her prosthetics. She doesn't view them as "fixing" something, but rather as augmentations. She wants them to be beautiful, to give her superpowers, to be parts of her body that people look at with admiration. With her public speaking and athletics, Mullins has popularized the idea that synthetic body parts are something to show off, rather than hide." (para. 4) The overall tone of the passage is
   a. sarcastic.   c. inspirational.
   b. melancholic.   d. concerned.

Exploring the Topic

Discuss the following questions to review the content of the article you have just read.

1. Mullins' doctors predicted that she would never be able to walk and would spend the rest of her life in a wheelchair. Despite this prognosis, Mullins became a successful athlete and inspired others to use prosthetic legs. Discuss what inspired Mullins to become an athlete.

2. According to the article, "What makes Mullins post-human is her attitude toward her prosthetics. She doesn't view them as "fixing" something, but rather as augmentations." (para. 4) Discuss what Mullins means by that.

3. We learn from the article that "Mullins has popularized the idea that synthetic body parts are something to show off, rather than hide." (para. 4) Why do you think people with synthetic body parts may want to hide their disability? Discuss what social forces influence our perception of people with a disability.

Post-Reading Vocabulary

Without using a dictionary, determine the meaning of the bolded words from the context.

1. "By age two, she had learned to walk on prosthetic legs, and spent her childhood doing the usual athletic activities of her **peers**: swimming, biking, softball, soccer, and skiing, always alongside 'able-bodied' kids." (para. 1)

   Peers means _____

2. "She enlisted the **expertise** of Frank Gagliano, one of the country's most respected track coaches." (para. 2)

   Expertise means _____

3. "Outfitted with woven carbon-fiber prostheses that were modeled after the hind legs of a cheetah, she went on to set World Records in the 100 meter, the 200 meter, and the long jump, sparking a **frenzy** over the radical design of her prototype sprinting legs." (para. 2)

   Frenzy means _____

What Does Autism Mean?

Preview Questions

1. According to the National Survey of Children's Health, 1 out of 100 children in the United States has autism, a developmental disorder causing impaired communication and emotional detachment. What is alarming is that the rate of autism is growing between 10% and 17% every year. Why do you think the rate of an autism spectrum disorder among young children in the United States is growing?

2. Children who have autism usually keep to themselves and are usually unable to communicate with others. What advice would you give the parents of these children so that they can help them communicate with other members of society? Be specific.

3. Why is it that some people consider people with autism inferior to their peers? Do you hold a similar view, or do you believe that they have the potential to outgrow their medical condition?

MyReadingLab™

Complete this **Exercise** at **myreadinglab.com**

Pre-Reading Vocabulary: Focus on Some Key Terms

Collaboration

Before beginning the reading selection, it may be helpful to focus on the meaning of some key words in the article. Working with a partner, try to guess the meaning of these words. Then look up the words in a dictionary.

Word	Your Definition	Dictionary Definition
glanced		
bother		
linking		
frustrating		
insist		

What Does Autism Mean?

The Nemours Foundation / KidsHealth®

1   When Stacey went over to her new friend Chelsea's house, she met Chelsea's 4-year-old brother, Shawn. "Hi," said Stacey, smiling. Shawn glanced at her and said nothing. Then he turned back to a toy he was holding. Later, in Chelsea's room, Stacey said, "I don't think your brother likes me."

2   "It's not your fault," explained Chelsea. "Shawn has autism."

3   Stacey wanted to know what autism meant, what causes it, what it's like to have autism, and more. Let's find out.

What Does Autism Mean?

4   Autism (say: aw-tih-zum) causes kids to experience the world differently from the way most other kids do. It's hard for kids with autism to talk with other people and express themselves using words. Kids who have autism usually keep to themselves and many can't communicate without special help.

5   They also may react to what's going on around them in unusual ways. Normal sounds may really bother someone with autism—so much so that the person covers his or her ears. Being touched, even in a gentle way, may feel uncomfortable.

6   Kids with autism often can't make connections that other kids make easily. For example, when someone smiles, you know the smiling person is happy or being friendly. But a kid with autism may have trouble connecting that smile with the person's happy feelings.

7   A kid who has autism also has trouble linking words to their meanings. Imagine trying to understand what your mom is saying if you didn't know what her words really mean. It is doubly frustrating then if a kid can't come up with the right words to express his or her own thoughts.

8   Autism causes kids to act in unusual ways. They might flap their hands, say certain words over and over, have temper tantrums, or play only with one particular toy. Most kids with autism don't like changes in routines. They like to stay on a schedule that is always the same. They also may insist that their toys or other objects be arranged a certain way and get upset if these items are moved or disturbed.

9   If someone has autism, his or her brain has trouble with an important job: making sense of the world. Every day, your brain interprets the sights, sounds, smells, and other sensations that you experience. If your brain couldn't help you understand these things, you would have trouble functioning, talking, going to school, and doing other everyday stuff. Kids can be mildly affected by autism, so that they only have a little trouble in life, or they can be very affected, so that they need a lot of help.

Adapted from "What Does Autism Mean?" © 1995–2012 The Nemours Foundation/
KidsHealth®. Reprinted with permission.

Reading Comprehension Check

MyReadingLab™
Complete this Exercise
at **myreadinglab.com**

1. "They might flap their hands, say certain words over and over, have temper **tantrums**, or play only with one particular toy." (para. 8) In this context, the word *tantrums* means
   a. an expression of joy.
   b. a sudden burst of anger.
   c. an appreciation of kindness.
   d. an acknowledgment of love.

2. The main idea of the passage is that
   a. some adults with autism get along with children who have autism.
   b. some children with autism are extremely sociable.
   c. children who have autism are easy to please.
   d. children with autism perceive the world around them differently.

3. "They also may react to what's going on around them in unusual ways. Normal sounds may really bother someone with autism—so much so that the person covers his or her ears. Being touched, even in a gentle way, may feel uncomfortable." (para. 5) It can be inferred from this passage that
   a. someone with autism is likely to enjoy loud music.
   b. children with autism like to be cuddled.
   c. it is probably wise not to make loud noises around a child with autism.
   d. when you are with a child with autism, it is a good idea to cover your ears.

4. "Autism (say: aw-tih-zum) causes kids to experience the world differently from the way most other kids do. It's hard for kids with autism to talk with other people and express themselves using words. Kids who have autism usually keep to themselves and many can't communicate without special help." (para. 4) The author's primary purpose is to
   a. entertain.   c. persuade.
   b. inform.   d. amuse.

5. "Autism causes kids to act in unusual ways. They might flap their hands, say certain words over and over, have temper tantrums, or play only with one particular toy. Most kids with autism don't like changes in routines. They like to stay on a schedule that is always the same. They also may insist that their toys or other objects be arranged a certain way and get upset if these items are moved or disturbed." (para. 8) The overall tone of the passage is

   a. objective.   c. melancholic.

   b. sarcastic.   d. humorous.

Collaboration

Exploring the Topic

Discuss the following questions to review the content of the article you have just read.

1. When they come across a child with autism, most children draw the wrong conclusion that the child is not sociable. Do you think adults arrive at the same conclusion when they meet a child with autism, or do you think they are more understanding and accepting of the child? Explain.

2. If you were an occupational therapist, what would you do to help a child with autism make sense of the world?

3. According to the article, "Kids can be mildly affected by autism, so that they only have a little trouble in life, or they can be very affected, so that they need a lot of help." (para. 9) What kind of help do you think these children need? Be specific.

Post-Reading Vocabulary

Without using a dictionary, determine the meaning of the bolded words from the context.

1. "They also may **react** to what's going on around them in unusual ways." (para. 5)

   React means _____

2. "Normal sounds may really bother someone with autism—so much so that the person covers his or her ears. Being touched, even in a **gentle** way, may feel uncomfortable." (para. 5)

   Gentle means _____

3. "Kids can be **mildly** affected by autism, so that they only have a little trouble in life, or they can be very affected, so that they need a lot of help." (para. 9)

   Mildly means _____

Kim Jones — An Interview with a Student in the Field of Occupational Therapy

University of Southern California

1. How did you find your path to majoring in occupational therapy?

It was a long process for me. I was working in entertainment and not enjoying sitting in an office, working for a corporation. I've always loved biology/psychology/research/etc., and I had some friends who were occupational therapists who really encouraged me to find out more and take the prerequisites. I eventually lost my job and was able to focus full time on the prerequisites and apply for a full-time program.

2. What was the biggest obstacle you faced in your study of occupational therapy?

For me it was adjusting from being a respected professional with a level of expertise in my field and a lot of appreciable skills to moving into an area where I knew almost nothing and was treated accordingly. Additionally, many occupational therapists are "big picture" people, whereas the corporate world I was in made me extremely detail-oriented and organized. I am learning a lot about a new way of looking at things. Another obstacle has been finding new and interesting ways of explaining to people what "occupational therapy" is!

3. What area(s) of occupational therapy in particular do you find most interesting?

I am very interested in the psychosocial aspects of rehab. Not just working in mental health, specifically, but how experiencing an injury or chronic condition can impact psychosocial aspects as well as the physical health of the person.

4. What specific skills are required of students who study occupational therapy?

I think you need to have a great level of compassion and desire to help people who can be in pretty difficult situations, so you also need great people skills! You need to have critical-reasoning skills and an understanding of biology, psychology, and human anatomy.

5. Other than teaching occupational therapy, what other career avenues are available for occupational therapy majors?

Being a practicing occupational therapist offers so many opportunities. You can live and work almost anywhere. You can work with different age ranges, from premature infants to geriatrics. You can work in mental health or physical disabilities; in hospitals or in private clinics; with a private company or a government agency. You can also work in administration, as a director of rehab or a hospital administrator. There are also a lot of opportunities to continue doing research and developing new evidence-based practice to further the profession in general.

READING

Carpal Tunnel—One Patient's Story

Reading Selection **3**

Blog

Preview Questions

1. Have you come across people who experience pain in their wrist and fingers? Discuss what causes this pain, and how it can affect what people do for a living.

2. What might an occupational therapist do to treat a person with pain in his or her wrist and fingers? Think of some exercises that may be helpful.

3. Why is it that sometimes humans do not understand the limits of their bodies and end up hurting themselves unintentionally? Give specific examples when this is the case.

MyReadingLab™
Complete this **Exercise** at **myreadinglab.com**

Collaboration

Pre-Reading Vocabulary: Focus on Some Key Terms

Before beginning the reading selection, it may be helpful to focus on the meaning of some key words in the article. Working with a partner, try to guess the meaning of these words. Then look up the words in a dictionary.

Word	*Your Definition*	*Dictionary Definition*
symptoms		
biceps		
irritated		
inflamed		
entrapped		

Carpal Tunnel—One Patient's Story

By Dr. Christopher Andrew

1   Great question from a patient this week: "If it's my wrist and fingers that hurt, how come my elbow is the problem?"

2   I was informing this patient that her carpal tunnel symptoms can be caused by more than just tightness at the wrist. The carpal tunnel is located near the wrist (see diagram on p. 349).

3   The median nerve is commonly responsible for these symptoms—but surprisingly, the carpal tunnel is not usually the problem! The median nerve begins in the upper arm near the biceps and has multiple locations where it can be irritated, inflamed, and entrapped. The most common location is as it crosses the elbow and weaves/dives between multiple muscles that control the forearm and wrist.

4   Individuals who sit at a desk for multiple hours in a day or work with repeating motions in their hands and arms are particularly at risk for carpal tunnel symptoms. Athletes in tennis, golf, and throwing sports also experience irritation in the carpal tunnel.

5   For the patient this week, she types for 6 hours/day for work and likes to bowl twice/week. When examined, her symptoms all appeared when testing muscles that control her elbow. After 3 treatments, she no longer has the numbness, tingling, and swelling she had experienced in her hand/wrist.

6   At home, you can help prevent carpal tunnel irritation—especially if you have a job that requires repetitive motion or long-term holding of your hands at a computer:

- Take regular breaks—stand up 3 times/hr., roll your shoulders back and let your arms fall back.

- Do 3 snow angel movements, keeping your hands open and rolling your thumbs backward.

- Extend your wrists, elbows, and arms while taking 3 slow deep breaths.

- Gently move and lightly stretch your palms, wrists, and forearms.

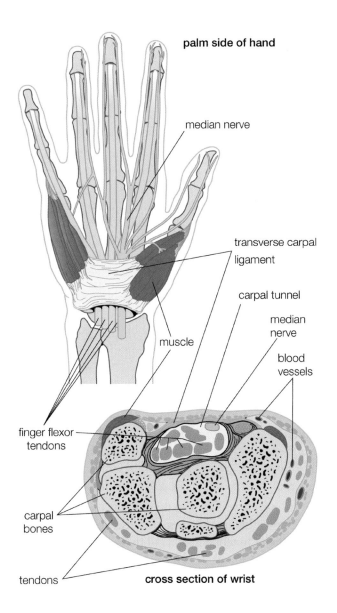

palm side of hand

median nerve

transverse carpal ligament

carpal tunnel

median nerve

blood vessels

muscle

finger flexor tendons

carpal bones

tendons   **cross section of wrist**

7   This should take 30 seconds and potentially save you from painful surgery and lengthy healing time. If you do have carpal tunnel symptoms, seek a physician who is able to properly diagnose the problem. Consider conservative treatment that looks at the entire median nerve, not just the Carpal Tunnel.

Reprinted by permission of Dr. Christopher Anthony, Tri-Synergy Chiropractic

Reading Comprehension Check

MyReadingLab™
Complete this Exercise
at **myreadinglab.com**

1. "At home, you can help **prevent** carpal tunnel irritation—especially if you have a job that requires repetitive motion or long-term holding of your hands at a computer." (para. 6) In this context, *prevent* means
    a. to aggravate a condition.
    c. to make something worse.
    b. to cause something negative.
    d. to keep from occurring.

2. The main idea of the passage is that
   a. tightness at the wrist is caused by a nerve in the back of the neck.
   b. carpal tunnel irritation cannot be treated at home.
   c. people doing sedentary jobs at a desk making repetitive motions with their hands are likely to have carpal tunnel symptoms.
   d. 30 minutes of exercise can save you from painful surgery.

3. "At home, you can help prevent carpal tunnel irritation—especially if you have a job that requires repetitive motion or long-term holding of your hands at a computer." (para. 6) A conclusion that can be drawn from this passage is that
   a. people who usually stay at home are likely to have carpal tunnel irritation.
   b. people who work on a computer regularly are at risk for carpal tunnel symptoms.
   c. some people who drive through a tunnel can be irritated and inflamed.
   d. most people get irritated if they have to work on a computer.

4. "The median nerve is commonly responsible for these symptoms—but surprisingly, the carpal tunnel is not usually the problem! The median nerve begins in the upper arm near the biceps and has multiple locations where it can be irritated, inflamed, and entrapped. The most common location is as it crosses the elbow and weaves/dives between multiple muscles that control the forearm and wrist." (para. 3) The author's primary purpose in this passage is to
   a. inform the reader that carpal tunnel irritation is usually caused by inflammation of the median nerve.
   b. convince the reader that they should flex their biceps every day.
   c. persuade the reader to take carpal tunnel irritation seriously.
   d. entertain the reader by telling an amusing story of carpal tunnel irritation.

5. "Individuals who sit at a desk for multiple hours in a day or work with repeating motions in their hands and arms are particularly at risk for carpal tunnel symptoms. Athletes in tennis, golf, and throwing sports also experience irritation in the carpal tunnel." (para. 4) The overall tone of this passage is
   a. objective.   c. humorous.
   b. sentimental.   d. subjective.

Collaboration

Exploring the Topic

Discuss the following questions to review the content of the blog you have just read.

1. The article begins with a question from a patient: "If it's my wrist and fingers that hurt, how come my elbow is the problem?" (para. 1) Why do you think the occupational therapist thinks it is a great question?

2. Even though athletes in tennis, golf, and throwing sports do not necessarily sit still at a desk and work on a computer all day, they experience carpal tunnel irritation. Discuss why this is so.

3. The author suggests, "If you do have carpal tunnel symptoms, seek a physician who is able to properly diagnose the problem. Consider conservative treatment that looks at the entire median nerve, not just the Carpal Tunnel." (para. 7) Why do you think the author recommends that the patient consider conservative treatment?

Post-Reading Vocabulary

Without using a dictionary, determine the meaning of the bolded words from the context.

1. "After 3 treatments, she no longer has the **numbness**, tingling, and swelling she had experienced in her hand/wrist." (para. 5)

Numbness means _____

2. "At home, you can help prevent carpal tunnel irritation—especially if you have a job that requires **repetitive** motion or long-term holding of your hands at a computer." (para. 6)

Repetitive means _____

3. "This should take 30 seconds and **potentially** save you from painful surgery and lengthy healing time." (para. 7)

Potentially means _____

SKILL FOCUS
Patterns of Organization

 LEARNING OBJECTIVE
Recognize patterns of organization and the transitional words related to each

When authors write an essay, they have a purpose in mind. Sometimes they want to compare and contrast similar and different things. For example, they may compare and contrast occupational therapists and occupational therapy assistants. They organize information in this way by using the compare and contrast pattern of organization. Sometimes their goal is to show the reader the effect of therapy on a certain patient. They may write about the effect on the health of a child with autism of teaching her to play music. This is the cause and effect pattern of organization. It is important to note that the author's purpose and patterns of organization go hand in hand.

In this section, you will learn how to recognize different patterns of organization. There are six major patterns of organizations that most authors use frequently:

1. Chronological order

2. Cause and Effect

3. Compare and Contrast

4. Definition and Example

5. Listing

6. Classification

There are other patterns of organization such as generalization and example, spatial order, and statement of clarification. However, for the purpose of this chapter, we will focus on the above-mentioned six most commonly used patterns of organization.

Here are some tips on how to identify the overall pattern of organization of a passage:

- **First, identify the topic and main idea.** It will help you to determine quickly what the author is writing about. Is it about a child with autism, or is it about carpal tunnel syndrome, or is it about treatment in a hospital setting? Once you identify the topic, try to find the main idea.
- **Second, find the supporting details.** See how the author provides details to support the main idea.
- **Next, pay attention to the transitional words to recognize the pattern of organization.** (See below.)
- **Finally, see how the different ideas are related to each other.**

If you follow these steps, you will be able to identify the correct pattern of organization. Learning the following transitional words that are related to specific patterns of organization will also help you.

Patterns of Organization	Transitional Words
Chronological Order	*first, second, next, finally, then, during, afterward, while*
Cause and Effect	*for this reason, as a result, cause, effect, therefore, because, since, accordingly*
Compare and Contrast	*similar, different, unlike, but, however, in comparison, yet, instead, opposite, on the one hand, on the other hand*
Definition and Example	*meaning, concept, defines, definition, example, for example*
Listing	*first, second, third, next, finally, meanwhile, during, afterward,*
Classification	*types, categories, classify, groups, kinds, style, classifications*

As you read a passage, look for these transitional words. If the author has used the cause and effect pattern of organization, for example, you are likely to come across transitional words such as "for this reason," "as a result," or "because."

Let's study the six most common patterns of organization now.

Chronological Order

The word *chronological* comes from the Greek word *chronos*, which means time. The **chronological order** pattern of organization arranges information as a sequence of events. For example, you may read a passage about when occupational therapy as a profession was founded and how it developed over time. Let's look at an example to understand this clearly.

Meyer (1922) mentions that the early founders of occupational therapy were concerned with the effect of occupation on children's health. Then, Christensen (1991) talks about letters that Barton and Dunton wrote to discuss why they chose the name *occupational therapy*. Next, Quiroga (1995) explains that the title was meant to cover different kinds of occupations that affect one's health. Finally, Kielhofner (2007) clarifies the concept of construct within the profession of occupational therapy.

Notice the progression of time in the above passage. First, it starts with 1922 when the field of occupational therapy was relatively new. Then, it mentions Christensen in 1991. We learn that in 1995 Quiroga explained what the term "occupational therapy" meant. Finally, we read that Kielhofner gave a clarification in 2007. We can see clearly that the author has used the chronological order pattern of organization in the passage.

EXERCISE 3   Chronological Order

Read the following paragraph and answer the question that follows.

According to Piaget, the child's sensory-motor development lasts from birth to 2 years of age. The second stage of the child's cognitive development happens between 2 through 7 years of age. The third stage of development takes place between the ages of 7 and 11 years. Finally, the fourth stage develops from age 12 through 16 years of age.

List the different stages of the child's development and the different age group when each stage occurs.

Stage of Development	*Age Group*	*Stage of Development*	*Age Group*
_____	_____	_____	_____
_____	_____	_____	_____

Cause and Effect

An author may choose to show you how one thing can cause many effects. Similarly, the author can show you how many causes may have one effect. Regardless of the events or the effects, the author's purpose is to use the **cause and effect** pattern of organization to show you how one event can cause another.

Here is an example of the cause and effect pattern of organization:

A child diagnosed as autistic may have difficulty reading or writing simple sentences. An experienced occupational therapist works with the child on identifying the alphabet first. Then the occupational therapist introduces monosyllabic words such as *game, food,* etc. Also, the therapist may play music or games with the child to improve her ability to read.

The author says that the child is having difficulty reading or writing. Obviously, something is causing the child to have this difficulty. The occupational therapist tries to provide an intervention by introducing the alphabet and by playing word games. In this case, the *cause* is intervention, and the *intended effect* is the child's improved ability to read and write.

EXERCISE 4   Cause and Effect

Read the following passage and answer the questions that follow.

> Some children and adolescents have sensory integration problems. In other words, they have difficulty hearing sounds, seeing things clearly, and touching and feeling objects. These sensory problems are caused by a mismatch between the brain and sensory information. Children and adolescents with sensory integration problems also struggle with language and speaking.

What causes sensory integration problems? —————————————————

——————————————————————————————————————

What are the effects of sensory integration problems? ——————————

——————————————————————————————————————

Compare and Contrast

An author might use the **compare and contrast** pattern of organization to compare and contrast the roles of an occupational therapist and an occupational therapist assistant or compare two theories of occupational therapy. In this pattern of organization, you are likely to find transitional words such as *in comparison*, *in contrast*, and *however*. Let's read the following example to see how the author uses the compare and contrast pattern of organization.

> The occupational therapist and the occupational therapy assistant play distinct roles during the process of evaluating a child's condition. The occupational therapist begins the occupational therapy evaluation of a child or adolescent with a disability. The occupational therapist collects and analyzes the data to plan an intervention. Then the occupational therapist may ask the occupational therapist assistant to do some parts of the evaluation. However, how much the occupational assistant can evaluate depends on state regulations. Some states do not allow the occupational assistant to do the evaluation. In those states, the occupational therapist must carry out the evaluation without the occupational therapist assistant.

The above passage makes it clear that the occupational therapist is primarily responsible for the evaluation of a child's treatment. As the title itself suggests, the occupational therapist assistant is only there to assist. In fact, some states do not allow the occupational therapist assistant to do the evaluation.

EXERCISE 5 Compare and Contrast

Read the passage and answer the questions that follow.

Erikson focused on psychosocial development across the life span. In contrast, Piaget examined cognitive development of children. Unlike Erikson, who proposed five stages of psychosocial development during the lifetime of an individual, Piaget offered four stages of cognitive development from birth through 16 years of age. In recent years, experts have criticized Erikson for mainly focusing on male development. They have also challenged Piaget's fixed notions of development.

Which scientists are compared and contrasted? _____

How are Erikson's and Piaget's theories different? _____

_____

_____

Why have experts criticized the two scientists recently? _____

_____

What transitional words helped you determine the pattern of organization?

_____

Definition and Example

As the name suggests, the **definition and example** pattern of organization defines a term and provides examples to help the reader understand it. For example, a passage may introduce the term *sensory integration* and explain it with an example or two. Let's look at an example to understand the definition pattern of organization clearly.

> Physical environments can be defined as places where individuals can come across and interact with each other. Examples of natural physical environments are rivers, forest, and oceans. Also, some physical environments can be man-made. For example, schools, hospitals, and community centers are considered physical environments.

Notice how the author first defines the term *physical environments* and then gives examples of both natural and man-made physical environments. It is important to remember that the definition and example pattern of organization defines a term and gives examples to clarify the term.

 **Definition and Example**

Read the following passage carefully and answer the questions that follow.

Occupational performance is defined as the actual action carried out in different occupations. For example, it is the actual action performed by individuals who fish, swim, and canoe on a river. Also, it is the actions of cooking, painting, dancing, and performing martial arts. These actions require motor skills, process skills, and communication and interaction skills.

What term is defined? _____

What is the definition of the term? _____

What examples are given to explain the term? _____

_____

What skills are required to perform the actions mentioned in the passage?

_____

What transitional words helped you recognize the pattern of organization?

_____

Listing

As the name suggests, the **listing** pattern of organization arranges information in a list, the particular order of which may or may not be important. This pattern of organization may be used to show the different ways an occupational therapist provides treatment to a child with autism. A list showing five different ways to provide an intervention to a child does not necessarily require the occupational therapist to go through them in a sequential order. However, in the following example, the particular sequential order does matter as signaled by the use of key transition words.

> Before they provide an intervention to a client, occupational therapists look at many factors. First, they find out about the client's beliefs. Then, they talk to the clients about their values. The therapists also take the client's spiritual background seriously. Next, they take into consideration the client's body functions. This includes examining the client's body parts.

The above passage shows what client factors an occupational therapist considers before moving on to a planned intervention. In other situations, the listing of items does not indicate the order in which items should appear or a task should be performed. For example, names of different types of occupational therapy or items needed to provide therapy do not need to be listed in a specific order.

EXERCISE 7 **Listing**

Read the following passage carefully and answer the questions that follow.

An occupational therapist plans an intervention to improve a client's ability to process information. The therapist mainly focuses on four visual-cognitive functions. First, the therapist pays attention to the client's visual memory, which includes both short- and long-term memory. Then, she considers visual attention, which includes alertness, selective attention, and divided attention. Next, the therapist looks at visual discrimination, which includes the ability to see, recognize, and match the differences in visual features. Finally, visual imagery involving the ability to remember objects without seeing them is examined.

What is the overall pattern of organization in this passage? _____

What functions are mentioned in the above passage?

1. _____

2. _____

3. _____

4. _____

Is there a specific order in which the occupational therapist must gather information about the client?

Yes _____

No _____

What transitional words are related to the pattern of organization?

_____

Classification

The **classification** pattern of organization divides ideas into different categories that share similar characteristics. Using this pattern an author may describe different types of intervention and their effects on a child's mental and physical health. That is to say, the author may put these types of intervention into different categories and describe each one of them.

Let's read the following example to see how the author uses the classification pattern of organization.

> Occupational therapists and occupational therapy assistants do different types of assessment before an evaluation. Some assessments are non-standardized. These types of assessment do not require a specific physical environment. The occupational therapist can conduct non-standardized assessments easily. Checklists, observations, interviews, charts, and questionnaires are examples of non-standardized assessments. Other assessments are standardized. These assessments are based on norms and criteria. Examples of standardized assessments are typical behaviors of a child by a certain age and performance on specific tests.

The author describes two types of assessments: *non-standardized* and *standardized.* They share similar characteristics because they are both used to find out more information about a child or client. However, they differ from each other, as non-standardized assessments can be done easily, but standardized assessments are more complicated.

EXERCISE 8   **Classification**

Read the following passage carefully and answer the questions. This exercise will help you recognize the classification pattern of organization easily.

From the early days of their lives, children engage in different types of play with their parents, caregivers, and peers. Infants engage in social play with their parents. This type of play includes cooing, smiling, and crying to get their parents' attention. They also begin exploratory play by repeatedly sucking their fists and kicking their legs. When they are between the ages of 12 months and 18 months, children engage in functional play. Functional play includes playing with cups or spoons or pushing a toy vacuum cleaner. Relational play begins at the same time and involves actions such as the child pulling a toy wagon with a stuffed animal in it. Children also engage in gross motor play during this same time. This category of play involves children exploring space and objects, running, swimming, and spinning. Two- and three-year-old children engage in symbolic play, using paper cutouts as birds, for instance. Another classification of play occurs when children begin to draw and solve puzzles. This type of play is called constructive play. Between the ages of three and five years, children begin fantasy play. They learn to use a stick as a fishing pole, for example. Rough-and-tumble play also emerges at this point, as children learn to climb, roll, and sled down hills. By 6 years of age, children begin to participate in competitive play. The purpose is to participate in organized sports, not necessarily to win or lose. The type of play children engage in during the first 6 years of life affects the types of play they enjoy as they grow older.

How many types of play are categorized in the above passage? _____
List the types of play and the activities related to each of them.

Type of Play	Activities

What transitional words in the above passage are related to the classification pattern of organization? _____

LANDMARK IN THE FIELD OF OCCUPATIONAL THERAPY

Individuals with Disability Education Act (1973–1974)

In the past, children with disabilities were not allowed to attend public schools. These children were blind, deaf, and some children were even called "emotionally disturbed" or "mentally retarded." U.S. public schools educated only 1 out of 5 children with disabilities. Children with disabilities were treated unfairly. Sadly, they were considered inferior to their peers without disabilities.

This attitude toward children with disabilities changed when the Individuals with Disabilities Education Act (IDEA) became a U.S. federal law in 1973. Since then, the IDEA has shaped how public and private schools provide special education to children with disabilities. The IDEA meets the educational needs of these children from birth to age 18 or sometimes 21. To receive special education, children must fit into one of at least fourteen categories of disability.

The IDEA only applies to those states that accept federal funding under the special act. Those states that do not accept such funding are not required by law to provide special education to children with disabilities. However, it is encouraging that all states have accepted federal funding and follow the IDEA.

The need for the IDEA arose from the denial of free public education to children

who were blind, deaf, or had some form of disability. The IDEA has been changed several times to meet children's special educational needs. Most recently, in 2004 the IDEA stated that students with disabilities must be provided a Free Appropriate Public Education (FAPE). The main purpose of FAPE is to prepare students with special needs for higher education, jobs, and independent living.

Public schools have since worked to meet the special needs of children with disabilities, making sure that children with special needs are prepared to function in the real world and make a decent living without depending on others.

It is important to note that having a disability does not automatically qualify a student for special education. The IDEA considers a child with disabilities such as deafness, blindness, autism, brain injury, or learning disabilities eligible for special education.

Since the IDEA became a federal law, we have come a long way in terms of treating children with disabilities fairly and equally. The IDEA has become a turning point in the history of public education. It gives children with disabilities a chance to benefit from special education and become successful in their lives.

Considering the Topic

Collaboration

Answer the following questions with a partner.

1. In your opinion, why were children with disabilities denied public education before the IDEA became a federal law? Think of specific examples to answer the question.

2. What made lawmakers aware of the simple fact that children with disabilities had the same right to get an education as did other children?

3. How has the IDEA affected the lives of students with unique educational needs and the people who teach them? Be specific.

Internet Connection

Research another landmark in the field of sociology, and fill out the section below.

prosthetic legs	accessible bathrooms
accessible buildings	war veterans' benefits
disabled sports	EAHCA

Landmark: _____

Question	*Answer*
When did this landmark become a reality?	
Who was involved in developing this landmark?	
What made this landmark special?	
How did this landmark change the way people view disabled people?	

READING

Reading Selection **4**

Article

Shields Valley Ranch Helps Rehabilitate Soldiers

Preview Questions

MyReadingLab™
Complete this **Exercise**
at **myreadinglab.com**

1. U.S. soldiers returning from war with physical injuries and emotional scars struggle with reintegrating into society. What can be done to help these soldiers regain their health and get on with their lives?

2. Soldiers fighting for their country in a foreign land leave behind their loved ones and risk their lives. Discuss why these unsung heroes are easily forgotten when they return home.

3. Injured soldiers returning home are not the only ones affected by war. Who else is affected by their injuries when they are back home? Think of specific examples to support your answer.

Collaboration

Pre-Reading Vocabulary: Focus on Some Key Terms

Before beginning the reading selection, it may be helpful to focus on the meaning of some key words in the article. Working with a partner, try to guess the meaning of these words. Then look up the words in a dictionary.

Word	Your Definition	Dictionary Definition
ranch		
rehabilitation		
therapeutic		
adapt		
dominant		

Shields Valley Ranch Helps Rehabilitate Soldiers

The Associated Press

John Masters smiles as he waits to begin a horseback ride on Howling Wolf Ranch in Shields Valley on Thursday. Masters is one of six wounded warriors who spent six days at the ranch, which uses outdoor activities to rehabilitate soldiers.

1   LIVINGSTON — The owner of a south-central Montana ranch is offering in-jured soldiers a chance to enjoy the outdoors as part of their rehabilitation. Bill Cohen said he was inspired to provide a place where servicemen could find "thera-peutic recreation and rehabilitation" after reading reports of similar efforts around the country. "I just knew there was a need out there," said Cohen, a retired manag-ing director of a Wall Street firm.

2   Cohen has converted his six-bedroom home into a guest lodge of sorts for servicemen. Groups of six to eight soldiers are invited to enjoy a six-night stay at Cohen's home and participate in activities such as horseback riding, fly fishing, ATV riding and trap shooting.

3   This summer, Cohen hosted three groups of servicemen from major military hospitals at his 520-acre ranch in the Shields Valley. "I've got this beautiful place here, why not share it with this great group of guys?" Cohen told the *Livingston Enterprise*.

4   The visitors from Sept. 14–20 include John Masters, who lost three fingers on his right hand in an explosion while serving as an Army staff sergeant in Afghanistan in January. The visit gave him the opportunity to adapt to an injury to his dominant hand. "To relearn things is hard enough," Masters said. "But learning to do something I didn't do already, like fly fish, helped me be more ambidextrous."

5   Last Saturday, the group went out for some target shooting. "They're soldiers," said Ross Colquhoun, who coordinates excursions for wounded soldiers at Walter Reed Army Medical Center in Washington, D.C. "They enjoy putting a weapon back in their hands."

6   Josh Rector, a 20-year-old Missouri Army specialist, has a prosthesis that allows him to operate a firearm after he lost his left hand and lower arm in the gears of a gun turret in Iraq four months ago. "There's a way to do everything I did before," he said. "It's just different." Rector said he grew up in the country, and being on the ranch reminds him of home. "This trip is great," Rector said. "I'm going to cry. We don't want to leave."

7   Maj. Garrick Rard, 38, a member of the U.S. Marine Corps, suffers from post-traumatic stress disorder and a lower back injury suffered in an IED blast in Iraq. Last spring, Rard was admitted to the Balboa Naval Medical Center in San Diego with PTSD. His symptoms include inability to complete tasks, a shortened temper and frequent nightmares that disturb his sleep.

8   Last weekend on the ranch, Rard slept for seven hours. "It was the first time I've slept that long in as long as I can remember," he said.

9   Cohen calls the program a "smashing success." "I just want to show them all that we all care," Cohen said.

"Shields Valley Ranch Helps Rehabilitate Soldiers" The Associated Press, September 25, 2010. Reprinted by permission of The YGS group.

MyReadingLab™
Complete this **Exercise**
at **myreadinglab.com**

Reading Comprehension Check

1. "Josh Rector, a 20-year-old Missouri Army specialist, has a **prosthesis** that allows him to operate a firearm after he lost his left hand and lower arm in the gears of a gun turret in Iraq four months ago." (para. 6) In this context, *prosthesis* means
   a. a shield to protect the body.
   b. a firearm for injured soldiers.
   c. a device to replace a missing body part.
   d. a gun turret in Iraq.

2. "The owner of a south-central Montana ranch is offering injured soldiers a chance to enjoy the outdoors as part of their rehabilitation." (para. 1) The overall pattern of organization in this sentence is
   a. definition.   c. chronological order.
   b. generalization.   d. classification.

3. "Bill Cohen said he was inspired to provide a place where servicemen could find 'therapeutic recreation and rehabilitation' after reading reports of similar efforts around the country." (para. 1) The overall pattern of organization in this sentence is
   a. comparison and contrast.   c. chronological order.
   b. cause and effect.   d. classification.

4. "Cohen has converted his six-bedroom home into a guest lodge of sorts for servicemen. Groups of six to eight soldiers are invited to enjoy a six-night stay at Cohen's home and participate in activities such as horseback riding, fly fishing, ATV riding and trap shooting." (para. 2) This is an example of the following pattern of organization:

a. compare and contrast.
b. definition and example.
c. cause and effect.
d. listing order.

5. "Josh Rector, a 20-year-old Missouri Army specialist, has a prosthesis that allows him to operate a firearm after he lost his left hand and lower arm in the gears of a gun turret in Iraq four months ago." (para. 6) The overall pattern of organization in this sentence is

a. chronological order.
b. classification.
c. definition and example.
d. cause and effect.

Exploring the Topic

Collaboration

Discuss the following questions to review the content of the article you have just read.

1. What inspired Bill Cohen to provide the injured servicemen his ranch for rehabilitation? Give specific examples to support your answer.

2. We learn that Major Garrick Rard suffers from post-traumatic stress disorder. Discuss how this disorder might affect a soldier, and what an occupational therapist might do to treat this soldier.

3. Cohen says, "I just want to show them all that we all care." (para. 9) Tell what a country can do to honor injured servicemen and show that it cares about them. Be specific.

Post-Reading Vocabulary

Without using a dictionary, determine the meaning of the bolded words from the context.

1. "This summer, Cohen **hosted** three groups of servicemen from major military hospitals at his 520-acre ranch in the Shields Valley." (para. 3)

Hosted means _____

2. "Bill Cohen said he was **inspired** to provide a place where servicemen could find 'therapeutic recreation and rehabilitation' after reading reports of similar efforts around the country." (para. 1)

Inspired means _____

3. "His **symptoms** include inability to complete tasks, a shortened temper and frequent nightmares that disturb his sleep." (para. 7)

Symptoms means _____

Collaboration

Panel Discussion on Teaching Students with Special Needs

Some college students who have been diagnosed as autistic or who have learning disabilities need more individual attention than do other students. Most professors do not know how to work with students with autism simply because they are not occupational therapists who are trained to work with such students. Some people feel that these students should be taught separately by professors who specialize in teaching students with special needs. Others believe that these students have the right to be taught by the same professors who teach other students. Parents of students with learning disabilities feel strongly that their children are not inferior to their peers and deserve the right to be educated in the same manner. Your college has asked you to participate in a panel to discuss this controversial issue. Choose a profile for yourself from the following list and prepare for the panel discussion accordingly.

1. mother of an autistic son
2. father of an autistic daughter
3. college president
4. college professor
5. freshmen coordinator
6. director of advisement
7. director of testing
8. in-class tutor
9. coordinator of the learning center
10. bookstore manager
11. director of daycare
12. head librarian

You may create more profiles that are suitable for the panel discussion. For example, you can play the role of a student who is diagnosed as "autistic," or you can be an occupational therapist or an occupational therapy assistant who provides therapy to the student.

As you participate in the panel discussion, use the following guiding questions to present your points of view and ask other panelists to reflect on the issues seriously.

1. Should there be a special class for students who are diagnosed as "autistic"?
2. If students with autism take classes with other students, how will it affect their and their peers' learning?
3. What type of special training must the college provide to the professors so that they can educate students with autism?
4. What accommodations and provisions must be made to meet the special needs of students with learning disabilities?
5. What set of skills must the tutors have in order to help students with learning disabilities complete their assignments successfully?

Keep in mind that a panel discussion is unlike a debate where the participants take a position, defend it, and challenge the opponents' points of view.

A panel discussion is a forum whereby the panelists express their opinions without worrying about winning or losing an argument. As you participate in the panel discussion, listen to the panelists with an open mind and present your points of view to have a lively discussion.

WRITING CONNECTIONS: *Keeping a Weekly Reading Guide*

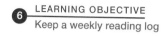

"The palest ink is better than the best memory."
—*Chinese proverb*

As a college student, you will be given many reading assignments. Regardless of the discipline you are studying, you will need to read chapters, academic essays, research papers and other material. Sometimes you may find it hard to keep track of everything you are learning. Keeping a weekly reading guide is an effective way to take stock of your learning and improve your vocabulary and reading comprehension.

Use the following questions to organize your thoughts as you complete your reading assignments. You may wish to include technical terms (jargon), key concepts and ideas, and vocabulary items in your reading guide.

1. What do I understand the reading to be about?
2. What is my opinion of what I read?
3. What is it about the text that piques my interest?
4. What descriptive words, phrases, and idiomatic expressions do I like?
5. What vocabulary items and ideas confuse me?
6. Why is this information important to me?
7. What do I need to remember for the next reading assignment?

As you can see, your weekly reading guide will become an ongoing learning log for you where you explore your thoughts in writing in response to what you read every week. Making it a weekly habit to write in your reading guide is a great way to become an active reader and a critical thinker.

READING

Democratic Party Ignores Handicapped Woman's Plea for Access to Downtown South Bend Headquarters

Reading Selection **5**

Article

Preview Questions

1. Do you think all residential and commercial buildings provide access to people with disabilities? If yes, discuss why it is important for them to have easy access to the building. If not, tell why people with disabilities are sometimes ignored by architects, builders, and government agencies.

MyReadingLab™
Complete this **Exercise**
at **myreadinglab.com**

2. Some people argue that though it is the government's legal obligation to provide full access to people in a wheelchair, it is not its moral obligation to do so. What do you think?

3. At what point in time do you think architects, builders, and government agencies became more aware of the accessibility needs of people with disabilities? What do you think brought about this awareness? Be specific.

Collaboration

Pre-Reading Vocabulary: Focus on Some Key Terms

Before beginning the reading selection, it may be helpful to focus on the meaning of some key words in the article. Working with a partner, try to guess the meaning of these words. Then look up the words in a dictionary.

Word	Your Definition	Dictionary Definition
plea		
volunteer		
campaign		
overlook		
commitment		

Democratic Party Ignores Handicapped Woman's Plea for Access to Downtown South Bend Headquarters

By Jason Aubry

1   SOUTH BEND, Ind. — The pleas of a wheelchair-bound woman are falling on deaf ears at the Democratic Party Headquarters in downtown South Bend. For nearly four years, Karen Brandy-Comer has tried to get St. Joseph County Democratic Party Chairman Butch Morgan to do something, anything, to help her have better access and service to the building. Brandy-Comer is a registered Democrat, unafraid of calling her own party out on this issue.

2   The first time Brandy-Comer experienced a problem was when she was running for a school board position during the 2008 General Election. "I wanted to go in the office to volunteer to possibly get some help with my campaign but I couldn't get in the office," said Brandy-Comer.

3   From the first time she attempted to gain access to the building, which has just two doors, both of which require the ability to navigate up stairs to reach them, she feels her needs have been overlooked. "That's just ridiculous; there should not be a building in the United States that I can't just roll into," said Brandy-Comer.

4   Brandy-Comer suffers from multiple sclerosis, and has been in a wheelchair for 23 years. She says getting the attention of someone inside the office is no easy task. "I can't even get to the front door to knock on the front door. And I can't get to the back door to knock on the back door. I have to beat on the window," said Brandy-Comer.

5   It was after one of these window assaults, during the mid-term elections of 2010, she thought her luck had changed. Brandy-Comer says, U.S. Congressman Joe Donnelly happened to be at the office and came to the door. After explaining her situation, and showing him the state both entryways were in, she says he made a commitment to her. "He said, 'I promise you I will fix this'," said Brandy-Comer. She also says, that was over a year and a half ago and nothing has changed since.

6   In the meantime, Brandy-Comer has made several trips in her motorized wheelchair to the party headquarters, trying to catch Morgan. She says, Morgan is a difficult man to get a hold of, "I've talked to Butch one time. And every other time I go over there, he's just left or he's in a meeting and he can't come to the door," said Brandy-Comer.

7   Jokingly, she bet we would get the same result when we arrived Wednesday afternoon. Sure enough, after she beat on the window a few times, someone came out to see what she wanted. After introducing ourselves, we were told Morgan was in a meeting. Brandy-Comer just laughed. For her, it was par for the course.

8   Brandy-Comer told us of the one time she did get to talk to the county chairman. She says, he promised to make a call and line up a portable ramp and install a doorbell that people could use to signal those in the office someone was waiting outside. As of Wednesday, no doorbells are present and no signs of a portable ramp have been seen. "He lied. He straight out lied, and it's obvious that he lied because there is no ramp, there's no starting to be a ramp, I mean there's nothing," said Brandy-Comer.

9   Brandy-Comer says Morgan's blatant attempts to ignore her concerns, and his refusal to accommodate her even with a face-to-face meeting, makes her feel like a second-class citizen. "They want us to be involved in our city's government. How can I be involved if I can't get in?" questioned Brandy-Comer. It's a question I posed to Mark Dubin, former senior trial attorney for the Department of Justice (DOJ), Civil Rights Division, Disability Rights Section from 1993 to 2005. Dubin was responsible for the enforcement of the Americans with Disabilities Act (ADA) and Section 504 during the same years.

10   Dubin found it startling that a political party, let alone the Democratic Party, would be the focus of such an allegation. He says, the Democratic Party has long been a strong supporter of the ADA and civil rights across the board. However, if the situation is as bad as it is described, he thinks the people in charge of the location simply need to be educated on the need for access and the ease with which it can be provided. Dubin goes on to say, the headquarters should be made accessible; and if it cannot be made accessible, it should move to a location that is. "The Democratic Party and the Republican Party both have a legal obligation and a moral obligation to ensure that the community can access whatever it is that they are offering," said Dubin.

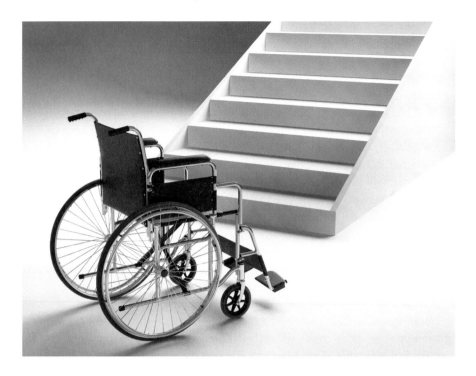

11   Dubin also raised the issue that many people who have these types of allegations levied against them often look at the issue as a building code violation. He says it is not, and should be approached as a civil rights matter.

12   Earlier this year Democratic Party candidate for U.S. Congress in Indiana's second district, Andrew Straw, filed a complaint, with the DOJ, against his own party because of this issue. Since then, the DOJ has responded to Straw, telling him they would do nothing about the situation. However, the correspondence goes on to inform Straw that the DOJ decision does not mean a violation does not exist and that there are other options he can exercise, including civil court. Straw has since filed a complaint with a civil liberties union and is awaiting a response from them.

13   Meanwhile, Brandy-Comer continues to want to participate in the democratic process with the Democratic Party and she does not want to be treated any differently than a person without a disability. "I was told at one time, 'well you can make calls from your house.' I don't want to do that. I want to get in [the Democratic Party Headquarters] building," said Brandy-Comer.

14   Still, what hurts Brandy-Comer the most is the betrayal from her own party. "They should be ashamed of themselves, they really should," said Brandy-Comer. Especially when, according to Brandy-Comer, helping her and the many other disabled voters that want to participate in the Democratic Party really is not that difficult. "I'm sure [Morgan] could get volunteers, Democratic [Party] volunteers, to donate materials or do whatever but he's not trying. I don't think Butch is trying," said Brandy-Comer. According to a confidential source inside the St. Joseph Democratic Party, Brandy-Comer's assessment may be right.

15   ABC 57 tried contacting Morgan several times on Tuesday and Wednesday this week, both by phone and in person at the party headquarters. A phone number was left with a staff member, and a request that he contact us as soon as possible was left with another.

16   On Wednesday, I was told Morgan was in the building but in a meeting. None of our requests for a phone call have been returned, and the voicemail on Morgan's cellular phone is full.

17   Repeated calls to the number we were provided went unanswered despite the fact a staffer had recently finished a telephone conversation with him, calling the same number.

Reprinted by permission of ABC57 News.

Reading Comprehension Check

MyReadingLab™
Complete this Exercise
at myreadinglab.com

1. "Dubin also raised the issue that many people who have these types of allegations levied against them often look at the issue as a building code violation." (para. 11) In this context, *allegations* means
   a. charges or claims.
   b. statements of denial.
   c. moral obligations.
   d. legal obligations.

2. "Earlier this year Democratic Party candidate for U.S. Congress in Indiana's second district, Andrew Straw, filed a complaint, with the DOJ, against his own party because of this issue. Since then, the DOJ has responded to Straw, telling him they would do nothing about the situation." (para. 12) This statement is an example of the following pattern of organization:
   a. chronological order
   b. cause and effect
   c. definition and example
   d. classification

3. "For nearly four years, Karen Brandy-Comer has tried to get St. Joseph County Democratic Party Chairman Butch Morgan to do something, anything, to help her have better access and service to the building." (para. 1) The duration of Brandy-Comer's plea is an example of the following pattern of organization in this passage
   a. definition and example.
   b. chronological order.
   c. cause and effect.
   d. compare and contrast.

4. "However, if the situation is as bad as it is described, he thinks the people in charge of the location simply need to be educated on the need for access and the ease at which it can be provided. Dubin goes on to say, the headquarters should be made accessible; and if it cannot be made accessible, it should move to a location that is." (para. 10) The author's overall pattern of organization in this passage
   a. shows the possible effects of a bad situation.
   b. contrasts the differences between accessible and non-accessible locations.
   c. summarizes the changes in the location.
   d. lists the changes in the location.

5. "ABC 57 tried contacting Morgan several times on Tuesday and Wednesday this week, both by phone and in person at the party headquarters. A phone number was left with a staff member, and a request that he contact us as soon as possible was left with another." (para. 15) The overall pattern of organization in this passage is
   a. definition and example.
   b. chronological order.
   c. comparison and contrast.
   d. generalization and example.

Collaboration

Exploring the Topic

Discuss the following questions to review the content of the article you have just read.

1. The article begins with the statement "The pleas of a wheelchair-bound woman are falling on deaf ears at the Democratic Party Headquarters in downtown South Bend." (para. 1) Discuss why the Democratic Party has ignored the woman's pleas.

2. "Dubin also raised the issue that many people who have these types of allegations levied against them often look at the issue as a building code violation. He says it is not, and should be approached as a civil rights matter." (para. 11) What does Dubin mean by the issue being a civil rights matter? Be specific.

3. The county chairman promised Brandy-Comer that he would call the Democratic Party Headquarters and urge them to build a portable ramp. However, he did not keep his promise. Do you think government officials only lie to people with disabilities, or do you believe they treat everyone the same way?

Post-Reading Vocabulary

Without using a dictionary, determine the meaning of the bolded words from the context.

1. "From the first time she attempted to gain access to the building, which has just two doors, both of which require the ability to **navigate** up stairs to reach, she feels her needs have been overlooked." (para. 3)

   Navigate means _____

2. "Brandy-Comer says Morgan's blatant attempts to ignore her concerns, and his refusal to **accommodate** her even with a face-to-face meeting, makes her feel like a second-class citizen." (para. 9)

   Accommodate means _____

3. "'The Democratic Party and the Republican Party both have a legal **obligation** and a moral obligation to ensure that the community can access whatever it is that they are offering,' said Dubin." (para. 10)

   Obligation means _____

TEXTBOOK APPLICATION | **Understanding the Domain and Process of Occupational Therapy**

The purpose of this exercise is to get you acquainted with the type of reading you will be required to do in college. First, listen to the lecture and take notes. You can listen to the lecture by scanning the QR code on the next page with your smart phone. Your professor may also read the selection or play the audio file in class. Make sure that you write down the important points of the lecture.

Collaboration

Group Discussion

Working in small groups of three to four students, answer the following questions. Your instructor may ask you to share your answers with your classmates. As you refer to your notes, it is best to write brief answers to each of the questions below using your own words. After the discussion, you will have an opportunity to share your findings with your peers.

1. Why has occupational therapy been important for the health and well-being of individuals? Give specific examples to answer this question.

2. According to the lecture, how is a construct built?

3. What is a concept, and how does the precise meaning of a concept change?

4. Do you think that work, leisure, and daily living have an impact on our health and overall wellness? If yes, explain how they affect our health in general.

5. In your opinion, how do "time, space, society, and culture intersect with each other to create conditions that affect what people do, and how and why they think and feel about what they do"? Use specific examples to support your answer.

6. Do you agree with the view that the physical space and location of a hospital can affect the physical and mental health of children and adults? Why or why not?

7. How do you think children think and feel about their health and safety, and how does it affect their occupational capacities?

Now that you have discussed the highlights of the lecture with your classmates, read the following selection and answer the multiple-choice questions that follow.

Understanding the Domain and Process of Occupational Therapy

By Janet V. DeLany and Margaret J. Pendzick

Scan this code using your smart phone to listen to an audio version of this reading

1   Occupational therapy focuses on the effect of occupation on the health of individuals. This focus on occupation has been at the cornerstone of occupational therapy. Occupational therapists and occupational therapy assistants work with people who may have health issues related to their occupation. According to Kramer, Hinojosa, & Royeen (2003), occupation is a complex construct, which is built from many concepts. *Merriam-Webster* (2007) defines a concept as an intangible idea built from many examples. Intelligence is an example of construct built on many things such as memory, thought, and perception. As the construct changes, the precise meaning of a concept can also change. Similarly, as the concept changes, the meaning of the construct also changes.

2   Meyer (1922) refers to the early founders of occupational therapy who were concerned with the influence of work, leisure, daily living and rest. They and other occupational therapists chose the title occupational therapy because they thought it covered a wide range of occupations affecting people's mental and physical health (Christensen, 1991; Kramer et al., 2003; Quiroga, 1995).

3   Experts have made it clearer for the common people to understand the concept of occupation. This clarification helps occupational therapists and their assistants work with children and adults and understand their clients' occupations. Kielhofner (2007) defines human occupation as:

> the doing of work, play, or activities of daily living with a temporal, physical, and sociocultural context that characterizes much of human life. … Time, space, society, and culture intersect with each other to create conditions that affect what people do, and how and why they think and feel about what they do (pp. 1–2).

4   Using this definition, occupational therapists look at how a hospital's setting affects the physical and mental health of children and adults. Similarly, occupational therapists and occupational therapy assistants who work with children and adults in an emergency shelter study the location of the shelter to understand its effect on the health of the children and adults. These experts examine how children think and feel about their health and safety in a particular occupational setting.

from Delany and Pendzick, *Working with Children and Adolescents:*
A Guide for the Occupational Therapy Assistant, 1e

Reading Comprehension Check

1. "This focus on occupation has been at the **cornerstone** of occupational therapy." (para. 1) In this context, *cornerstone* means
   a. something that is unnecessary.
   c. something that is expensive.
   b. something that is essential.
   d. something that is dispensable.

2. "*Merriam-Webster* (2007) defines a concept as an **intangible** idea built from many examples." (para. 1) In this context, *intangible* means
   a. easily understandable.
   c. not clear to the mind.
   b. crystal clear.
   d. a number of unclear examples.

3. "As the construct changes, the **precise** meaning of a concept can also change." In this context, *precise* means
   a. strictly defined.
   c. not exact.
   b. not clearly defined.
   d. loosely stated.

4. The main idea of the essay is that
   a. occupational therapy is essential for weight loss.
   b. people's height and weight is at the cornerstone of occupational therapy.
   c. occupational therapy is primarily concerned with the health and well-being of individuals.
   d. occupational therapy focuses on the rising cost of therapy for multiple sclerosis.

5. In the second paragraph, the example of the early founders of the profession of occupational therapy is offered to support the idea that
   a. they chose the profession of occupational therapy for personal gains.
   b. occupational therapists in the past did not know that people's occupations affected their health and well-being.
   c. they chose the title occupational therapy to address the mental and physical health of individuals in occupations.
   d. they were least concerned about the health and well-being of individuals in different occupations.

6. "Occupational therapy focuses on the effect of occupation on the health of individuals. This focus on occupation has been at the cornerstone of occupational therapy." (para. 1) What is the overall pattern of organization?
   a. cause and effect
   c. listing
   b. classification
   d. definition

7. "According to Kramer, Hinojosa, & Royeen (2003), occupation is a complex construct, which is built from many concepts. *Merriam-Webster* (2007) defines a concept as an intangible idea built from many examples." (para. 1) What is the overall pattern of organization?

    a. listing

    b. chronological order

    c. cause and effect

    d. definition

8. "Intelligence is an example of construct built on many things such as memory, thought, and perception." (para. 1) The overall pattern of organization is

    a. comparison and contrast.

    b. example.

    c. definition.

    d. cause and effect.

9. "Meyer (1922) refers to the early founders of occupational therapy who were concerned with the influence of work, leisure, daily living and rest." (para. 2) What is the overall pattern of organization?

    a. cause and effect

    b. classification

    c. listing

    d. example

10. "Using this definition, occupational therapists look at how a hospital's setting affects the physical and mental health of children and adults. Similarly, occupational therapists and occupational therapy assistants who work with children and adults in an emergency shelter study the location of the shelter to understand its effect on the health of the children and adults. These experts examine how children think and feel about their health and safety in a particular occupational setting." (para. 4) The overall pattern of organization is

    a. cause and effect.

    b. example.

    c. classification.

    d. comparison and contrast.

INTERNET FACT SEARCH

Occupational Therapy

The Internet can be a powerful and effective research tool once you have learned how to successfully limit your information searches and have learned how to interpret the results of your search with a critical lens.

Instructions: First try to use logic and background knowledge in guessing the correct answers to the following data questions. Then, go online and search for the relevant data. Be sure to write the Web source next to your research finding.

1. What percentage of young children in the United States are diagnosed as autistic?

    a. 1%

    b. 5%

    c. 10%

    d. 15%

Your guess: _____ Research finding: _____

Web source: _____

2. How many years of school are required to become an occupational therapist?

    a. 1 year

    b. 2 years to 6 years

    c. 3 years to 8 years

    d. 5 years to 9 years

Your guess: _____ Research finding: _____

Web source: _____

3. How much does occupational therapy cost per hour for multiple sclerosis, a chronic disease of the central nervous system?
   a. $25–$50
   b. $40–$60
   c. $65–$300
   d. $350–$500

   Your guess: _____   Research finding: _____

   Web source: _____

4. How much does a prosthetic (artificial) leg cost?
   a. between $1000 and $2000
   b. between $1500 and $2000
   c. between $3500 and $4000
   d. between $6000 and $8000

   Your guess: _____   Research finding: _____

   Web source: _____

5. How often are artificial limbs usually replaced due to wear and tear?
   a. every 4 to 6 months
   b. every 6 months to 1 year
   c. every 3 to 4 years
   d. every 5 to 6 years

   Your guess: _____   Research finding: _____

   Web source: _____

FORMAL PRESENTATION PROJECTS

You will be given the opportunity to present on one of the topics related to this chapter's discipline. Topics could relate to one of the questions you have checked off in the "Follow Your Interests" section at the beginning of the chapter. If you wish, your instructor can help you browse through the chapter and choose an appropriate topic related to occupational therapy.

For more help with **Reading for Meaning, Critical Thinking Skills,** and **Patterns of Organization,** go to your learning path in **MyReadingLab.com.**

U.S. HISTORY

Learning Objectives

IN THIS CHAPTER, YOU WILL LEARN TO . . .

1. Describe the discipline of U.S. history
2. Define key terms in the field of U.S. history
3. Read actively
4. Effectively interpret the instructions in your class assignments
5. Recognize an author's bias

INTRODUCTION TO THE DISCIPLINE OF U.S. HISTORY

1 LEARNING OBJECTIVE
Describe the discipline
of U.S. history

Robert Penn Warren once wrote: "History cannot give us a program for the future, but it can give us a fuller understanding of ourselves, and of our common humanity, so that we can better face the future." Through the study of history we can better understand our world, the places we inhabit, and our cultural heritage.

This chapter will focus on U.S. history. In its pages you will read about some remarkable characters and the historical events that transformed their lives. You will have the chance to rethink the role of Christopher Columbus in "discovering America." You will read about the journey of John and Sally Peters, a slave couple caught in between the lines of the British and the colonists during the American Revolution. You will also examine how new technologies such as the personal bathtub and the phonograph changed many Americans' everyday lives in the late nineteenth century. Finally, you will read profiles of ten great women of the twentieth century and gain a better understanding of why some historians have called this past hundred years, "The Women's Century."

Collaboration

Reading into a Photo

Working in a small group, examine the following photograph and answer the questions that follow.

1. In your opinion, what is the relationship between the people in the line and the billboard?

2. What message does this image convey to you?

Follow Your Interests

Collaboration

Review the set of questions below that history scholars might explore. Check off the three to four questions that are most interesting to you.

1. George Santayana (1863–1952), a Spanish philosopher, wrote the famous statement: "Those who cannot remember the past are condemned to repeat it." In your view, what is the idea behind this line? Can you think of any examples of history repeating itself?

2. Many middle school and high school students complain that history classes are boring for them. Do you think these students feel down about history because everything that happened in the past is uninteresting, or is it the case that history teachers are not teaching history in a stimulating manner? How could teachers change their strategy to make history come alive?

3. American history can be broken down into many subfields such as African-American history, war history, women's history, business history, history of technological changes, labor history, music history, and constitutional history. Which subfields of American history do you find most interesting and why?

4. If you had the opportunity to go back in time with the help of a time machine, what period of history would you go back to? What famous people in history would you want to interview?

5. Technology is always progressing: ten years ago, we did not have social networking sites. Twenty-five years ago we didn't have cell phones. Fifty years ago, we did not have personal computers. One hundred years ago, you could not take a commercial airplane flight. Which technologies invented in the last hundred years do you think you would have the most trouble living without? Explain your choices.

6. American history is filled with great names and great lives that have left their permanent imprint on what it means to be American. How many of the following names do you recognize? With a partner, try to briefly state what made each of them legendary. If you are not sure, you could always do a quick Google search to find out.

   a. Sitting Bull
   b. Benjamin Franklin
   c. Lewis and Clark
   d. Frederick Douglass
   e. Robert E. Lee
   f. Thomas Edison
   g. Susan B. Anthony
   h. Joe Hill
   i. Eleanor Roosevelt
   j. Martin Luther King Jr.
   k. Elvis Presley

7. American history has been marked by many wars and international conflicts from the Revolutionary War to the War of 1812, from the Civil War to the Spanish-American War, and onward to World War I and II, the Korean and Vietnam Wars, the Persian Gulf War, and the war in Iraq. Thinking back to all of these military conflicts, do you think war is a natural state of affairs, or can war be avoided? Explain your opinion.

8. If we compare everyday life today with the way people lived their lives two hundred years ago, would you say that our lives have gotten better or worse? Justify your answer with an example or two.

9. Frederick Douglass, the great civil rights statesman, once wrote: "If there is no struggle, there can be no progress." Do you agree or disagree that things only get better when people fight for change? In other words, do you agree that change happens from "the bottom up," and not from "the top down"? Explain your viewpoint.

10. American culture is famous across the world for being a culture of great creative innovation. From Hollywood movies to Apple computers to the invention of hip hop and R&B, the United States has led the way. Why do you think American cultural innovation has played such a significant role on the world stage?

11. The role of women in society has changed dramatically throughout the course of American history. Not very long ago, women did not have the right to vote, and only recently have the majority of women been able to enter into the workplace. Will the twenty-first century be a time of great progress for women's rights? What significant gains do you foresee for women in the next hundred years?

12. Someone once wrote: "History is something that happens to other people." Yet, it seems to be the case that historical events, both great and small, often do have a direct effect on our everyday lives. Can you think of some examples of how your life has been affected by a historical event?

Now, share your choices with a small group of classmates and discuss why these particular questions are most interesting to you. You may wish to discuss these questions with them and ask which questions they found interesting.

Key Terms in the Field of History

LEARNING OBJECTIVE
②
Define key terms in the field of U.S. history

The following key terms are frequently used in the discipline of history. If you take a college-level course in history, it will be important for you to remember these words and to use them in your speech and writing. Review the words below and answer the multiple-choice questions that follow.

civil rights	nativist	subjective
colonization	populism	temperance
Confederate	primary source	tenant farmer
constitutional	revolution	welfare state
inevitable	sit-in	yellow press

EXERCISE 1   Inferring Meaning from Context

Read each sentence below and try to derive the meaning of the italicized key terms from the context. Circle the correct definition of each italicized term.

1. When you read about an episode in history, always keep in mind that all perspectives are *subjective*.
   a. factual
   b. personal; seen through an individual's lens
   c. about a subject
   d. confused and off-topic

2. The American *Revolution* gave birth to a new nation.
   a. movement
   b. a critical moment without bloodshed
   c. the overthrow and replacement of an established government
   d. a discussion of new ideas

3. Many believe that due to the multiple developing tensions between the North and the South, the Civil War was *inevitable*.
   a. impossible to avoid   c. an error in human history
   b. could have been stopped   d. worthy of closer study

4. The invasion of online privacy was not judged as *constitutional*.
   a. deemed to be fair and just
   b. in accordance with the Constitution
   c. illegal
   d. relative to the laws of one or more states

5. The British Empire secured its claim to the riches of many lands through *colonization*.
   a. creating conflict through war-like behavior
   b. the organization of work relationships
   c. business model for global networking
   d. the establishment of permanent settlements and political control over foreign lands

6. Not allowing someone to enter a commercial establishment based on their skin color is a *civil rights* violation.
   a. city or local regulations
   b. business suits related to racial discrimination
   c. rights related to personal liberty and equality under the law
   d. a code of conduct set out clearly in our educational system

7. When historians do research, they rely mostly on *primary sources*.
   a. most important episodes
   b. documents or objects made during the period being studied
   c. textbooks
   d. secondary sources of information

8. The *Nativist* Party wanted to close the doors on new immigrants.
   a. someone who is native to a given land
   b. the idea of advocating for immigrant rights
   c. the concept that all power must be in the hands of a strong leader
   d. the belief that the interests of native inhabitants must be protected over those of immigrants

9. A *populist* candidate for governor promised to put power back in the hands of the common man.
   a. political movement that offers unorthodox solutions or policies and appeals to the common person
   b. someone who is popular
   c. the idea of supporting big business interests over the rights of everyone else
   d. the belief that corporate lobbying and big spending on political ads on TV are the answer to America's problems

10. The university students organized *sit-in* to protest the increase in college tuition.
    a. a peaceful protest in which participants occupy premises and refuse to leave
    b. sitting down in a public building
    c. an angry movement of young people against the political system as a whole
    d. a desire to change the political system through violent methods

11. In the post-slavery period in the South, many African-American *tenant farmers* lived in dire poverty.
    a. people who live on farms
    b. wealthy owners of farmhands
    c. minority farmers who worked long hours
    d. farmers who rent rather than own the land

12. The *temperance* movement in the United States succeeded in bringing about the prohibition of alcohol during the 1920s.
    a. the idea of helping people control their tempers
    b. total abstinence from alcoholic beverages
    c. moderation of all activities
    d. defining actions in terms of alcohol abuse

13. Conservatives generally argue against government intervention and the growth of a *welfare state*.
    a. a free market state where there is minimal government intervention and taxes are kept relatively low
    b. a state in which the majority of citizens are accepting welfare assistance checks
    c. a state in which the welfare of the people in such matters as social security, health and education, and housing is the responsibility of the government
    d. a government focus on deficit spending during a recession

14. The *yellow press* follows celebrity activity in order to get the latest scoop.
    a. newspapers that are designed to appeal to college students
    b. a dishonest newspaper column
    c. a type of journalism that uses eye-catching headlines to sell more newspapers
    d. fashion magazines that have entered the digital age

15. The *Confederate* army surrendered at Appomattox Court House in April 1865.
    a. the army of the southern states during the Civil War
    b. the slave-holding system of the South
    c. the Union army of the northern states
    d. an economic system based on a small-business model developed in the nineteenth century

 **EXERCISE 2** **Creating Meaningful Sentences with the Key Terms**

Collaboration

Working with a partner, choose five of the key terms in history and write an original sentence about each one.

1. Word = _____

_____

_____

2. Word = _____

_____

_____

3. Word = _____

_____

_____

4. Word = _____

_____

_____

5. Word = _____

_____

_____

Active Reading

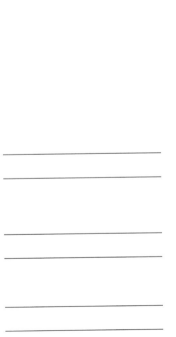

Collaboration

③ LEARNING OBJECTIVE
Read actively

Asking Pertinent Questions of the Text

It is helpful to think of reading as an interactive activity. If you are sitting alone and holding a textbook or novel, you may ask, *Who exactly am I interacting with?* Good question! The answer is that if you are engaged in active reading, you are interacting with the words on the page by asking questions about the ideas and information coming at you. It is human nature to be curious, and when you start to read about a particular topic, your mind begins to formulate key questions in an effort to figure out what is going on. So for example, you might glance at a newspaper and the headline reads:

Three School Children Suspended for Bad Behavior in San Diego

Automatically, you begin to ask questions of the text in an effort to fill in the details of the story.

Practice: With a partner, write down three questions about the headline you would like to know the answers to. When you are done, share your answers with the class.

1. _____

2. _____

3. _____

Putting the Skill into Action

Let's read about the violent draft riots that occurred in New York City during the Civil War. As you read each new sentence, write down a question that is forming in your mind in the sidebar to the left of the text.

> In July 1863, as the Civil War grew more bloody, the streets of Manhattan suddenly erupted in violence.
> The working classes, mainly Irish immigrants, resented the military draft, which conscripted soldiers for duty in the Civil War.
> The riots developed into a major battle in some spots of the city, with mobs fighting it out with NYC police and even federal troops. By the time it was over, much damage had been done to city buildings, and hundreds of protesters were wounded or killed.
> The nation was shocked to be reading about masses of angry men battling police and soldiers in the streets of New York. The news appeared on the front pages of newspapers and magazines across the country.

The Last Word

Asking pertinent questions as you read, along with note-taking and annotation, is a key way to interact with text. Active reading serves many purposes. It helps keep you focused and connected to what you are reading. As a result, you are better able to navigate and comprehend the text in front of you.

READINESS FOR COLLEGE SUCCESS
Understanding Your Class Assignments

4 LEARNING OBJECTIVE
Effectively interpret the
instructions in your class
assignments

You have a U.S. History 1 take-home final due in the morning. You stay up all night reviewing the text chapters and composing your answers to the exam questions. You run to class, hand in the final, only to have your work handed back to you a moment later by the professor, who tells you, "This was NOT the assignment."

This is a very common occurrence. Students often do not read the assignment instructions carefully enough and thus do not follow the specific guidelines outlined by the professor in the assignment handout. To make sure that your work is in line with your professor's expectations, pay attention to the following set of strategies for reviewing a class assignment.

Strategies for Understanding Class Assignments

- **Read over the exact details of the assignment very carefully.** When an instructor gives you an assignment, whether it be in the form of a handout written on the board or a message posted on Blackboard, you need to spend some time with it. Do not rush through your reading of it.

- **While reviewing the assignment, ask yourself:**
  o What is this assignment asking me to do?
  o How many steps are involved?
  o What is the expected time frame for each stage of the assignment?
  o If it is a written assignment, is the expected length of the paper specifically mentioned?

- **For written assignments, pay attention to specific formatting requests.** The instructor might specify that an essay must follow standard formatting (written in Microsoft Word, Times New Roman 12 font, double-spaced), or might ask you to follow other formatting instructions. You might be asked to submit your work as an e-mail attachment or be asked to post your work online by a certain date.

- **Pay attention to the topic parameters of the assignment.** Many class assignments leave some choices up to the student, but you cannot do research on kangaroo mothers if the instructor is asking you to focus on animals within the reptile family! If you are asked to write an essay on the history of your family's immigration to the United States, do not spend a paragraph sharing your feelings about your mother. Do not go off-topic.

- **After reviewing the assignment, if there is ANYTHING that you do not completely understand, ask your instructor to explain his or her instructions more clearly.** Do not sit quietly in your seat, wondering what to do. If you miss the moment in class, do not hesitate to send your instructor an e-mail or to visit him or her during office hours to request clarification of the assignment.

Let's Practice! Carefully review the following three U.S. history assignments and take notes on the key set of instructions contained within each. The notes for Assignment 1 have been done for you, and should serve as a model for the remaining assignments.

Assignment 1: Review of a History Textbook

Option 1: Write a book review of an academic history book (chosen from the lists provided at the College Library Reserve Reading Room). For this option, you must choose at least one other historical text (for example, an article on the same topic) to place this work in comparative perspective. This will allow you to better evaluate the author's point of view and conclusions.

Option 2: Write an analysis of a piece of historical fiction (either chosen from the course list or approved by your teaching assistant). Since you are evaluating a piece of fiction, you must consult at least two outside sources (for example, a textbook, a history book or an article on the period) in order to evaluate the accuracy and historical relevance of the novel under review.

Key Points in the Instructions
1. *You have two options to choose from. You do not have to do both options.*
2. *(for option 1) The academic history book to be reviewed must come from the reserve reading room of the college library.*
3. *(for option 1) The book to be reviewed must be compared with another text/article on the same topic.*
4. *(for option 2) You must choose a piece of historical fiction to review from the class list OR get instructor approval for one not on the list.*
5. *(for option 2) Two nonfiction readings on the same period as the fiction piece must be reviewed and incorporated into the discussion of the work of fiction.*

Assignment 2: Immigration Children's Book Project

The Task: You will use imagination and research to create a historical fiction book for children through which you tell the story of a specific group of American immigrants. The grading rubric and research links are at the bottom of this page. Your book must include the following:

Content Guidelines

Why They Came

1. PUSH factor as to why your characters left their homeland.

2. PULL factor as to why they came here.

Preparation to Leave

1. What possessions did they take?

2. Who did they take?

The Journey to America

1. What was the trip across the ocean, or across the mountains, like?

2. When they arrived, were they allowed to enter the country?

Where Did They Settle?

1. Where in the United States did they settle? Why did they choose this place?

2. What conditions did they find here?

How Were They Treated?

1. What attitudes did they face as newcomers?

2. How did they deal with their treatment?

Trials and Tribulations

1. Provide at least three problems they faced in America.

2. How did they overcome these problems?

Research Links

Type the following key words into your search engine to find additional information on the topic:

Digital History: The Huddled Masses

German Immigration to America

French Emigration to America

Chinese Immigrants and the
   Transcontinental Railroad

Irish Immigration

The Korean American Experience

Library of Congress

Italian Immigration to America

Immigration from England

Russian Emigration to America

Immigration from Mexico

Key Points in the Instructions
1. _____
2. _____
3. _____
4. _____

Assignment 3: The Causes and Effects of the American Revolution

Read David McCullough's *1776*. Write a roughly eight to ten page paper addressing the following question:

What were the ideas and issues surrounding the American Revolution through 1776, and how do you think they affected the outcome of the war as well as the formation of early American government and society?

In answering this question, you should consider several of the following topics for discussion:

- What were the feelings of those involved in the struggle? Consider common soldiers, leaders, and non-combatants.
- What were those involved in the conflict trying to accomplish?
- What role did the leadership of certain individuals play?
- What problems and advantages existed on each side?
- How did the British government view the conflict?
- What measures did the American government take and why?
- How did the battles that took place in New England, New York and New Jersey affect the outcome of the war?

You may use outside resources to complete the assignment, but be sure to cite them correctly. In addition, citations of any information from any source (the assigned text or outside sources) should be in parenthetical citations. Your paper should also include a bibliography. Keep in mind that this paper will count as your first quarter project/paper assignment, and is thus a significant part of your grade.

Courtesy of Ron Watkins.

Key Points in the Instructions
1. _____
_____
_____
2. _____
3. _____
_____
4. _____
5. _____

Reading Selection **1**

Article

MyReadingLab™
Complete this **Exercise**
at **myreadinglab.com**

Adapted from "Rethinking Columbus and His Day"

Preview Questions

Discuss the following questions with a small group of classmates.

1. Someone once wrote that "history is written by the winners." What is the idea behind this quotation? Do you agree? Explain.

2. What facts did you learn in school about the explorer Christopher Columbus?

3. Do you think Columbus deserves a national holiday? Can you think of a heroic figure in American history that should have a holiday named after him or her?

Collaboration

Pre-Reading Vocabulary: Focus on Some Key Terms

Before beginning the reading selection, it may be helpful to focus on the meaning of some key words in the article. Working with a partner, try to guess the meaning of these words. Then look up the words in a dictionary.

Word	Your Definition	Dictionary Definition
monarchy		
faulty		
vicious		
pave (the way)		
heritage		

Adapted from "Rethinking Columbus and His Day"

By Sharon Short
October 10, 2011

"In 1492, Columbus sailed the ocean blue …"

1   Thus goes the elementary school chant I remember learning years ago.

2   And, of course, the version of history that we learned was a cleaned-up, Euro-centric view. Good old Christopher Columbus, discovered the Americas and thus established a connection between Europe and our American turf.

3   Except that's not quite how things happened.

4   Columbus was actually trying to reach Asia on behalf of Spain's monarchy to establish trade routes for spices. But, since he was sailing with faulty maps (and didn't have the 21st century advantage of a GPS), he was off by about 10,000 miles. He and his ships landed in the Caribbean, on an island called Hispaniola. This island contains the present-day countries of the Dominican Republic and Haiti. It was on the shores of Hispaniola that his flagship, the *Santa Maria*, sank. He nevertheless insisted he'd landed in India, and thus tagged the natives as Indians. His rule as governor of settlements in Hispaniola was—by his own accounts—vicious and brutal to the native peoples of the land. Eventually, he fell out of favor with the Spanish crown, and was dismissed as governor.

5   What's more, since people were already living there, we cannot say that Columbus discovered the land. He can't really take credit as the first European to have landed upon American continental shores either. That credit actually goes to Leif Ericson. Ericson was a Norseman who sailed to and established a settlement on the northern peninsula of Newfoundland, Canada. This happened in the year 1002 or 1003, nearly 500 years before Columbus.

6   Columbus does get credit for making four round-trip voyages between Spain and the Americas. While his voyages paved the way for the American colonies, he wasn't quite the good-guy discoverer that he's cracked up to be in simplified history stories.

7   So … why does digging into the history of Columbus matter? Why not merrily chant "In 1492, Columbus sailed the ocean blue," and hit a few Columbus Day sales?

8   Because understanding our heritage and history shouldn't just be reduced to a few sound bites. Truly honoring our history means understanding it, as much as possible, both the good and the ugly. And that's important because, as the famous quote goes, "Those who cannot remember the past are condemned to repeat it."

9   In that spirit, there are plenty of resources for exploring the deeper, richer history behind Columbus's sailing that ocean blue. Two good places to start: the History Channel's Columbus page and *Time* magazine's article on the history of Columbus Day.

Reading Comprehension Check

1. What is the author's purpose in writing this article about Columbus?
   a. to give instructions
   b. to show that all of the facts we have learned about Columbus are true
   c. to convince readers that much of what we have learned about Columbus is not true
   d. to prove that Columbus did not exist

2. In paragraph 3, we read, "Except that's not quite how things happened." In this context, what does the word *that* refer to?
   a. the idea that Columbus discovered America
   b. America
   c. Europeans
   d. the idea that Europe and America are the same

3. According to the article, why did Columbus call the people he met "Indians"?
   a. He liked the sound of the word.
   b. He was on the island of Hispaniola.
   c. Columbus wanted to sail to India after this voyage.
   d. He mistakenly believed he had sailed to India.

4. According to the author, how can we best honor history?
   a. by reading about Columbus
   b. by celebrating historical holidays
   c. by understanding it
   d. by researching our heritage

5. What is the main idea of the article?
   a. History starts with a holiday.
   b. It is important to dig into the facts behind historical events.
   c. We must always read more and more about history.
   d. Columbus Day is an important American holiday.

Collaboration

Exploring the Topic

Discuss the following questions to review the content of the article you have just read.

1. What does the author mean when she writes "the version of history that we learned was a cleaned-up, Euro-centric view"? (para. 2)

2. Columbus's governorship of the island of Hispaniola is described as "vicious and brutal." (para. 4) What crimes do you think Columbus committed against the native population of the island? Explain.

3. The author argues that it is important for us to understand both the "good and the ugly" (para. 8) of American history. Can you share an example of a "good" and an "ugly" episode in our history?

Post-Reading Vocabulary

Without using a dictionary, determine the meaning of the bolded words from the context.

1. "Good old Christopher Columbus, discovered the Americas and thus established a connection between Europe and our American **turf**." (para. 2)

    Turf means _____

2. "Columbus was actually trying to reach Asia **on behalf of** Spain's monarchy" (para. 4)

    On behalf of means _____

3. "While his voyages paved the way for the American colonies, he wasn't quite the good-guy discoverer that he's **cracked up** to be in simplified history stories." (para. 6)

    Cracked up means _____

The Journey of Tom and Sally Peters

Reading Selection **2**

Book Excerpt

Preview Questions

1. If you were a slave living in the colonies during the American Revolution, do you think you would agree to fight for the British Loyalists in exchange for your freedom? Explain your viewpoint.

2. The Declaration of Independence clearly states that "all men are created equal." Yet, when this document was signed and America became an independent country, the enslavement of black people continued. How can this contradiction between words and deeds be explained?

3. In what ways can the outbreak of war disrupt family life?

MyReadingLab™
Complete this **Exercise**
at **myreadinglab.com**

Pre-Reading Vocabulary: Focus on Some Key Terms

Collaboration

Before beginning the reading selection, it may be helpful to focus on the meaning of some key words in the excerpt. Working with a partner, try to guess the meaning of these words. Then look up the words in a dictionary.

Word	Your Definition	Dictionary Definition
rebel		
prosperous		
abduction		
petition		
odyssey		

The Journey of Tom and Sally Peters

By Jacqueline A. Jones, Peter H. Wood, Thomas Borstelmann,
Elaine Tyler May, and Vicki L. Ruiz

Focusing on the lives of real people brings history to life. The following story of an eighteenth-century family brings together two of the most significant events in U.S. history: the slave trade and the American Revolution.

1   In 1760, a young man, aged twenty-two, was taken from his home in what is now Nigeria. He was shipped to Louisiana aboard the slave ship *Henri Quatre*. The young man was forced to cut sugar cane. He rebelled so often that he was sold to a prosperous Scottish immigrant in Wilmington, North Carolina. He was then put to work, operating a grist mill. The African took an English name, Thomas Peters. He then started a family with a young woman named Sally.

2   During the fifteen years between Peters's abduction from Africa and the outbreak of hostilities between America and Britain in 1775, nearly 225,000 people had poured into the British mainland colonies. Nearly half of these individuals had been purchased in Africa and were enslaved in the coastal South. As open warfare erupted, Tom and Sally Peters's lives were thrown into confusion. The young couple experienced hardships, opportunities, and enormous dislocations.

3   Late in 1775, Virginia's governor, Lord Dunmore, offered freedom to slaves who would take up arms for the British. So when ships from the Royal Navy arrived at the Cape Fear River in March, Tom and Sally Peters risked arrest to gain their personal liberty. They bolted to the British vessels. Peters was with the British when General Clinton's forces tried to take Charleston, South Carolina, in June 1776.

4   Throughout the war, Peters served the British in a unit called the Black Pioneers. Wounded twice, he rose to the rank of sergeant. Peters earned the promise of a farm in Canada. In 1783, as defeated Loyalists left New York City at the end of the war, he and his family joined other ex-slaves aboard a ship bound for Nova Scotia. Departing in November, the ship was blown off course by foul weather. Tom and Sally, with their twelve-year-old daughter Clairy and eighteen-month-old son

John, spent the winter sheltered at Bermuda. Finally, in 1784, they were able to join 3,500 other black Loyalists in Nova Scotia.

5   But the odyssey of the Peters family did not end in Nova Scotia. Peters and others were denied their promised farmland. So, in 1790 Thomas ventured to London as an advocate for these former slaves. He protested their treatment and petitioned for relief. He also met with British abolitionists planning a colony of former slaves in West Africa. Eager for his family to join the effort, he returned to Canada and led 1,200 African-Americans to Sierra Leone. Peters lived the rest of his life there and died in Freetown in 1792.

6   During a life that began and ended in Africa, Peters had seen New Orleans, Wilmington, Charleston, Philadelphia, New York, Bermuda, Halifax, and London. He survived sixteen years of enslavement and fought his own war for the freedom and safety of family and friends.

adapted from Jones et al., *Created Equal: A History of the United States*, Brief Ed., Vol. 1, 3e.

Reading Comprehension Check

MyReadingLab™
Complete this **Exercise** at **myreadinglab.com**

1. What phenomena is the focus of the second paragraph?
   a. the abduction of the Peters family
   b. the slave trade
   c. the mass of people coming into the British colonies in America in the period before the American Revolution
   d. the rights of African migrants to fight for the Loyalist army

2. Why did Lord Dunmore, the governor of Virginia, offer slaves their freedom?
   a. He was a kind soul who believed that slavery was evil.
   b. He had made a special deal with Thomas Jefferson.
   c. He refused to offer liberty to any African males.
   d. He wanted more soldiers to fight to defend the English colonies.

3. Who were the Black Pioneers?
   a. black fighters for the revolutionary army
   b. settlers on the western plain
   c. the first Africans to obtain farmland in Canada
   d. a British unit made up of black soldiers

4. Why were the Peters and others denied their farmlands in Nova Scotia?
   a. The article does not specify the reason.
   b. They were considered traitors.
   c. They did not have enough money to buy the land.
   d. They were ignored because of their skin color.

5. What is the author's tone?
   a. objective   c. indifferent
   b. angry   d. pessimistic

Exploring the Topic

Discuss the following questions to review the content of the book excerpt you have just read.

Collaboration

1. What risks did Peters take in his quest for freedom?

2. Why do you think the Peters family was denied their promised farmland in Canada?

3. Do you think Peters made a wise move in agreeing to return to Africa, his native continent? Explain the pros and cons of such a choice.

Post-Reading Vocabulary

Without using a dictionary, determine the meaning of the bolded words from the context.

1. "During the fifteen years between Peters's abduction from Africa and the outbreak of **hostilities** between America and Britain in 1775, nearly 225,000 people had poured into the British mainland colonies." (para. 2)

   Hostilities means _____

2. "As open warfare **erupted**, Tom and Sally Peters's lives were thrown into confusion." (para. 2)

   Erupted means _____

3. "So, in 1790 Thomas ventured to London as an **advocate** for these former slaves." (para. 5)

   Advocate means _____

Jeanelle Hope   An Interview with a Student in the Field of History

California State University-Long Beach

1. How did you find your path to majoring in history?

While in high school I found myself gravitating toward the subject after encountering a phenomenal history teacher who made the subject extremely interesting, relevant, and relatable.

2. What was the biggest obstacle you faced in your study of history?

The biggest obstacle that I have faced has been with writing and reading. Because of the dense amount of reading that is required of history majors, I have virtually had to learn how to read again, because often primary sources and scholarly historical articles and monographs are quite complex and difficult to understand. Additionally, writing has been an obstacle as I am always working toward making my work more credible and scholarly, which is a huge never-ending task.

3. What area(s) of history in particular do you find most interesting?

I enjoy researching and learning about the unknown as well as providing a voice for areas in history that go overshadowed or lack representation.

4. What specific skills are required of students who study history?

-Great Writer	-Passion for the Subject
-Critical Thinking	-Enjoy Reading
-Analyzing	-Memorization

5. Other than teaching history, what other career avenues are available for history majors?

-Historian	-Researcher
-Author	-Journalist
-College Administrator	-Archivist
-Historian for Films	-Librarian
-Activist	-Lawyer

John C. Calhoun's 1848 Speech Warning Against Incorporating Mexico into the United States

Preview Questions

1. If two nations are at war and one defeats the other, is the victor entitled to annex land from the defeated? In other words, is the concept of taking "the spoils of war" a just one? Explain.

2. The "founding fathers" of this new nation argued passionately against colonial rule and were strongly in favor of individual rights. Yet, 70 years after gaining independence, the United States invaded Mexico, the first of many occupations of sovereign nations to our south. In pursuing land and colonial possessions abroad, did the United States, in your opinion, betray its original cause?

3. If you glance at a map, the original 13 colonies encompassed just a quarter of the entire continent. How did the United States succeed in developing westward all the way to the Pacific coast?

MyReadingLab™

Complete this Exercise at **myreadinglab.com**

Collaboration

Pre-Reading Vocabulary: Focus on Some Key Terms

Before beginning the reading selection, it may be helpful to focus on the meaning of some key words in the speech. Working with a partner, try to guess the meaning of these words. Then look up the words in a dictionary.

Word	Your Definition	Dictionary Definition
incorporate		
anarchy		
noble		
civilized		
endurance		

John C. Calhoun's 1848 Speech Warning Against Incorporating Mexico into the United States

Public Document

The Mexican–American War broke out in 1846. The conflict began after President Tyler annexed the Mexican state of Texas into the Union. The war lasted less than two years, ending with Mexico's surrender. In the Treaty of Guadalupe Hidalgo the United States gained Mexican territory that comprises present-day New Mexico, Arizona, Utah, Nevada, and California.

In 1848, Senator John C. Calhoun delivered a speech warning against incorporating all of a conquered Mexico into the United States.

Note to Reader: *The following is an example of a "primary source." Primary sources are documents, recordings, or other sources of information that were created by people who witnessed and/or recorded the events being studied. They are critical to the study of history. They are often tricky to read as they are written in the tone of the period they were produced. Be patient in your reading of primary sources. It is worth the effort. Primary sources bear a lot of fruit.*

1 | "RESOLVED, That to conquer Mexico and to hold it, either as a province or to incorporate it into the Union, would be inconsistent with the avowed object for which the war has been prosecuted; a departure from the settled policy of the Government; in conflict with its character and genius; and in the end subversive of our free and popular institutions."

2 | The next reason which my resolutions assign, is, that it is without example or precedent, wither to hold Mexico as a province, or to incorporate her into our Union. No example of such a line of policy can be found. We have conquered many of the neighboring tribes of Indians, but we have never thought of holding them in subjection—never of incorporating them into our Union. They have either been left as an independent people amongst us, or been driven into the forests.

3 | I know further, sir, that we have never dreamt of incorporating into our Union any but the Caucasian race—the free white race. To incorporate Mexico, would be the very first instance of the kind of incorporating an Indian race; for more than half of the Mexicans are Indians, and the other is composed chiefly of mixed tribes. I protest against such a union as that! Ours, sir, is the Government of a white race. The greatest misfortunes of Spanish America are to be traced to the fatal error of placing these colored races on an equality with the white race. That error destroyed the social arrangement which formed the basis of society. The Portuguese and ourselves have escaped—the Portuguese at least to some extent—and we are the only people on this continent which have made revolutions without being followed by anarchy. And yet it is professed and talked about to erect these Mexicans into a Territorial Government, and place them on an equality with the people of the United States. I protest utterly against such a project.

4 | Sir, it is a remarkable fact, that in the whole history of man, as far as my knowledge extends, there is no instance whatever of any civilized colored races being found equal to the establishment of free popular government, although by far the largest portion of the human family is composed of these races. And even in the savage state we scarcely find them anywhere with such government, except it be our noble savages—for noble I will call them. They, for the most part, had free institutions, but they are easily sustained among a savage people. Are we to overlook this fact? Are we to associate with ourselves as equals, companions, and fellow-citizens, the Indians and mixed race of Mexico? Sir, I should consider such a thing as fatal to our institutions.

5 | But, Mr. President, suppose all these difficulties removed; suppose these people attached to our Union, and desirous of incorporating with us, ought we to bring them in? Are they fit to be connected with us? Are they fit for self-government and for governing you? Are you, any of you, willing that your States should be governed by these twenty-odd Mexican States, with a population of about only one million of your blood, and two or three millions of mixed blood, better informed, all the rest pure Indians, a mixed blood equally ignorant and unfit for liberty, impure races, not as good as Cherokees or Choctaws?

6 | We make a great mistake, sir, when we suppose that all people are capable of self-government. We are anxious to force free government on all; and I see that it has been urged in a very respectable quarter, that it is the mission of this country to spread civil and religious liberty over all the world, and especially over this continent. It is a great mistake. None but people advanced to a very high state of moral and intellectual improvement are capable, in a civilized state, of maintaining free government; and amongst those who are so purified, very few, indeed, have had the good fortune of forming a constitution capable of endurance. It is a remarkable fact in the history of man, that scarcely ever have free popular institutions been formed by wisdom alone that have endured.

Reading Comprehension Check

1. What connection does Calhoun make (para. 2) between the treatment of Indians and that of Mexicans?
   a. He makes the point that both the Mexicans and the Indians were assimilated into the country.
   b. He argues that, as with the Indians, the conquered Mexicans should not be brought into the Union as citizens.
   c. He argues that all men are created equal, regardless of race.
   d. He makes the point that both Indian leaders and Mexican leaders could be brought to a compromise.

2. Calhoun writes, "I know further, sir, that we have never dreamt of incorporating into our Union any but the Caucasian race—the free white race." (para. 3) We can infer from this statement that
   a. Calhoun clearly held racist views.
   b. Calhoun had struggled against the slave system.
   c. Calhoun wanted Mexicans to be enslaved in the American South.
   d. Calhoun demanded that all of Mexico submit to U.S. control.

3. "Are we to associate with ourselves as equals, companions, and fellow-citizens, the Indians and mixed race of Mexico?" (para. 4) Calhoun's tone in the above statement can be described as
   a. elitist.   c. objective.
   b. egalitarian.   d. satisfied.

4. What mistaken idea does Calhoun refer to in the final paragraph?
   a. the concept of a nation divided against itself
   b. that Mexicans are Indians
   c. that liberty should only exist for Americans
   d. the belief that all people are capable of self-government

5. What is the main idea of Calhoun's speech?
   a. that the white race is superior
   b. that democracy must be spread to all parts of the world
   c. that to bring Mexico into the Union would be a grave error
   d. that the slave system should not be threatened

Exploring the Topic

Discuss the following questions to review the content of the primary source excerpt you have just read.

Collaboration

1. Calhoun states, "Ours, sir, is the Government of a white race." (para. 3) In your opinion, what would Calhoun think of twenty-first-century, multicultural America? How much have things changed in the United States since Calhoun made this speech in 1848?

2. In describing U.S. policy toward Native Americans, Calhoun writes, "They have either been left as an independent people amongst us, or been driven into the forests." (para. 2) How does Calhoun use the example of Indians to make his case about U.S. policy toward Mexicans?

3. Calhoun was a strong proponent of westward expansion. From your knowledge of U.S. history, what were some of the advantages and disadvantages of the U.S. government seeking new lands to the west?

Post-Reading Vocabulary

Without using a dictionary, determine the meaning of the highlighted words from the context.

1. "I protest **utterly** against such a project." (para. 3)

   Utterly means _____

2. "The greatest misfortunes of Spanish America are to be **traced** to the fatal error of placing these colored races on an equality with the white race." (para. 3)

   Traced means _____

3. "Are we to associate with ourselves as equals, companions, and fellow-citizens, the Indians and mixed race of Mexico? Sir, I should consider such a thing as **fatal** to our institutions." (para. 4)

   Fatal means _____

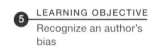

SKILL FOCUS
Author's Bias

⑤ LEARNING OBJECTIVE
Recognize an author's bias

"We want a better America, an America that will give its citizens, first of all, a higher and higher standard of living so that no child will cry for food in the midst of plenty."

—Sidney Hillman (1887–1946), first president (1914–1946) of
Amalgamated Clothing Workers of America

"I can hire one half of the working class to kill the other half."

—Jay Gould, nineteenth-century railroad executive

We are all biased by nature. How we express ourselves, whether in speech or in writing, is flavored by our life experience, our belief systems, our political leanings, and our cultural favoritism.

Observe the two competing quotations about American labor above:

a. Which of the writers has a bias against laborers?

b. Compare the two quoted individuals' positions in society. How does each of their professions connect to their personal bias? Explain.

It is very important to be aware of an author's bias when you are reading just about anything—from commercial ads to history books, from daily newspapers to weekly magazines. It is very easy to be misled if you do not consider an author's bias.

If you read an advertisement that says, "Jamaica is the most beautiful place on earth," would you cancel your trip to Mexico? Why not?

If you took out a book from the library entitled *The Great Vietnam War* and all of the people interviewed in the book said positive things about this war, would you then believe that everything about the Vietnam War was positive? Why not?

Being aware of an author's bias makes you a more critical reader and brings you to a better understanding of the topics you are reading about and the author's perspective on these particular topics.

When trying to determine an author's bias, ask yourself the following questions:

- What is the author's profession/position in society? What type of bias would someone in this position most likely hold? (For example, a bank executive might favor lower taxes. A young student might favor lower tuition.)

- What position is the author taking or favoring regarding a particular topic?

- Is the author only presenting facts in favor of one view on the topic?

It is often difficult to tell what an author's bias is on a subject unless you know more about the subject than just that author's writing. This is why it is important to read multiple sources on a given subject so that you are exposed to various perspectives on the issue.

Practice 1: Imagining Different Perspectives on the American Civil War

The American Civil War (1861–1865) was a war fought within the United States. In response to the election of Abraham Lincoln as president of the United States, 11 Southern slave states declared their secession from the United States and formed the Confederate States of America; the other 25 states supported the federal government ("the Union"). After four years of warfare, mostly within the Southern states, the Confederacy surrendered and slavery was outlawed everywhere in the nation.

With a classmate, imagine what each of the following eight people— living over 150 years ago—might have thought about the start of the Civil War in 1861. Would they most likely have been in favor of the war, against it, loyal to the North or to the South? In other words, how would each be biased, in one way or another, in their relation to the war?

Collaboration

Nineteenth-Century Character	Bias toward War (and Why?)
A. An 18-year-old slave working in a cotton field in Louisiana	
B. A Christian minister living in New England	
C. A Confederate general based in Atlanta	
D. The owner of a cotton plantation in Texas	
E. A New York banker heavily invested in textile manufacturing	
F. A poor, unemployed white man living in South Carolina	
G. A new mother in Connecticut married to her 20-year-old husband	
H. An American-Indian chief living just on the border between the Northern and Southern states	

Practice 2: Imagining Different Perspectives on the American Civil War

Collaboration

Read the following primary-source quotations written during the time of the American Civil War. Then answer the questions that follow, focusing on each author's bias.

1. "Four score and seven years ago our fathers brought forth upon this continent a new nation, conceived in Liberty, and dedicated to the proposition that all men are created equal. Now we are engaged in a great civil war, testing whether that nation, or any nation so conceived and so dedicated, can long endure. We are met on a great battle-field of that war. We have come to dedicate a portion of that field, as the final resting place of those who here gave their lives that that nation might live. It is altogether fitting and proper that we should do this period. …"

   —Abraham Lincoln, Gettysburg Address

   Lincoln's bias could be described as
   a. in favor of slavery.
   b. in favor of fighting a war to reunite the country.
   c. against both the Northern and Southern states.
   d. as opposed to any type of aggression.

   Discuss your choice with a partner. Which words keyed you into the author's bias?

2. "War is cruelty. There is no use trying to reform it. The crueler it is, the sooner it will be over."

   —General William Tecumseh Sherman

General Sherman's bias could be described as

a. anti-war.

b. in favor of fighting an aggressive war.

c. in favor of slavery.

d. against any effort to speed up the war.

Discuss your choice with a partner. Which words keyed you into the author's bias?

3. "The North Cannot subdue us. We are too determined to be free. They have no right to confiscate our property to pay debts they themselves have incurred. Death as a nation, rather than Union on such terms. We will have our rights secured on so firm a basis that it can never be shaken. If by power of overwhelming numbers they conquer us, it will be a barren victory over a desolate land."

—Sarah Morgan Dawson
Confederate Girl's Diary, p. 32

Sarah Morgan's bias could be described as

a. strongly pro-South.

b. in favor of a Northern victory.

c. against the war.

d. against slavery.

Discuss your choice with a partner. Which words keyed you into the author's bias?

4. "Multiply the above by scores, aye hundreds—verify it in all the forms that different circumstances, individuals, places, could afford—light it with every lurid passion, the wolf's, the lion's lapping thirst for blood—the passionate, boiling volcanoes of human revenge for comrades, brothers slain—with the light of burning farms, and heaps of smutting, smouldering black embers— and in the human heart everywhere black, worse embers—and you have an inkling of this war."

—Walt Whitman
Prose Works

Walt Whitman's bias could be described as

a. pro-war.

b. pro-Southern states.

c. very anti-war.

d. anti-business.

Discuss your choice with a partner. Which words keyed you into the author's bias?

5. "I expose slavery in this country, because to expose it is to kill it. Slavery is one of those monsters of darkness to whom the light of truth is death."

—Frederick Douglass

Frederick Douglass's bias could be described as

a. pro-slavery.

b. against the war.

c. anti-slavery.

d. in favor of the Southern states.

Discuss your choice with a partner. Which words keyed you into the author's bias?

LANDMARK IN THE FIELD OF U.S. HISTORY

The Digitization of Books

In the old days, libraries took great care in preserving rare books and documents. It was not easy to access these old documents. One had to go through huge archives and find a book that was out of print. With the digitization of rare documents, it is now possible for people to download, read, and save them rather easily.

In the absence of documents detailing how an ancient city was built thousands of years ago, it was extremely difficult for historians to revisit the city. Thanks to sophisticated architectural software, a city that was completely destroyed by a natural disaster can now be rebuilt electronically and maps showing streets and by lanes can be drawn.

Similarly, in the past, if a researcher wanted to obtain information about a particular individual, say Abraham Lincoln, s/he would have to go to a library and spend countless hours going through its stacks and archives. Digitization has made it possible to sift through enormous amounts of data and find information about an individual's birth and death, lineage, marriage, relatively quickly.

When Google, the world's most frequently used search engine, launched

Google Books, a repository of scanned and digitized books, researchers welcomed the revolutionary idea. Though some publishers were not pleased with this service, most students and scholars around the world embraced Google Books wholeheartedly.

Despite the fact that some publishers complained about copyright infringement and tried to block Google from digitizing their books, Google Books has survived their initial resistance and has become one of the most frequently visited digital libraries. As more and more scholars and researchers use Google Books, it has become one of the largest online resources of digitized knowledge, especially of unique books. For example, by March 2012 Google Books had digitized more than 20 million books, an astounding number.

Google says that it is far from done in terms of digitizing most of the rare books. In the year 2010, Google said that there were approximately 130 million rare books in the world, and that its goal was to digitize most, if not all, of them by the year 2020. It should be noted that while most of the digitized books can be downloaded for free, there is a small charge for some books.

Collaboration

Considering the Topic

Answer the following questions with a partner.

1. In what ways has the digitization of books and documents changed the way historians do research?

2. Many new technologies such as book digitization have to deal with copyright issues. What copyright concerns are involved with book digitization? What other new technologies infringe on copyright law?

3. Google Books promises to scan and digitize over 130 million books by 2020. Why do you think this company has invested so much time and so many resources carrying out this revolutionary project? What is in it for Google?

Internet Connection

Research another landmark in the field of U.S. history, and fill out the section below.

the women's rights movement	the Emancipation Proclamation
Ground Zero	Pearl Harbor
the printing press	Thomas Edison's inventions

Landmark: _____

Question	Answer
When did this landmark become a reality?	
Who was involved in developing this landmark?	
What made this landmark special?	
How did this landmark change the way people interact?	

Luxury Domestic Products Become "Necessities": Late Nineteenth Century Technologies

Preview Questions

1. Before the invention of Edison's phonograph, the only way people could listen to music was when it was played live. How do you think access to recorded music changed people's everyday lives? How has the technology of recorded music evolved since the birth of the phonograph?

2. It is hard to imagine that little more than 100 years ago, only the rich had access to ownership of their own bathtub. By what means did poorer members of society wash themselves at that point in history?

3. The late nineteenth century saw the growth of heavy marketing of consumer products through newspaper and magazine advertising. How often do you spend time reading product advertising? Do these ads influence your choice of purchases? Explain.

MyReadingLab™

⚙ **Complete** this **Exercise** at **myreadinglab.com**

Pre-Reading Vocabulary: Focus on Some Key Terms

Collaboration

Before beginning the reading selection, it may be helpful to focus on the meaning of some key words in the advertisements. Working with a partner, try to guess the meaning of these words. Then look up the words in a dictionary.

Word	Your Definition	Dictionary Definition
prevent		
boon		
amuse		
sanitary		
equipped		

Luxury Domestic Products Become "Necessities": Late Nineteenth Century Technologies

These two advertisements, for the Edison phonograph and for a bathtub, are examples of the growth of consumer-product advertising in the late nineteenth century. Businesses tried to persuade people that a wide array of products, previously considered luxuries, were now necessities. From this period forward, we begin to see companies making use of sophisticated psychological techniques to lure potential customers to the purchase of their goods.

An Edison Home Phonograph and a romantic couple are shown in an advertisement dated 1906.

Advertisement for Standard porcelain enameled baths and one-piece lavatories. Line engraving, English, 1905.

Reading Comprehension Check

1. Examine the Edison Phonograph advertisement. It can be inferred that the $10 price
   a. was a bargain.
   b. was a lot of money at the time (but cheaper than earlier models).
   c. was negotiable.
   d. did not include all the parts of the phonograph machine.

2. "To appreciate the marked superiority of Edison Phonographs and Gold Moulded Records hear them at your dealer's, free of charge." In this context, the word *superiority* means
   a. inferiority in quality.   c. cheaper quality.
   b. similarity in quality.   d. greater quality.

3. Examine the advertisement for the bathtub. What audience is this ad aimed at?
   a. families with children   c. single women
   b. single men   d. divorced men

4. In the bathtub ad, the text reads: "The complete equipment can be bought and installed at a very moderate cost." In this context, the word *moderate* means
   a. unreasonably expensive.   c. reasonable.
   b. extremely costly.   d. very cheap.

5. Both of these ads aim to reach a large audience by
   a. focusing on very wealthy clients.
   b. making the point that luxury goods can be affordable.
   c. appealing to the business class.
   d. focusing on regional tastes.

Exploring the Topic

Discuss the following questions to review the content of the advertisements you have just read.

Collaboration

1. Reviewing the bathtub ad, what do we do learn about the product from the line, "Your House is not Modern Without a Bathroom Equipped With "Standard" Ware"?

2. Reexamining the phonograph ad, what other products are being advertised? What are the benefits of including these other products in this ad?

3. Taking these two ads from the late nineteenth century as good examples of the time period, how has product marketing changed over time?

Post-Reading Vocabulary

Without using a dictionary, determine the meaning of the bolded words from the context.

1. "It is **sanitary** because its snowy surface is non-porous without crack or crevice for dirt to lodge." (bathtub ad.)

   Sanitary means _____

2. "From this period forward, we began to see companies making use of sophisticated psychological **techniques** to lure potential customers to the purchase of their goods."

   Techniques means _____

3. "From this period forward, we begin to see companies making use of sophisticated psychological techniques **to lure** potential customers to the purchase of their goods."

   To lure means _____

READING

Reading Selection **5**

Biographies

The Women's Century: Short Biographies of Influential Women of the 20th Century

Preview Questions

1. If someone asked you to name three of the most influential women of the past hundred years, who would come to mind? What is each of these women famous for?

2. Some historians would argue that one of the greatest changes that took place in the United States during the twentieth century involved the status of women. From your knowledge of history, what are some concrete examples of how life changed for women in America between 1900 and 2000?

3. Compare the opportunities women from your generation have with those your great-grandmother and grandmother had during their times. What has changed?

Collaboration

Pre-Reading Vocabulary: Focus on Some Key Terms

Before beginning the reading selection, it may be helpful to focus on the meaning of some key words in the biographies. Working with a partner, try to guess the meaning of these words. Then look up the words in a dictionary.

Word	*Your Definition*	*Dictionary Definition*
contribute		
dedication		
suffrage		
authoritative		
contaminate		

The Women's Century: Short Biographies of Influential Women of the 20th Century

From the National Women's History Project Web site

Some historians view the 20th century as the "Women's Century." At the beginning of the century, women did not have the right to vote and few had roles in public life. Most women lived their lives behind the scenes. Their options were limited, beyond raising children and serving their husbands. As the 20th century progressed, women's rights became a rallying call for the Women's Rights Movement. The role of women in American society changed dramatically.

The following short profiles of ten remarkable women offer a window into the gains women have made through the 20th century and moving into the 21st. There are countless other women, both famous and unknown, who have contributed to the rise of women in American society.

1. Jane Addams (1860–1935)

Social Worker

Addams founded Hull House in Chicago in 1889, America's first settlement house. Hull House provided English language classes, health education, and recreational programs for poor immigrant families. From 1919 until her death, Addams was president of the Women's International League for Peace and Freedom. She won the Nobel Peace Prize in 1931. Addams was the first American woman so honored. She was chosen for her dedication to the causes of peace and social justice.

2. Mary Anderson (1872–1964)

Labor Activist

Anderson had strong negotiating skills. Her success in defending working women won her a critical appointment. In 1920 she became the first director of the Women's Bureau in the U.S. Department of Labor. During her 24 years there, she played a major role in winning federal minimum wage and maximum hour laws for women. After retiring in 1944, Anderson continued to advocate on behalf of working women.

3. Mary McLeod Bethune (1875–1955)

Educator, Presidential Advisor

In 1904, Bethune opened a school for black girls in Daytona Beach. The school became Bethune-Cookman College in 1929. She was its president until 1942. In 1935, she founded the National Council of Negro Women and was its president until 1949. From 1936 to 1944, Bethune served as advisor to President Roosevelt on minority affairs. She was vice-president of the NAACP from 1940 to 1955. In 1945, she attended the organizing conference of the United Nations.

4. Jacqueline Cochran (1910–1980)

World-Renowned Pilot

Cochran started flying in 1932. She began competing in the Bendix Transcontinental Air Race in 1935. She won it in 1938. In 1941, she was a flight captain in the British Air Transport Auxiliary. Returning to America, she became the director of the Women's Air Force Service Pilots. In 1945, she was awarded the Distinguished Service Medal. In 1953, Cochran became the first woman to break the sound barrier. Cochran received more than 200 awards as a pilot.

5. Felisa Rincon (1897–1994)

Political Activist

Rincon began her political activism campaigning for women's suffrage in Puerto Rico. This was won in 1932. She joined the Popular Democratic Party and in 1938 was president of its San Juan committee. From 1946 to 1968, she was mayor of San Juan. In her open government, many schools, daycares, and health centers were built. She was on the National Committee of the U.S. Democratic Party. She served as a delegate to the national party conventions until 1992.

6. Alice Paul (1885–1977)

Suffragist, Founder of the Congressional Union

Paul was arrested six times and jailed three times for suffrage protests in England. She returned to the United States with radical ideas for the American movement. In 1913, she staged a huge parade in Washington, D.C. Four years later she organized pickets at the White House. Paul drafted the Equal Rights Amendment (ERA) in 1923. For over fifty years, she led the movement to have the ERA become part of the Constitution.

7. Marian Wright Edelman (1939–)

Children's Rights Advocate, Civil Rights Activist

From her earliest years, Edelman was encouraged to give hope and aid to others. She has served as a lawyer, civil rights activist, and founder of the Children's Defense Fund. She has always provided a strong authoritative voice for those who have been denied the power to speak for themselves. She has advocated for quality health care, nutritious food, and educational opportunities. For almost forty years, she has provided hope and possibility to countless numbers of people.

8. Sarah Buel (1953–)

Domestic Violence Activist, Attorney

Buel escaped domestic violence in her own life. Later she became an impassioned advocate for the legal rights of battered women and abused children. She set her goal to attend Harvard Law School so she could position herself to best defend and advocate for battered women and their children. She now runs a legal clinic for battered women. She is also co-founder and co-director of the National Training Center on Domestic and Sexual Violence.

9. Rachel Carson (1907–1964)

Biologist, Pioneer Environmentalist

Carson's research and writings awakened worldwide concern for our environment. In 1962, *Silent Spring* detailed the dangers of DDT and other pesticides. She warned that these chemicals contaminate humans, animals, and the entire "web of life." She wrote that "the central problem of our age has therefore become the contamination of [the] total environment." Her ideas were considered very controversial at the time. These ideas became the foundation of the modern environmental movement.

10. Amy Goodman (1957–)

Journalist

Goodman is a well-respected journalist for *Democracy Now*. She has interviewed leaders throughout the world about the pressing issues of war and peace. She has also focused on global warming and its related impact. In her coverage of these global stories, she has braved some of the most intense world crises. Her goal as a journalist is to inform her audience about the threats to the planet.

Items 1–10 adapted from the National Women's History Project Web site:
http://nwhp.org/resourcecenter/biographycenter.php

MyReadingLab™
Complete this **Exercise**
at **myreadinglab.com**

Reading Comprehension Check

1. What do the ten women profiled all have in common?
   a. They were born in California.
   b. They all served in Washington.
   c. They all worked directly for women's rights.
   d. They all made major contributions to society.

2. Review the profile of Jane Addams. Which of the following was NOT one of the services offered at Hull House?
   a. workshops on buying a home
   b. health education
   c. English language classes
   d. recreational programs

3. What can we infer from reading the profile of Mary McLeod Bethune?
   a. She was from a rich family.
   b. She held many leadership roles.
   c. She was a strong supporter of the U.S. military.
   d. She worked hard to gain the support of business leaders.

4. When we read sentences like, "She set her goal to attend Harvard Law School so she could position herself to best defend and advocate for battered women and their children" (Sarah Buel), or "she has braved some of the most intense world crises" (Amy Goodman), what do we learn about the author's bias?
   a. The author is very critical of these women.
   b. The author takes a neutral position toward these female figures.
   c. The author has a positive view of these women.
   d. There is not enough information on which to base an opinion.

5. In reading the profile of the journalist, Amy Goodman, we can draw the conclusion that
   a. she is someone who might run for political office.
   b. she is an advocate for the environment.
   c. she enjoys covering wars around the globe.
   d. she doubts the role of women in society.

Exploring the Topic

Collaboration

Discuss the following questions to review the content of the biographies you have just read.

1. What were some of the risks Alice Paul took in her life? Do you think it is worth taking such risks for the belief in a cause? Explain your view.

2. What do we learn about the relationship between Sarah Buel's personal and professional experience? Do you think it is wise to connect different parts of our lives as she has done? Explain.

3. All of the women profiled made a tremendous contribution to American society. Which of the ten, in your view, made the most lasting contribution? Justify your choice(s).

Post-Reading Vocabulary

Without using a dictionary, determine the meaning of the bolded words from the context.

1. "Anderson continued to advocate **on behalf of** working women." (Mary Anderson)

   On behalf of means _____

2. "For almost forty years, she has provided hope and possibility to **countless** numbers." (Marian Wright Edelman)

   Countless means _____

3. "Her ideas were considered very **controversial** at the time." (Rachel Carson)

   Controversial means _____

Panel Discussion on the Future: What Will Life Be Like in the Year 2100?

Collaboration

One of the advantages of studying history is that we can use our knowledge of the past to predict what will happen in the future.

You have been invited to a special meeting where you will be given a few minutes to share your vision of the future. Each member of the panel will be asked to focus on a specific topic area. To prepare for the panel discussion, first decide as a class who will speak about which topic area. Then, prepare some notes before the meeting and practice what you are going to say in advance.

Choose ONE topic focus from the list below:

1. The future of computer technology
2. The future of home entertainment and telecommunications
3. The changing role of women in the future
4. The future of transportation technology

5. The future of world peace

6. The future of the global economic situation

7. The future of the American employment situation

8. The future of race relations in America

9. The future of fashion

10. The future of everyday relationships (romantic/family/friendships)

Feel free to create more topics that are appropriate for the focus of the panel discussion.

WRITING CONNECTIONS: *Imagining the Future—A Short Essay*

You have just taken part in a panel discussion about life in the year 2100 and heard your classmates sharing their ideas on their chosen topic area. Now, while all of these ideas are floating around in your head, share your vision for the future in a short essay.

Choose THREE of the topics from the panel discussion list, and devote one paragraph to each. Include a short introduction before jumping into your three chosen topics.

To enrich your writing, remember:

- To use descriptive adjectives to make your writing more lively

- To include clear examples to illustrate each of your ideas

- To offer specific details to help explain each of your points

---

READING

Reading Selection **6**

Interview

MyReadingLab™
Complete this **Exercise**
at **myreadinglab.com**

Zelda Anderson, One of the First Black Women to Enter the U.S. Women's Army Auxiliary Corps (1942), Shares Her Story

Preview Questions

1. Until the time of the Korean War, the U.S. army was racially segregated. What do you think the rationale was behind this policy of segregation?

2. What changed to bring about the integration of the army?

3. In your opinion, what role should women play in the U.S. military? Should women serve in combat missions?

Pre-Reading Vocabulary: Focus on Some Key Terms

Before beginning the reading selection, it may be helpful to focus on the meaning of some key words in the interview. Working with a partner, try to guess the meaning of these words. Then look up the words in a dictionary.

Collaboration

Word	*Your Definition*	*Dictionary Definition*
segregate		
recruits		
rations		
demeaning		
chaos		

Zelda Anderson, One of the First Black Woman to Enter the U.S. Women's Army Auxiliary Corps (1942), Shares Her Story

By Zelda Anderson, ca. 1945

Zelda Anderson

Zelda Anderson (1921–2010) was one of the first black women to enter the military service in the Women's Army Auxiliary Corps (later renamed the Women's Army Corps, or WAC). Following her experience with the army, she went to graduate school and received her M.Ed. and her Ed.D. and worked in education. Anderson was interviewed by Victoria Ford for the University of Nevada Oral History Program in 1995.

1   I reported for duty in January 1942. Until then everything had been done over the phone and in writing, and it was only when I reported at the recruiting office in Baltimore that they saw that I was black. Because we had a segregated army back then they sent me home until March, when they had enough black recruits to make up an all-black unit.

2   They put me in charge of fifteen black WAACs [Women's Auxiliary Army Corps, later the Women's Army Corps] from Baltimore, and sent us to Fort Des Moines, Iowa. This was so exciting to me. We had black officers, and our basic training was the same as for men. They would simply tell us, "You wanted to be in a man's army, so now you've got to do what the men do." We learned military courtesy, history, how to shoot an M-1, go on bivouac, bathe in a teacup of water, eat hardtack rations.

3   Every evening troops of male soldiers would march by our barracks en route to the mess hall. I told the commanding officer that we would like to have some shades at the windows, "Oh, no. You wanted to be in the man's army. Fine you have to do what the men do."

4   I told all the girls, "Listen, they won't give us any shades. So I want you to get right in front of the windows buck naked." The next day we had shades at all the windows. [laughter]

5   They pulled me out of basic training the third week and sent me to officer training in Des Moines. All of the instructors were white, but white and black officers were being trained in the same facility, in the same classes, and we slept in the same barracks. After OCS [Officer's Candidate School] I was assigned to a laundry unit.

6   A black enlisted WAAC could either be in the laundry unit or she could be in the hospital unit. In the laundry unit, if she had a college degree she could work at the front counter, giving the laundry out and taking the laundry in. If she had less than that, then she did the laundry—very demeaning. And in the hospital unit they let her wash walls, empty basins, wash windows—all that menial work.

7   In the laundry unit we were constantly asking for promotions for our girls. The white troops were steadily being promoted, but they would tell us that all of the promotions were frozen. We learned that you can skip all that chain of command and go to the inspector general and action will be taken. Three of us officers asked the girls to cooperate with us. We took off our officer uniforms and went to work right beside them for two weeks. We told the girls, "If you have a backache, if you have a headache, if you have any kind of ache, go on sick call, because we want this to be part of our report." We had so many girls going on sick call!

8   We sent our report to the inspector general, and, as a result, they rewrote the rules about what women could do in the service: They could no longer lift over a certain number of pounds; they could no longer wash the windows. We couldn't do it by the book, because they weren't going to listen to us. We had to find another route, but we got it done.

9   I started applying for every opportunity to take additional training advertised on the bulletin board. Everywhere I went, a president quit. At Purdue University I took a course in personnel administration, and the president quit. At William and Mary College in Virginia, the president quit. I was sent to Washington and Lee University, to become a special service officer—the president quit. Schools had to agree that all trainees would stay in the same facilities, and I was the only black each time. It was unthinkable for a black person to walk up and down those "halls of ivy" without a broom in his hand. "Sleep in our beds? Oh, no!"

10   I was assigned to duty at Fort Breckenridge, Kentucky. The post commander's name was Colonel Throckmorton. In a pronounced southern accent he told me, "You're going over to that colored WAC company, and you're going to be the mess officer."

11   I said, "Sir, I have not had any mess training."

12   "All you nigras know how to cook."

13   I said, "You just met one who does not know how to cook; but if you send me to Fort Eustis, Virginia, for training I will come back and be the best mess officer you have on this post."

14   "I ain't sending you to no school, and you're going over there to be a mess officer." When I about-faced, I kept on going. I didn't even salute him.

15   In the days of slavery there was always a black slave who would shuffle up to the master and tell him anything that was going on among the blacks, an informant. Usually they had a handkerchief tied around their head for perspiration, so that's where the slang expression "handkerchief head" came from. This woman in our barracks was a handkerchief head. She told Colonel Throckmorton things about me … that I went out without my hat on, trivial things.

16   He said, "Now, I sent you over to that colored WAC company to be the mess officer, and I understand you don't even eat in there."

17   I said, "Well sir, if I didn't eat in there, where would I eat? I can't eat in Mess Number One because that's for white officers."

18   He pointed at me, and when he did that I grabbed his finger and said, "As long as you live, don't you ever point your finger in my face. I am an officer and a gentleman by the same act of Congress that commissioned you."

19   They finally decided to send some black WACs to Europe, and everybody was calling me from all over the country: "I see your name is on the list to go to Europe. I'll see you at Ft. McClellan." But I never got any orders. Finally I went to Colonel Throckmorton. I said, "All of these people are calling me saying my name is on a list to go overseas, but I have not received any orders."

20   Now he tells me the real truth: "We had your name taken off of the list to go overseas, because you wanted to show me that you can be the best mess officer on this post."

21   "I told you I would be the best mess officer you have on this post if you sent me to Fort Eustis, and I've been waiting on my orders," I said.

22   Instead, he made me the assistant to the post publications officer. But there was no post publication officer! I was the assistant to a nonexistent position to organize books of Army regulations. When the books come out, a train delivers them to a warehouse on the post; they simply dump them in the building. I had twelve WACs, two German prisoners of war (to kill the rats), and a white civilian fellow who the colonel had planted there to really be in charge. The first order I gave this young man, he said, "Uh-uh. Negroes don't talk like that to white folks."

23   So I said, "Well, darling, if you can't stand the heat, get out of the kitchen," and he left.

24   Our job was to make some order out of all of that chaos. I have a whole scrapbook of letters of commendation on the good job that I did there. We not only made order of the chaos, but I got every one of those girls a promotion to PFC [Private First Class] or corporal. Meanwhile, I'm still a second lieutenant. Oh, it took a new act of congress to get a promotion for me! [laughter]

25   Not too long after that, as the war was de-escalating, they closed Camp Breckenridge, and they sent me to Fort Knox. Lo and behold, that's where they had sent Colonel Throckmorton as post commander! When I went up to greet him, he said, "Now, Lieutenant, I think we understand each other, and so that there won't be any friction, I will make you the post special service officer. Your office will be right here in headquarters."

26   I groaned, "Oh, no!"

27   "This will be your secretary and your driver, and you will be assigned a station wagon."

28   My job was to act as a liaison between the big entertainers in the civilian world and the military, to bring them to the post to entertain the troops. Duke Ellington, Stan Kenton, Lena Horne, Earl Hines, Jimmy Lunsford, Cab Calloway, Count Basie—the legends. They put on good shows, and they were good for morale, because it was a release from this day-to-day, humdrum life of the military. I met their planes and found rooms for them, because they couldn't stay on the post or in the white hotels. They would stay at colored hotels or rooming houses or in the homes of private citizens. One of the places was a doctor's wife's home—the doctor had died, and she was living by herself in this three-bedroom house.

29   As a result of our relationship, the colonel would come to me for advice. One of the things that he wanted advice on was whether all officers, black and white, should use the same mess hall and theater. I told him that segregation has not allowed white

people to know black people. "We know you very intimately, but you don't know how we think, how we react, and so you just try to push your stuff on us, not giving a damn about how we feel about this. And then when we rebel, or you meet somebody like me who decides that you can't do this to me, then you think I'm cantankerous; you think I'm an agitator. I'm just trying to give you an education. All we want to know is that we can use these facilities." I said, "It's degrading to us to have gone through officer training school, and then we have to go to the enlisted men's club or the non-coms' [non-commissioned officers'] club if we want to have a drink with our friends."

30   I lived out the rest of my days very happy in the army. If I had succumbed to the treatment that they had given other blacks before and not spoken up for myself, my morale would have been down, and I would have been doing work that I did not like. In this life you've got to speak up for yourself.

Used by permission of the University of Nevada Oral History Program, University of Nevada, Reno.

MyReadingLab™
Complete this **Exercise**
at **myreadinglab.com**

Reading Comprehension Check

1. According to the introduction, how old was Ms. Anderson when she was interviewed?
   a. 21   b. 24   c. 74   d. 95

2. Why was the recruiting office in Baltimore unaware that Zelda was black?
   a. She was very light-skinned.
   b. She had only communicated with them by phone and in writing.
   c. She had lied to the office in her letter.
   d. At that point in time, the Army did not care about the racial profile of new recruits.

3. What assignment options did a black female army recruit have in Zelda's time?
   a. to clean dishes or to do combat duty
   b. to manufacture weapons
   c. to work in the laundry room or in a hospital unit
   d. to work in the laundry room or to fly fighter planes

4. It is implied that the reason college presidents kept quitting each time Zelda took a training position was
   a. they didn't want to work with someone black.
   b. these were men who were probably recruited by the army.
   c. it was just a coincidence each time and bad luck for Zelda.
   d. we do not have enough information to answer this question.

5. What action prompted Zelda to tell off the white army officer?
   a. He asked her to wear a handkerchief.
   b. He commanded her to work in a mess hall.
   c. He tried to remove her from the U.S. Army.
   d. He pointed his finger at her.

6. What life lesson did Zelda learn from her experience in the military?
   a. Women can do anything a man can do.
   b. Segregation sometimes makes sense.
   c. You have to speak up for yourself.
   d. Power is held by those who seize power.

Exploring the Topic

Collaboration

Discuss the following questions to review the content of the interview you have just read.

1. What types of strategies did Zelda use when she faced cases of discrimination in the military?

2. How did Zelda react when the colonel asked her advice about desegregating the mess hall and theater?

3. During the interview, Zelda discusses the expression "handkerchief head." (para. 15) What does it mean? Why do you think this expression has disappeared from the language?

Post-Reading Vocabulary

Without using a dictionary, determine the meaning of the bolded words from the context.

1. "And in the hospital unit they let her wash walls, empty basins, wash windows—all that **menial** work." (para. 6)

   Menial means _____

2. "I am an officer and a gentleman by the same act of Congress that **commissioned** you." (para. 18)

   Commissioned means _____

3. "I have a whole scrapbook of letters of **commendation** on the good job that I did there." (para. 24)

   Commendation means _____

Interview with Historians Peter H. Wood and Elaine Tyler May   **TEXTBOOK APPLICATION**

The purpose of this exercise is to get you acquainted with the type of reading you will be required to do in college. First, listen to the lecture and take notes. You can listen to the lecture by scanning the QR code on the next page with your smart phone. Your professor may also read the selection or play the audio file in class. Make sure that you write down the important points of the lecture.

Group Discussion

Collaboration

Working in small groups of three to four students, answer the following questions. Your instructor may ask you to share your answers with your classmates. As you refer to your notes, it is best to write brief answers to each of the questions below using your own words. After the discussion, you will have an opportunity to share your findings with your peers.

1. What does the historian say about the idea of equality in America?
2. In your opinion, are all people "created equal"? Explain.

3. According to the historian, what is the "deepest American theme"?

4. What is the central idea in the quotation from Thomas Paine?

5. According to the historian, who has made change throughout American history?

6. The historian says that it is important to study American history in a truly global context. What does this mean? Do you agree? Why or why not?

7. What was the most interesting idea discussed in this short lecture?

Now that you have discussed the highlights of the lecture with your classmates, read the following selection and answer the multiple-choice questions that follow.

Interview with Historians Peter H. Wood and Elaine Tyler May

Scan this code using your smart phone to listen to an audio version of this reading

The following excerpt is from interviews with historians Peter H. Wood and Elaine Tyler May, two of the authors of a U.S. history textbook entitled Created Equal.

1   We all recognize the phrase "created equal" from the Declaration of Independence, but we rarely ponder it. For me it represents an affirmation of humanity, the family of mankind. But it also raises the deepest American theme: the endless struggles over defining whose equality will be recognized. I suppose you could say that there is equality in birth and death, but a great deal of inequality in between. Many of those inequities—and their partial removal—drive the story of American history.

2   Tom Paine understood this in 1776 when he published *Common Sense*. Months before the Declaration of Independence appeared, Paine put it this way: "Mankind being originally equal in the order of creation, the equality could only be destroyed by some subsequent circumstance."

3   *Created Equal* brings together aspects of the nation's story that are usually examined separately. It demonstrates that the people who make change are not only those in major positions of power; they are also ordinary Americans from all backgrounds. We illuminate ways that diverse Americans have seized opportunities to improve their lives and their nation. We also address the ongoing interaction between the United States and the rest of the world, examining the nation in a truly global context.

4   We started with an understanding that the North American land itself is a major player in the story—the environment, the different regions, and the ways in which people, businesses, public policy and the forces of nature have shaped it. Our emphasis on the process of globalization over time helps to broaden that perspective. As American citizens inhabiting a shrinking planet, we are all learning to think harder than ever about complex links between the local and the global—past, present and future.

from Jones et al., *Created Equal: A History of the United States*, Brief Ed., Vol. 1, 3e

Reading Comprehension Check

1. What is the authors' purpose in this reading?
   a. to persuade readers that American history is similar to European history
   b. to frighten readers away from studying American history
   c. to entertain readers with humorous stories from U.S. history classes
   d. to inform readers about some of the themes in their history textbook

2. "I suppose you could say that there is equality in birth and death, but a great deal of inequality in between." (para. 1) From this statement, we might say
   a. the authors take a neutral tone.
   b. the authors' bias is against societal inequality.
   c. the authors are biased in favor of social inequality.
   d. the authors are biased against death.

3. One of the historians states: "… the people who make change are not only those in major positions of power; they are also ordinary Americans from all backgrounds." (para. 3) The above is a
   a. statement of opinion.   c. both fact and opinion.
   b. statement of fact.   d. lie.

4. One of the writers argues that because we inhabit a "shrinking planet," (para. 4) we need to
   a. look at history more globally.   c. study American history every day.
   b. combat other cultures.   d. dig our heels in the sand.

5. "We illuminate ways that diverse Americans have seized opportunities to improve their lives and their nation." (para. 3) The word *illuminate* could be replaced with the term
   a. build a fire.   c. make clear.
   b. argue against.   d. discuss.

6. According to the writers, one of the major players in America's story is
   a. family relationships.   c. business.
   b. psychology.   d. the land.

7. "Our **emphasis** on the process of globalization over time helps to broaden that perspective" (para. 4). A synonym for the word *emphasis*, as used in this context, is
   a. excitement.   c. focus.
   b. anger.   d. limitation.

8. We can infer from the reading that
   a. American history should be studied in isolation from world history.
   b. these historians do not believe in true equality.
   c. both of the historians are interested in sharing the stories of ordinary Americans, and not just of the powerful.
   d. the historians have a pessimistic view of U.S. history.

9. What is the topic of the reading?
   a. history   c. the North American land
   b. key themes in American history d. equality

INTERNET FACT SEARCH

U.S. History

Instructions: First try to use logic and background knowledge in guessing the correct answers to the following data questions. Then, go online and search for the relevant data. Be sure to write the Web source next to your research finding.

1. In the history of the United States, which war saw the highest number of U.S. casualties?

   a. World War I   c. the Vietnam War
   b. the Civil War   d. World War II

   Your guess: _____   Research finding: _____

   Web source: _____

2. Which decade had the highest level of immigration to the United States?

   a. 1990–2000   c. 1790–1800
   b. 1900–1910   d. 1920–1930

   Your guess: _____   Research finding: _____

   Web source: _____

3. In what year did women get the right to vote in the United States?

   a. 1901   c. 1970
   b. 1850   d. 1920

   Your guess: _____   Research finding: _____

   Web source: _____

4. Which American president served the longest term in the White House?

   a. George Washington   c. Franklin Roosevelt
   b. Abraham Lincoln   d. Andrew Jackson

   Your guess: _____   Research finding: _____

   Web source: _____

5. When did the practice of slavery officially end in the United States?

   a. 1943   c. 1863
   b. 1910   d. 1776

   Your guess: _____   Research finding: _____

   Web source: _____

FORMAL PRESENTATION PROJECTS

You will be given the opportunity to present on a topic of your interest pertinent to one of the text's chapter disciplines. Topics could relate to one of the questions you checked off in the "Follow Your Interests" section at the beginning of the chapter. Your instructor may ask you to browse through the chapters to guide you toward a given discipline focus.

MyReadingLab™   For more help with **Active Reading** and **Recognizing Bias**, go to your learning path in **MyReadingLab.com**.

TRAVEL AND TOURISM

10

"Travel makes a wise man better, but a fool worse."
—American proverb

Learning Objectives

IN THIS CHAPTER, YOU WILL LEARN TO . . .

1 Describe the discipline of tourism

2 Identify key terms pertinent to the field of tourism

3 Sharpen your memory skills

4 Choose academic courses

5 Recognize question types within a combined-skills reading test

INTRODUCTION TO THE DISCIPLINE OF TRAVEL AND TOURISM

1 LEARNING OBJECTIVE
Describe the discipline of tourism

Travel and tourism is a vibrant field, which opens up the world to those who step inside. Whether one is a tour guide, runs a travel agency, works on business travel tours, or acts as an interpreter for foreign tourists, a career in travel and tourism offers you the opportunity to interact with travelers, providing them with the quality services that will make their travel experiences special.

In this chapter, you will read about the mishaps of a tour operator in Alaska. You will travel to Antarctica and consider the perils of ecotourism. The chapter will also focus on the importance of properly marketing tourist destinations, and we will visit some Mayan sites as we read about how government involvement can help with tourism planning. We will consider the challenges of managing tourism in such crowded places.

Reading into a Photo

Working in a small group, examine the following photograph and answer the questions that follow.

1. In your opinion, what brought this man to the lake?
2. What message does this image convey to you about tourism?

Follow Your Interests

Collaboration

Review the set of questions below that travel and tourism experts might explore. Check off the three or four questions that are most interesting to you.

1. The chapter begins with an American proverb, "Travel makes a wise man better, but a fool worse." What does the proverb seem to imply?

2. What tourist sites would you recommend to someone visiting your area? Are there any destinations that you would not recommend? Explain why.

3. If you received a $5,000 travel voucher that was valid for only one week, where would you go and why? Be specific.

4. Imagine you are a travel agent. What age group–specific activities would you recommend to your clients? Think of young children, adults, and elderly people.

5. Why do you think people go on vacation in the first place? In other words, what are the motivating factors that lead someone to go on a trip?

6. Why is it that when most people think of vacation, they tend to choose a beach destination such as Honolulu, Acapulco, or Rio de Janeiro?

7. What would motivate a tourist to avoid the ever-popular beach destinations and choose another vacation option? For example, why would a tourist not go to South Beach in Florida in favor of another destination?

8. What are the most effective ways to market a tourist destination? What sources of media appeal to a tourist who might be choosing between a number of tourist locations?

9. Fifty years ago, how do you think tourists found out about travel options? In what ways was organizing a vacation more difficult than it is today?

10. Nowadays people are always thinking about saving money. What advice would you give a tourist who is on a tight budget?

11. Ecotourism, which involves responsible travel to natural areas without hurting the environment, is gaining in popularity. Can you explain this increased interest in ecotourism? Would you personally get involved in promoting ecotourism? Why or why not?

12. Approximately 20% of Americans have a valid passport. Most Americans choose domestic travel destinations over international travel. Can you explain this phenomenon?

13. When Americans do travel abroad, they tend to choose European destinations such as Paris, London, and Rome and avoid non-European countries. Discuss the reason for this cultural preference.

14. A famous Persian philosopher once wrote, "Much travel is needed before the raw one is ripened." Explain.

Now, share your choices with a small group of classmates and discuss why these particular questions are most interesting to you. You may wish to discuss these questions with them and ask which questions they found interesting.

LEARNING OBJECTIVE
Identify key terms
pertinent to the field
of tourism

Key Terms in the Field of Travel and Tourism

The following key terms are frequently used in the discipline of tourism. If you take a college-level course in tourism, it will be important for you to remember these words and to use them in your speech and writing. Review the words below and answer the multiple-choice questions that follow.

attractions	hospitality	revenue
conservation	heritage	safari
convention	package	sanctuary
demographics	pilgrimage	sustainable
domestic	promotional	time-share

EXERCISE 1   Inferring Meaning from Context

Read each sentence below and try to derive the meaning of the italicized key terms from the context. Circle the correct definition of each italicized term.

1. California has major *attractions* such as Universal Studios and Disneyland that draw tourists from all over the world.
   a. magnets
   b. landscapes
   c. tourist traps
   d. places that provide pleasure

2. Most U.S. cities have a *convention* center where meetings and events are held.
   a. a meeting of representatives of a church, political party, or organization
   b. rules of behavior in a big city
   c. large building which is very convenient to use
   d. a nunnery

3. As people from many parts of the world buy homes in Florida, the state is adapting to the area's *demographics* by offering tour guides who speak in different languages.
   a. exchanging foreign currencies
   b. the statistical data of a population
   c. the languages people speak
   d. multilingual tour guides

4. A recent surge in tourism to Alaska has been good for the *hospitality* industry.
   a. a factory where clothes for tourists are made
   b. providing free shuttles to the pilots of major airlines.
   c. receiving and treating guests in a warm and friendly way
   d. offering free food to tourists at the airport

5. Millions of adults say that they plan vacations around *heritage* activities.
   a. something that belongs to one by birth
   b. any property that one purchases anywhere
   c. a piece of land that an architect buys
   d. something that is given to someone as a gift

6. When tourists visit a particular site in large numbers, they generate *revenue* for the state.
   a. tourism-related expenses
   b. the costs of renovating a site
   c. returning tourists
   d. income

7. The famous hummingbird *sanctuary* in Costa Rica draws tourists from many parts of the world.
   a. a farm where salmon is raised for food purposes
   b. a protected place where animals can breed without interference
   c. a factory where stuffed animals, especially birds, are made
   d. a huge place where animals are slaughtered for consumption

8. The *conservation* of historic sites such as old castles and museums is important for the tourism industry.
   a. demolition
   b. building
   c. depletion of old buildings
   d. restoration and preservation

9. In their old age, some people like to go on a religious *pilgrimage*.
   a. a long flight to a beach destination
   b. a long journey made to a rock concert
   c. a long journey made to a holy place
   d. a short trip to a circus

10. Travel search engines such as Expedia and Orbitz offer *package* deals to tourists, giving them huge discounts on flight, hotel, and rental car reservations.
   a. free Internet access
   b. one price for several items
   c. discounts for pets
   d. different rates for foreigners

11. Kenya is one of the most popular destinations for *safari* vacations, offering tourists scenic beauty and abundant wildlife.
   a. a visit to an African mosque
   b. a train ride to a hill station
   c. a journey for hunting and viewing wildlife
   d. a guided tour of a central library

12. A growth in tourism is not *sustainable* if a government does not promote its places of tourist attractions through advertising and marketing.
   a. able to be maintained
   b. easy to discontinue
   c. profitable
   d. competitive

13. Peter Chen and his friends bought a condominium in Hawaii, and they *time-share* at different times of the year.
   a. take turns going on vacation
   b. go on a guided tour with friends and family
   c. make hotel reservations for close friends
   d. use a residence for a specified time each year

14. Hotels often offer tourists a *promotional* incentive such as a free night's stay or complimentary breakfast to compete with other businesses.
    a. something designed to discourage tourists
    b. something offered to advertise a product or service
    c. something excluded to discontinue a product or service
    d. something planned to reduce the flow of tourists

15. Many American tourists prefer to take *domestic* vacations, traveling to attractions like the Grand Canyon and Yosemite.
    a. relating to one's country of origin
    b. relating to a foreign country
    c. relating to one's house
    d. relating to the kitchen

Collaboration

EXERCISE **2**   Creating Meaningful Sentences with the Key Terms

Working with a partner, choose five of the key terms in travel and tourism and write an original sentence about each one.

1. Word = _____

_____

_____

2. Word = _____

_____

_____

3. Word = _____

_____

_____

4. Word = _____

_____

_____

5. Word = _____

_____

_____

COLLEGE STUDY SKILLS
Sharpening Your Memory

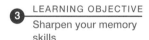

LEARNING OBJECTIVE
3
Sharpen your memory skills

As a college student, you will need to remember many things. For example, you have to be mindful of the deadlines for different assignments. You also will have to keep in mind when a certain professor wants to meet with you to go over your research paper. If you have a good memory, you will go a long way in your academic career. If you tend to forget important deadlines and assignments, your college experience can be unpleasant. Sharpening your memory while you are in college will help you succeed as a student.

Psychologists suggest many effective ways to improve one's memory. One of them is to keep learning new information, which will cause your brain to adapt, change, and develop new neural pathways. Since you are already in college taking new courses every semester, this is an easy task for you. As you learn new information and work to retain it, you will notice an improvement in your memory. Taking notes while you listen to a professor's lecture and going over them at home is an effective strategy for doing this.

It is important to note that both short- and long-term memory are involved in learning, integrating, and analyzing information. Memory is strengthened and maintained through use.

There are three stages your brain goes through when it receives new information:

1. **Sensory memory:** Information we receive from our senses is stored for only a few seconds in this first stage of memory. Information we attend to passes into short-term memory.

2. **Short-term memory:** In this stage of memory, we remember what we are paying attention to or are currently thinking about for approximately 20–30 seconds. The average person can hold seven items in this stage of memory. Attending to specific information leads to it being stored in our long-term memory.

3. **Long-term memory:** It is believed that information stored in long-term memory is organized into clusters of related information, which is what allows us to remember and retrieve specific details when needed.

Strategies for Improving Your Memory

Here are some strategies you can use to sharpen your memory in a short period of time. If you use these strategies, you will be surprised by the improvement in your memory.

1. **Take a new route to your classroom.** This may seem simple or even comical to you, but reaching the same destination using a different route every week will increase your memory tremendously.

2. **Learn something new every week.** This strategy is probably the easiest to use. You are already in the classroom exposed to new ideas. Just try to store new information in an organized way, as it will sharpen your memory.

3. **Read a chapter, a short story, or an essay out loud.** Your parents or friends may find it annoying, but do not worry about them. Reading out loud can help you listen and learn at the same time.

4. **Learn no more than seven things at one time.** Remember that you cannot store more than seven items in your short-term memory. Practice making lists and categories with only seven items. You will slowly become expert at organizing information with a great deal of accuracy.

5. **Teach your peers what you have learned.** Research shows that students learn new information by teaching it to their classmates. Speak to your professor about leading class discussions. Teaching information you have internalized to your peers will sharpen your memory.

6. **Exercise regularly.** When you exercise, more blood flows to your brain. This will make you sharper and more attentive. As a result, you will be able to retrieve information more easily.

7. **Eat fresh, natural foods.** Your tight schedule may make it difficult for you to eat fresh foods. However, eating healthy, fresh foods loaded with antioxidants will give your brain the adequate nutrition it needs to function properly.

Putting the Skill into Action

As you know, practice makes perfect. If you are enrolled in a reading course, read an essay or a reading selection carefully. Then close your book and eyes, and try to recall some of the key ideas. In fact, it is not a bad idea to take mental notes and prepare an outline in your mind. Then open your eyes and write the outline in your notebook. When in doubt, you can always refer back to your book and check your outline for missing information. The more you practice sharpening your memory, the more you will be able to retain information when you need it with ease and success. Remember to use most of the above-mentioned strategies every day in college.

The Last Word

Using all of these strategies may seem a bit daunting to you, but they are not as difficult as they seem. Since you are already a college student, you are likely to be bombarded with new information in most of your classes. All you have to do is store that new information in an organized way. You may use as many strategies as you need to sharpen your memory. It is only a matter of time and practice before you can retrieve information easily. The great American football coach Vince Lombardi once said, "The only place where success comes before work is in the dictionary." So, work hard on improving your memory, and you will succeed in college.

READINESS FOR COLLEGE SUCCESS
Choosing Your Classes for Next Semester

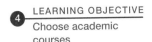

LEARNING OBJECTIVE
4 Choose academic courses

Now that you have started your academic journey, you know how important it is to balance your current course load with your plans for the upcoming semester. It is critical to see an advisor early to make plans for the coming semester in order to avoid a last-minute rush. You do not want to learn that the chemistry course you need to fulfill a science requirement is full or only has sections available at times when you have to work.

Collaboration

Task: With a classmate, read through the list of ways to best prepare for the coming semester on page 427 and discuss how you would accomplish each task. Then take time to each draw up your own to-do list to ensure you meet your course requirements and balance your school, work, and family responsibilities.

How Best to Prepare for the Coming Semester

1. Seek early advisement so as to beat the registration rush.

2. Print out a copy of your college transcript and study it carefully.

3. If you have not declared a major, review the list of required courses you still need to take to satisfy your liberal arts degree.

4. If you have declared your major, carefully review the list of required courses you still need to take.

5. Think about your out-of-class, work, and family responsibilities in determining your course load. Do not try to bite off more than you can chew!

6. In organizing your course load, try to balance very demanding courses (such as Organic Chemistry 301) with lighter courses (such as Volleyball 1).

7. Make room in your schedule for any courses you are currently taking that you may need to repeat, due to the possibility of receiving a very low grade or failing the course.

8. Using Microsoft Word, create a schedule of a typical week, filling in time slots where you are unable to attend classes due to work and family responsibilities. Your advisement office may offer a schedule grid for you to work with.

9. In choosing your class sections, think about the times of the day when your mind is most focused. Some students work well in the early morning; others are at their best later on in the day.

10. Try to avoid big gaps in your daily course schedule. If you register for an 8 AM course, it may be wise to look for a second course that runs just after at 10 AM.

Dispatch, Alaska: Tour Leaders' Enthusiasm Shines Through

Reading Selection **1**

Web Article

Preview Questions

1. What kinds of seasonal summer jobs are available to college students?

2. What skills are needed to be an effective tour guide? Explain.

3. Think about your own skills set. Do you think you would make a quality tour guide? Why or why not?

MyReadingLab™
Complete this **Exercise**
at **myreadinglab.com**

Collaboration

Pre-Reading Vocabulary: Focus on Some Key Terms

Before beginning the reading selection, it may be helpful to focus on the meaning of some key words in the article. Working with a partner, try to guess the meaning of these words. Then look up the words in a dictionary

Word	Your Definition	Dictionary Definition
embark		
contagious		
mediocre		
genuinely		
raved		

Dispatch, Alaska: Tour Leaders' Enthusiasm Shines Through

By Johanna Jainchill

Cruise Editor Johanna Jainchill has embarked on a land-cruise tour of Alaska and the Yukon territory. She will be filing dispatches detailing her adventures there.

1   Dispatch 2, Whitehorse, Yukon: I am constantly amazed at the ability of the tour director and driver/guides on this trip to remain so cheerful, so positive and so excited by every curve on this very long road. So who are these young men and women, who for one week become the faces of a once-in-a-lifetime vacation?

2   Rachel Wright, 22, our group's tour director, is a recent college graduate from Mississippi spending her second season in Alaska with Holland America. As a tour director, she basically does everything except drive the bus. If there's a problem, it's her problem. If you need something, she gets it for you. And no matter how obnoxious someone is acting, she smiles. "You have to," said Wright. "You'd go crazy if you didn't."

3   Her colleagues agreed.

4   Pat Whaley, 24, our bus' current driver/guide (the tour directors stay on an entire tour, while driver/guides change), and Justin Jasperson, 27, the driver/guide on the bus behind us, are responsible for being tour guides while driving motor coaches over very long stretches of road. They learned quickly that their outlook is contagious. "There is no room for a mediocre attitude," said Jasperson (far right in photo, with Wright and Whaley). "People paid to have a good time. A lot of that falls on you and your attitude."

5   It helps that these three staffers love what they do and genuinely want their groups to have a good time.

"It's Alaska. Some people have been waiting 73 years to make this trip," Whaley said. "We get to make it happen for them. It's so rewarding."

6   Alaska's summer workforce swells with staffers who take seasonal jobs in tourism. Wright drove nine hours for her interview with Holland America two years ago. Jasperson was recruited at college in his native Utah, where he studies aviation science. Whaley knew someone that knew someone, and the job was a fit for his degree in recreation and leisure services.

7   All three appreciate experiencing Alaska while they are working, something that comes through in their narratives, such as the story of the Chilkoot Trail (the treacherous, 33-mile trail that stampeders used to travel from Skagway to the Klondike goldfields during the gold rush) or in their enthusiasm about a certain view from the road.

8   I've heard very few complaints on this tour, and they have mostly been about the food. The group has only raved about the staff. "People are OK with whatever happens as long as you warn them about it," said Wright. "This is Alaska, so we tell people right away that we run on 'ish time,' as in we leave at seven-ish. And they understand."

9   Whaley agreed and repeated one of the jokes he tells every motorcoach group to prepare them for the rutted Alaska and Yukon roads. "The road will be bumpy," he said. "It's not my fault. It's not your fault. It's the asphalt."

"Dispatch, Alaska: Tour Leaders' Enthusiasm Shines Through," by Johanna Jainchill. *Travel Weekly*, June 3, 2008. Reprinted by permission of the YGS Group.

Reading Comprehension Check

1. Why does the writer describe Rachel Wright's work in the following manner, "As a tour director, she basically does everything except drive the bus"? (para. 2)
    a. Rachel doesn't have a driver's license.
    b. Rachel handles nearly all the tour operator responsibilities.
    c. Rachel is a volunteer.
    d. The writer doesn't have enough information.

2. What is the topic of the article?
    a. travel
    b. a writer taking a job as a tour guide
    c. Alaska
    d. tour guides' experience in Alaska

3. What is the author's tone?
    a. very serious
    b. light and optimistic
    c. pessimistic
    d. frightened

4. It can be inferred from the reading that
    a. these tour guides have no time for fun.
    b. Alaska is very hot in the summer.
    c. each of the tour guides has a sense of adventure.
    d. the cost of a plane ticket to Alaska is expensive.

5. What is Pat Whaley's point in the last sentence of the article?
    a. Alaska has some tough terrain and does not always offer full comfort.
    b. A tour guide is responsible to make sure all of her/his clients are comfortable.
    c. The roads in Alaska are very well paved.
    d. Some tourists like to blame each other for rough conditions.

Collaboration

Exploring the Topic

Discuss the following questions to review the content of the story you have just read.

1. Each of the tour guides made a choice to embark on this Alaska adventure? What do you think are the pluses and minuses of being a summer tour guide in Alaska?

2. One of the tour guides says, "This is Alaska, so we tell people right away that we run on 'ish time.'" (para. 8) What do they mean by "ish time"? In your part of the country, do some people run on "ish" time? Explain.

3. The writer is keeping a blog/dispatch about her travels? What would motivate someone to share a daily account of their travel adventures?

Post-Reading Vocabulary

Without using a dictionary, determine the meaning of the bolded words from the context.

1. "They learned quickly that their **outlook** is contagious." (para. 4)

   Outlook means _____

2. "Alaska's summer workforce **swells** with staffers who take seasonal jobs in tourism." (para. 6)

   Swells means _____

3. "Whaley agreed and repeated one of the jokes he tells every motorcoach group to prepare them for the **rutted** Alaska and Yukon roads." (para. 9)

   Rutted means _____

Reading Selection 2

Article

MyReadingLab™
Complete this **Exercise**
at **myreadinglab.com**

How Ecotourism Is Destroying Antarctica

Preview Questions

1. Ecotourism began because of a concern about the impact of tourists on natural resources such as a waterfall or a canyon. What negative impacts might a tourist have on the environment? Think of specific examples as you answer the question.

2. When you go on a trip to see unspoiled natural resources, what do you do to have a minimal impact on the environment? How do you think your actions as a tourist may harm the natural resources? Be specific.

3. Antarctica, the continent surrounding the South Pole, is uninhabited by humans. Some people think that we must preserve Antarctica's natural beauty by not allowing tourists to visit the continent. Others believe that there is nothing wrong in letting tourists visit Antarctica. Which of the views do you agree with and why? Explain.

Pre-Reading Vocabulary: Focus on Some Key Terms

Collaboration

Before beginning the reading selection, it may be helpful to focus on the meaning of some key words in the article. Working with a partner, try to guess the meaning of these words. Then look up the words in a dictionary

Word	Your Definition	Dictionary Definition
inevitable		
unspoiled		
vulnerable		
pollute		
invasive		

How Ecotourism Is Destroying Antarctica

By Andy Stone

1   Problems were inevitable for Antarctic tourism from the start. Seen by many as the last unspoiled landmass on earth, the unique and vulnerable ecosystem is

what attracts people to our southernmost continent. How do we handle tourism to a place whose only appeal to most of us is its lack of large-scale human contact? Doesn't that defeat the purpose?

2   Dutch researchers have thought the same thing, and believe they have a solution: limit and then auction off visiting rights to Antarctica.

Gentoo penguin rookery with cruise ship in background

3   In some ways, their logic is sound. Tourist limits are needed; not only for future tourism to work, but for the Antarctic's own sake. People pollute, disturb the animals and carry eggs, spores, rodents and other living matter that can spread. Even those few thousand trained scientists have unwittingly brought in numerous invasive species—what can we expect from tens or perhaps hundreds of thousands of possibly ignorant tourists? And as more and more tourists and companies line up to get in, they will only be harder to monitor.

4   At the same time, their plan does give an unfair advantage to the super-rich. While far from cheap today, at least now everyone theoretically has an equal chance of getting to Antarctica. But people with way too much money and no concept of its value are the bane of less fortunate auction goers everywhere—haven't these researchers ever used eBay or seen how much Picassos sell for? If the auctions were well publicized, which these would be, the final price tags

Tourists photographing Gentoo penguins

could be well out of reach for all but the very well-to-do. Is that fair? No. But this is a tricky proposition as reducing supply inevitably means higher cost. Ticket prices will be high no matter what they do.

5   If scientists get their way, there will be limits placed on the number of people who can visit Antarctica and the days they can go. This particular solution is better than nothing, but hopefully the final plan will have everyone in mind.

Environmental Graffiti Ltd. Reprinted by permission.

Reading Comprehension Check

MyReadingLab™
Complete this **Exercise**
at **myreadinglab.com**

1. The author's main idea is that
    a. Dutch researchers do not have an effective plan to preserve Antarctica.
    b. ecotourism is gradually damaging Antarctica's many natural resources.
    c. ecotourism in Antarctica is an excellent way to preserve its unspoiled natural resources.
    d. it is better if only the "super-rich" are allowed to be ecotourists.

2. "How do we handle tourism to a place whose only appeal to most of us is its lack of large-scale human contact? Doesn't that defeat the purpose? Dutch researchers have thought the same thing, and believe they have a solution; limit and then auction off visiting rights to Antarctica." (para. 1 and 2) What is the overall pattern of organization?
    a. classification
    b. compare and contrast
    c. cause and effect
    d. definition and example

3. Which of the following sentences is a statement of opinion?
    a. "People pollute, disturb the animals and carry eggs, spores, rodents and other living matter that can spread."
    b. "Dutch researchers have thought the same thing, and believe they have a solution: limit and then auction off visiting rights to Antarctica."
    c. "Ticket prices will be high no matter what they do."
    d. "Even those few thousand trained scientists have unwittingly brought in numerous invasive species."

4. "Tourist limits are needed; not only for future tourism to work, but for the Antarctic's own sake. People pollute, disturb the animals and carry eggs, spores, rodents and other living matter that can spread." (para. 3) For this passage, the author uses the overall pattern of organization that
    a. shows tourism to Antarctica in a chronological order.
    b. defines the term *ecotourism* and gives appropriate examples.
    c. contrasts Antarctica with the tourists.
    d. tells how the tourists are and will affect Antarctica's natural resources.

5. "At the same time, their plan does give an unfair advantage to the super-rich. While far from cheap today, at least now everyone theoretically has an equal chance of getting to Antarctica. But people with way too much money and no concept of its value are the bane of less fortunate auction goers everywhere—haven't these researchers ever used eBay or seen how much Picassos sell for? If the auctions were well publicized, which these would be, the final price tags could be well out of reach for all but the very well-to-do." (para. 4) What is the overall pattern of organization?

    a. compare and contrast
    b. chronological order
    c. listing
    d. classification

Collaboration

Exploring the Topic

Discuss the following questions to review the content of the essay you have just read.

1. The article begins with the statement, "Problems were inevitable for Antarctic tourism from the start." (para. 1) What problems does the author refer to, and why do you think they were inevitable?

2. Dutch researchers have proposed a solution to the problems of handling tourism in Antarctica. Do you agree with the proposal? Why or why not?

3. Why does the author believe that the Dutch researchers' plan gives an unfair advantage to the "super-rich"? (para. 4) Explain.

Post-Reading Vocabulary

Without using a dictionary, determine the meaning of the bolded words from the context.

1. "Even those few thousand trained scientists have **unwittingly** brought in numerous invasive species." (para. 3)

    Unwittingly means _____

2. "And as more and more tourists and companies line up to get in, they will only be harder to **monitor**." (para. 3)

    Monitor means _____

3. "But people with way too much money and no concept of its value are the **bane** of less fortunate auction goers everywhere." (para. 4)

    Bane means _____

Dominic Jaramillo

California State Polytechnic University, Pomona

1. How did you find your path to majoring in hospitality management?

I started in culinary school in 2005. While studying there I was made aware of the fact that you could actually get a recognized bachelor's degree in hospitality.

2. What is the biggest obstacle you face in your study of hospitality?

The biggest obstacle I faced in studying hospitality is the fact that people automatically assume that means either I'm a chef or I work at the front desk of a hotel.

3. What area(s) of hospitality in particular do you find most interesting?

The areas of hospitality that I find most interesting are corporate social responsibility and how it's implemented in the industry. I'm also interested in food and beverage management.

4. What specific skills are required of students who study hospitality?

Students that study hospitality should be able to multi-task. They should begin becoming comfortable with speaking before crowds of people. But most importantly hospitality students must be able to work in teams of people, especially with people they may not always get along with.

5. What career avenues are available for hospitality majors?

The hospitality industry has so many different opportunities it's difficult to sum them all up in a few sentences. There's food and beverage management, hotel operations management, beverage sales and consulting, we have sommeliers and cicerones, there are chefs, there are event coordinators. There are advocacy groups for third-world nations trying to develop tourism interests in today's market; there are so many different career paths to choose from in this industry.

Tourism Marketing Strategies

Preview Questions

1. Imagine one of the world's most beautiful beaches with just a handful of tourists coming each week. In a world full of thirsty sun-seekers, how could a gorgeous beach be mostly empty?

2. If you worked for a tourist marketing firm and you were conducting a survey on students' travel habits, what types of questions would you include in your questionnaire?

3. Think about three of America's most popular tourist destinations, Disneyland, New York City, and Yosemite National Park. How is each marketed differently to bring in the highest number of visitors each year?

MyReadingLab™

Complete this **Exercise** at **myreadinglab.com**

Collaboration

Pre-Reading Vocabulary: Focus on Some Key Terms

Before beginning the reading selection, it may be helpful to focus on the meaning of some key words in the blog. Working with a partner, try to guess the meaning of these words. Then look up the words in a dictionary.

Word	Your Definition	Vocabulary Definition
essential		
spur		
boost		
entice		
impact		

Tourism Marketing Strategies

By Laura Acevedo, eHow Contributor

Successful tourism marketing strategies increase outside awareness of your destination and overall tourism dollars. Whether your property is a beachside resort or a historic landmark, a well-crafted marketing plan is essential to the long-term success and profitability of your destination. The best tourism marketing strategies encourage group attendance and spur repeat visits.

Conventions

1   Market your tourist destination to groups, organizations and businesses that sponsor conventions. Create comprehensive information packages that focus on meeting spaces, hotel availability, catering options, local activities and entertainment options. Distribute these packages through website requests and targeted direct mail campaigns and in welcome centers. Offer customized convention planning services to help lure larger conventions. Conventions can be a boon to a local economy through a large increase in spending by convention attendees. If you properly position your activities and location options, you can increase the number of family members and guests that accompany the convention attendee. Conventions boost your tourism profile, which can lead to increases in non-convention visitors and tourism dollars.

Promotions

2   Offer promotions to entice tourists to visit your destination. Consider offering group discounts, coupons, off-season specials and free items to entice tourists to spend their holiday dollars with you. Work with multiple attractions to create a bigger package and steeper discounts. If you are a small tourist town, work with the trolley car tour, museums and other attractions to offer package discounts. Consider half-price options if visitors purchase at least two activities. For a more

comprehensive approach, bundle lodging, food and activities into savings packages that target families, honeymooners or seniors. The increase in visitors can
offset discounts and can increase tourists choosing your destination over rival
locations.

Experience

3   Target travelers based on their vacation preferences. Offer activities
and options for visitors who want learning experiences, activity-based experiences, shopping, relaxation or family bonding. Realize each tourist has a
different vision for her vacation, so the more experience options you create,
the greater chance you will connect with more potential visitors. Market your
experience options through your website and targeted pamphlets. On your
website, create well-defined sections that highlight each experience. For example, a water-based tour operator for a historical river could highlight the
nature experience, the river history experience and even an action experience. By targeting multiple experiences, potential clients are more likely to
bond with your tourism option and choose to spend their vacation with you.
To maximize the impact of this strategy, offer customized activities for each
experience.

Demand Media.

Reading Comprehension Check

MyReadingLab™
Complete this **Exercise**
at **myreadinglab.com**

1. The main idea of the reading is that
   a. tourist destinations can only remain popular if they are marketed wisely.
   b. effective tourism marketing strategies can increase destination awareness
      and tourism revenue.
   c. identifying your target audience is a key step in marketing a tourist
      destination.
   d. marketing a tourist destination is important to generate revenue.

2. The sentence "Conventions boost your tourism profile, which can lead to
   increases in non-convention visitors and tourism dollars" (para. 1) is a statement of
   a. fact.   c. opinion.
   b. guess.   d. fact and opinion.

3. "Conventions can be a **boon** to a local economy through a large increase in
   spending by convention attendees." (para. 1) In this context, the word *boon* means
   a. blessing.   c. shortcoming.
   b. disadvantage.   d. flaw.

4. What is the author's purpose in writing this article?
   a. to offer some facts about the tourism industry
   b. to persuade the reader to visit a particular tourist site
   c. to humor the reader with entertaining stories about marketing and
      tourism
   d. to give advice on how to most effectively market a tourist destination

5. "For a more comprehensive approach, bundle lodging, food and activities into savings packages that target families, honeymooners or seniors. The increase in visitors can offset discounts and can increase tourists choosing your destination over rival locations." (para. 2) It can be inferred from this passage that
   a. seniors are not interested in vacation packages.
   b. single men and women are not interested in vacation packages.
   c. only honeymooners are interested in vacation packages.
   d. most families do not care much about vacation packages.

Collaboration

Exploring the Topic

Discuss the following questions to review the content of the essay you have just read.

1. Who is the intended audience for this reading? In other words, who is the writer giving advice to?

2. Reread the article again. Clearly, the writer has a lot of experience in the travel field and many pieces of advice to offer. However, there must be some helpful travel marketing tips that she left out. What other advice would you offer the Department of Tourism in your town or city to attract more tourists?

3. The writer mentions offering clients half-price options and other types of travel discounts. What might be a downside to a travel business of focusing on discount plans and half-off coupons?

Post-Reading Vocabulary

Without using a dictionary, determine the meaning of the bolded words from the context.

1. "Offer customized convention planning services to help **lure** larger conventions." (para. 1)

   Lure means _____

2. "For a more comprehensive approach, **bundle** lodging, food and activities into savings packages." (para. 2)

   Bundle means _____

3. "Work with multiple attractions to create a bigger package and **steeper** discounts." (para. 2)

   Steeper means _____

SKILL FOCUS
Combined Skills

⑤ LEARNING OBJECTIVE
Recognize question types within a combined-skills reading test

Throughout this text, each chapter has focused on one particular reading skill. The chart below maps out both the academic disciplines and the focus skills for Chapters 1–9.

Chapter 1	Sociology	Vocabulary in Context
Chapter 2	Biology	Main Idea and Topic
Chapter 3	Personal Finance	Supporting Details
Chapter 4	Economics	Making Inferences
Chapter 5	Literature	Author's Purpose and Tone
Chapter 6	Mathematics	Logical Relationships
Chapter 7	Architecture	Facts and Opinion
Chapter 8	Occupational Therapy	Patterns of Organization
Chapter 9	US History	Author's Bias

You have learned a lot about working with vocabulary in context. You should now be better able to distinguish between main idea and topic, to identify major and minor details, and also to understand an author's purpose and tone. In the second half of the text, you learned about logical relationships within a text, how to distinguish fact from opinion, how to identify different patterns of organization and finally how to better understand an author's bias.

Most standardized reading exams do not isolate skills but rather offer multiple-choice tests with various question types included for each reading passage. Therefore, it is critical that you have ample opportunity to practice with combined-skill questions. Moreover, sharpening your ability to identify and label question types in a combined-skills reading will better prepare you for success with these exams.

Creating a Reading Selection Map

One way to measure your overall understanding of a reading passage is to break down some key aspects of the reading through mapping. Read the passage below, and examine the "reading selection map" that follows.

Corporate Profile: Carnival Cruise Lines

The name Carnival Cruise Lines is a good indication of what the company is all about. Festive, yet casual, and affordable to all, Carnival is the company that brings fun to cruising. Starting in 1972 with only one ship named the *Mardi Gras*, entrepreneur Ted Arison realized his vision of making cruising available to the wider population and not to only the very rich. Fifteen years later, Carnival had, with seven ships in service, become the first cruise line on network TV (1984), earned its distinction as "Most Popular Cruise Line in the World," carried more passengers than any other cruise line, and undertook its initial public offering on Wall Street to raise capital for expansion.

from John Walker and Josielyn Walker, *Tourism: Concepts and Practices*, p. 444

Reading Selection Map	
Topic	Carnival Cruises
Main Idea	Carnival began as a modest operation, but is now one of the largest cruise lines in the world.
Supporting Detail	In 1987, Carnival had seven ships in its service.
A Fact	Carnival was the first cruise line on network TV.
An Opinion	Carnival cruises are "festive, yet casual, and affordable to all."
Author's Tone	Positive; informative
Author's Purpose	To market; to inform
One Pattern of Organization Used	Compare/contrast (Carnival in the beginning with only one ship and later as a huge operation)
An Inference	We can infer that Carnival's TV advertising paid off.

Collaboration

EXERCISE 1   Practicing Mapping

Let's read another passage focusing on the tourism industry, and practice mapping its key aspects (topic, main idea, supporting details, and so on).

Six Flags Theme Parks, Inc.

Six Flags is a world-renowned theme-park operation. The company owns and operates 20 different parks spread out over North America, Latin America and Europe. Locations include Mexico City, Belgium, France, Spain, Germany and most major metropolitan areas in the United States. In fact, 74% of the continental United States parks are located within a six-hour drive. Six Flags has earned the title of the world's largest theme park company. Annually, more than 25 million visitors are reported to entertain themselves at Six Flags theme parks worldwide, 90% of which reported a desire to return.

from John Walker and Josielyn Walker, *Tourism: Concepts and Practices*, p. 266

With a classmate, please fill out the reading selection map below.

Reading Selection Map	
Topic	
Main Idea	
Supporting Detail	
A Fact	
An Opinion	
Author's Tone	
Author's Purpose	
One Pattern of Organization Used	
An Inference	

EXERCISE 2   Identifying Key Elements in a Passage

Now that you have reviewed many key skill areas, read the following passage, and label each question type to indicate which key element of the passage it is asking about BEFORE you answer the multiple-choice questions. The first one is completed for you.

New York is an example of a community that has reaped the benefits of cultural and heritage tourism. Many destinations related to cultural and heritage tourism, such as the Statue of Liberty and Ellis Island, attempt to provide experiences that are unique only to that community. Attraction planners in the city help tourists to experience New York's vibrant culture and history through exhibits, museums and monuments. To have continued success in the future, New York City tourism planners and destinations will need to ensure that they maintain the authenticity of the attractions and manage guests appropriately so as not to destroy the destination. New York City, with so many cultural and heritage destinations, seems prepared for success in the future because of expected growth rates in cultural and heritage tourism and increasing numbers of tourists in New York City.

Statue of Liberty and Ellis Island

from John Walker and Josielyn Walker, *Tourism: Concepts and Practices*, p. 295

1. The Statue of Liberty and Ellis Island are mentioned

   Question Type: _____ *supporting detail*
   a. to prove the point that New York is a great city.
   b. as examples of cultural and heritage tourism sites.
   c. in terms of their central location.
   d. in relation to world tourism.

2. We can infer from the reading that

   Question Type: _____
   a. city tourist officials want New York to be destroyed by too much tourism.
   b. tourism planners in NYC are putting a great focus on cultural and heritage tourism.
   c. tourism planners do not want to set limits on the numbers of tourists coming to a given site.
   d. most tourists come to New York for entertainment.

3. "To have continued success in the future, New York City tourism planners and destinations will need to ensure that they maintain the authenticity of the attractions and manage guests appropriately so as not to destroy the destination." Which pattern of organization is exemplified in the above sentences?

   Question Type: _____
   a. chronological order   c. cause and effect
   b. compare and contrast   d. listing

4. The word "authenticity" in line 8 of the passage could be replaced with

   Question Type: _____
   a. genuineness.
   c. depth.
   b. falsehood.
   d. collateral.

5. What is the main idea of the reading passage?

   Question Type: _____
   a. The Statue of Liberty is an example of a cultural and heritage site.
   b. New York's future looks good.
   c. City planners do not want over-tourism to destroy New York's tourism industry.
   d. Cultural and heritage tourism has benefitted the New York City tourism industry.

LANDMARK IN THE FIELD OF TRAVEL AND TOURISM

Online Travel Agencies (OTAs)

Before the Internet was invented, most tourists depended on travel agents to make hotel and flight reservations. They went to brick-and-mortar travel agencies to book a hotel, purchase flight tickets, and sometimes even rent a car. For years, these travel agencies dominated the hotel and flight reservation markets. They collected as much as a 10% commission from the hotels for each customer. In addition, they also earned a commission from the airlines.

All of that changed when Hotel Reservations Network (HRN) created the first Online Travel Agency (OTA) in 1991. Tourists finally had a much easier alternative. HRN started Hotels.com, which became very popular in a short time. Travelers and tourists were no longer at the mercy of a travel agent. Thanks to the Internet, travel agencies finally had stiff competition.

OTAs gained popularity in the 2000s. They provided many travel options within a few clicks. Tourists could choose from many hotels and compare airline ticket prices. They did all of this from the comfort of their homes. Slowly more and more people began to learn about the many benefits of OTAs.

Other businesses saw OTAs as a great opportunity to make profits. They followed suit and launched many OTAs. For example, Microsoft

launched the OTA Expedia in 1995 and bought Hotels.com. Under the Expedia umbrella are Venere.com, Hotwire.com, Egencia, TripAdvisor, Expedia Local Expert, Classic Vacations, and eLong.

Other companies that launched OTAs are Priceline (1998), Orbitz (2001), TripAdvisor (2005), and Travelocity (2007). Kayak.com is a recent addition to the existing OTAs. It is different from an OTA because it is an OTA search engine. It provides tourists with different hotel, flight, and car rental prices offered by the OTAs. Tourists can then make a final decision after comparing these prices.

Together, Expedia, Hotels.com, Travelocity, Priceline, Orbitz, and TripAdvisor control over 90% of the market. They compete with each other for a share of the market. However, this competition is healthy for tourists. They can pick and choose from many options. They can now access airline databases with ease. They can also book and purchase without the help of a travel agent or broker. Thanks to OTAs, tourists can now check in online, print out their boarding passes, and board a plane without any hassles. It is clear that OTAs are here to stay.

Considering the Topic

Answer the following questions with a partner.

Collaboration

1. The first OTA was launched in 1991 by Hotel Reservations Network. However, it took consumers almost 10 years to feel comfortable making hotel and flight reservations online. Why do you think OTAs did not become commonplace right away? In other words, what was it about this landmark that kept most people from purchasing tickets online comfortably?

2. We learn that travel agencies finally had stiff competition from the OTAs. Do you think OTAs will cannibalize traditional travel agencies? In your opinion, how do you think travel agencies can survive?

3. It is reasonable to assume that there will be more innovations in the tourism industry. Discuss the future of the industry with your peers and make predictions as to what it will be like 20 years from now.

Internet Connection

Research another landmark in the field of tourism, and fill out the section below.

chartered planes	ecotourism
tourism for the disabled	travel information center
time-share	guided tours

Landmark: _____

Question	Answer
When did this landmark become a reality?	
Who was involved in developing this landmark?	
What made this landmark special?	
How did this landmark change the way people travel?	

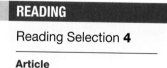
READING

Mexico Launches Tourism Plan for Mayan Sites

Reading Selection **4**

Article

Preview Questions

1. Why is it that most tourists choose popular destinations such as Las Vegas, Hawaii, or Acapulco, but that few go off the beaten path and visit places that are forgotten? Think logically and give specific reasons.

MyReadingLab™
Complete this **Exercise**
at **myreadinglab.com**

2. If you were the director of the Department of Tourism, what would you do to attract tourists to less frequented tourist sites in your country? How would you plan activities to promote these often forgotten sites? Be specific.

3. In your opinion, is it important to preserve and promote ruins that are an integral part of a country's cultural heritage as tourism destinations?

Pre-Reading Vocabulary: Focus on Some Key Terms

Before beginning the reading selection, it may be helpful to focus on the meaning of some key words in the article. Working with a partner, try to guess the meaning of these words. Then look up the words in a dictionary.

Word	*Your Definition*	*Dictionary Definition*
trail		
invest		
promote		
generate		
campaign		

Mexico Launches Tourism Plan for Mayan Sites

Published on January 13, 2012

1. Mexico City, Mexico (NTN24)—Gloria Guevara, Minister of Tourism in Mexico, said that the country plans to build a trail that will connect 70 Mayan sites in southern Mexico, Belize, El Salvador, Guatemala, and Honduras. She hopes that the trail will attract more tourists and help Mexico's economy.

2. Guevara said Mexico will invest 8 million US dollars to promote Mayan sites. She said the goal is to draw 52 million tourists. Also, she hopes that the promotion will generate billions of pesos for Mexico. "Together with governors we are promoting investment in different tourist destinations in different states in this region. What's the estimated impact? We predict we will bring 52 million people to this region as a consequence of this initiative, both national and international tourists generating 200 billion pesos," Guevara said.

Temples of Tikal

3   The campaign organizers hope that the initiative will spark tourists' interest in Mayan culture. The Mayans predicted that the world would end in 2012. The organizers think that Mexico will compete with Greece and Egypt as a hot tourist destination, especially in the year 2012. "It's also a great opportunity to position Mayan culture to the level of Egyptian and Greek cultures so that it generates a lot of tourism to this region. There are a number of very important and valuable assets in the region. The Mayan world covers five countries including five Mexican states and there are six sites in our country which have been declared world heritage sites," added Guevara.

4   The Mayan civilization flourished from 300 AD to 900 AD. During this period they predicted that the world would come to an end on December 21, 2012. Interestingly, the Mayan calendar ends on the same date. Tourism officials in Mexico believe that tourism will boom in December 2012. They think that Guatemala and Belize will also benefit from the boom.

5   The proposed tourist trail is called "Mayan World." It will connect many archaeological zones. Mexican officials plan to improve transport to link these Mayan ruins.

6   The Maya are famous for building towering temples and magnificent palaces in Central America. They dominated the region for approximately 2,000 years. Their downfall began in 900 AD when they mysteriously abandoned their cities.

Reprinted by permission of NTN22 USA Inc.

Reading Comprehension Check

MyReadingLab™
Complete this Exercise
at myreadinglab.com

1. What is the author's main idea?
   a. The Maya predicted that the world would come to an end in December 2012.
   b. Mexico is promoting Mayan sites to improve its economy.
   c. Guevara is excited about the campaign to promote Mayan sites in southern Mexico.
   d. Campaign officials believe that Mexico, Guatemala, and Belize will be destroyed on December 21, 2012.

2. It is a fact that
   a. Mexico will spend 8 million dollars to promote Mayan sites.
   b. Guevara does not want Guatemala's economy to improve.
   c. Mexico's economy will not improve without the trail.
   d. Mayan culture is inferior to Egyptian and Greek cultures.

3. "Gloria Guevara, Minister of Tourism in Mexico, said that the country plans to build a trail that will connect 70 Mayan sites in southern Mexico, Belize, El Salvador, Guatemala, and Honduras. She hopes that the trail will attract more tourists and help Mexico's economy." (para. 1) What is the overall pattern of organization of this passage?
   a. compare and contrast
   b. classification
   c. definition and example
   d. cause and effect

4. What is the author's purpose?
   a. to convince
   b. to persuade
   c. to inform
   d. to entertain

5. "The Maya are famous for building towering temples and magnificent palaces in Central America. They dominated the region for approximately 2,000 years. Their downfall began in 900 AD when they mysteriously abandoned their cities." (para. 6) What is the overall pattern of organization of this passage?
   a. listing
   b. chronological order
   c. classification
   d. compare and contrast

Collaboration

Exploring the Topic

Discuss the following questions to review the content of the article you have just read.

1. We learn that Guevara plans to connect 70 Mayan sites in southern Mexico, Belize, Guatemala, El Salvador, and Honduras to attract more tourists in order to generate revenue. Do you think she will succeed in her plan? Why or why not?

2. Imagine you are a tourist who travels frequently. What would attract you to see a site that is not visited by many tourists? Be specific.

3. What is the link between the Mayan prediction of the world ending in December 2012 and the timing of the tourism campaign in Mexico? Explain.

Post-Reading Vocabulary

Without using a dictionary, determine the meaning of the bolded words from the context.

1. "Together with governors we are promoting investment in different tourist **destinations** in different states in this region." (para. 2)

   Destinations means _____

2. " 'We predict we will bring 52 million people to this region as a **consequence** of this initiative, both national and international tourists generating 200 billion pesos,' Guevara said." (para. 2)

   Consequence means _____

3. "The Maya are famous for building **towering** temples and magnificent palaces in Central America." (para. 6)

   Towering means _____

Focus on Attractions and Entertainment

Preview Questions

1. What challenges do you think managing a world-famous tourist attraction would hold? Do you think you are the kind of person who could help meet this type of challenge? Explain.

2. Some tourists complain that famous tourist attractions such as Disney World are more a nuisance than a joy during the overcrowded holiday season. Is it Disney World's responsibility to reduce the effects of overcrowding, or is this just the reality of supply and demand? Can you think of any practical solutions to this problem?

3. Do you think it is wiser to visit a popular U.S. tourist attraction within two hours of your residence by car or by mass transit? What are the advantages of each mode of transportation?

MyReadingLab™

⚙—Complete this Exercise
at myreadinglab.com

Collaboration

Pre-Reading Vocabulary: Focus on Some Key Terms

Before beginning the reading selection, it may be helpful to focus on the meaning of some key words in the excerpt. Working with a partner, try to guess the meaning of these words. Then look up the words in a dictionary.

Word	*Your Definition*	*Dictionary Definition*
account for		
rationale		
sustain		
restrict		
flow		

Focus on Attractions and Entertainment

By John Walker and Josielyn Walker

1   Attractions and entertainment are an important part of the tourism system. They account for much of the rationale for tourism by "pulling" people to them. Many of the components of the tourist trip are demands derived from the consumer's desire to enjoy what a destination has to offer in terms of things to see and do.

The Taj Mahal

2   Attractions are first characterized as natural or built environments. Then they are examined in terms of ownership—public or private. Historically certain attractions became popular, among them the original Seven Wonders of the World, as declared by Philon of Byzantium in 200 BCE: the Hanging Gardens of Babylon, the Great Pyramids of Egypt, the Statue of Zeus at Olympia, the Temple of Artemis at Ephesus, the Mausoleum at Halicarnassus, the Colossus of Rhodes and the Lighthouse at Alexandria.

3   More recent lists include hundreds of so-called Wonders of the World. Among the more popular are the Great Wall of China, the Taj Mahal, the Serengeti Migration, the Galapagos Islands, the Grand Canyon, Bali, the Amazon rain forest and the Great Barrier Reef. It is interesting to note the difference between the original Seven Wonders of the World and the more recent popular wonders. The originals were mostly of the built environment compared to the more recent that are more natural.

4   The management of attractions presents several challenges and opportunities for tourism officials. These challenges and opportunities include infrastructure (water, waste management, utilities, communications, roads). They also include services usually provided by the government; and superstructure (rail, auto and bus transportation, hotels, resorts, restaurants, entertainment places, shopping centers, museums). These services are usually provided by corporations or privately. Other issues include overcrowding, seasonality and sustaining the site for the future enjoyment of tourists. For example, one of the biggest challenges for the planners of the Super Bowl is where to park the hundreds of corporate jets that fly in.

5   Restricting the flow and number of tourists visiting an attraction can be a challenge. Consider how many tour buses can be parked in Oxford, England, or in one of the beautiful squares in Paris. At times they seem to overwhelm the very places that tourists want to see. To reduce traffic many attractions have instituted a park-and-ride approach to better control the flow of visitors. The travel and tourism distribution chain also helps by offering special deals on off-peak travel to selected destinations.

from John T. Walker and Josielyn T. Walker, *Tourism: Concepts and Practices*, 1e.

Reading Comprehension Check

1. According to the excerpt, what is the difference between the original "Seven Wonders of the World" and the updated list of world wonders?
   a. The more recent list has more man-made sites.
   b. The more recent list offers more natural sites.
   c. The earlier list of "Wonders" includes more natural sites.
   d. Neither list is environmentally friendly.

2. The Super Bowl is mentioned as an example of
   a. an overcrowded disaster.
   b. a site which presents parking challenges for corporate jets.
   c. one of the "Seven Wonders of the World."
   d. an ancient site.

3. The author's tone is
   a. humorous.   c. neutral.
   b. persuasive.   d. shocked.

4. Which pattern of organization is utilized in paragraphs two and three?
   a. chronology   c. definition
   b. cause and effect   d. listing

5. What is the main idea of the final paragraph?
   a. One of the great challenges tourist sites face is controlling the flow of visitors.
   b. Tourists must be restricted from entering certain attractions during high season.
   c. There are many beautiful squares in Paris.
   d. Travel discounts for off-peak travel is one solution to overcrowding.

Exploring the Topic

Discuss the following questions to review the content of the book excerpt you have just read.

Collaboration

1. Examining the updated list of the "Seven Wonders of the World," which would you most like to visit? Explain your choice.

2. The excerpt mentions the difficulty of maintaining a tourist site's infrastructure. Which infrastructure item (water, waste management, utilities, communications, roads) might present the greatest challenge to site management? Explain.

3. What can a site management company do in the case that tourists tire of a particular, famous tourist site (e.g., the Statue of Liberty)? How can they bring tourists back?

Post-Reading Vocabulary

Without using a dictionary, determine the meaning of the bolded words from the context.

1. "At times they seem to **overwhelm** the very places that tourists want to see." (para. 5)

   Overwhelm means _____

2. "Other issues include overcrowding, **seasonality** and sustaining the site for the future enjoyment of tourists." (para. 4)

   Seasonality means _____

3. "It is interesting to **note** the difference between the original Seven Wonders of the World and the more recent popular wonders." (para. 3)

   Note means _____

Collaboration

Panel Discussion on Planning to Attract Tourists to the Forgotten Town of Solitude

The town of Solitude has seen a sharp decline in its economy recently. Most of the townspeople have moved on to greener pastures because of the sluggish economy. However, you have chosen to stay in Solitude because it is your birthplace and this is where your ancestors lived. Interestingly, your town has been recently in the news because of the discovery of ancient ruins by a team of archaeologists from Excavation University. In fact, the archaeologists believe that the ruins belong to a once thriving empire.

Mayor Gloomberg sees this discovery as a great opportunity to revive the economy. She has asked the townspeople to participate in a panel discussion to brainstorm ideas to promote tourism to Solitude. The mayor is more than willing to entertain unusual ideas, because her main concern is to generate revenue for the town. Obviously, your loyalty is with the town, and you want to do your part by participating in the panel. However, you are concerned about the safety of the townspeople, as the tourists will be flocking to Solitude from all over the world. Here are some profiles of the townspeople. You may wish to create a list of ideas and write your short speech for the discussion.

1. mayor
2. local businessperson
3. director of transportation
4. environmentalist
5. hotel manager
6. travel agent
7. social activist
8. business tycoon
9. police chief
10. tour guide
11. taxi driver
12. rental car company agent

Be creative and think of more profiles that are appropriate for the purposes of the panel discussion.

You may use the following questions to prepare for the panel discussion. You also may wish to work with your peers and formulate appropriate questions to be raised during the discussion.

1. How would Solitude promote the ruins to draw tourists from different parts of the world? What would be the role of the hospitality industry in promoting tourism?

2. How would the townspeople be impacted by the overflow of national and international tourists? In other words, is it in the townspeople's best interest to have swarms of tourists?

3. What would Solitude do with the revenue? Would there be a profit-sharing model? Who would benefit most from the surge in tourism?

4. What would the tourists gain from visiting Solitude? That is to say, what's in it for them? Why should they spend their hard-earned money on Solitude to begin with?

5. What can you do as a resident of Solitude to turn the economy around?

Remember that a panel discussion is unlike a debate where you must win or lose. A panel discussion is more like a forum in which people participate and present their points of view without worrying about winning or losing an argument. Whether or not you play an active role in promoting tourism is irrelevant for the purpose of the discussion. What is more important is that you keep an open mind and have an open discussion about the pros and cons of promoting tourism to Solitude.

WRITING CONNECTIONS: *Budget Allocation*

You are working for a travel agency in your current city or town of residence. You receive the following e-mail from the principal of the local high school.

From: Meredith Young [YoungM@school.edu]

Sent: Thursday, March 09, 2013 11:59

To: Borden's Travel Agency

Subject: Student Trip to London in Easter 2014

Our school is planning to reward our top ten students with a free trip to London, England, next spring during Easter vacation. We would like to work with your agency in organizing our travel arrangements. We have a limited budget and would like to keep the total cost of the trip to under $1,300 a student. We would like our trip to London to run for five days and five nights. We are willing to stay in a budget hotel and the students can double up in their rooms, of course. In terms of food, as long as breakfast is included, we can make do with some extra travel money set aside to cover our lunch and dinner costs. We mainly want our budget allocation to cover transportation, hotel accommodation, and at least one tour of a famous site in London.

There will be two adult chaperones, so we will be twelve travelers in all.

Please do investigate and give us a rough estimate of how much such a trip will cost. We look forward to working with you.

Sincerely,

Ms. Young

School Principal

Stage One: Internet Research. With a classmate, research the cost of each component of this London excursion. Use the chart below.

Travel Item	Estimated Cost per Person
Round-trip airfare from current location to London, England	
Hotel cost for five nights (including breakfast)	
Other transportation costs	
Tour of a famous site in London	
Additional costs	
Total	

Stage Two. Now that you and your partner have done your research, reply to the principal's e-mail message. Outline the trip information in a clear letter written in paragraph form.

To: Meredith Young [YoungM@school.edu]

Sent:

From:

Subject:

Definition of Tourism

The purpose of this exercise is to get you acquainted with the type of reading you will be required to do in college. First, listen to the lecture and take notes. You can listen to the lecture by scanning the QR code below with your smart phone. Your professor may also read the selection or play the audio file in class. Make sure that you write down the important points of the lecture.

Group Discussion

Working in small groups of three to four students, answer the following questions. Your instructor may ask you to share your answers with your classmates. As you refer to your notes, it is best to write brief answers to each of the questions below using your own words. After the discussion, you will have an opportunity to share your findings with your peers.

Collaboration

1. What points were included in the definition of tourism offered?
2. What examples are given of infrastructure components?
3. What examples are given of superstructure components?
4. According to the lecture, what is an example of lodging?
5. What two types of attractions are compared?
6. What are the most frequently used vehicles by tourists?
7. What do we learn about rail service in the United States, Europe, and in parts of Asia?

Now that you have discussed the highlights of the lecture with your classmates, read the following selection and answer the multiple-choice questions that follow.

Definition of Tourism

Scan this code using your smart phone to listen to an audio version of this reading

1   The United Nations World Tourism Organization (UNWTO) states that tourism comprises *the activities of persons travelling to, and staying in places outside their usual environment for not more than one consecutive year for leisure, business and other purposes*. This is the definition of tourism that we use throughout the book.

2   Also tourism is frequently considered in terms of the demand side, meaning the tourists' motivations, and the supply side, the sectors that satisfy tourist needs. Other important terms associated with tourism are *infrastructure*, the components that an area's residents rely on such as roads, bridges, communications networks, markets and supermarkets, and so on; and *superstructure*, facilities that have been built to accommodate the needs of tourists such as cruise terminals, airports, and convention centers (although these also support the area's residents), hotels, resorts, restaurants, and car rentals.

Tourism Industry Sectors

3   Several interactive industries make up the tourism system, including lodging attractions, transportation and foodservice:

4   **Lodging:** Lodging includes all the different types of accommodations that tourists use, from camping spots and cabins in a national park, to resorts and hotels, to bed-and-breakfast inns, to all-suite properties.

5   **Attractions:** Attractions are differentiated as natural attractions, as in Mount Fuji, a park, or a beach, and man-made attractions, as in the Euro-Disney theme park. Destinations are also attractions: cities such as Athens, Hong Kong, Rome, Paris and London receive millions of tourists every year.

6   **Transportation:** Transportation is by automobile, ship, rail or air. Personal autos, rental cars, and coaches are the most frequently used vehicles by tourists. Cruises include exotic ports of call to add interest and on-board entertainment to add excitement for passengers. Rail travel has decreased in the United States, but in Europe and parts of Asia the trains are a convenient way to sightsee and travel between major cities. Air travel has made distant locations seem much closer. By air, Europe and Asia are only a few hours away, and with the newer Airbus 380 and Boeing's Dreamliner, long-haul flights, such as New York to Singapore or Hong Kong, are now non-stop.

7   **Foodservice:** Foodservice related to tourism mostly includes restaurants and cafes that cater to tourists as well as people living in the tourist area. The choice of dining available likely reflects the type of food and service that the target market wants.

from by John Walker and Josielyn Walker, *Tourism: Concepts and Practices*, pp. 7, 12–13

Reading Comprehension Check

1. A synonym for the term *lodging* might be
   a. food service.
   b. travel option.
   c. a temporary place to stay.
   d. air transport.

2. According to the UNWTO's definition of tourism, someone could be considered a tourist
   a. up to a week.
   b. up to a month.
   c. up to a decade.
   d. up to a year.

3. What pattern of organization is used in discussing infrastructure and superstructure?
   a. compare and contrast
   b. chronology
   c. cause and effect
   d. none of the above

4. "Lodging includes all the different types of accommodations that tourists use." (para. 4) This sentence is
   a. a statement of fact.
   b. a statement of opinion.
   c. a statement of both fact and opinion.
   d. neither fact nor opinion.

5. How are "attractions" differentiated?
   a. between land and sea
   b. between expensive and cheap
   c. between man-made and natural
   d. They are not differentiated at all.

6. What is the topic of the reading?

    a. tourism

    b. natural travel

    c. modes of travel transportation

    d. Tourists have many options to choose from.

7. We can infer from the reading that before the Boeing Dreamliner and Airbus 380,

    a. travelers flying halfway around the world had fewer options to fly non-stop.

    b. no American companies were flying around the world.

    c. there were no modes of transportation.

    d. travelers had inexpensive flight options.

8. Rail travel in the United States has

    a. gone up.

    b. not kept up with the amount of tourists coming into the country.

    c. stayed at the same level.

    d. gone down.

9. Cruises are mentioned

    a. in relation to foodservice options.

    b. as one mode of tourist transport.

    c. as a challenge in terms of lodging.

    d. as being great for your health.

10. "The choice of dining available likely reflects the type of food and service that the target market wants." (para. 7) In this sentence, the term *reflects* could be replaced by

    a. contrasts.   c. meditates.

    b. gives in to.   d. parallels.

The Internet can be a powerful and effective research tool once you have learned how to successfully limit your information searches and have learned how to interpret the results of your search with a critical lens.

Instructions: First try to use logic and background knowledge in guessing the correct answers to the following data questions. Then, go online and search for the relevant data. Be sure to write the Web source next to your research finding.

1. How many Americans have a passport?

    a. 10%   c. 37%

    b. 15%   d. 55%

Your guess: _____   Research finding: _____

Web source: _____

2. According to the U.S. Travel Association, how many foreign tourists visited the United States in 2010?
   a. 26 million
   b. 26.4 million
   c. 30 million
   d. 30.5 million

   Your guess: _____   Research finding: _____

   Web source: _____

3. What is America's most popular destination?
   a. The Las Vegas Strip, Nevada
   b. Disney World's Magic Kingdom, Florida
   c. Times Square, New York City
   d. National Mall and Memorial Parks, Washington, D.C.

   Your guess: _____   Research finding: _____

   Web source: _____

4. Which of the following is not one of America's top 10 tourist attractions?
   a. The Mall of America, Minnesota
   b. Faneuil Hall Marketplace, Boston
   c. Disneyland Park, California
   d. Golden Gate National Recreation Area, San Francisco

   Your guess: _____   Research finding: _____

   Web source: _____

5. How many people visit the Statue of Liberty National Monument and Ellis Island in New York each year?
   a. 3.5 million
   b. 4 million
   c. 4.5 million
   d. 5 million

   Your guess: _____   Research finding: _____

   Web source: _____

FORMAL PRESENTATION PROJECTS

You will be given the opportunity to present on a topic of your interest pertinent to one of the text's chapter disciplines. Topics could relate to one of the questions you checked off in the "Follow Your Interests" section at the beginning of the chapter. Your instructor may ask you to browse through the chapters to guide you toward a given discipline focus.

MyReadingLab™   For more help with **Test-Taking**, go to your learning path in **MyReadingLab.com**.

Below are 10 lists of academic words organized by frequency of use. Those that are used most often are listed first (Sublist 1), followed, in descending order of usage, by Sublists 2–10.

Sublist 1—Most Frequent Words in Families

This sublist contains the most frequent words of the Academic Word List in the Academic Corpus.

analysis
approach
area
assessment
assume
authority
available
benefit
concept
consistent
constitutional
context
contract
create
data
definition
derived
distribution
economic
environment
established
estimate
evidence
export
factors
financial
formula
function
identified
income
indicate
individual
interpretation
involved

issues
labor
legal
legislation
major
method
occur
percent
period
policy
principle
procedure
process
required
research
response
role
section
sector
significant
similar
source
specific
structure
theory
variables

Sublist 2—Most Frequent Words in Families

This sublist contains the second most frequent words in the Academic Word List in the Academic Corpus.

achieve
acquisition
administration
affect
appropriate
aspects

assistance
categories
chapter
commission
community
complex
computer
conclusion
conduct
consequences
construction
consumer
credit
cultural
design
distinction
elements
equation
evaluation
features
final
focus
impact
injury
institute
investment
items
journal
maintenance
normal
obtained
participation
perceived
positive
potential
previous
primary
purchase
range
region

regulations
relevant
resident
resources
restricted
security
sought
select
site
strategies
survey
text
traditional
transfer

Sublist 3—Most Frequent Words in Families

This sublist contains the third most frequent words of the Academic Word List in the Academic Corpus.

alternative
circumstances
comments
compensation
components
consent
considerable
constant
constraints
contribution
convention
coordination
core
corporate
corresponding
criteria
deduction
demonstrate
document
dominant
emphasis
ensure
excluded
framework
funds
illustrated
immigration
implies
initial
instance

interaction
justification
layer
link
location
maximum
minorities
negative
outcomes
partnership
philosophy
physical
proportion
published
reaction
registered
reliance
removed
scheme
sequence
sex
shift
specified
sufficient
task
technical
techniques
technology
validity
volume

Sublist 4—Most Frequent Words in Families

This sublist contains the fourth most frequent words of the Academic Word List in the Academic Corpus.

access
adequate
annual
apparent
approximated
attitudes
attributed
civil
code
commitment
communication
concentration
conference
contrast

cycle
debate
despite
dimensions
domestic
emerged
error
ethnic
goals
granted
hence
hypothesis
implementation
implications
imposed
integration
internal
investigation
job
label
mechanism
obvious
occupational
option
output
overall
parallel
parameters
phase
predicted
principal
prior
professional
project
promote
regime
resolution
retained
series
statistics
status
stress
subsequent
sum
summary
undertaken

Sublist 5—Most Frequent Words in Families

academic
adjustment

alter
amendment
aware
capacity
challenge
clause
compounds
conflict
consultation
contact
decline
discretion
draft
enable
energy
enforcement
entities
equivalent
evolution
expansion
exposure
external
facilitate
fundamental
generated
generation
image
liberal
licence
logic
marginal
medical
mental
modified
monitoring
network
notion
objective
orientation
perspective
precise
prime
psychology
pursue
ratio
rejected
revenue
stability
styles
substitution
sustainable
symbolic

target
transition
trend
version
welfare
whereas

Sublist 6—Most Frequent Words in Families

abstract
accurate
acknowledged
aggregate
allocation
assigned
attached
author
bond
brief
capable
cited
cooperative
discrimination
display
diversity
domain
edition
enhanced
estate
exceed
expert
explicit
federal
fees
flexibility
furthermore
gender
ignored
incentive
incidence
incorporated
index
inhibition
initiatives
input
instructions
intelligence
interval
lecture
migration
minimum

ministry
motivation
neutral
nevertheless
overseas
preceding
presumption
rational
recovery
revealed
scope
subsidiary
tapes
trace
transformation
transport
underlying
utility

Sublist 7—Most Frequent Words in Families

adaptation
adults
advocate
aid
channel
chemical
classical
comprehensive
comprise
confirmed
contrary
converted
couple
decades
definite
deny
differentiation
disposal
dynamic
eliminate
empirical
equipment
extract
file
finite
foundation
global
grade
guarantee
hierarchical

identical
ideology
inferred
innovation
insert
intervention
isolated
media
mode
paradigm
phenomenon
priority
prohibited
publication
quotation
release
reverse
simulation
solely
somewhat
submitted
successive
survive
thesis
topic
transmission
ultimately
unique
visible
voluntary

Sublist 8—Most Frequent Words in Families

abandon
accompanied
accumulation
ambiguous
appendix
appreciation
arbitrary
automatically
bias
chart
clarity
conformity
commodity
complement
contemporary
contradiction
crucial
currency

denote
detected
deviation
displacement
dramatic
eventually
exhibit
exploitation
fluctuations
guidelines
highlighted
implicit
induced
inevitably
infrastructure
inspection
intensity
manipulation
minimised
nuclear
offset
paragraph
plus
practitioners
predominantly
prospect
radical
random
reinforced
restore
revision
schedule
tension
termination
theme
thereby
uniform
vehicle
via
virtually
widespread
visual

Sublist 9—Most Frequent Words in Families

accommodation
analogous
anticipated
assurance
attained
behalf

bulk
ceases
coherence
coincide
commenced
incompatible
concurrent
confined
controversy
conversely
device
devoted
diminished
distorted/distortion—*equal figures*
duration
erosion
ethical
format
founded
inherent
insights
integral
intermediate
manual
mature
mediation
medium
military
minimal
mutual
norms
overlap
passive
portion
preliminary
protocol
qualitative
refine
relaxed
restraints
revolution
rigid
route
scenario
sphere
subordinate
supplementary
suspended
team
temporary

trigger
unified
violation
vision

Sublist 10—Most Frequent Words in Families

This sublist contains the least frequent words of the Academic Word List in the Academic Corpus.

adjacent
albeit
assembly

collapse
colleagues
compiled
conceived
convinced
depression
encountered
enormous
forthcoming
inclination
integrity
intrinsic
invoked
levy

likewise
nonetheless
notwithstanding
odd
ongoing
panel
persistent
posed
reluctant
so-called
straightforward
undergo
whereby

Chapter 1: Sociology

Sociology is the study of human behavior in society, including the study of the organization, institutions, and development of human society. As you can tell, human behavior is quite complex, so sociologists study various aspects of it such as race and ethnicity, gender and age, families, education and religion, and environment and urbanization. In this chapter, you will read several reading selections dealing with a wide range of topics such as gender differences in communication, social networking and teenagers, choosing a life partner, successful parenting, and parenting teenagers. We hope that after completing the chapter, you will arrive at a basic understanding of how different social factors determine and influence human behavior.

Key Terms in the Field of Sociology

acculturation	deviance	social class
assimilation	mores	social justice
competition	peer group	social networking
conflict	polygamy	status
cultural relativism	prejudice	survey

Landmark in the Field of Sociology:
Chat Rooms

Not many years ago, before text messaging and online chatting, if someone wanted to communicate with another person in writing they had to write a letter and mail or fax it. Thus, if the letter was mailed, there would be a significant gap in time from the composition of the message to its reception. This was particularly true if the receiver was in another part of the world. The ability to communicate via e-mail and chat sessions fundamentally changed written communication.

Online chat is a form of communication in which people send text messages to other people in the same chat room in real time. Some chat rooms now offer both text and voice simultaneously, as well as live video capability.

The first online chat rooms were created by an English college student named Roy Trubshaw in 1978. Trubshaw's program allowed others to play a fantasy game called Multi-User Dungeon (MUD) from their home computers. MUD spread from Trubshaw's network of friends. It inspired others to create their own versions. By the mid 1990s, there were hundreds of MUDs on the Internet covering all kinds of shared interests.

In 1991, a team of computer engineers began work on an Internet programming language. This eventually became what is known today as Java. Java chat was distinct in that it allowed people to participate in chat rooms from their Internet browser. Java technology advanced over the years. By 2003 its usage reached over 500 million computers. Java chat now has many uses, from recreational and personal chatting to customer service chat rooms.

Instant messaging, such as Yahoo! Messenger, soon developed, and private chat room users could invite others into their chat sessions. More recently, voice chat combined with video conferencing has allowed users to both see and hear one another during chat sessions.

Chat rooms have changed our perceptions of what it means to communicate with someone both in written and in spoken form. They have blurred the distinction between telephone-like conversation and written messages. People can send and receive written responses as fast as they can type them or text them through cell phones. Chat rooms are in many ways the updated telephone of the twenty-first century. They connect us instantly to those in our own social networks and to strangers with shared interests.

Chapter 2: Biology

Biology is the study of life and of all living organisms, including their function, growth, origin, evolution, and distribution. Biologists study human biology as well as carbohydrates, lipids, proteins, structure and function of cells, ecosystems, evolution, and the origin of life. In this chapter, the reading selections address several topics such as cloning, weight loss, genetically modified foods, reversing the process of aging, and organ donation. After reading the selections in this chapter, you will have a deeper appreciation of the variety of life, the role of science in society, and how human activities affect the lives of all living organisms.

Key Terms in the Field of Biology

anemia	cloning	molecule
antioxidants	genetics	neurons
arteries	hormones	organisms
cancerous	immune	plasma
cardiac	leukemia	transplant

Landmark in the Field of Biology:
Organ Transplant

In the nineteeth century, if a person's organs, such as the heart, liver, kidneys, or lungs, failed to function, there was not much doctors could do to save his or her life. The patient was usually given medicine to treat the ailing organ, but had no choice but to await a slow and painful death. Family members prayed for recovery, but there was no way around it. Death was coming.

The beginning of the twentieth century brought about a revolution in the field of medical science. Eduard Konrad Zirm, an Austrian, performed the first successful cornea transplant on December 7, 1905. The cornea recipient was a blind worker from a small town in the Czech Republic. The patient was able to see again after the transplant.

Zirm became a role model for surgeons all over the world trying to perform organ transplants. However, it took another 50 years for this dream to be realized. In 1954 Joseph Murray transplanted a kidney successfully for the first time. This feat was followed by the first successful pancreas transplant in 1966. Thomas Starzl followed with a liver transplant in 1967. Later in the same year, Christiaan Barnard performed the first successful heart transplant in South Africa.

An organ transplant is considered a landmark in the field of biology for obvious reasons. Who would have thought in the past that a patient whose kidneys were not functioning could receive a healthy kidney from another person? With the progress in science and technology, it is now possible to transfer an organ from one person to another and save someone's life.

There are at least 100,000 patients in the United States waiting for a suitable organ donor. However, only a few of them are lucky enough to receive an organ from a donor. For example, when Steve Jobs, founder of Apple Inc., was ill, he was lucky to receive a liver from a 23-year-old who had recently died in a car accident. As you can imagine, not everyone is as fortunate as Steve Jobs was. Most patients awaiting an organ do not get a second chance to live. There simply aren't enough organ donors.

Chapter 3: Personal Finance

Personal finance is about planning your spending habits, financing, and investing to improve your overall financial situation. You may not realize the importance of personal finance, but it is a fact that the everyday decisions you make about spending your hard-earned money can have a positive or negative effect on your savings and financial health in the long term. This chapter introduces you to the fundamentals of personal finance and touches on topics such as personal savings, using credit cards, tenant protection from foreclosure, online banking, student loan issues, and college and careers. After reading the several different selections in this chapter, you will arrive at a better understanding of how to manage your financial situation well and will hopefully make sound decisions to build a stable financial future.

Key Terms in the Field of Personal Finance

allocation	disability	investing
assessing	estate	managing
assets	financing	mutual funds
bonds	forecasting	planning
budgeting	implement	stocks

Landmark in the Field of Personal Finance:
Online Banking

Just a few decades ago you had to go to a bank location and wait on line for a teller in order to do most banking transactions. Not so today. Online banking, along with the ATM, has changed the way we interact with banks.

Online banking allows individuals to perform many banking applications through the Internet. The common features fall into two categories:

- **Transactional**: You can transfer money from one account to another. You can pay most of your bills online. It is possible to apply for a bank loan. You can also set up a new account online.

- **Non-transactional**: You can check your online statements to find out how much funds you have in a particular account. You can confirm whether a particular transaction went through. This might be a bill payment, a transfer of funds from account to account, a wiring of funds, etc...

Online banking services began in New York in 1981. This was when four of the city's major banks offered home banking services using the videotex system. This early effort was a failure as videotex technology never really caught on. In the 1990s the time was ripe for banks to offer their services online. Internet usage was already popular. In 1994, Stanford Federal Credit Union was the first bank to offer Internet banking services to all of its members. The idea was quickly picked up by other banks such as Wells Fargo and Chase Manhattan.

Today there are many banks that are "Internet only" banks. These banks try to differentiate themselves from brick-and-mortar bank branches. They do this by offering better interest rates and convenient online banking features.

Online banking does present some security risk to users. There have been many cases of account theft and even identity theft. The main security method used for online banking is the PIN/TAN system. The PIN represents a password for the login. The TANs are used for one-time passwords to authenticate a transaction.

The inventors of online banking predicted that online banking would soon completely replace traditional banking. The facts prove that this is not what happened. Many customers still prefer visiting their local bank. They distrust any system of money transaction which does not involve face-to-face interaction. This being said, the number of online banking customers has been increasing at a very quick rate. It seems that the younger generation prefers to do its banking transactions from the comfort of home.

Chapter 4: Economics

You may not know it, but economics has an effect on our everyday life. Economists, experts who study economics, look at what goods and services are offered to meet people's needs. They are also interested in finding out how and why the decisions to make goods and services are made. Soft drinks, fast-food items, and shoes are some of the examples of goods that people want, and businesses produce them. In this chapter, you will learn about supply and demand, profit and loss, competition and government policy, markets and government, globalization and economic growth, and money. We hope that after reading this chapter, you will understand how economics affects life every day.

Key Terms in the Field of Economics

capitalism	incentive	production
competition	inflation	profit
consumption	loss	recession
demand	policy	scarcity
employment	prediction	supply

Landmark in the Field of Economics:
The Social Security Act

In the old days, the American people had to work very hard and save for rainy days. Even if they were still in good health in their old age, many people had to keep working to make ends meet. There were no government programs to help them.

That changed on August 14, 1935 when President Roosevelt signed the Social Security Act to help older people economically. The act also gave money to those who had lost their jobs and were having a hard time living a normal life. Some people did not like the idea and said that the act would cause a loss of jobs. However, those who supported the act argued that it would encourage older people to retire and make it easier for younger people to find jobs.

The Social Security program is the largest government program in the world and is right now the largest social program in the United States (37% of the government budget is spent on Social Security benefits). Money is paid every year to older people, to those who have lost their jobs, and to the husbands, wives, and children of workers who have passed away. The program keeps about 40% of the American people who are at least 65 years old out of poverty. The headquarters of the Social Security Administration is based in Woodlawn, Maryland.

In recent years, some people have become really worried that when they retire, there will be no Social Security benefits for them. This is a real issue as it is the contributions of younger, current workers into the program that support retirees. As large numbers of baby boomers retire and more young people have difficulty finding work, there will be an increasing imbalance between money coming in and benefits being paid out. There are other factors that harm the Social Security program. These are the rising costs of goods and services and much lower economic growth in the last ten years.

The government is well aware of this problem, and Congress has made some changes in Social Security to make sure that older people will be taken care of when they retire in the future. It is hoped that the government will find a way to keep helping the people who need money for their basic needs.

Chapter 5: Literature

Literature depicts life in all its shining colors. Whether we are reading a poem or a play, reading a story or a novel, love and hate, romance and tragedy, jealousy and compassion take center stage and challenge the way we see the world around us. In this chapter, you will have a chance to read some poems, a story, a scene from a play and a chapter from a great novel. You will also read about how technology, in the form of audio and e-books, is changing the way we interact with literature.

Key Terms in the Field of Literature

alliteration	irony	scene
character	metaphor	setting
conflict	personification	stanza
dialogue	plot	symbolism
foreshadowing	point of view	tone

Landmark in the Field of Literature:
Audio Books

If William Shakespeare came back to life four hundred years after writing some of his best plays, he would be shocked to learn that some of his current fans are listening to his plays alone in their cars on the way to work! Yes, the age of the audio book has arrived.

Many people believe that audio books are a recent invention because of the technical terms mentioned when discussing them. These include CDs, downloadable digital formats, MP3s and PDAs. But, in fact, recording of books in audio formats has been around for a long time. In 1933 anthropologist J.P. Harrington drove through the country recording oral histories of Native American tribes on aluminum discs. The Library of Congress made recordings of literary works for use by the blind more than fifty years ago.

The transition of the recording of books into audiocassette tapes happened in the late 1970s. Yet, it wasn't until the invention of CD technology that the concept of audio books really took off. Now audio book technology has joined the digital age with downloadable formats that can be heard on your computer. Audio files of text can be transferred to a portable audio player or burned to a CD.

In the 1980s a major effort was made by large publishing houses to attract book retailers to the concept of the audio book. As more and more publishers entered the world of spoken-word publishing, audio books appeared on retail bookstore bookshelves. In 2005 cassette-tape sales were 16% of the audio book market, with CD sales accounting for 74% of the market. Downloadable audio books accounted for about 9%.

The future looks bright for audio books. In the age of multitasking, today's audio books allow readers to listen to a romance novel while cooking, or to enjoy detective fiction (or a Shakespeare tragedy) on their way to work.

Chapter 6: Mathematics

Arthur Michelson, the author of the first reading selection in the chapter (p. 238) believes that mathematics is not just important for practical reasons. He argues that math knowledge can open our minds to logic and beauty as well. In this chapter, you will have the opportunity to consider how important math is in your own lives. You will read about the nature of coincidence. What are the chances of a mother having seven girls in a row? You can study some humorous math formulas that can be used to help you find the right marriage partner. You will read about how basic calculators evolved into the high-tech scientific calculators that we use in most math and science courses today. One reading will explore how best to calculate your real hourly wage (taking into account your transportation costs, food costs, etc.). Finally, the chapter will also focus on both how to analyze graphs and how to create graphs using Microsoft Excel.

Key Terms in the Field of Mathematics

correlation	graph	probability
deduce	inductive	sequence
equation	inverse	statistics
estimate	logical	subset
factoring	parallel	volume

Landmark in the Field of Mathematics:
Scientific Calculator

A scientific calculator is used mostly in solving problems in the math field. It has special features that make number crunching much easier. One key feature is the floating point in arithmetic. It also offers some basic functions in trigonometry.

Imagine trying to solve math problems without using a scientific calculator! The very first calculator was an adding and subtracting machine. Pascal invented it in 1642. Not much has changed over the years in terms of how numbers are calculated. However, there is one main difference. The evolution has come in the speed and variety of calculations that can be completed using a scientific calculator.

The modern age of calculators began in the nineteenth century. Early inventors faced many limitations in making better calculators. These challenges resulted in many early calculators not functioning correctly, if at all. However, with the birth of the twentieth century, reliable mechanical calculators began to be built and operated. Some of the milestones in calculator technology included the following:

- In 1901, Hopkins developed the standard calculator by utilizing two rows of five buttons, representing the digits 0 through 9.
- In 1911, a Swede named Sundstrand designed the standard ten-digit keyboard we are familiar with today.
- In 1914, the first commercial calculators entered the business world. After this, the use of calculators became commonplace.

Calculator technology continued to improve through the twentieth century. The first scientific calculator, the Hewlett-Packard HP-9100A, came out in 1968. The HP-35, introduced in 1972, was the world's first handheld scientific calculator. It cost $395 and was considered very expensive for its time. Since then, the price of scientific calculators has decreased. This is due to competition among the makers.

Scientific calculators are often required for math classes from the middle school level through college. They are generally required on many standardized tests covering math and science subjects. As a result, many are sold into educational markets.

Chapter 7: Architecture

Architecture is a field that focuses on designing buildings, both private and commercial, communities, and artificial constructions. It often includes designs of furnishings and decorations, and the restoration and renovation of older buildings. In this chapter, you will come across reading selections that touch upon various aspects of architecture, such as the prairie style created by the legendary American architect Frank Lloyd Wright; Scandinavian architecture; earthquake-proof homes; connecting the urban, suburban, and rural environments; and design students participating in city planning. We hope that this chapter will help you understand the interplay between humans and nature in the field of architecture.

Key Terms in the Field of Architecture

appliances	decorative	patios
attic	design	preservation
basement	flooring	renovate
cabinets	furnishings	roofing
decks	interiors	woodwork

Landmark in the Field of Architecture:
The Golden Gate Bridge in San Francisco

It is said that a trip to San Francisco is not complete without seeing the breathtaking Golden Gate Bridge. When it was completed in 1937, it was the longest suspension bridge in the world. The bridge connects San Francisco to Marin County. The Golden Gate Bridge is seen around the world as a symbol of San Francisco, California, the United States of America. The American Society of Civil Engineers has called the Golden Gate Bridge one of the modern Wonders of the World.

In 1916, an engineering student, James Wilkins, offered a proposal to build the bridge. At that time, people used to take a ferry to go from San Francisco to Marin County. The trip cost $1.00 and took 20 minutes. At first, some people did not like the idea of building the bridge. However, car manufacturers saw a great opportunity to sell more cars and supported the proposal. In 1917, M. M. O'Shaughnessy, city engineer of San Francisco, called the bridge the Golden Gate Bridge.

Many engineers were responsible for the huge project. Joseph Strauss, Irving Morrow, Charles Alton Ellis, and Leon Moisseiff designed the bridge together. However, it was Strauss who got credit for designing the Golden Gate Bridge. It was not until 2007 that the Golden Gate Bridge District gave credit to Ellis for the design of the bridge.

Work on the bridge started on January 5, 1933. It cost more than $35 million to build the bridge. Strauss remained in charge of the project. During construction, eleven workers were killed. Nineteen workers who fell from the bridge were saved by a net. The Golden Gate Bridge was finished in April 1937.

After much waiting, the bridge was opened on May 27, 1937. Celebrations lasted one week. Before cars were allowed to cross the bridge, about 200,000 people crossed the bridge by foot. A song, "There's a Silver Moon on the Golden Gate," was played to mark the occasion. On May 28, 1937, President Roosevelt pushed a button in Washington, D.C. to start vehicle traffic over the bridge officially. Since its opening, the Golden Gate Bridge has appeared in books, films, documentaries, musical shows, and television series. According to the Frommer's travel guide, it is "possibly the most beautiful, certainly the most photographed bridge in the world."

Chapter 8: Occupational Therapy

Occupational therapy focuses on the health and well-being of individuals, especially children and adolescents. Occupational therapists and occupational therapy assistants provide services to individuals and address their mental and physical condition related to their occupations. In this chapter, you will read selections on how to use an artificial limb, autism, repetitive motion injuries, rehabilitating veterans returning from war, and the legal rights of the disabled. Reading and discussing the subject matter of these selections will help you understand the importance of occupation for the physical and mental health of individuals.

Key Terms in the Field of Occupational Therapy

behavior	disability	outcome
client	ethics	rehabilitation
cognitive	evaluation	sensory
context	intervention	theory
developmental	occupation	therapy

Landmark in the Field of Occupational Therapy:
Individuals with Disability Education Act (1973–1974)

In the past, children with disabilities were not allowed to attend public schools. These children were blind, deaf, and some children were even called "emotionally disturbed" or "mentally retarded." U.S. public schools educated only 1 out of 5 children with disabilities. Children with disabilities were treated unfairly. Sadly, they were considered inferior to their peers without disabilities.

This attitude toward children with disabilities changed when the Individuals with Disabilities Education Act (IDEA) became a U.S. federal law in 1973. Since then, the IDEA has shaped how public and private schools provide special education to children with disabilities. The IDEA meets the educational needs of these children from birth to age 18 or sometimes 21. To receive special education, children must fit into one of at least fourteen categories of disability.

The IDEA only applies to those states that accept federal funding under the special act. Those states that do not accept such funding are not required by law to provide special education to children with disabilities. However, it is encouraging that all states have accepted federal funding and follow the IDEA.

The need for the IDEA arose from the denial of free public education to children who were blind, deaf, or had some form of disability. The IDEA has been changed several times to meet the needs of children's special educational needs. Most recently, in 2004 the IDEA stated that students with disabilities must be provided a Free Appropriate Public Education (FAPE). The main purpose of FAPE is to prepare students with special needs for higher education, jobs, and independent living.

Public schools have since worked to meet the special needs of children with disabilities, making sure that children with special needs are prepared to function in the real world and make a decent living without depending on others.

It is important to note that having a disability does not automatically qualify a student for special education. The IDEA considers a child with disabilities such as deafness, blindness, autism, brain injury, or learning disabilities eligible for special education.

Since the IDEA became a federal law, we have come a long way in terms of treating children with disabilities fairly and equally. The IDEA has become a turning point in the history of public education. It gives children with disabilities a chance to benefit from special education and become successful in their lives.

Chapter 9: U.S. History

Robert Penn Warren once wrote: "History cannot give us a program for the future, but it can give us a fuller understanding of ourselves, and of our common humanity, so that we can better face the future." Through the study of history we can better understand our world, the places we inhabit, and our cultural heritage.

This chapter will focus on U.S. history. In its pages you will read about some remarkable characters and the historical events that transformed their lives. You will have the chance to rethink the role of Christopher Columbus in "discovering America." You will read about the journey of John and Sally Peters, a slave couple caught in between the lines of the British and the colonists during the American Revolution. You will also examine how new technologies such as the personal bathtub and the phonograph changed many Americans' everyday lives in the late nineteenth century. Finally, you will read profiles of ten great women of the twentieth century and gain a better understanding of why some historians have called this past hundred years, "The Women's Century."

Key Terms in the Field of U.S. History

civil rights	nativist	subjective
colonization	populism	temperance
Confederate	primary source	tenant farmer
constitutional	revolution	welfare state
inevitable	sit-in	yellow press

Landmark in the Field of U.S. History:
The Digitization of Books

In the old days, libraries took great care in preserving rare books and documents. It was not easy to access these old documents. One had to go through huge archives and find a book that was out of print. With the digitization of rare documents, it is now possible for people to download, read, and save them rather easily.

In the absence of documents detailing how an ancient city was built thousands of years ago, it was extremely difficult for historians to revisit the city. Thanks to sophisticated architectural software, a city that was completely destroyed by a natural disaster can now be rebuilt electronically and maps showing streets and by lanes can be drawn.

Similarly, in the past, if a researcher wanted to obtain information about a particular individual, say Abraham Lincoln, s/he would have to go to a library and spend countless hours going through its stacks and archives. Digitization has made it possible to sift through enormous amounts of data and find information about an individual's birth and death, lineage, marriage, relatively quickly.

When Google, the world's most frequently used search engine, launched Google Books, a repository of scanned and digitized books, researchers welcomed the revolutionary idea. Though some publishers were not pleased with this service, most students and scholars around the world embraced Google Books wholeheartedly.

Despite the fact that some publishers complained about copyright infringement and tried to block Google from digitizing their books, Google Books has survived their initial resistance and has become one of the most frequently visited digital libraries. As more and more scholars and researchers use Google Books, it has become one of the largest online resources of digitized knowledge, especially of unique books. For example, by March 2012 Google Books had digitized more than 20 million books, an astounding number.

Google says that it is far from done in terms of digitizing most of the rare books. In the year 2010, Google said that there were approximately 130 million rare books in the world, and that its goal was to digitize most, if not all, of them by the year 2020. It should be noted that while most of the digitized books can be downloaded for free, there is a small charge for some books.

Chapter 10: Travel and Tourism

Travel and tourism is a vibrant field, which opens up the world to those who step inside. Whether one is a tour guide, runs a travel agency, works on business travel tours, or acts as an interpreter for foreign tourists, a career in travel and tourism offers you the opportunity to interact with travelers, providing them with the quality services that will make their travel experiences special.

In this chapter, you will read about the mishaps of a tour operator in Alaska. You will travel to Antarctica and consider the perils of ecotourism. The chapter will also focus on the importance of properly marketing tourist destinations, and we will visit some Mayan sites as we read about how government involvement can help with tourism planning. We will consider the challenges of managing tourism in such crowded places.

Key Terms in the Field of Travel and Tourism

attractions	hospitality	revenue
conservation	heritage	safari
convention	package	sanctuary
demographics	pilgrimage	sustainable
domestic	promotion	time-share

Landmark in the Field of Travel and Tourism:
Online Travel Agencies (OTAs)

Before the Internet was invented, most tourists depended on travel agents to make hotel and flight reservations. They went to brick-and-mortar travel agencies to book a hotel, purchase flight tickets, and sometimes even rent a car. For years, these travel agencies dominated the hotel and flight reservation markets. They collected as much as a 10% commission from the hotels for each customer. In addition, they also earned a commission from the airlines.

All of that changed when Hotel Reservations Network (HRN) created the first Online Travel Agency (OTA) in 1991. Tourists finally had a much easier alternative. HRN started Hotels.com, which became very popular in a short time. Travelers and tourists were no longer at the mercy of a travel agent. Thanks to the Internet, travel agencies finally had stiff competition.

OTAs gained popularity in the 2000s. They provided many travel options within a few clicks. Tourists could choose from many hotels and compare airline ticket prices. They did all of this from the comfort of their homes. Slowly more and more people began to learn about the many benefits of OTAs.

Other businesses saw OTAs as a great opportunity to make profits. They followed suit and launched many OTAs. For example, Microsoft launched the OTA Expedia in 1995 and bought Hotels.com. Under the Expedia umbrella are Venere.com, Hotwire.com, Egencia, TripAdvisor, Expedia Local Expert, Classic Vacations, and eLong.

Other companies that launched OTAs are Priceline (1998), Orbitz (2001), TripAdvisor (2005), and Travelocity (2007). Kayak.com is a recent addition to the existing OTAs. It is different from an OTA because it is an OTA search engine. It provides tourists with different hotel, flight, and car rental prices offered by the OTAs. Tourists can then make a final decision after comparing these prices.

Together, Expedia, Hotels.com, Travelocity, Priceline, Orbitz, and TripAdvisor control over 90% of the market. They compete with each other for a share of the market. However, this competition is healthy for tourists. They can pick and choose from many options. They can now access airline databases with ease. They can also book and purchase without the help of a travel agent or broker. Thanks to OTAs, tourists can now check in online, print out their boarding passes, and board a plane without any hassles. It is clear that OTAs are here to stay.

Photo Credits

Text Credits

Chapter 1

p. 19: Janice Allen, "Is This the One? Choosing the Right Mate." Fox 17 News, October 28, 2011. Reprinted by permission.

p. 22: From Alex D. Thio., *Sociology: A Brief Introduction*, 7th Ed., © 2009. Reprinted and Electronically reproduced by permission of Pearson Education, Inc., Upper Saddle River, New Jersey.

p. 23: From Alex D. Thio., *Sociology: A Brief Introduction*, 7th Ed., © 2009. Reprinted and Electronically reproduced by permission of Pearson Education, Inc., Upper Saddle River, New Jersey.

p. 24: From Alex D. Thio., *Sociology: A Brief Introduction*, 7th Ed., © 2009. Reprinted and Electronically reproduced by permission of Pearson Education, Inc., Upper Saddle River, New Jersey.

p. 28: Kathryn Kvols, "Ten Keys to Successful Parenting." Kathryn Kvols is an international speaker and author of the book "Redirecting Children's Behavior." Visit her web site www.incaf.com or call 877-375-6498.

p. 32: Larry Meeks, "Troubles with Raising Teenage Son." © 2011 Creators.com. By permission of Larry Meeks and Creators Syndicate, Inc.

p. 37: From Alex D. Thio, *Sociology: A Brief Introduction*, 7th Ed., © 2009. Reprinted and Electronically reproduced by permission of Pearson Education, Inc., Upper Saddle River, New Jersey.

Chapter 2

p. 48: From Michael D. Johnson, *Human Biology: Concepts And Current Issues*, 6th Ed, © 2012. Reprinted and Electronically reproduced by permission of Pearson Education, Inc., Upper Saddle River, New Jersey.

p. 52: Valerie Coskrey, "An Ode to Dolly Re Global Warming." © 2006 by Valerie Coskrey in http://vmemos .flobspot.com/2008/12/poem-about-cloning-and-global-warming.html. Reprinted by permission of the author, from vforteachers.com

p. 54: Kathleen Blanchard, RN, "What's the Best Way to Lose belly Fat?" EmaxHealth.com

p. 57: From Michael D. Johnson, *Human Biology: Concepts And Current Issues*, 6th Ed, © 2012. Reprinted and Electronically reproduced by permission of Pearson Education, Inc., Upper Saddle River, New Jersey.

p. 58: From Michael D. Johnson, *Human Biology: Concepts And Current Issues*, 6th Ed, © 2012. Reprinted and Electronically reproduced by permission of Pearson Education, Inc., Upper Saddle River, New Jersey.

p. 59: From Michael D. Johnson, *Human Biology: Concepts And Current Issues*, 6th Ed, © 2012. Reprinted and Electronically reproduced by permission of Pearson Education, Inc., Upper Saddle River, New Jersey.

p. 60: From Michael D. Johnson, *Human Biology: Concepts And Current Issues*, 6th Ed, © 2012. Reprinted and Electronically reproduced by permission of Pearson Education, Inc., Upper Saddle River, New Jersey.

p. 61: From Michael D. Johnson, *Human Biology: Concepts And Current Issues*, 6th Ed, © 2012. Reprinted and Electronically reproduced by permission of Pearson Education, Inc., Upper Saddle River, New Jersey.

p. 64: "Organ Donation: Don't Let These Myths Confuse You." Reprinted with permission from MayoClinic.com. All rights reserved.

p. 70: Brennan Lingsley, "Monkeys live longer on low-cal diet; would humans?" The Associated Press, July 9, 2009. Reprinted by permission of the The YGS Group.

p. 74: Michael Pollan, "A Field of Corn," from *The Omnivore's Dilemma: Young Readers Edition* by Michael Pollan, copyright © 2009 by Michael Pollan. Used by permission of Dial Books for Young Readers, a division of Penguin Group (USA) Inc.

p. 79: Michael D. Johnson, *Human Biology: Concepts And Current Issues*, 6th Ed, © 2012. Reprinted and Electronically reproduced by permission of Pearson Education, Inc., Upper Saddle River, New Jersey.

Chapter 3

p. 89: From Jeff Madura, "How You Benefit from an Understanding of Personal Finance, Personal Finance, 4th Ed., © 2011. Reprinted and Electronically reproduced by permission of Pearson Education, Inc., Upper Saddle River, New Jersey.

p. 93: Jeremy Vohwinkle, "The Importance of Creating a Savings Account." Reprinted by permission of the author.

p. 97: "Credit Card Smarts." Copyright © 2005. The College Board. www.collegeboard.org. Reproduced with permission.

p. 102: "Tenants Facing Foreclosure." Demand Media.

p. 105: From Jeff Madura, *Personal Finance*, 4th Ed., © 2011. Reprinted and Electronically reproduced by permission of Pearson Education, Inc., Upper Saddle River, New Jersey.

p. 107: From Jeff Madura, *Personal Finance*, 4th Ed., © 2011. Reprinted and Electronically reproduced by permission of Pearson Education, Inc., Upper Saddle River, New Jersey.

p. 108: From Jeff Madura, *Personal Finance*, 4th Ed., © 2011. Reprinted and Electronically reproduced by permission of Pearson Education, Inc., Upper Saddle River, New Jersey.

p. 109: From Jeff Madura, *Personal Finance*, 4th Ed., © 2011. Reprinted and Electronically reproduced by permission of Pearson Education, Inc., Upper Saddle River, New Jersey.

p. 110: From Jeff Madura, *Personal Finance*, 4th Ed., © 2011. Reprinted and Electronically reproduced by permission of Pearson Education, Inc., Upper Saddle River, New Jersey.

p. 111: From Jeff Madura, *Personal Finance*, 4th Ed., © 2011. Reprinted and Electronically reproduced by permission of Pearson Education, Inc., Upper Saddle River, New Jersey.

Chapter 4

Chapter 5

p. 204: Jamaica Kincaid, from *Lucy* by Jamaica Kincaid. Copyright © 1990 by Jamaica Kincaid. Farrar, Straus and Giroux, LLC.

p. 211: August Wilson, from *The Piano Lesson* by August Wilson, copyright © 1988, 1990 by August Wilson. Used by permission of Dutton Signet, a division of Penguin Group (USA) Inc.

p. 220: Robert McCrum, "Are Real Books Nearing the End of Their Shelf Life?" *The Observer*, February 8, 2009. Copyright Guardian News & Media Ltd. 2009. Reprinted by permission.

p. 223: From Sylvan Barnet; William E. Burto; William E. Cain, *Introduction to Literature, an*, 6th Ed. © 2011. Reprinted and Electronically reproduced by permission of Pearson Education, Inc., Upper Saddle River, New Jersey.

p. 223: *Writers at Work: The Paris Review Interviews*, Second Series.

p. 224: *Esquire*, December 1934, page 68.

Chapter 6

p. 233: From Robert F. Blitzer, *Thinking Mathematically*, 5th Ed., © 2011. Reprinted and Electronically reproduced by permission of Pearson Education, Inc., Upper Saddle River, New Jersey.

p. 234: From Robert F. Blitzer, *Thinking Mathematically*, 5th Ed., © 2011. Reprinted and Electronically reproduced by permission of Pearson Education, Inc., Upper Saddle River, New Jersey.

p. 235: From Robert F. Blitzer, *Thinking Mathematically*, 5th Ed., © 2011. Reprinted and Electronically reproduced by permission of Pearson Education, Inc., Upper Saddle River, New Jersey.

p. 238: Arthur Michelson, "Why Math Always Counts: It Can Open Our Minds to Logic and Beauty." Courtesy of Arthur Michelson

p. 241: From Robert F. Blitzer, *Thinking Mathematically*, 5th Ed., © 2011. Reprinted and Electronically reproduced by permission of Pearson Education, Inc., Upper Saddle River, New Jersey.

p. 246: Garth Sundem, "Marriage Equations, from *Geek Logic*, by Garth Sundem. © Garth Sundem. Garth Sundem is the author of books including *Brain Trust* and *The Geeks' Guide to World Domination*. Reprinted by permission.

p. 252: From Jeffrey O. Bennett; William L. Briggs, *Using and Understanding Mathematics: A Quantitative Reasoning Approach*, 5th Ed., © 2011. Reprinted and Electronically reproduced by permission of Pearson Education, Inc., Upper Saddle River, New Jersey.

p. 253: From Jeffrey O. Bennett; William L. Briggs, *Using and Understanding Mathematics: A Quantitative Reasoning Approach*, 5th Ed., © 2011. Reprinted and Electronically reproduced by permission of Pearson Education, Inc., Upper Saddle River, New Jersey.

p. 254: From Jeffrey O. Bennett; William L. Briggs, *Using and Understanding Mathematics: A Quantitative Reasoning Approach*, 5th Ed., © 2011. Reprinted and Electronically reproduced by permission of Pearson Education, Inc., Upper Saddle River, New Jersey.

p. 255: From Jeffrey O. Bennett; William L. Briggs, *Using and Understanding Mathematics: A Quantitative Reasoning Approach*, 5th Ed., © 2011. Reprinted and Electronically reproduced by permission of Pearson Education, Inc., Upper Saddle River, New Jersey.

p. 256: From Jeffrey O. Bennett; William L. Briggs, *Using and Understanding Mathematics: A Quantitative Reasoning Approach*, 5th Ed., © 2011. Reprinted and Electronically reproduced by permission of Pearson Education, Inc., Upper Saddle River, New Jersey.

p. 257: From Jeffrey O. Bennett; William L. Briggs, *Using and Understanding Mathematics: A Quantitative Reasoning Approach*, 5th Ed., © 2011. Reprinted and Electronically reproduced by permission of Pearson Education, Inc., Upper Saddle River, New Jersey.

p. 260: From Jeffrey O. Bennett; William L. Briggs, *Using and Understanding Mathematics: A Quantative Reasoning Approach*, 5th Ed., © 2011. Reprinted and Electronically reproduced by permission of Pearson Education, Inc., Upper Saddle River, New Jersey.

p. 264: "How to Calculate Your Real Hourly Wage." wikiHow Reprinted by permission.

p. 269: From Jeffrey O. Bennett; William L. Briggs, *Using and Understanding Mathematics: A Quantative Reasoning Approach,*, 5th Ed., © 2011. Reprinted and Electronically reproduced by permission of Pearson Education, Inc., Upper Saddle River, New Jersey.

p. 270: From Jeffrey O. Bennett; William L. Briggs, *Using and Understanding Mathematics: A Quantative Reasoning Approach,*, 5th Ed., © 2011. Reprinted and Electronically reproduced by permission of Pearson Education, Inc., Upper Saddle River, New Jersey.

p. 271: Flowtown. © Demandforce. Reprinted by permission

p. 275: Graph, "Average Estimated Undergraduate Budgets," from Trends in College Pricing. Copyright © 2008. The College Board www.collegeboard.org. Reproduced with permission.

p. 276: Graph, "U.S. Age Distribution," from Bennett, Jeffrey O.; Briggs, William L., *Using and Understanding Mathematics: A Quantative Reasoning Approach*, 5th Ed., © 2011. Reprinted and Electronically reproduced by permission of Pearson Education, Inc., Upper Saddle River, New Jersey.

p. 278: From Jeffrey O. Bennett; William L. Briggs, *Using and Understanding Mathematics: A Quantitative Reasoning Approach*, 5th Ed., © 2011. Reprinted and Electronically reproduced by permission of Pearson Education, Inc., Upper Saddle River, New Jersey.

Chapter 7

p. 293: "Frank Lloyd Wright: Prairie Style" Wright on the Web http://www.delmars.com/wright/flw2.htm Reprinted by permission.

p. 297: Text and photos from blog entitled "Scandinavian Architecture: From Country to City" http://inspireyourlife-style.wordpress.com/2011/02/25/scandinavian-architecture/. Reprinted by permission of Style & Shoot LLC

p. 301: William Browning, "Japan Quake Aftermath: How to Earthquake-Proof Your House." Reprinted with permission from Yahoo! inc. 2012 Yahoo! Inc. YAHOO! and the YAHOO! logo are trademarks of Yahoo! Inc.

p. 315: Jeremiah Russell, adapted from "Urban vs. Suburban." R|One Studio Architecture, LLC Reprinted by permission.

p. 322: Kevin Canfield, "OU Design Students Hope to Play a Role in Revitalizing North Tulsa." *Tulsa World.* April 9, 2011. http://www.tulsaworld.com/news/article.aspx?subjectid=16&articleid=20110409_16_A17_ULNSam694979. Reprinted by permission.

pp. 322–323: From Buie Harwood; Bridget May; Curt Sherman, *Architecture And Interior Design From The 19th Century, Volume II,* 1st Ed., © 2009. Reprinted and Electronically reproduced by permission of Pearson Education, Inc., Upper Saddle River, New Jersey.

p. 390: From Jacqueline A. Jones; Peter H. Wood; Thomas Borstelmann; Elaine Tyler May; Vicki L. Ruiz, *Created Equal: A History of The United States, Brief Edition,* Volume 1, 3rd Ed., © 2011. Reprinted and Electronically reproduced by permission of Pearson Education, Inc., Upper Saddle River, New Jersey.

p. 396: Sidney Hillman, reported in *The New Republic,* Vol. 115 (1946), p. 379.

p. 405: © 2012 The National Women's History Project www.nwhp.org

p. 411: Zelda Anderson, "Zelda Anderson, One of the First Black Woman to Enter the U.S. Women's Army Auxiliary Corps (1942), Shares Her Story." Used by permission of the University of Nevada Oral History Program, University of Nevada, Reno.

p. 416: From Jacqueline A. Jones; Peter H. Wood; Thomas Borstelmann; Elaine Tyler May; Vicki L. Ruiz, *Created Equal History Story of the United States, Brief Edition,* Volume 1 3rd Ed., © 2011. Reprinted and Electronically reproduced by permission of Pearson Education, Inc., Upper Saddle River, New Jersey.

Chapter 8

p. 340: Annalee Newitz, "Portraits in Posthumanity: Aimee Mullins," by Annalee Newitz, i.o9.com, May 10, 2010. Reprinted by permission.

p. 344: Adapted from "What Does Autism Mean?" © 1995–2012 The Nemours Foundation/KidsHealth®. Reprinted with permission.

p. 348: Dr. Christopher Anthony, "Carpal Tunnel—One Patient's Story," Reprinted by permission of Dr. Christopher Anthony, Tri-Synergy Chiropractic.

p. 361: "Shields Valley Ranch Helps Rehabilitate Soldiers" The Associated Press, September 25, 2010. Reprinted by permission of The YGS group.

p. 366: Jason Aubrey, "Democratic Party Ignores Handicapped Woman's Plea for Access to Downtown South Bend Headquarters." Reprinted by permission of ABC57 News.

p. 371: From Delany, Janet V.; Pendzick, Margaret J., *Working With Children And Adolescents: A Guide for the occupational Therapy Assistant,* 1st Ed., © 2009. Reprinted and Electronically reproduced by permission of Pearson Education, Inc., Upper Saddle River, New Jersey.

Chapter 9

p. 385: Assignment 3: The Causes and Effects of the American Revolution. Courtesy of Ron Watkins

p. 387: Sharon Short, adapted from "Rethinking Columbus and His Day." *Dayton Daily News* October 10, 2011. Reprinted with permission from the Dayton Daily News

Chapter 10

p. 428: Johanna Jainchill, "Dispatch, Alaska: Tour Leaders' Enthusiasm Shines Through." *Travel Weekly,* June 3, 2008. Reprinted by permission of the YGS Group.

p. 431: Andy Stone, "How Ecotourism is Destroying Antarctica." Environmental Graffiti Ltd. Reprinted by permission.

p. 436: Laura Acevedo, "Tourism Marketing Strategies." Demand Media.

p. 439: From John R. Walker; Josielyn T. Walker, *Tourism: Concepts and Practices,* 1st Ed., © 2011. Reprinted and Electronically reproduced by permission of Pearson Education, Inc., Upper Saddle River, New Jersey.

p. 440: From John R. Walker; Josielyn T. Walker, *Tourism: Concepts and Practices,* 1st Ed., © 2011. Reprinted and Electronically reproduced by permission of Pearson Education, Inc., Upper Saddle River, New Jersey.

p. 441: From John R. Walker; Josielyn T. Walker, *Tourism: Concepts and Practices,* 1st Ed., © 2011. Reprinted and Electronically reproduced by permission of Pearson Education, Inc., Upper Saddle River, New Jersey.

p. 444: "Mexico Launches Tourism Plan for Mayan Sites." Reprinted by permission of NTN22 USA Inc.

p. 447: From John R. Walker; Josielyn T. Walker, *Tourism: Concepts and Practices,* 1st Ed., © 2011. Reprinted and Electronically reproduced by permission of Pearson Education, Inc., Upper Saddle River, New Jersey.

p. 453: From John R. Walker; Josielyn T. Walker, *Tourism: Concepts and Practices,* 1st Ed., © 2011. Reprinted and Electronically reproduced by permission of Pearson Education, Inc., Upper Saddle River, New Jersey.